The Harbrace Guide to Writing

CONCISE SECOND EDITION

Cheryl Glenn
The Pennsylvania State University

WADSWORTH
CENGAGE Learning™

Australia • Brazil • Japan • Korea • Mexico • Singapore • Spain • United Kingdom • United States

WADSWORTH
CENGAGE Learning™

The Harbrace Guide to Writing,
Concise Second Edition
Cheryl Glenn

Senior Publisher: Lyn Uhl

Executive Editor: Monica Eckman

Acquisitions Editor: Margaret Leslie

Senior Development Editor: Leslie
Taggart

Development Editor: Stephanie
Pelkowski Carpenter, LLC

Assistant Editor: Amy Haines

Senior Editorial Assistant: Elizabeth
Ramsey

Marketing Director: Jason Sakos

Associate Media Editor: Janine
Tangney

Senior Marketing Communications
Manager: Stacey Purviance

Marketing Coordinator: Ryan
Ahern

Content Project Manager:
Rosemary Winfield

Art Director: Jill Ort

Print Buyer: Susan Spencer

Rights Acquisition Specialist,
Images: Jennifer Meyer Dare

Rights Acquisition Specialist, Text:
Katie Huha

Production Service: Lifland et al.,
Bookmakers

Text Designer: Lillie Caporlingua,
Bill Smith Group

Cover Designer: Lillie Caporlingua,
Bill Smith Group

Cover Image: David Prentice, *Night
Light* / Bridgeman Art

Compositor: PreMediaGlobal

For product information and
technology assistance,
contact us at
**Cengage Learning Customer & Sales Support,
1-800-354-9706.**

For permission to use material from this text or product,
submit all requests online at **www. cengage.com/permissions**.
Further permissions questions can be emailed to
permissionrequest@cengage.com.

Library of Congress Control Number: 2010932593

ISBN-13: 978-0-495-91399-3

ISBN-10: 0-495-91399-5

Wadsworth
20 Channel Center Street
Boston, MA 02210
USA

Cengage Learning is a leading provider of customized learning solutions with office locations around the globe, including Singapore, the United Kingdom, Australia, Mexico, Brazil, and Japan. Locate your local office at **international.cengage.com/region**.

Cengage Learning products are represented in Canada by Nelson Education, Ltd.

For your course and learning solutions, visit
www.cengage.com.

Purchase any of our products at your local college store or at our preferred online store **www.cengagebrain.com**.

Printed in China
3 4 5 14 13 12

The
Harbrace
Guide
to Writing

CONCISE SECOND EDITION

BRIEF CONTENTS

CONTENTS

© 2007 Steven Lunetta Photography.

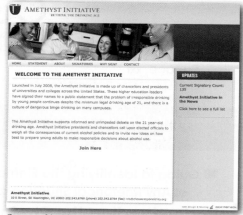

Courtesy of Amethyst Initiative.

2 Identifying a Fitting Response 29

© iStockphoto.com/Andres Peiro Palmer

AP Photo/Paul Sakuma.

AP Photo/Sara D. Davis

Arnold Newman/Getty Images

Daniel Eatock/Eatock Ltd.

© Cheryl Glenn, 2007

Large Still Life Frieze, Joseph Ablow. Copyright © Joseph Ablow. Reprinted by permission of Pucker Gallery.

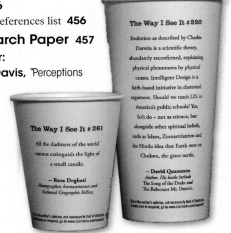

Steven Lunetta Photography, 2007

PREFACE

We live in a world in which many things are other than they should be: public schools are deeply segregated by race and income; professional athletes pull down bigger salaries than medical researchers; human-caused ecological disasters occur on a regular basis with devastating consequences; Palestine and Israel continue to bomb each other, while our own country continues to bomb Iraq and Afghanistan.

Fortunately, we also live in a world of resolution and possibility, often contingent on the appropriate words being delivered to the appropriate person. Thus, more than ever before, we need to learn how to use language ethically, effectively, and appropriately to address and ultimately resolve conflict—so we can move ahead together and make our world a better place. We need to learn how to use rhetoric purposefully.

The Harbrace Guide to Writing, Concise Second Edition, helps students do just that: It helps them use rhetoric to move forward by addressing and resolving problems, whether those problems are social, academic, or work-related. A comprehensive and richly flexible guide for first-year writers—and their teachers—*The Harbrace Guide to Writing,* Concise Second Edition, includes a rhetoric, a reader, and a research manual. *The Harbrace Guide to Writing,* Concise Second Edition, distinguishes itself from other writing guides on the market by its sustained focus on the rhetorical situation and on the specific rhetorical techniques that allow writers to shape their ideas into language that is best suited for their audience and most appropriate for their situation. This writing guide is theoretically sophisticated yet practical: Students will see writing and speaking—using language purposefully—as integral parts of daily life, in and out of school.

In each of its four parts, *The Harbrace Guide to Writing,* Concise Second Edition, translates rhetorical theory into easy-to-follow (and easy-to-teach) techniques that help sharpen the ability to decide which words, assertions, or opinions might work best with a particular audience in a specific situation. In this edition, you'll find many innovations (large and small) that help students understand how to evaluate a rhetorical situation, to identify and respond to an opportunity, and to address a problem. With a sustained focus on authentic issues and opportunities within students' local communities—issues that merit response—this edition offers guidance that supports student writers as they create fitting responses using all of the means of delivery available to them.

How Does the Book Work?

First, the two chapters in Part 1, **Entering the Conversation: The Rhetorical Situation,** introduce students to the rhetorical principles that underlie all writing situations and provide them with a basic method for using those principles:

▶ To recognize when writing in any of its forms is the best response

▶ To consider strategically their audience and their purpose

▶ To identify language that fits the context and delivers the intended message

Second, the six chapters in Part 2, **Rhetorical Situations for Composing**, offer writing projects that engage students in responding to real situations:

▶ Assignment options at the start of each chapter prompt students to consider the visual, audio, digital, and print options for responding to the rhetorical situation.

▶ A selection of readings and photos illustrate how others have responded to the same subjects.

▶ An example of writing within a familiar genre (such as a memoir, an investigative report, or a proposal) demonstrates how the genre frames an appropriate response to many similar situations.

▶ Writing in Three Media features refer students to multimodal examples of the genre on the book's English CourseMate Web site.

▶ A step-by-step guide to writing helps students bring it all together to establish the elements of their rhetorical situation and work within a genre to create a fitting response.

Part 3, **Strategies for Composing**, offers strategies for approaching the writing process, including the use of the rhetorical methods and multimedia. The Part 3 chapters help students learn

▶ to pay close attention to their own writing processes, from recognizing an opportunity for change to revising, editing, and proofreading;

▶ to use the rhetorical methods to develop their paragraphs and essays;

▶ to use effective strategies for peer review;

▶ to recognize when multimedia is part of a fitting response and when print is most appropriate; and

▶ to use rhetorically effective processes for communicating via Web sites, blogs, wikis, podcasts, Facebook, and even YouTube.

The research manual in Part 4, **A Guide to Research**, draws students into research as a rhetorical activity. Students learn to see a research assignment, not as a set of rules and requirements, but as an effective way of responding to certain rhetorical opportunities. The chapters in Part 4 offer

▶ help in finding print and electronic sources in the library, online, and through databases;

▶ a comprehensive introduction to field research, with examples of observation, interviews, and questionnaires; and

▶ information on reading, evaluating, and responding to sources and help with creating summaries and working bibliographies.

Key Features

▶ **Brings the rhetorical situation to life**. *The Harbrace Guide to Writing*, Concise Second Edition, introduces students to the rhetorical principles that underlie all writing situations, providing them with a basic method for using those principles. This introduction to rhetoric is adaptable to any composition classroom, and the principles it teaches are transferable to students' other writing tasks.

▶ **Guides students easily through the writing process**. Step-by-step writing guides help students through the processes outlined in Part 1. Students identify an opportunity for change and create a fitting response that takes advantage of all of their available means. In this way, manageable tasks build toward a larger writing project in direct, incremental ways.

▶ **Offers activities to help students think rhetorically and act locally**. Activities in **Identifying an Opportunity** and **Community Connections** help students consider openings for composing in various media within their communities. **Analyzing the Rhetorical Situation** activities help students understand the elements of a response to a rhetorical situation, and **Your Writing Experiences** and **Write for Five** connect everyday writing with more extensive writing projects.

▶ **Presents research as a rhetorical response**. Rather than offering a series of lock-step procedures for students to follow as they approach a research project, the research manual in Part 4 draws students into research as a rhetorical activity. Because different research questions require different research methods, the research manual includes information on library, online, and field research.

NEW to This Edition

- **Rhetorical concepts updated for the twenty-first century**. *The Harbrace Guide to Writing*, Concise Second Edition, uses student-friendly language to help students apply rhetorical principles to all of their writing situations and bring the rhetorical situation to life.

- **New focus on multimodal options for writing.** New assignment options at the start of each Part 2 chapter prompt students to consider the visual, audio, digital, and print options for responding to the rhetorical situation. Students will understand immediately that the elements of the rhetorical situation must guide all considerations when they are forming a fitting response.

- **New chapter on composing with multimedia.** Chapter 10, **Responding with Multimedia**, was created to help students not only to understand how to create multimedia compositions, but also to appreciate when and where such multimedia composition is most effective. The chapter begins with scenarios calling for multimedia responses and then addresses the composition process for Web sites, blogs, wikis, podcasts, and postings on Facebook and YouTube.

- **Engaging new readings**. New readings show students the rhetorical considerations at the heart of such responses as presidential speeches, Steve Jobs's multimedia presentations, and even canvas tote bags.

- **More emphasis on student research**. New student-written **Tricks of the Trade** features offer valuable tips for research—such as when to paraphrase or summarize rather than quote and how the bibliography of a good source can yield additional relevant sources. Chapter 13, **Research in the Field**, includes a transcript of a new student-conducted interview, and an audio recording of the full interview is available at the book's companion Web site.

- **New English CourseMate Web site.** The guide's new English CourseMate Web site features multimodal examples of student and professional writing for each Part 2 writing project. Interactive guides prompt students to consider and map out each element of their rhetorical situation—characteristics of their audience, the message, and themselves as writers. Access the English CourseMate via cengagebrain.com.

- **Clear support of the Council of Writing Program Administrators' (WPA) objectives and outcomes.** To help instructors and students consider shared goals, this edition incorporates the WPA objectives and outcomes. A complete description follows.

How Does *The Harbrace Guide to Writing,* Concise Second Edition, Help Students Achieve the WPA Outcomes?

On the following pages, each of the five primary outcomes of the **WPA Outcomes Statement for First-Year Composition** is followed by an explanation and illustration of how—and where—*The Harbrace Guide to Writing,* Concise Second Edition, supports that outcome.

Rhetorical Knowledge

By the end of first year composition, students should

- ▶ Focus on a purpose
- ▶ Respond to the needs of different audiences
- ▶ Respond appropriately to different kinds of rhetorical situations
- ▶ Use conventions of format and structure appropriate to the rhetorical situation
- ▶ Adopt appropriate voice, tone, and level of formality
- ▶ Understand how genres shape reading and writing
- ▶ Write in several genres

From the WPA Outcomes Statement

The Harbrace Guide to Writing, Concise Second Edition, begins with a full introduction to the elements of the rhetorical situation. Examples and activities help students consider the opportunity for change, the writer, the audience, the purpose, the message, and the context, making the book's first two chapters a user-friendly mini-guide to the rhetorical situation.

The writing projects in Part 2 guide students in making decisions about the genres and methods of delivery that are most appropriate to their audience and purpose.

■ GUIDE TO RESPONDING TO THE RHETORICAL SITUATION

Understanding the Rhetorical Situation

When you want to share your understanding of somebody with an audience, consider composing a profile. Profiles commonly have the following features:

- Profiles have as their subject someone readers will find compelling or interesting.
- Profiles provide descriptive details to help readers imagine how the subject looks, sounds, or acts.
- Profiles includes several direct quotations from the subject or others that help readers understand the person's opinions and perspectives.
- Profiles draw on evidence and insights from a variety of sources, such as personal observations, interviews, and research.
- Profiles present several anecdotes about the subject that show readers the background and experiences that have shaped the subject.
- Profiles lead readers to a particular emotional response or logical conclusion about the subject.

The following sections will help you compose a profile about someone who is successful with words. To work with an online guide to the elements of the rhetorical situation, access your English CourseMate through CengageBrain.com.

Critical Thinking, Reading, and Writing

By the end of first year composition, students should

- ▶ Use writing and reading for inquiry, learning, thinking, and communicating

- ▶ Understand a writing assignment as a series of tasks, including finding, evaluating, analyzing, and synthesizing appropriate primary and secondary sources

- ▶ Integrate their own ideas with those of others

- ▶ Understand the relationships among language, knowledge, and power

From the WPA Outcomes Statement

Each chapter of *The Harbrace Guide to Writing*, Concise Second Edition, offers activities to help students think rhetorically and yet act locally. Activities in **Identifying an Opportunity** and **Community Connections** help students consider openings for composing within their communities—for addressing or even resolving a problem through the use of language. **Analyzing the Rhetorical Situation** activities help students understand the elements of a fitting response to a rhetorical situation, and **Your Writing Experiences** and **Write for Five** connect everyday writing with more extensive writing projects.

> ANALYZING THE RHETORICAL SITUATION

Based on the excerpt from Susan Orlean's essay, answer the following questions.

1. If Orlean's purpose is to find the extraordinary in the ordinary, what is her rhetorical opportunity?
2. How does she work to respond to that opportunity through her language? How does her language fit the problem?
3. What are the available means she taps to form her response? Where and how does she use the rhetorical appeals of ethos, pathos, and logos?

To help students integrate their ideas with those of others, the chapters in **A Guide to Research** (Part 4) guide students in finding, reading, evaluating, and responding to sources at the library, online, and in the field. These five chapters provide many opportunities for students to approach researched writing incrementally by creating a research log, partial and full summaries, and working and annotated bibliographies.

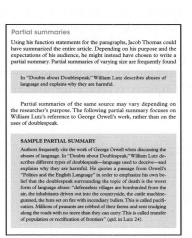

Processes

By the end of first year composition, students should

▶ Be aware that it usually takes multiple drafts to create and complete a successful text

▶ Develop flexible strategies for generating, revising, editing, and proofreading

▶ Understand writing as an open process that permits writers to use later invention and re-thinking to revise their work

▶ Understand the collaborative and social aspects of writing processes

▶ Learn to critique their own and others' works

▶ Learn to balance the advantages of relying on others with the responsibility of doing their part

▶ Use a variety of technologies to address a range of audiences

From the WPA Outcomes Statement

Part 3, **Strategies for Composing**, offers support for approaching traditional and multimodal writing processes, from recognizing an opportunity for change to revising, editing, and proofreading. Activities for exploring, drafting, peer reviewing, revising, and editing—as well as help in developing rhetorically effective processes for working with digital media—make Part 3 a concise resource for understanding processes.

Strategies
for **Composing**

Questions for a peer reviewer
1. To what opportunity for change is the writer responding?
2. Who might be the writer's intended audience?
3. What might be the writer's purpose?
4. What information did you receive from the introduction? How effective is the introduction? What suggestions do you have for the writer for improving the introduction?
5. Note the writer's thesis statement. If you cannot locate a thesis statement, what thesis statement might work for this argument?
6. Note the assertions the writer makes to support the thesis. Are they presented in chronological or emphatic order? Does the writer use the order that seems most effective? Would you re-order some of the assertions?
7. If you cannot locate a series of assertions, what assertions could be made to support the thesis statement?
8. Note the supporting ideas (presented through narration, cause-and-effect analysis, description, exemplification, process analysis, or definition) that the writer uses to support his or her assertions.
9. How does the writer establish ethos? How could the writer strengthen this appeal?
10. What material does the writer use to establish logos? How might the writer strengthen this appeal (see questions 6–8)?
11. How does the writer make use of pathos?
12. What did you learn from the conclusion that you didn't already know after reading the introduction and the body? What information does the writer want you to take away from the argument? Does the writer attempt to change your attitude, action, or opinion?
13. What section of the argument did you most enjoy? Why?

Of course, students are called on to observe and implement these strategies no matter which part of the book they happen to be working within, whether they are reflecting on their writing experiences in Part 1 (**Your Writing Experiences** activities), working through the **Guides to Responding** in Part 2, trying out clustering methods with peers in Part 3, or generating multiple responses to sources in Part 4.

Knowledge of Conventions

By the end of first year composition, students should

► Learn common formats for different kinds of texts

► Develop knowledge of genre conventions ranging from structure and paragraphing to tone and mechanics

► Practice appropriate means of documenting their work

► Control such surface features as syntax, grammar, punctuation, and spelling

From the WPA Outcomes Statement

Annotated examples of each featured genre in Part 2 identify and describe the conventions common to that genre. Additionally, each **Guide to Responding** begins with a list that identifies features typically found in the genre under discussion; as students work to shape their writing project, a helpful illustration reminds them of how a piece of writing in that genre is commonly shaped or organized.

Introduction	**Body**	**Conclusion**
▶ Shows readers that the subject is someone they need to know more about ▶ Highlights some key feature of the subject's personality, character, or values	▶ Presents a fuller description of the subject and his or her life's work ▶ Includes details that help readers to visualize the subject's actions and hear the subject's words ▶ Provides logical appeals in the form of examples that show how the individual's work affects the lives of people like the readers themselves	▶ Often contains one final quote or anecdote that nicely captures the essence of the individual ▶ May bring readers into the present day, if the profile has had a historical scope

In Part 4, Chapter 15, **Acknowledging Sources**, discusses MLA and APA style to help students identify the conventions specific to the academic essay genre—and to understand why those conventions exist.

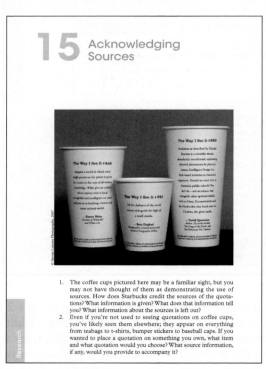

Composing in Electronic Environments

Writing in the twenty-first century involves the use of digital technologies for several purposes, from drafting to peer reviewing to editing. Therefore, although the *kinds* of composing processes and texts expected from students vary across programs and institutions, there are nonetheless common expectations.

By the end of first-year composition, students should

▶ Use electronic environments for drafting, reviewing, revising, editing, and sharing texts

▶ Locate, evaluate, organize, and use research material collected from electronic sources, including scholarly library databases; other official databases (e.g., federal government databases); and informal electronic networks and internet sources

▶ Understand and exploit the differences in the rhetorical strategies and in the affordances available for both print and electronic composing processes and texts

From the WPA Outcomes Statement

The Harbrace Guide to Writing, Concise Second Edition, emphasizes rhetorical situations that students are likely to encounter every day, from writing a text message to a friend to participating in a course wiki. Because many of these rhetorical situations have digital contexts, *The Harbrace Guide to Writing* features examples of those contexts in its chapters and provides an interactive digital environment for viewing multimodal examples and mapping out elements of students' rhetorical situations. The English CourseMate Web site can be accessed via cengagebrain.com.

Rhetorical Situation

Guide to Identifying the Elements of Any Rhetorical Situation

© Steven Lunetta Photography, 2007

As a responsible writer and speaker, you need to understand the elements of any rhetorical situation you decide to enter. Chapters 1 and 2 will help you identify those elements using the following steps.

▶ Identify the opportunity for change that encourages you to enter the situation. Ask yourself: What is it that tugs at me? Why do I feel the need to speak, write, take a photo, share an image? What attitude, action, or opinion do I want to change?

▶ Connect the opportunity to make change with your purpose. Ask yourself: What can I accomplish with rhetoric? How can words or visuals allow me to respond to this opportunity?

▶ Knowing that your purpose is tethered to the nature and character of the audience, carefully consider the composition of that audience: Who are its members? What are they like? What opinions do they hold? What are their feelings about this opportunity to resolve a problem, to make change? How will they react to the message? Different audiences have different needs and expectations, which the responsible writer or speaker tries to meet.

▶ Take into account whatever else has already been said on the subject: Who has been speaking or writing, and what do they say?

▶ Whatever the form of its delivery (spoken, written, or electronic), you'll want your response to be fitting (or appropriate). By calibrating the tone of your response, you can control the attitude you project to your intended audience. When shaping a fitting response, you need to be fully aware that you can come only as close to persuasion as the rhetorical situation allows. A responsible speaker or writer cannot do or expect more.

Assignment options at the start of each Part 2 chapter prompt students to consider the visual, audio, digital, and print options for responding to the rhetorical situation. When students begin writing, they can access examples in each medium online.

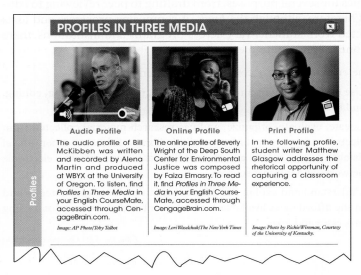

PROFILES IN THREE MEDIA

Audio Profile

The audio profile of Bill McKibben was written and recorded by Alena Martin and produced at WBYX at the University of Oregon. To listen, find *Profiles in Three Media* in your English CourseMate, accessed through CengageBrain.com.

Image: AP Photo/Toby Talbot

Online Profile

The online profile of Beverly Wright of the Deep South Center for Environmental Justice was composed by Faiza Elmasry. To read it, find *Profiles in Three Media* in your English Course-Mate, accessed through CengageBrain.com.

Image: Lori Waselchuk/The New York Times

Print Profile

In the following profile, student writer Matthew Glasgow addresses the rhetorical opportunity of capturing a classroom experience.

Image: Photo by Richie Wireman, Courtesy of the University of Kentucky.

Responding with Multimedia (Chapter 10) highlights rhetorical situations calling for multimedia responses and addresses the composition process for Web sites, blogs, wikis, podcasts, and postings on Facebook and YouTube.

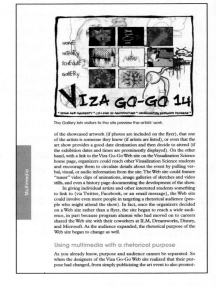

The Gallery lets visitors to the site preview the artists' work.

of the showcased artwork (if photos are included on the flyer), that one of the artists is someone they know (if artists are listed), or even that the art show provides a good date destination and then decide to attend (if the exhibition dates and times are prominently displayed). On the other hand, with a link to the Viza Go-Go Web site on the Visualization Science home page, organizers could reach other Visualization Science students and encourage them to circulate details about the event by pulling verbal, visual, or audio information from the site. The Web site could feature "teaser" video clips of animations, image galleries of sketches and video stills, and even a history page documenting the development of the show.

In giving individual artists and other interested students something to link to (via Twitter, Facebook, or an email message), the Web site could involve even more people in targeting a rhetorical audience (people who might attend the show). In fact, once the organizers decided on a Web site rather than a flyer, the site began to reach a wide audience, in part because program alumni who had moved on to careers shared the Web site with their coworkers at ILM, Dreamworks, Disney, and Microsoft. As the audience expanded, the rhetorical purpose of the Web site began to change as well.

Using multimedia with a rhetorical purpose

As you already know, purpose and audience cannot be separated. So when the designers of the Viza Go-Go Web site realized that their purpose had changed, from simply publicizing the art event to also promot-

The Harbrace Guide to Writing, Concise Second Edition, also helps students take advantage of technology for research, whether they are locating materials through library databases and the Internet, evaluating and citing those materials, or using a word-processing program to keep track of different sources.

Supplements

Instructor's Manual for Glenn's *The Harbrace Guide to Writing,* Concise Second Edition

The comprehensive Instructor's Manual includes detailed syllabi, sample syllabi, and chapter-by-chapter suggestions for using the guide in your classroom. The detailed syllabi comprise three annotated course plans that can be followed or consulted when teaching with this text in programs that focus on academic writing, writing in the disciplines, or service learning. Activities, exercises, and journal-writing prompts are provided for each class meeting, along with suggested goals and materials for instructors to review. If your course is organized around genres, themes, or rhetorical methods, you'll find each of these approaches addressed by sample syllabi and journal-writing prompt—all created for *The Harbrace Guide to Writing.*

Enhanced InSite for Glenn's *The Harbrace Guide to Writing,* Concise Second Edition

You can easily create, assign, and grade writing assignments with Enhanced InSite™ for Glenn's *The Harbrace Guide to Writing*, Concise Second Edition. From a single, easy-to-navigate site, you and your students can manage the flow of papers online, check for originality, and conduct peer reviews. Students can access a multimedia eBook that offers a text-specific workbook, private tutoring options, and resources for writers, including anti-plagiarism tutorials and downloadable grammar podcasts. Enhanced InSite™ provides the tools and resources you and your students need, plus the training and support you want. Learn more at www.cengage.com/insite.

CourseMate for Glenn's *The Harbrace Guide to Writing,* Concise Second Edition

Printed Access Card
ISBN-10: 111176607X; ISBN-13: 9781111766078
Instant Access Code
ISBN-10: 1111766088; ISBN-13: 9781111766085
Cengage Learning's English CourseMate brings course concepts to life with interactive learning, study, and exam preparation tools that support the printed textbook. Students' comprehension will soar as your class works with the printed textbook and the textbook-specific Web site. English CourseMate goes beyond the book to deliver what you need! Learn more at cengage.com/coursemate.

Multimedia eBook for Glenn's *The Harbrace Guide to Writing,* Concise Second Edition

Students can do all of their reading online or use the eBook as a handy reference while they're completing coursework. The eBook includes the full text of the print version with interactive exercises; an integrated text-specific workbook; user-friendly navigation, search, and highlight tools; and links to videos that enhance the text content.

Acknowledgments

All books demand time, talent, and plenty of hard work. For that reason, I could not have produced this textbook without the help and support of a number of colleagues and friends. I found myself calling on their expertise at various times throughout the creation of this book. Stacey Sheriff, Rosalyn Collings Eves, John Belk, and Heather Adams gave generously of their time and wisdom as teachers, scholars, and writers, working with me to create assignments and exercises to which students will want to respond. They helped me conduct research into multimedia sources and locate new readings as well as contributors for various parts of the book. Cristian Nuñez, Alyse Murphy Leininger, and Keith Evans created Tricks of the Trade features. Undergraduate interns Brooke Senior, Sierra Stovall, Emilie Sunndergrun, Daniel Leayman, Monique Williams, Hannah Lewis, and Matt Conte helped with various research and proofreading duties, all demonstrating a professionalism beyond their years. I remain grateful to them all.

At Cengage, Leslie Taggart oversaw the development of the project, relying (as we all have) on the good sense and keen insights of publisher Lyn Uhl, vice-president P. J. Boardman, and, of course, acquisitions editor Margaret Leslie. A recent Cengage hire, Jason Sakos has already demonstrated his marketing prowess. Editorial assistant Elizabeth Ramsey and English Sales Specialist Sherry Robertson helped launch the substantive improvements to this edition. For their painstaking production of this book, I thank Rosemary Winfield, Cengage production editor; Jane Hoover and Quica Ostrander, copyeditors at Lifland et al., Bookmakers; Sarah Bonner, image permissions editor; Martha Hall, text permissions editor; and Lillie Caporlingua, the book's designer. My especial thanks go to Stephanie Pelkowski Carpenter, my constant intellectual companion and out-of-this-world development editor.

Finally, I have learned from a phenomenal group of reviewers, including the following instructors who offered their guidance on this second edition:

Jeff Andelora, *Mesa Community College*
Amy Azul, *Chaffey College*
Andrea Bewick, *Napa Valley College*
Lee Brewer-Jones, *Georgia Perimeter College*
Sue Briggs, *Salt Lake Community College*
Mark Browning, *Johnson County Community College*
Mary Burkhart, *University of Scranton*
Mary Carden, *Edinboro University of Pennsylvania*
Jo Cavins, *North Dakota State University*
Ron Christiansen, *Salt Lake Community College*
Stephanie Dowdle, *Salt Lake Community College*
Rosalyn Eves, *Brigham Young University*
Eugene Flinn, *New Jersey City University*
Patricia Flinn, *New Jersey City University*
Rebecca Fournier, *Triton College*
Powell Franklin, *Jackson State Community College*
Kevin Griffith, *Capital University*
Anna Harrington, *Jackson State Community College*
Martha Holder, *Wytheville Community College*
Dawn Hubbell-Staeble, *Bowling Green State University*
James Mayo, *Jackson State Community College*
Kate Mohler, *Mesa Community College*
Randy Nelson, *Davidson College*
Dana Nkana, *Illinois Central College*
Eden Pearson, *Des Moines Area Community College*
Jason Pickavance, *Salt Lake Community College*
Jeff Pruchnic, *Wayne State University*
Amy Ratto-Parks, *University of Montana*
Wendy Sharer, *East Carolina University*
Noel Sloboda, *Pennsylvania State University-York*
David Swain, *Southern New Hampshire University*
Sharon Tash, *Saddleback College*
Michael Trovato, *Ohio State University–Newark*
Cynthia VanSickle, *McHenry County College*

Cheryl Glenn
July 2010

Entering the Conversation: The Rhetorical Situation

Too often, the word *rhetoric* refers to empty words, implying manipulation, deception, or persuasion at any cost. But as you'll learn in this book, rhetoric and rhetorical situations are not negative and not manipulative. They are everywhere—as pervasive as the air we breathe—and play an essential role in our daily lives as we work to get things done efficiently and ethically. The following two chapters define rhetoric and the rhetorical situation and show you how such situations shape the writing process. You'll begin to develop your rhetorical skills as you work through these chapters, but you'll continue to sharpen them all through your college career and into the workplace. The important point to remember is this: you're probably already pretty good at using rhetoric. So let's build on what you know—and go from there.

Guide to Identifying the Elements of Any Rhetorical Situation

As a responsible writer and speaker, you need to understand the elements of any rhetorical situation you decide to enter. Chapters 1 and 2 will help you identify those elements using the following steps.

- ▶ Identify the opportunity for change that encourages you to enter the situation. Ask yourself: What is it that tugs at me? Why do I feel the need to speak, write, take a photo, share an image? What attitude, action, or opinion do I want to change?

- ▶ Connect the opportunity to make change with your purpose. Ask yourself: What can I accomplish with rhetoric? How can words or visuals allow me to respond to this opportunity?

- ▶ Knowing that your purpose is tethered to the nature and character of the audience, carefully consider the composition of that audience: Who are its members? What are they like? What opinions do they hold? What are their feelings about this opportunity to resolve a problem, to make change? How will they react to the message? Different audiences have different needs and expectations, which the responsible writer or speaker tries to meet.

- ▶ Take into account whatever else has already been said on the subject: Who has been speaking or writing, and what do they say?

- ▶ Whatever the form of its delivery (spoken, written, or electronic), you'll want your response to be fitting (or appropriate). By calibrating the tone of your response, you can control the attitude you project to your intended audience. When shaping a fitting response, you need to be fully aware that you can come only as close to persuasion as the rhetorical situation allows. A responsible speaker or writer cannot do or expect more.

Understanding the Rhetorical Situation 1

Rhetoric Surrounds Us

Every day, you use rhetoric. You use it as you read course syllabi and assignments, the directions for hooking up your stereo system, and your mail, as well as emails, social network postings, and instant messages. You also use it as you write: when you submit written assignments, answer quiz questions in class, leave notes for your roommate, and send text messages to your friends. Every day, you are surrounded by rhetoric and rhetorical opportunities. In fact, you've been participating in rhetorical situations for most of your life.

> ### > WRITE FOR FIVE
>
> 1. Take a few minutes to list the kinds of writing you do every day. Include all instances when you write down information (whether on paper, white board, chalk board, or computer screen). Beside each entry, jot down the reason for that type of writing. Be prepared to share your answers with the rest of the class.
> 2. Consider five of the types of writing you identified in the first activity. Who is your audience for these different kinds of writing? In other words, to whom or for whom are you writing? What is your purpose for each kind of writing? What do you hope to achieve?

Rhetoric: The Purposeful Use of Language and Images

Rhetoric is the purposeful use of language and images. That definition covers a great deal of territory—practically every word and visual element you encounter every day. But it's the word *purposeful* that will guide you through the maze of words and images that saturate your life. When you use words or images to achieve a specific purpose—such as explaining to your supervisor why you need next weekend off—you are speaking, writing, or conveying images rhetorically.

The Greek philosopher Aristotle coined an authoritative definition of *rhetoric* over 2,500 years ago: "Rhetoric is the art of observing in any given situation the available means of persuasion." Let's take this definition apart and examine its constituent elements.

The art of observing in any given situation

"Rhetoric is the art [or mental ability] of observing . . . ." Notice that Aristotle does not call for you to overpower your **audience** (your readers or listeners) with words or images, nor does he push you to win an argument. Instead, he encourages you (as a *rhetor*, or user of rhetoric, such as a **writer** or speaker) to observe, as the first step in discovering what you might say or write. For Aristotle, and all of the rhetorical thinkers who have followed, observing before speaking or writing is primary. You need to observe, to take the time to figure out what kind of rhetorical situation you're entering. Whom are you speaking or writing to? What is your relationship to that person or group of people? What is the occasion? Who else is listening? What do you want your language to accomplish (that is, what is your **purpose**)? By answering these questions, you are establishing the elements of the "given situation."

The available means of persuasion

When you consider "the available means," you evaluate the possible methods of communication you might use. You want to choose the one that will best make **meaning** that helps you achieve your purpose. In other words, should you deliver your **message** orally (face to face or over the telephone), in writing (using a letter or note, an email or instant message, or a Web page), or via film, video, still images, or other visuals? Where might you most successfully deliver that message: in class, at church, at the coffee shop, at a town meeting?

The spoken word is sometimes most appropriate. If you and a good friend have had an argument, you might not want to put your feelings into writing. It might be better if you simply pick up the telephone and say, "I'm sorry." If you're attending a funeral, you'll want to offer your spoken condolences directly to the bereaved, even if you've already sent a card or flowers. However, if your professor expects you to submit a three-page essay recounting your experiences with technology (a technology autobiography, so to speak) you cannot announce that you'd rather tell her your story over coffee in the student union. The only means available in this situation is the written word. Or is it? Your professor might be impressed if you prepared an electronic presentation to accompany your written essay, complete with video or audio clips. Your available means of communicating are seemingly endless.

The last phrase in Aristotle's definition of *rhetoric* is "of persuasion." Persuasion is not a zero-sum game, with the winner taking all. Think of persuasion as a coming together, a meeting of the minds. Ideally, persuasion results in you and your audience being changed by the experience of understanding one another. When both parties are changed (if only by expanding their understanding of an issue), the rhetorical interaction isn't one-sided: both sides are heard, and both the sender and the receiver(s) benefit.

Aristotle tells us that rhetoric's function is not solely successful persuasion; rather, it is to "discover the means of coming as near such success as the circumstances of each particular case allow." If your only persuasive purpose is to get your own way, you may sometimes succeed; more often, truth be told, you'll find yourself disappointed. But if you think about persuasion in terms of understanding, invitation, and adjustment, you can marshal your rhetorical know-how to achieve success in a broader sense.

Persuasive writers (and speakers) rely on observation in order to get a sense of the **rhetorical situation**, the context in which they are communicating. They know that no two situations are ever exactly the same. Every **context** includes distinctive **resources** (positive influences) and **constraints** (obstacles) that shape the rhetorical transaction:

► what has already been said on the subject (by whom and to whom);

► when, where, and how the rhetorical exchange takes place;

► the writer's credibility; and

► the appropriateness of the message in terms of both content and delivery.

Thus, every rhetorical situation calls for you to take note of the available means of persuasion as well as the contextual resources and constraints that will affect your persuasive success.

>ANALYZING THE RHETORICAL SITUATION

Choose two of the following situations and note their similarities and differences in terms of speaker or writer, purpose, audience, and available means (including any resources and constraints). Be prepared to share your observations with the rest of the class.

1. It's time for you to talk with your parents about how you'll spend the coming summer.
2. For the first time, your rent check will be late. You need to explain the reason to your landlord in such a way that the usual late fee will be waived.
3. Your boss has asked you to compose a sign for the store entrance, one that politely asks customers to turn off their cell phones.

4. Your professor has assigned a three-page technology autobiography for Monday.
5. You and your fiancé(e) need to show proof of citizenship or student visas to receive a marriage license.

Analyzing the Rhetorical Situation

You encounter rhetoric—and rhetorical situations—every day, all through the day, from the minute you turn on the morning news to the moment you close your textbook, turn off the light, and go to sleep. In order to develop your skills of persuasion, you need to be able to recognize the elements of rhetorical situations and gauge your own rhetoric accordingly.

As noted above, a rhetorical situation is the context for communicating, the context a writer (or speaker) enters into in order to shape a message that can address a problem and reach an intended audience to change an attitude, action, or opinion. The writer identifies that problem as an **opportunity** to make change through the use of language, whether visual, written, or spoken. Such a problem or opportunity is also known as an *exigence*. For instance, by asking a question, your instructor creates an opportunity for change in the classroom (usually a change in everyone's understanding). The question just hangs there—until someone provides an appropriate response, a **fitting response** in terms of timing, medium of delivery, tone, and content. Similarly, if the company you work for loses online business because its Web site is outdated, that problem can be resolved only through appropriate use of text and visuals. Once the fitting response comes into being, the opportunity for making a change ("I need an answer" or "We need to update our Web site") is either partially removed or disappears altogether; then you have responded to the invitation for change.

Sample analysis of a rhetorical situation

If the idea of a rhetorical situation still seems unfamiliar, consider a wedding invitation. Each invitation is rhetorical, embodying every element of a rhetorical situation: opportunity for change, a writer, an audience, a purpose, the message itself, and a context. The need (or desire, in this case) to invite family and friends to their wedding—the problem—provides the happy couple with a rhetorical opportunity. Whether sent to the audience of potential wedding guests through the mail or electronically, the invitation is a response, a way to resolve the specific problem. The meaning of a wedding invitation resonates within a specific context: it announces a joyous celebration for specific people.

Above is a generic representation of the rhetorical situation. For help visualizing the elements of *specific* rhetorical situations—including those you will encounter in the assignments in Part 2 of this book—access the English CourseMate via CengageBrain.com.

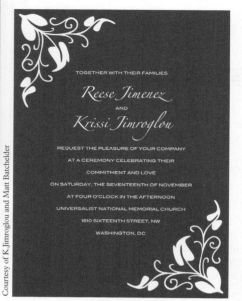

TOGETHER WITH THEIR FAMILIES

Reese Jimenez

AND

Krissi Jimroglou

REQUEST THE PLEASURE OF YOUR COMPANY

AT A CEREMONY CELEBRATING THEIR

COMMITMENT AND LOVE

ON SATURDAY, THE SEVENTEENTH OF NOVEMBER

AT FOUR O'CLOCK IN THE AFTERNOON

UNIVERSALIST NATIONAL MEMORIAL CHURCH

1810 SIXTEENTH STREET, NW

WASHINGTON, DC

Courtesy of K. Jimroglou and Matt Batchelder

Every invitation, such as this one for a commitment ceremony, is rhetorical.

Often, one fitting response sparks another opportunity. Imagine that you have received a wedding invitation. The invitation provides you with an opportunity to resolve a specific problem through language: in this case, to respond by informing the couple whether you will attend the wedding. Your response could be as simple as checking a box on a card included with the invitation, indicating that you will attend. If you are close to the couple and have decided you cannot attend the wedding, you might give them a phone call, in addition to checking the "must decline with regret" box on the reply card. The appropriateness of your response depends on your relationship to the couple (your *audience*, in this rhetorical situation) and your purpose in responding.

> ### > ANALYZING THE RHETORICAL SITUATION

For each of the rhetorical situations below, try to identify the opportunity, writer, audience, message, purpose, and context.

1. A guy you met last summer has invited you to be his Facebook friend.
2. You are applying for a scholarship and need three letters of recommendation.
3. As a member of a wedding party, you are expected to make a toast at the reception.
4. You need to request permission to enroll in a class that is already full but is required for your field of study.

The decision to engage

Rhetorical situations may call for your attention, as when you receive a wedding invitation, or they may arise from your interpretation of some event. For instance, if you're in the market for a new car, you might be tantalized by an advertised price for a car that interests you, only to arrive at the dealership and discover that the marked price is higher than the advertised price. If the price discrepancy catches your attention—enough that you want to enter the rhetorical situation—then that's your opportunity.

You'll next have to decide if you want to attempt to change the situation through the use of rhetoric. If you choose to say something about the discrepancy, you'll have to decide on your purpose, what message you want to send, how to send it, and to whom. You'll also need to take into consideration the constraints on your message: perhaps the advertised car had higher mileage than the one on the dealer's lot, or perhaps the advertised price had a time limit. Therefore, if you decide to enter the rhetorical situation, you'll need to shape it in a way that allows you to send a message. If you're annoyed by the price discrepancy but walk away because you don't want to discuss it, let alone negotiate with the car dealership, then you've chosen not to act rhetorically.

On a daily basis, you'll encounter dozens of opportunities to enter rhetorical situations. Some situations you'll decide to enter, and some you'll decide to pass by. If you witness a car accident, for example, you are an observer; you may decide to volunteer to testify about it and thus become a speaker. If you identify an old friend from a newspaper photograph (observer), you may decide to email him (writer). You might hear a song (observer) and decide to perform it and post a video of your performance on YouTube (speaker). Or you might decide to begin introducing yourself to people in an online video game (observer, audience, and writer). Whatever the situations are and however they are delivered (whether spoken, printed, online, or in some other way), you can decide how or whether you want to act on them.

> YOUR WRITING EXPERIENCES

1. To whom have you written today? Why did you write to that person? Take five minutes to describe that rhetorical situation and transaction, identifying the elements of the rhetorical situation (opportunity, writer, audience, purpose, message, constraints, and resources), the means of communication (handwriting or word processing), and means of delivery (mail, email, note on a slip of paper). How did you make your response a fitting one for the rhetorical situation, even if you did so unconsciously?

2. Think of a time when you identified an opportunity to address a problem but didn't respond. Write for five minutes, describing that opportunity for change and explaining why you didn't write or speak in response to it. If you could do it over, how might you respond? How would you take into consideration each element of the rhetorical situation, in order to come as close to persuasion as conditions allowed?

3. What have you learned from reading this section that you didn't know when you started? How might the information about the rhetorical situation help you? Is there a rhetorical situation that is tugging at you now? If you decide to enter that rhetorical situation, how will you do so? How will you take into consideration each element of the rhetorical situation?

Shaping Reasons to Write

Now that you have begun to identify the constituent elements of a rhetorical situation, take a closer look at each of these elements, along with examples from diverse contexts.

What is a rhetorical opportunity for change?

A rhetorical opportunity (sometimes called an *exigence*) is an opening you identify to address or resolve a problem through spoken or written language. In the example on the facing page, student Collin Allan has identified a rhetorical opportunity in his need for a letter of recommendation. His response to that need is in the form of an email (written language) sent to his instructor.

In writing to Dr. Eves, Collin has created a response to his own need (the need for a letter of recommendation). He's also doing his best to present a rhetorical opportunity to which his instructor will respond. After all, he clearly wants his instructor to consider writing him a positive letter of recommendation. Thus, he has set out to resolve his problem using words. Although he has composed an email, he could have written Dr. Eves a letter or spoken to her over the phone or during an office visit. Whether he used spoken or written words, he would not lose sight of the fact that his audience is his instructor and his purpose is to obtain a letter that gives him a good recommendation.

The medium of delivery—spoken or written (with or without visual elements other than text)—is always up to the sender of a message, who must decide which medium of delivery is most appropriate and timely. Suppose you're applying for a scholarship and need some help from your academic advisor. If the semester isn't yet under way, your best option may be to send an email message to your advisor, which he can access remotely. If you see your advisor almost daily and have taken several classes from him, it might make sense to begin with a spoken request. You could then mail him a set of written documents that include official materials he must fill out and your own materials (illustrating your interests and strengths) that pertain to the application. The materials you supply and the medium you use to communicate with your advisor depend on the elements of the specific rhetorical situation.

Another important characteristic of a rhetorical opportunity for change is that the writer or speaker believes that change can be brought about through language that is spoken or written (or some combination of the two, perhaps combined with visual elements). The woman who picks up the phone to tell her friend she's sorry, the couple who want guests at their wedding, the student who composes an email asking his instructor for a letter of recommendation—all believe that their

> From: Collin Allan <csallan2111@hotmail.com>
> Date: August 13, 2009 1:19 PM
> Subject: Letter of recommendation
> To: Rosalyn Eves <rosalyn.eves@gmail.com>
>
> Dear Dr. Eves,
>
> I will be applying to law school this coming semester. Having
> worked with you both as a student and as a Writing Fellow,
> I thought that you might be willing to provide a letter of
> recommendation for me. Most schools require two letters of
> recommendation from an academic source. If you feel you
> could write a positive letter of recommendation for me, I would
> be honored and would deeply appreciate it. I will be out of town
> until school starts, but, if you are willing, I will get you the necessary
> information upon my return. I hope that I have contacted you far
> enough in advance to give you an opportunity to consider writing
> the letter before the grind of the semester really starts.
>
> Thank you,
>
> Collin Allan

Collin Allan chose email as the most appropriate medium for delivering
his request for a letter of recommendation.

problems can be resolved through language. If any of these problems
were *certain* to be resolved, however, there would be no need to craft
a response to them. If a problem could never be resolved, there would
also be no point in responding to it.

> ANALYZING THE RHETORICAL SITUATION

Decide whether each problem listed below is also a rhetorical
opportunity. Be prepared to share the reasoning behind your
responses with the rest of the class.

1. The Internal Revenue Service is charging you $2,000 in back
   taxes, asserting that you neglected to declare the income from
   your summer job.
2. Your college library has just sent you an email informing you
   that you're being fined for several overdue books, all of which
   you returned a month ago.
3. After Thanksgiving dinner is served, your brothers and mother
   resume their ongoing argument about U.S. politics: health care,
   the wars, and the economy.

4. In the student section at the football stadium, some fans throw empty soda cans, toss beach balls, boo the opposing team, and stand during most of the game. You're quickly losing interest in attending the games.

5. If the university's child care center raises its rates again this year, you will have to look elsewhere for affordable child care.

> YOUR WRITING EXPERIENCES

1. Write for five minutes about a specific school-related assignment that created a rhetorical opportunity for you. In other words, try to remember an assignment that posed a problem to which you *wanted* to respond and *felt a need* to respond with spoken or written words or visuals. Be prepared to share your memory of this assignment with the rest of the class.

2. Consider a school-related assignment that you've been given in recent weeks. In your own words, write out the assignment, paying careful attention to the problem you think the assignment is asking you to resolve with language. Does this assignment establish an opportunity that calls for your response? Do you *want* to respond? If so, explain why. If not, explain how the assignment could be rewritten in such a way that you would feel an authentic reason to write. Be prepared to share your ideas with the rest of the class.

Reading a text for rhetorical opportunity

The following essay, "Why I Want a Wife," by Judy Brady, was first published forty years ago, in the inaugural issue of *Ms.* magazine. It remains one of the most widely anthologized essays in the United States. As you read this short essay, try to imagine American domestic life forty years ago. What specific details does the author provide to feed your imagination? Try to determine Brady's reason for writing this essay. What might have been the rhetorical opportunity that called for her written response?

> Why I Want a Wife
Judy Brady

I belong to that classification of people known as wives. I am a Wife. And, not altogether incidentally, I am a mother.

Not too long ago a male friend of mine appeared on the scene from the Midwest fresh from a recent divorce. He had one child, who is, of course, with his ex-wife. He is obviously looking for another wife. As I thought about him while I was ironing one evening, it suddenly occurred to me that I, too, would like to have a wife. Why do I want a wife?

I would like to go back to school, so that I can become economically independent, support myself, and, if need be, support those dependent upon me. I want a wife who will work and send me to school. And while I am going to school I want a wife to take care of my children. I want a wife to keep track of the children's doctor and dentist appointments. And to keep track of mine, too. I want a wife to make sure my children eat properly and are kept clean. I want a wife who will wash the children's clothes and keep them mended. I want a wife who is a good nurturant attendant to my children, arranges for their schooling, makes sure that they have an adequate social life with their peers, takes them to the park, the zoo, etc. I want a wife who takes care of the children when they are sick, a wife who arranges to be around when the children need special care, because, of course, I cannot miss classes at school. My wife must arrange to lose time at work and not lose the job. It may mean a small cut in my wife's income from time to time, but I guess I can tolerate that. Needless to say, my wife will arrange and pay for the care of the children while my wife is working.

I want a wife who will take care of my physical needs. I want a wife who will keep my house clean. A wife who will pick up after my children, a wife who will pick up after me. I want a wife who will keep my clothes clean, ironed, mended, replaced when need be, and who will see to it that my personal things are kept in their proper place so that I can find what I need the minute I need it. I want a wife who cooks the meals, a wife who is a good cook. I want a wife who will plan the menus, do the necessary grocery shopping, prepare the meals, serve them pleasantly, and then do the cleaning up while I do my studying. I want a wife who will care for me when I am sick and sympathize with my pain and loss of time from school. I want a wife to go along when our family takes a vacation so that someone can continue to care for me and my children when I need a rest and a change of scene.

I want a wife who will take care of details of my social life. When my wife and I are invited out by my friends, I want a wife who will take care of the babysitting arrangements. When I meet people at school that I like and want to entertain, I want a wife who will have the house clean, will prepare a special meal, serve it to me and my friends, and not interrupt when I talk about the things that interest me and my friends. I want a wife who will have arranged that the children are fed and ready for bed before my guests arrive so that the children do not bother us. I want a wife who takes care of the needs of my guests so that they feel comfortable, who makes sure that they have an ashtray, that they are passed the hors d'oeuvres, that they are offered a second helping of the food, that their wine glasses are replenished when

continued

"Why I Want a Wife" *(continued)*

necessary, that their coffee is served to them as they like it. And I want a wife who knows that sometimes I need a night out by myself.

I want a wife who is sensitive to my sexual needs, a wife who makes love passionately and eagerly when I feel like it, a wife who makes sure that I am satisfied. And, of course, I want a wife who will not demand sexual attention when I am not in the mood for it. I want a wife who assumes the complete responsibility for birth control, because I do not want more children. I want a wife who will remain sexually faithful to me so that I do not have to clutter up my intellectual life with jealousies. And I want a wife who understands that my sexual needs may entail more than strict adherence to monogamy. I must, after all, be able to relate to people as fully as possible.

If, by chance, I find another person more suitable as a wife than the wife I already have, I want the liberty to replace my present wife with another one. Naturally, I will expect a fresh, new life; my wife will take the children and be solely responsible for them so that I am left free.

When I am through with school and have acquired a job, I want my wife to quit working and remain at home so that my wife can more fully and completely take care of a wife's duties.

My God, why wouldn't I want a wife?

After reading Brady's essay, you may want to spend some class time discussing the merits of her argument, for both the 1970s and today. You may also want to consider her pervasive use of irony (her tongue-in-cheek attitude toward her subject), the extent to which she's being serious, and the potential sexism of the essay. Few readers of this essay can resist registering their agreement or disagreement with its author; you may want to register yours as well.

Whether or not you agree with Brady, it's important for you to be able to analyze her rhetorical situation, starting with the reason she may have written this essay in the first place. Why would she keep repeating "I want a wife . . ."? Why would she write from the husband's point of view? Why would she describe a wife who does all the "heavy lifting" in a marriage? What kind of husband does she evoke? What effects do her rhetorical choices have on you as a reader?

Write your responses to the following questions. In doing so, you are practicing what's known as *rhetorical analysis*.

1. *What does this essay say?* Compile the details of a wife's daily life and describe the writer's feelings about a husband's expectations; then write one sentence that conveys Brady's main argument.

2. *Why does the essay say that?* Drawing on your previous answer, write three or four assertions that support Brady's argument.

3. *Who composed this message?* What information does the writer supply about her identity?

4. *What rhetorical opportunity called for the writing of this essay?* State that opportunity in one sentence.

5. *How does the essay respond to that opportunity? What change in attitude, opinion, or action does the author wish to influence?*

Reading an image for rhetorical opportunity

Responses to rhetorical opportunities are not always verbal. Visual responses to rhetorical opportunities constantly bombard us—from advertisements and promotions to cards from friends and political messages. If you think the Callout Card here addresses the problem of electronic harassment, then you view it as a fitting response to a rhetorical opportunity for change. Obviously, the sender of "David, wrapped in a towel" does not want to receive visuals that are "naughty," maybe even pornographic. When you consider this image and text in terms of a rhetorical response, you are analyzing it rhetorically, "reading" it more thoroughly than you might have otherwise.

Reading for rhetorical opportunity helps you develop your skills as an active, informed reader and as a rhetorical analyst. Respond to the same questions you answered about "Why I Want a Wife," but this time focus on the Callout Card:

Sponsored and co-created by the Family Violence Prevention Fund, the Office on Violence Against Women, and the Ad COUNCIL.

This Callout Card, available at Thatsnotcool.com, is a visual response to a rhetorical opportunity.

1. *What does the visual "say"—and how?* Describe the visual in one sentence, paying attention to both the statue and the brightly colored text that accompanies it.

2. *Why does the visual say that?* Consider the contexts in which you might usually see a statue such as Michelangelo's *David*. Compare those contexts with this one.

3. *Who composed this message?* Consider what you know or can find out about the groups responsible for the message: the Family Violence Prevention Fund, the Office on Violence Against Women, and the Ad Council for the Web site Thatsnotcool.com.

4. *What is the rhetorical opportunity that called for the creation of this visual?* Using the information you've compiled in response to questions 1, 2, and 3, identify the opportunity that calls for this visual response.

5. *How does the visual respond to the opportunity?* What message does this visual send to viewers? How might this visual work to address the problem you described in the previous answer? It might help to keep in mind that Callout Cards can be shared through email, Facebook, and MySpace.

Whether you're reading an essay, listening to a speech, or looking at a visual, you'll understand the message better if you begin by determining the rhetorical opportunity that calls for specific words or visuals. Very often, the responses you're reading or viewing call for even further responses. For instance, you may feel a strong urge to respond to "Why I Want a Wife" or to the Callout Card, which are responses in themselves. Whether your response is spoken, written, or composed visually, its power lies in your understanding of the rhetorical opportunity.

Creating or Finding a Rhetorical Opportunity

Unless you perceive something as an opportunity, you cannot respond to it. In other words, *something* needs to stimulate or provoke your interest and call for your response. When you take an essay examination for an American history midterm, you might be given the choice of answering one of three questions:

1. The great increase in size and power of the federal government since the Civil War has long been a dominant theme of American history. Trace the growth of the federal government since 1865, paying particular attention to its evolving involvement in world affairs and the domestic economy. Be sure to support your argument with relevant historical details.

2. Compare and contrast the attempts to create and safeguard African American civil rights in two historical periods: the first era of reconstruction (post–Civil War years to the early twentieth century) and the second era of reconstruction (1950s to 1970s). Consider government policies, African American strategies, and the responses of white people to those strategies.

3. "When the United States enters a war, it does so in the defense of vital national interests." Assess the accuracy of this statement with reference to any three of the following: the Spanish-American War, World War I, World War II, the Cold War, and the Vietnam War. Be sure to define "national interests" and to support your argument with relevant historical details.

If you're lucky, one of the above questions will call for your response, given your interests and knowledge. You can ignore the other two questions and turn your energies to the one you've chosen. Think of every college writing situation as a rhetorical opportunity for you to use language in order to resolve or address a problem.

Online opportunities

In addition to the spoken and written rhetorical opportunities we encounter, online opportunities greet us nearly every time we turn on our computers. If you're familiar with the Web site Facebook.com, for instance, you know that it presents numerous opportunities for response. If "Become a Fan" or "What's on Your Mind" doesn't tantalize you, other opportunities will, such as "Status Updates." In other words, different people respond to different online rhetorical opportunities—and those opportunities exist nearly everywhere you browse online.

The family of missing college student Cindy Song, for instance, has resorted to online opportunities in the hope of receiving information about Song, who disappeared on Halloween 2001. Despite an extended, intensive search, an ongoing FBI investigation, and a feature on the TV series *Unsolved Mysteries,* Song's family has no leads. So they have set up a Web page (page 19), which asks anyone who might remember any detail about the night Song went missing to contact the local police. Each of the news stories, in addition to the appeal on the Web, creates an opportunity for people to respond with language. Every time you come across a story like Song's, you may wish you could respond—but you probably cannot. You have no

David J. Green-lifestyle themes/Alamy

Social networking sites offer many rhetorical opportunities.

information about the missing person. Therefore, despite the opportunity, you don't respond (even though you wish you could).

> ## > YOUR WRITING EXPERIENCES

1. When was the last time you identified a rhetorical opportunity to which you felt compelled to respond? Write for five minutes or so, describing the opportunity in terms of the rhetorical situation and how you addressed it. Share your response with the rest of the class.

2. Consider a time when you indentified a rhetorical opportunity to which you did not or could not respond. Describe this opportunity and explain what prevented you from responding.

Everyday rhetorical opportunities

Cindy Song's disappearance serves as one of many daily chances you will have to respond to rhetorical opportunities, some joyous, others heartbreaking. If your good friend applies for and gets the job of her dreams, the situation calls for a response. How will she know that you're happy for her unless you send her a congratulatory card, give her a phone call, invite her to a celebratory lunch—or all three? The death of your neighbor creates an opportunity to respond with a letter to the family or a bouquet of flowers and an accompanying condolence note. A friend's illness, an argument with a roommate, a tuition hike, an essay exam, a sales presentation, a job interview, a sorority rush, or children's misbehavior—these are all situations that provide opportunities for response through spoken or written words or through visuals.

Whether you choose to recognize—let alone speak to—a rhetorical opportunity is usually up to you, as are whether you create an elaborate or a simple response and how you deliver your message—whether you choose to write a letter to the editor of the campus newspaper, make a phone call to your state representative's office, prepare a PowerPoint presentation, create a fact sheet, or interrupt someone else and speak. You often have a choice, but not always. Sometimes you're forced to respond and to do so in a specific way.

> ## > ANALYZING THE RHETORICAL SITUATION

1. What is one rhetorical opportunity you are currently considering? Write for a few minutes, describing the overall situation, the problem that can be addressed with language, and the specific call for language.

2. From whom would you like a response? Why is that person (or group) the best source of a response? Write for a few minutes, connecting your answer with that for question 1.

Hyun Jong Song

MPCCN Case File: 1529F00

Above Images: Song, circa 2001

Vital Statistics at Time of Disappearance

- **Missing Since:** November 1, 2001 from State College, Pennsylvania
  - **Classification:** Endangered Missing
    - **Date Of Birth:** February 25, 1980
      - **Age:** 21 years old
      - **Height and Weight:** 5'1-5'3, 110-130 pounds
- **Distinguishing Characteristics:** Black hair, brown eyes. Song is of Korean descent. Her ears and navel are pierced. Song's nickname is Cindy. Her middle name may be spelled "Jung." Song's first name may be spelled "Hyunjong" or "Hyunjung."

Details of Disappearance

Song was raised in Seoul, South Korea. She moved to the United States in 1995 to live with relatives in Springfield, Virginia near Alexandria. Song graduated from high school and enrolled in Pennsylvania State University, where she majored in integrated arts. She was scheduled to graduate during the spring of 2002.

Song attended a Halloween party during the early morning hours of November 1, 2001 at the *Player's Nite Club* in the 110 block of West College Avenue. She departed from the party at 2:00 a.m., then stopped by a friend's home for two hours. Another friend dropped Song off outside of her residence in *State College Park Apartments* in the 340 block of West Clinton Avenue at approximately 4:00 a.m. She had been drinking that evening and was mildly intoxicated when taken to her apartment. She was last seen wearing her costume, which consisted of a pink sleeveless shirt with a rabbit design imprinted on the front, rabbit ears, a white tennis skirt with a cotton bunny tail attached to the back, brown suede leather knee-

Web sites such as this one for missing children try to create an opportunity to which viewers want to respond.

3. What content and medium of response would you prefer? How will people know your preference? Expand on what you wrote for questions 1 and 2 and explain why your preferred content and medium form the best response to this rhetorical opportunity.
4. How might language be a way to respond to the opportunity for making change? In other words, what exactly might language do to relieve or resolve the problem in your life? Add your answer to this question to what you've already written. Be prepared to share your overall analysis with the rest of the class.
5. In class, listen carefully to your classmates' analyses, and take notes. Be prepared to provide suggestions for improving their concepts of rhetorical opportunity, response, and resolution.

Selecting a Rhetorical Audience and Purpose

No doubt many of you have received mailings targeted to you based on your interests and purchases. The message on the following page was sent via email by Barnes & Noble in anticipation of the publication of the last novel in the Harry Potter series. The message was sent to many people—but not to just anyone—for one purpose: to persuade them to

Rhetorical Situation

© Barnes & Nobles, Inc., 2007

Messages such as this one from Barnes & Noble are created with a *rhetorical audience* in mind.

come to a celebration at a Barnes & Noble store, and to buy their copy of *Harry Potter and the Deathly Hallows* there, too.

Of course, not everyone is interested in Harry Potter, let alone in attending a late night party in costume, just to be among the first to get a copy of the newest book in the series. So Barnes & Noble sent this email message to people who had purchased other Harry Potter books or calendars, notebooks, and so on, anticipating that they would be familiar with the tradition of arriving at a store hours ahead of the book's release ("Join us . . . as you count down the final moments to Harry's arrival!"). Additionally, because Barnes & Noble is reaching these people through the medium of email, the message includes information about ordering the book online—just a click away for those already reading email. Thus, the specific audience for the email (people who had purchased Harry Potter items in the past) was closely related to its purpose (enticing these people to purchase Harry Potter items in the near future).

Audience versus rhetorical audience

Audience is a key component of any rhetorical situation. After all, you'll direct your writing, speaking, or visual display to a specific audience in an attempt to change some opinion, attitude, or action. But even as you tailor your verbal or visual language to a specific audience, you must keep in mind that that person or group may not be a rhetorical audience. A **rhetorical audience** consists of *only* those persons who are capable of being influenced by verbal or visual discourse and of bringing about change, either by acting themselves or by influencing others who can create change. The following examples will help clarify the concept of rhetorical audience.

Not every person who received the invitation to come to the Harry Potter party was persuaded to attend, let alone buy the new book. No matter how enticing the email might have been, some people did not even read it: they were not open to being influenced by the message. Others may have looked it over quickly, considered the offer, and *then* deleted it. Still others probably waited to discuss the invitation with their friends before deciding whether to attend. Those who did accept the invitation were capable of bringing about the change that made them guests at the party and consumers of the product.

Now consider the Saab advertisement. Clearly, the purpose of all advertising is to sell a product, so every advertiser must keep a buying audience in mind. The Saab ad tantalizes readers with visual and verbal details, including the $39,995 price tag. The audience for this ad consists of people who appreciate Saabs and perhaps admire Saab owners. Some of them might yearn for a Saab themselves but feel they cannot afford one. The rhetorical audience for this ad, however, consists of those people who can either buy a Saab or influence someone else to buy one. These people can use words to negotiate specific features (color, engine, wheel design, model, and so on) and price if they decide to purchase a Saab. Or they can use words to influence someone else to purchase a Saab. Either way, their actions have been influenced by the ad. But, not every reader of the ad will be influenced by it.

Not every person who listens to a presidential hopeful's speech, watches a Super Bowl ad, or reads about impending tuition hikes is part of a rhetorical audience. After

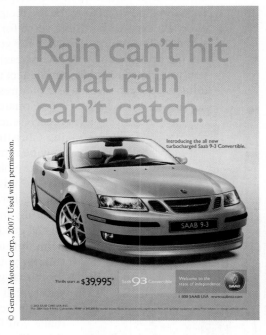

© General Motors Corp., 2007. Used with permission.

Magazine advertisements such as this one seek to persuade those who can buy the product advertised or those who can influence someone else to buy it.

all, not every person is open to being influenced by the discourse and bringing about change or influencing those who can make a change. But some people *are* open to influence. The delegates at the Republican National Convention are a rhetorical audience: they listen to speeches and cast their votes. When the delegates choose the presidential and vice presidential candidates, they eliminate all the other Republican candidates, thereby influencing the voting options of millions of Americans.

Similarly, many more people are upset—and affected—by tuition hikes than are willing to try to do something about them. Those in the rhetorical audience write or telephone their state representatives, their university's board of trustees, and the university administration to protest tuition hikes. They feel empowered as agents of change and believe that their words can change the minds of the people who determine tuition rates.

The message—whether verbal or visual—can influence a rhetorical audience. You apply this knowledge every time you stand in front of a large display of greeting cards and spend what seems like more time choosing "just the right card" than you spent choosing the gift. You evaluate each card's visual elements and greeting, considering and rejecting cards in rapid succession as you match up the features of the card with the interests of the recipient. After all, you want your influence to be positive, to make the recipient feel appreciated. Whether you choose a card with a Bible verse for your religious friend, a picture of a black lab catching a Frisbee for your dog-loving roommate, or a romantic greeting for your sweetheart, your choice reflects the message you want to send to your audience, the person who is capable of being influenced by the words and pictures that you chose.

© Steven Lunetta photography, 2007

Even when choosing a birthday card, you're considering a rhetorical audience.

Consider the pile of holiday cards you receive each winter. Some may be celebrating Christmas, Hanukkah, or Kwanzaa; some may be reminders of lesser-known holidays— Winter Solstice, Yule, or Ásatrú. Others may just be wishing you "Happy Holidays" or hoping for "Peace on Earth." Whatever the greeting and visual, you are the audience for all the cards you receive. You are capable of being influenced by any of them. But, in actuality, you'll be influenced by only a few: those that give you special pleasure, motivate you to call the sender, surprise you because you don't celebrate *that* particular holiday, or make you feel sentimental about the holiday at hand or friends who are not.

As a member of a rhetorical audience, you're not only capable of being influenced (or changed) by the situation, but also capable of bringing about change as a result of the situation. You can bring about change on your own, or you can influence the people who can make the change.

You are bringing about change, for example, when you pick up the phone to apologize for a long-standing misunderstanding after you read a former friend's moving handwritten message at the bottom of a "Peace on Earth" card. After receiving a "Happy Holidays" card from your brother announcing that he'll be home from Iraq for the holidays, you might recruit all his old buddies for a surprise welcome. Both decisions render you part of the rhetorical audience. When your English instructor writes comments on your drafts, you can become part of her rhetorical audience by following her instructions and writing better essays.

Considering purpose in terms of rhetorical audience

Many writers equate purpose with their reason for writing: they're fulfilling an assignment or meeting a deadline; they want a good grade or want to see their essay in print; they want to make money or win a contest. When you're writing with a **rhetorical purpose**, however, you move beyond such goals to one of influencing your rhetorical audience. In order to achieve this influence, you'll need to keep in mind the nature of your audience (their control, power, and status) and their character (sympathetic or unsympathetic to, opposed to or in favor of your message).

You already know that rhetorical audience and purpose cannot be separated. You always try to send your message to someone who can be influenced to change an attitude, action, or opinion or resolve a problem of some kind. For example, when you enter a department store to return defective merchandise, you know that you need to speak to a department supervisor or maybe go to the service desk. You don't want to waste your time talking with people who cannot help you.

Once you reach your rhetorical audience, you try to shape your message in terms of content, tone, examples, and timeliness in order to enhance its chances of influencing that audience. Whether you're talking to your instructor, one of your parents, or your physician, you try to keep in mind the kind of information you should deliver—as well as how and when to deliver it. Balancing audience and purpose is a skill you can work to improve.

Reading a cartoon for rhetorical audience and purpose

In June 2009, the re-election of President Mahmoud Ahmadinejad prompted many Iranians to cry foul. Although the government quickly blocked oppositional Web sites and text messaging services,

This cartoon responds to a political opportunity for change.

many Iranians found another available means for getting the word out about the protests that developed in response to the apparently rigged elections: Twitter posts (tweets). Thanks to the 140-character Twitter reports and the YouTube videos from Iranians, the rest of the world became aware of what they could not see on traditional media outlets.

The cartoon represents an Iranian Lady Liberty, who, like the Statue of Liberty, wears a stola (a dress worn over her tunic) and a radiant crown. Instead of a lit torch, she lifts up her cell phone (displaying a photo of a lit torch), a primary tool in the Iranian people's fight to be heard. Like the Statue of Liberty, she also carries a tablet in her left hand. But instead of being engraved with the date of the U.S. Declaration of Independence, it is inscribed with the word *VOTE* and the date of the elections that launched the protests, June 12.

> ANALYZING THE RHETORICAL SITUATION

1. Reread the cartoon, and then write for five minutes about it. List all the information you can possibly glean from its visual and verbal details.

2. Compare your answers to question 1 with those of one or two classmates and write a joint account of the visual and verbal details of the cartoon and its overall impact.

3. What rhetorical opportunity does the cartoon offer? To what rhetorical opportunity does it respond?

4. Who is the intended audience for the cartoon? In what ways does that audience fulfill the definition of a rhetorical audience?

5. Account for your response to the cartoon. Are you a member of the rhetorical audience? If so, list the ways you fulfill the role of a rhetorical audience. Be prepared to share your answer with the rest of the class.

6. What specific visual or verbal details reveal something about the character of the cartoonist? Appeal to your emotions (positively or negatively)? Shape an argument, even if it's one you don't agree with?

Reading a book introduction for rhetorical audience and purpose

English professor Michael Bérubé writes widely about academic matters: curriculum, teaching loads, classroom management, tenure, and cultural studies. But with the birth of his second son, James (Jamie), Bérubé ventured into another kind of writing, writing aimed at a wider audience. The following excerpt is from the introduction to *Life as We Know It: A Father, a Family, and an Exceptional Child*, a chronicle of his family's experiences with Jamie, who has Down syndrome.

Excerpt from

> Life as We Know It

Michael Bérubé

© Steve Tressler, 2006

My little Jamie loves lists: foods, colors, animals, numbers, letters, states, classmates, parts of the body, days of the week, modes of transportation, characters who live on Sesame Street, and the names of the people who love him. Early last summer, I hoped his love of lists—and his ability to catalogue things *into* lists—would stand him in good stead during what would undoubtedly be a difficult "vacation" for anyone, let alone a three-year-old child with Down syndrome: a three-hour drive to Chicago, a rush-hour flight to LaGuardia, a cab to Grand Central, a train to Connecticut—and *then* smaller trips to New York, Boston, and Old Orchard Beach, Maine. Even accomplishing the first of these mission objectives—arriving safely at O'Hare—required a precision and teamwork I do not always associate with my family. I dropped off Janet and nine-year-old Nick at the terminal with the baggage, then took Jamie to long-term parking with me while they checked in, and then entertained Jamie all the way back to the terminal,

continued

via bus and shuttle train. We sang about the driver on the bus, and we counted all the escalator steps and train stops, and when we finally got to our plane, I told Jamie, *Look, there's Mommy and Nick at the gate! They're yelling that we're going to lose our seats! They want to know why it took us forty-five minutes to park the car!*

All went well from that point on, though, and in the end, I suppose you could say Jamie got as much out of his vacation as might any toddler being whisked up and down New England. He's a seasoned traveler, and he thrives on shorelines, family gatherings, and New Haven pizza. And he's good with faces and names.

Then again, as we learned toward the end of our brief stay in Maine, he doesn't care much for amusement parks. Not that Nick did either, at three. But apparently one of the attractions of Old Orchard Beach, for my wife and her siblings, was the small beachfront arcade and amusement park in town, which they associated with their own childhoods. It was an endearing strip, with a roller coaster just the right size for Nick—exciting, mildly scary, but with no loop-the-loops, rings of fire, or oppressive G forces. We strolled among bumper cars, cotton candy, games of chance and skill, and a striking number of French-Canadian tourists: perhaps the first time our two little boys had ever seen more than one Bérubé family in one place. James, however, wanted nothing to do with any of the rides, and though he loves to pretend-drive and has been on bumper cars before, he squalled so industriously before the ride began as to induce the bumper cars operator to let him out of the car and refund his two tickets.

Jamie finally settled in next to a train ride designed for children five and under or thereabouts, which, for two tickets, took its passengers around an oval layout and over a bridge four times. I found out quickly enough that Jamie didn't want to *ride* the ride; he merely wanted to stand at its perimeter, grasping the partition with both hands and counting the cars—one, two, three, four, five, six—as they went by. Sometimes, when the train traversed the bridge, James would punctuate it with tiny jumps, saying, "Up! Up! Up!" But for the most part, he was content to hang onto the metal bars of the partition, grinning and counting—and, when the train came to a stop, pulling my sleeve and saying, "More, again."

This went on for about half an hour, well past the point at which I could convincingly share Jamie's enthusiasm for tracking the train's progress. As it went on my spirits began to sink in a way I do not recall having felt before. Occasionally it will occur to Jane or to me that Jamie will always be "disabled," that his adult and adolescent years will undoubtedly be more difficult emotionally—for him and for us—than his early childhood, that we will never *not* worry about his future, his quality of life, whether we're doing enough for him. But usually these moments occur in the relative comfort of abstraction, when Janet and I are lying in bed at night and wondering what will become of us all.

When I'm *with* Jamie, by contrast, I'm almost always fully occupied by taking care of his present needs rather than by worrying about his future. When he asks to hear the Beatles because he loves their cover of Little Richard's "Long Tall Sally," I just play the song, sing along, and watch him dance with delight; I do not concern myself with extraneous questions such as whether he'll ever distinguish early Beatles from late Beatles, Paul's songs from John's, originals from covers. These questions are now central to Nick's enjoyment of the Beatles, but that's Nick for you. Jamie is entirely *sui generis*, and as long as I'm with him I can't think of him as anything but Jamie.

I have tried. Almost as a form of emotional exercise, I have tried, on occasion, to step back and see him as others might see him, as an instance of a category, one item on the long list of human subgroups. *This is a child with Down syndrome,* I say to myself. *This is a child with a developmental disability.* It never works: Jamie remains Jamie to me. I have even tried to imagine him as he would have been seen in other eras, other places: *This is a retarded child.* And even: *This is a Mongoloid child.* This makes for unbearable cognitive dissonance. I can imagine that people might think such things, but I cannot imagine how they might think them in a way that prevents them from seeing Jamie *as* Jamie. I try to recall how I saw such children when I was a child, but here I guiltily draw a blank: I don't remember seeing them at all, which very likely means that I never quite saw them *as* children. Instead I remember a famous passage from Ludwig Wittgenstein's *Philosophical Investigations:* "'Seeing-as' is not part of perception. And for this reason it is *like* seeing, and then again *not* like." Reading Wittgenstein, I often think, is something like listening to a brilliant and cantankerous uncle with an annoying fondness for koans. But on this one, I know exactly what he means.

> ANALYZING THE RHETORICAL SITUATION

1. To what rhetorical opportunity might Bérubé be responding?
2. Who is the intended audience for Bérubé's book? In what ways does that audience fulfill the definition of a rhetorical audience? How do you know?
3. What rhetorical opportunity does Bérubé offer his audience? Are there specific ways in which his rhetorical audience could be open to effecting change or influencing others who could make change?
4. If you were writing an essay about a remarkable person, whom would you choose to write about? Who would make up your audience? What rhetorical opportunity might you create or perceive in order to shape a fitting response? What would be your purpose? Freewrite for ten minutes and be prepared to share your thoughts with the rest of the class.

COMMUNITY CONNECTIONS

1. Bring a copy of your local or campus newspaper to class. Spend time with a classmate looking over the cartoons, columns, and letters on the editorial page. Choose one of the editorials or cartoons and determine the rhetorical opportunity for change that it presents. Who is the rhetorical audience for the editorial or cartoon? In what specific ways might that audience be influenced to change? What is the overall purpose of the editorial? What does the artist or writer want the rhetorical audience to do with the information? Be prepared to share your answers with the rest of the class.

2. Work with one or two classmates to consider someone with influence in your school or community (whether in politics, education, sports, medicine, or the arts) and a rhetorical opportunity for change to which he or she has responded. Describe that opportunity and the person's response. What group of people comprise the rhetorical audience for the response? What would the person have his or her rhetorical audience do? Be prepared to share your answers with the rest of the class.

3. What problem do you face today that can be addressed or resolved through language? What is a possible fitting response to your problem? Who is the rhetorical audience for the response? How would you like that person or those people to be influenced or changed? Write for a few minutes, describing the elements of this rhetorical situation.

4. Consider yourself as a rhetorical audience. For whom do you function as such? In what ways are you considered capable of being influenced by the language of someone else? Capable of implementing change? Capable of influencing those who can make change? Write for five minutes, describing yourself as a rhetorical audience. Prepare to discuss your answer with the rest of the class.

Identifying a Fitting Response 2

Confronted with the problem of bird extinction, amateur birdwatcher and professor of English Christopher Cokinos began writing *Hope Is the Thing with Feathers*. Cokinos considered his new book to be a fitting response to the rhetorical opportunity for change that called to him. After all, most people knew nothing about important North American birds, particularly those birds that had become extinct, and his book could educate them. He knew he couldn't restore the Carolina parakeet or any of the other five bird species that had been hastened into extinction by logging, the millinery trade, unregulated hunting, and bird collecting. But Cokinos could "restory" these lost beings to human consciousness at the same time as he energized conservation efforts for other endangered nonhuman species.

The beautiful and extinct Carolina parakeet.

On an afternoon in late September, in a brisk prairie wind, I watched a bird I'd never seen before, a bird that had strayed far from its usual skies a continent away. Nearly epic in memory, that day began my journey, though I didn't know it then. The journey would take years and retrieve many things: first among them the name of the bird I had watched and didn't know—an escaped parrot that didn't "belong" in Kansas.

Seeing this bird led me to learn of—and revere—America's forgotten Carolina Parakeet, which once colored the sky "like an atmosphere of gems," as one pioneer wrote. The more I learned of the Carolina Parakeet's life, its extinction and its erasure from our memory, the more I wondered: How could we have lost and then forgotten so beautiful a bird? This book is, in part, an attempt to answer those questions and an effort to make certain that we never again forget this species nor the others of which I write.

—Christopher Cokinos, from *Hope Is the Thing with Feathers*

In writing answers to the following questions, think back to a time when you responded to a rhetorical opportunity through some form of writing.

1. In what ways did your response reach and satisfy your intended audience?
2. In what ways was it an appropriate response to the problem you identified?
3. What other appropriate responses would have been possible?

What Is a Fitting Response?

Chapter 1 stressed the importance of identifying the elements of a rhetorical situation (opportunity, purpose, writer, message, audience, and context). Now that you can identify these elements, you can begin evaluating the wide range of possible responses you can offer. The goal of every person who responds rhetorically to a situation is to shape a **fitting response**, a visual or verbal (written or spoken) response that

▶ addresses the opportunity for change,

▶ is appropriate in content, tone, and timing,

▶ is delivered in an appropriate medium, and thus

▶ reaches, satisfies, and maybe even changes the actions, opinions, or attitudes of the intended audience.

Was Christopher Cokinos's book on the extinction of bird species a fitting response? Yes.

Was his the *only* possible fitting response? No.

Had Cokinos been a different sort of person, having different resources and interests and imagining different rhetorical audiences, he might have made a feature film about these birds, one starring Robert Pattinson and Reese Witherspoon as either hunters or conservationists. He might have put together a public television special, underwritten by the U.S. Department of the Interior. Or maybe he could have induced PIXAR Studios to make an animated children's movie about these birds, with voiceovers by Angelina Jolie, Will Ferrel, and Forest Whitaker. Depending on the problem, responses in different media may reach and satisfy the rhetorical audience.

A fitting response suits the problem

As you know by now, the prime characteristic of a rhetorical situation is that it presents an opportunity for change. Another key feature of a rhetorical situation is that it invites a fitting response. The fitting response is dictated by the situation: by the specific opportunity for response, the writer's relationship with the audience, the constitution of the audience, what that audience might do, the available means of delivering a message, and other constraints and resources of the rhetorical situation. For instance, if you were bothered by your friend's weekend alcohol consumption, you'd want to find a good time and place to talk with her about it, focusing on the dangers to her own well-being or discussing the pros and cons of drinking by college students. This situation invites such a response. On the other hand, the situation does not invite a subpoena, lawsuit, or visit from a physician—at least not yet.

Fraternity parties, post-game celebrations, and spring break have long been part of the college experience. Some have said that these events serve as rites of passage for students as they move from high school into adulthood. But the alcohol consumption that so often accompanies these rites presents a major public health issue. Underage and binge drinking often lead to drunk driving, alcohol dependence, risky sexual behavior, physical injuries, and even death.

According to the Center on Alcohol Marketing and Youth (CAMY), American teenagers are particularly vulnerable to the effects of alcohol. A fact sheet published by the organization indicates that nine U.S. teens are killed each day from alcohol-related causes (including drunk driving). Drinking before the age of twenty-one is believed to impair critical stages of adolescent brain development. Twenty-three percent of sexually active teens and young adults (aged 15–24) blamed having had unprotected sex on drinking (or drug use). Finally, CAMY reports that "alcohol use plays a substantial role in all three leading causes of death among youth—unintentional injuries (including motor vehicle fatalities and drownings), suicides and homicides." Those are just the physical consequences. As you might imagine, the social consequences of underage and binge drinking are innumerable.

One response to the rhetorical situation presented by irresponsible drinking has been a reexamination of drinking practices. The U.S. medical community, for example, has summarized a list of prevention strategies, with the full realization that those strategies can be instituted only within supporting social, political, and economic infrastructure. To that end, the minimum drinking-age laws must be enforced; alcohol tax must be increased; young people must be excluded as targets of alcohol advertising; and educational programs must be instituted. And that's just a start.

Across the United States, college and university administrators have come together in the hope of sparking a national conversation on drinking. They want to work together to discuss the effects of a minimum drinking age and reopen the public debate on what that age should be. These efforts have given rise to what has come to be called the Amethyst

AP Photo/Toby Talbot

Amethyst Initiative's founder
John McCardell.

Initiative (from the ancient Greek *a methustos,* or "not intoxicated").

Part of the conversation proposed by the Amethyst Initiative is reconsideration of current laws and policies and the creation of a plan for instilling in young people responsible decision making about alcohol use. Toward these ends, college administrators framed an invitational statement expressing their views, a statement that, rather than prescribing specific actions or changes, serves as an invitation for their colleagues across the nation to discuss the possibilities for positive change in the actions, attitudes, and opinions of young people. The statement invites supporters to join the cause—and the conversation. Consider the ways in which the statement constitutes a fitting response to the problem of irresponsible drinking.

> It's Time To Rethink the Drinking Age

The Amethyst Initiative

In 1984 Congress passed the National Minimum Drinking Age Act, which imposed a penalty of 10% of a state's federal highway appropriation on any state setting its drinking age lower than 21.

Twenty-four years later, our experience as college and university presidents convinces us that . . .

Twenty-one is not working

A culture of dangerous, clandestine "binge-drinking"—often conducted off-campus—has developed.

Alcohol education that mandates abstinence as the only legal option has not resulted in significant constructive behavioral change among our students.

Adults under 21 are deemed capable of voting, signing contracts, serving on juries and enlisting in the military, but are told they are not mature enough to have a beer.

By choosing to use fake IDs, students make ethical compromises that erode respect for the law.

AMETHYST INITIATIVE
RETHINK THE DRINKING AGE

HOME   STATEMENT   ABOUT   SIGNATORIES   WHY SIGN?   CONTACT

WELCOME TO THE AMETHYST INITIATIVE

Launched in July 2008, the Amethyst Initiative is made up of chancellors and presidents of universities and colleges across the United States. These higher education leaders have signed their names to a public statement that the problem of irresponsible drinking by young people continues despite the minimum legal drinking age of 21, and there is a culture of dangerous binge drinking on many campuses.

The Amethyst Initiative supports informed and unimpeded debate on the 21 year-old drinking age. Amethyst Initiative presidents and chancellors call upon elected officials to weigh all the consequences of current alcohol policies and to invite new ideas on how best to prepare young adults to make responsible decisions about alcohol use.

Join Here

UPDATES

Current Signatory Count:
135

Amethyst Initiative in the News

Click here to see a full list

Amethyst Initiative
10 E Street, SE Washington, DC 20003 202.543.8760 (phone) 202.543.8764 (fax) info@chooseresponsibility.org

web design & hosting UNION STREET MEDIA

Courtesy of Amethyst Initiative

One means available to the Amethyst Initiative for creating a fitting response is this Web site.

How many times must we relearn the lessons of Prohibition?

We call upon our elected officials:

> To support an informed and dispassionate public debate over the effects of the 21 year-old drinking age.
>
> To consider whether the 10% highway fund "incentive" encourages or inhibits that debate.
>
> To invite new ideas about the best ways to prepare young adults to make responsible decisions about alcohol.

We pledge ourselves and our institutions to playing a vigorous, constructive role as these critical discussions unfold.

Please add my signature to this statement:

Name _____

Signature _____

Institution _____

A fitting response is delivered in a medium and genre that reach the audience

In addition to comprising a suitable response to the problem at hand, the Amethyst Initiative's statement was delivered through an easily accessed medium that immediately reached a wide audience: the World Wide Web. College administrators and faculty, parents and organizations, students and citizens alike can read the online document, or they can download and print a PDF version of the statement. But not all who read the statement are invited to sign it. At the bottom of the petition, the writers clearly indicate their rhetorical audience: *Currently, membership in the Amethyst Initiative is limited to college and university presidents and chancellors. If you are not a president or chancellor, but would like to become part of this larger effort, please sign up here.* The sentence ends with a link to the Web site of a broader organization called Choose Responsibility. A rhetorical audience is not only capable of being influenced by the message, but capable of acting upon it or influencing others to do so. The writers of the Amethyst Initiative's statement realize that college and university presidents and chancellors are those most capable of starting campus-wide conversations about policies that can encourage responsible alcohol use, and so they chose this group as their rhetorical audience.

The chosen medium of delivery did not limit the **genres** (the kinds of writing) available to these university administrators. Rather than delivering a statement, the World Wide Web could have delivered anything from a blog entry to a streaming video. But the rhetorical opportunity for change (the need to work toward a national strategy for establishing responsible alcohol use) and other elements of the rhetorical situation (including all the strong arguments surrounding the current drinking age itself) called for a kind of writing that promoted concern, research, and participation, rather than judgment.

By calling on the rhetorical audience to sign the statement, the Amethyst Initiative's writers made use of a genre with a long history—the petition. Consider petitions that you have seen or read, many of which are connected with social activism, all of which involve inviting others to join in the movement for halting or supporting legislation; boycotting or supporting manufacturers, products, or companies; or applauding or protesting decisions. Key characteristics of petitions are

► an explicit statement of the problem,

► essential background information,

► a statement of what should be done to resolve the problem,

► a named audience who can initiate change (that is, a rhetorical audience),

- a request for signatures or support, and
- strategic delivery of the message, often accompanied by some kind of publicity.

Every petition is a response to a rhetorical opportunity for change that calls for spreading the effort more widely. Those who read and sign the petition will likely understand the public nature of the petition because they have encountered that genre before. In other words, the genre has created expectations in readers.

A fitting response satisfies the intended audience

The Amethyst Initiative's petition—fitting response that it is—works on several levels to satisfy the intended audience:

- On a basic level, the petition identifies some of the irresponsible drinking behaviors that constitute health and safety problems— well-known behaviors that worry parents, teachers, and health care professionals, as well as school administrators.
- On a second level, the petition implies that these problems are sufficient cause to reconsider the current drinking age of twenty-one.
- Finally, the authors of the petition don't judge drinkers or drinking behaviors. Rather, they use calm and everyday language, and they call on elected officials to support "informed and unimpeded debate" for the purpose of inviting "new ideas about the best ways to prepare young adults to make responsible decisions about alcohol."

All of these features—identifying a problem, offering an engaged response, and inviting audience participation—are key features of the petition genre that often make such a document a fitting response.

>ANALYZING THE RHETORICAL SITUATION

For each of the following problems, decide whether you could shape a response that fulfills the three requirements for being fitting: language that suits the problem, is delivered in an appropriate medium, and satisfies the intended audience. Be prepared to share your answers with the rest of the class.

1. Your university's football coach, whom you have long admired, is receiving a great deal of negative press because the football team is losing.
2. When you and your friends get together, they always try to persuade you to join their church.

3. Your history instructor has assigned a research paper that is due on the same day as your biology midterm.
4. After taking your LSATs, you receive mailings from more than twenty law schools.
5. In order to obtain a green card (indicating U.S. permanent resident status), your Romanian friend wants to arrange a fraudulent American marriage.

Recognizing a Fitting Response

The Amethyst Initiative triggered "push back" from several groups: Mothers Against Drunk Driving (MADD), the Center for Science in the Public Interest (CSPI), the National Institute on Alcohol Abuse and Alcoholism (NIAAA), and the Community Anti-Drug Coalitions of America (CADCA), among others. These national organizations support the current minimum drinking age of twenty-one. Although the Amethyst Initiative suggests that lowering the minimum drinking age will allow multiple educational interventions focusing on responsible drinking, the opposed organizations argue that an overwhelming amount of research has already indicated positive health and safety effects of making twenty-one the minimum drinking age.

The Center for Science in the Public Interest, for instance, posted an online response in the form of a statement given at a press conference by George A. Hacker, Director of CSPI's Alcohol Policies Project. As you read the statement, consider what makes it a fitting response.

Statement by George A. Hacker on Minimum Drinking Age Law

One reason CSPI gives for keeping the current drinking age addresses the Amethyst Initiative's call for response.

Since its adoption throughout the United States in the late 1980s, we have learned enough about the benefits of the 21 minimum legal drinking age to know that it would be a disastrous mistake to lower it. Doing so would merely doom many more thousands of young people to premature death and other severe alcohol-related problems. Despite wishful thinking on the part of some, there is no evidence that a lower drinking age would result in fewer alcohol-related problems among young people, and quite a bit of evidence that refutes that view. Since passage of the National Minimum Purchase Age Act in 1983, the percent of high school seniors who report any alcohol use in the past year has dropped nearly 20% (from 88% in 1983 to 73% in 2006) and the proportion who report binge drinking has declined nearly 40% (from 41% in 1983 to 25% in 2006).

Simply having age-21 laws on the books, however, is no panacea. Confronting deeply ingrained alcohol problems requires a real commitment to an effective, comprehensive national prevention strategy. The National Academies of Science Institute of Medicine outlined that evidence-based strategy in a 2003 report to Congress. Among other elements, that groundbreaking report highlighted the need for:

▶ a well-financed, visible, adult-focused national media campaign to discourage underage drinking;

▶ higher taxes on alcoholic beverages, especially on beer, to deter youthful drinking and provide funding for prevention and treatment programs; and

▶ stronger coordination among federal agencies that manage programs addressing underage drinking issues.

The Congress took an important first step toward implementing some of that report's recommendations when it passed the modest Sober Truth on Preventing (STOP) Underage Drinking Act in December, 2006. Much more needs to be done.

The director articulates what CSPI considers the larger issue.

The NASIM is a source the audience of college administrators and others will likely respect.

Rather than inviting "informed and unimpeded public debate," as the Amethyst Initiative did, NASIM (and CSPI) offers specific actions.

For CSPI, the time for debate is past. It's now time to take action.

CSPI spokesperson George A. Hacker delivered a fitting response to the rhetorical opportunity, but not the only possible one. Whether or not this response can be considered the best one depends on the context, the audience, the purpose, and so on. Even if the response was not the best one, it was nevertheless a well-researched and well-executed response, one that invited a cascade of responses from other interested parent, professional, and university groups.

All through your life, you have been and will continue to be faced with rhetorical opportunities for change that call for a fitting response of some kind. Right now, as a college student, you are regularly asked to shape fitting responses to opportunities, many of which come in the form of assignments, social dilemmas, and political or religious challenges. In your first-year writing class, your instructor will direct you to a number of opportunities for change that you'll need to analyze and then address in writing. It's doubtful that only one person in the class will shape the perfect resolution for any rhetorical opportunity; more than likely, a number of students will shape fitting responses to each assignment, succeeding even though their responses vary.

The following list of questions can help you evaluate responses to determine whether or not they are fitting.

What makes a response fitting?

If any of the following conditions are not met, you have a problem that is not a rhetorical opportunity for change or a response that is not fitting.

► Is the problem one that can be addressed through language (spoken or written) or visual images?

► Is the response verbal or visual?

► Does the situation invite this response?

► Is this response delivered in an appropriate medium that reaches its intended audience?

► Is the intended audience also a rhetorical audience? (See chapter 1.)

► Does this response successfully satisfy the intended audience?

> YOUR WRITING EXPERIENCES

1. Think back to one of the most fitting rhetorical responses you've encountered. What, exactly, made that response memorable? Fitting? List its characteristics.

2. When you submit a piece of writing to your instructor, what kind of response do you like most to receive (other than praise, of course)? Answer the following questions to formulate a description of a fitting response to your academic writing:

   a. In what medium (or media) do you like to receive responses to your writing? Verbally, in a conference? In an email message or online course discussion forum? Handwritten in ink on your printed page?

   b. Do you like comments throughout your text or just at the end? Do you like your instructor to correct mechanical errors for you, point them out, or allude to them in a final comment?

   c. What do you want to learn from your instructor's comments and markings?

3. Think of a time when you gave a fitting response to someone else's writing. How exactly did your response address the rhetorical opportunity for change that the writing offered? Describe how your response fit the problem, why the medium you used was appropriate, and how the response successfully satisfied the intended audience.

Reading a resolution as a fitting response

As you already know, people shape different responses to the same rhetorical opportunity for change. Some responses may seem to you more fitting than others, but it can be hard to pinpoint where one falls short and others succeed. To help you become more comfortable evaluating fitting responses, this section presents three different responses to the verdict in the 1992 trial of the white Los Angeles police officers charged with use of excessive force in the arrest of Rodney King, a black man.

On March 3, 1991, after a high-speed chase, two California Highway Patrol (CHP) officers pulled King over for speeding and prepared to arrest him, guns drawn. Four LAPD officers intervened, and three of those officers struck King more than fifty times with their metal batons before handcuffing him and putting him in an ambulance. From a nearby apartment, George Holliday videotaped the entire episode, providing a local television station with nearly nine-and-a-half minutes of footage, including the first ninety seconds when the beatings took place. After much public controversy, involving charges of racism and incompetence against the LAPD, the nearly three-month-long trial began, resulting in the acquittal of all four LAPD officers. (In a federal trial one year later, two of the officers who had struck King were found guilty and were sentenced to serve time in prison.)

The verdict of the trial astounded many Americans. Commentators, news analysts, and race-relations experts rushed to the airwaves, the printed page, and cyberspace to provide what they thought were fitting responses to the verdict. The Academic Senate at San Francisco State University (SFSU), for example, posted a public resolution, questioning "whether the American system of justice treats people equitably under the law." As you read this resolution, which follows, consider how fitting a response it is.

> Resolution Regarding the Rodney King Verdict

Academic Senate of San Francisco State University

At its meeting of May 5, 1992, the Academic Senate approved the following resolution regarding the Rodney King verdict:

WHEREAS The April 29, 1992, verdict in the case of the officers charged with beating Rodney King has raised questions about whether the American system of justice treats people equitably under the law; and

WHEREAS The powerlessness born of having an unequal voice and inadequate representation begets frustration sometimes leading to violence; and

continued

"Resolution Regarding The Rodney King Verdict" *(continued)*

WHEREAS San Francisco State University, through the efforts of its Commission on Human Relations, Working Committee on Multicultural Perspectives in the Curriculum, and other projects has placed a high priority on implementing the principles embodied in its recently adopted statement, "Principles for a Multicultural University"; and

WHEREAS The hostile climate generated by the verdict in this case imperils the foundations of reason, common sense, morality, and compassion which underlie the academic enterprise as well as the larger society which this enterprise serves and is inimical to the equity and diversity goals of this campus; therefore be it

RESOLVED That the San Francisco State University Academic Senate decry the verdict in the case of the officers charged with beating Rodney King; and be it further

RESOLVED That the San Francisco State University Academic Senate reaffirm its commitment to a governance process which actively encourages the participation of all members of the academic community; and be it further

RESOLVED That the San Francisco State University Academic Senate reaffirm its commitment, and redouble its efforts, to provide an academic environment which promotes the empowerment, embraces the diverse viewpoints, and celebrates the contributions of all members of the community which the University serves; and be it further

RESOLVED That this resolution be distributed to the SFSU Campus community, the Chair of the Academic Senate, CSU and to the Chairs of the CSU Campus Senates.

Reading the Los Angeles riots as a fitting response

Although dramatic by academic standards, the SFSU Academic Senate resolution pales in comparison to the most powerful response of all: the three-day riots that began in Los Angeles within two hours after the initial verdict was announced. Arson, looting, and fighting spread throughout South Central Los Angeles, and riots also broke out in several other cities, as far away as Atlanta, Georgia. By the end of the rioting more than 50 people had been killed, over 4,000 injured, and over 12,000 arrested in Los Angeles alone. Many participants in the riots, as well as some onlookers, felt that the riots were, indeed, a fitting response to the opportunity for change offered by the verdict. What do you think?

AP Photo/Nick Ut

An immediate response to the Rodney King verdict.

> ANALYZING THE RHETORICAL SITUATION

1. Use the questions listed under "What Makes a Response Fitting?" (on page 38) to determine whether the Los Angeles riots and the SFSU Academic Senate resolution were fitting responses to the Rodney King verdict. Be sure to respond to all questions for each of the responses.
2. Which response(s) do you consider fitting? If both are fitting, why do you think such different responses can both be fitting? If only one response is fitting, what makes it more fitting than the other?

Reading political commentary as a fitting response

If you argue that the Los Angeles riots were, in and of themselves, a kind of visual rhetoric, you might believe them to be the most fitting of all the various responses to the Rodney King verdict. Columnist and activist Barbara Smith certainly believed that the riots were the most fitting response to a terrible verdict. In fact, as the riots waned, Smith commented on their political potential: "the insurrection in Los Angeles will galvanize unprecedented organizing." She also wrote about her own simmering fury. Recounting King's beating and a catalogue of brutalities that preceded it, Smith forged her fury into a verbal response that she felt fit the occasion.

Excerpt from

> The Truth That Never Hurts

Barbara Smith

What I felt at the King verdict and its aftermath was all too familiar. I felt the same gnawing in the pit of my stomach and in my chest when sixteen-year-old Yusuk Hawkins was gunned down on the streets of Bensonhurst, Brooklyn, in 1989. I felt the same impotent rage when the police murdered sixty-seven-year-old Eleanor Bumpurs with a shotgun in the process of evicting her from her Bronx apartment in 1984. I choked back the same bitter tears when I heard the verdict in the 1991 rape case involving a Black woman student and several white male students at St. John's University on Long Island. I was just as terrified when they murdered four Black school girls (my age peers) by bombing a church in Birmingham, Alabama, in 1963. And even though I was too young to understand its meaning, I learned Emmett Till's name in 1955 because of witnessing my family's anguish over his lynching in Mississippi.

So what do we do with all this fury besides burn down our own communities and hurt or kill anyone, white, Black, brown, or yellow who gets in our way? Figuring out what to do next is the incredibly difficult challenge that lies before us.

Above all, the events in Los Angeles have made it perfectly obvious why we need a revolution in this country. Nothing short of a revolution will work. Gross inequalities are built into the current system and Band-Aids, even big ones, won't cure capitalism's fundamental injustice and exploitation.

We need, however, to build analysis, practice, and movements that accurately address the specific ways that racism, capitalism, and all the major systems of oppression interconnect in the United States. It's not a coincidence that the most dramatic political changes have so often been catalyzed by race. In the United States, racism has shaped the nature of capitalism and race relations.

It is our responsibility as Black activists, radicals, and socialists to create vibrant new leadership that offers a real alternative to the tired civil rights establishment and to the bankrupt "two-party" system. It is our responsibility as we build autonomous Black organizations to make the connections between all of the oppressions and to work in coalition with the movements that have arisen to challenge them.

Recognizing the leadership of radical women of color, feminists, and lesbians is absolutely critical from this moment forward. Women of color are already building a movement that makes the connections between race, class, gender, and sexual identity, a movement that has the potential to win liberation for all of us.

It is past the time to talk. I really want to know how the white left, the white feminist, and the white lesbian and gay movements are going to change now that Los Angeles is burned. It's not enough to say what a shame all of this is or to have a perfect intellectual understanding of what has occurred. It's time for all the white people who say they're committed to freedom to figure out what useful antiracist organizing is and to put it into practice.

Smith says, "Figuring out what to do next is the incredibly difficult challenge that lies before us." You might think of "figuring out what to do next" as the challenge of shaping a fitting response to the opportunity for change within any rhetorical situation. Smith, a socialist, explores a number of options, all of which are "fitting" and some of which are more revolutionary than others.

Look again at Smith's final sentence: "It's time for all the white people who say they're committed to freedom to figure out what useful antiracist organizing is and to put it into practice." That sentence, the last one in her fitting response, opens up another rhetorical opportunity that invites yet another response. In fact, like the Amethyst Initiative's petition regarding the legal drinking age (see page 32), Smith's writing actually prescribes a response, going so far as to dictate the form that response should take.

> ANALYZING THE RHETORICAL SITUATION

1. Is the problem Smith is responding to a rhetorical opportunity for change?
2. Is the response verbal or visual?
3. Does the problem invite this response?
4. Is this response delivered in a medium that reaches its intended audience?
5. Does this response successfully satisfy the intended audience?

Compare your answers with those of your classmates, and then decide, as a class, if Smith's response was fitting for the rhetorical situation. You may also want to consider what result Smith hoped to achieve through her writing.

COMMUNITY CONNECTIONS

1. Your campus or town undoubtedly has unrest or upheaval of some kind, strong dissatisfaction related to economics, employment, politics, justice, race, athletics, or gender. Look through your local newspaper and identify one such incident of unrest. What rhetorical opportunity for change does this incident present? What is one possible fitting response to that opportunity? Be prepared to share your answer with the rest of the class.

2. Celebrations—birthdays, engagements, weddings, commitment ceremonies, graduations, family reunions, athletic victories, and holiday gatherings—invite responses. Fitting responses take the form of letters, cards, songs, speeches, and toasts. Draft a fitting response for an event that you're going to attend soon.

3. Think about the fitting response you drafted for question 2. Choose a different kind of event and explain how you would need to alter your response in order to make it a fitting one for that event. Would you need to change the medium in which you plan to deliver your response? Its length? The specific kind of language used?

Using the Available Means of Persuasion

In chapter 1, you learned that Aristotle defined *rhetoric* as "the art [mental capacity] of observing in any given situation the available means of persuasion." When you consider the available means, you think about the possible methods of communication you might use, whether those are oral (speaking face to face or over the telephone), written (using paper, email, instant messaging, or a Web page), visual (using film, video, or still images), digital, or some combination of oral, written, and visual.

You've already had years of experience identifying available means of persuasion and selecting the most appropriate means, whatever the rhetorical situation and whoever the audience. Humans were doing just that long before Aristotle wrote his *Rhetoric*. In fact, one of the earliest examples of humans tapping an available means of persuasion can be found in cave paintings, such as the ones in Lascaux, France, which depict stories of hunting expeditions that took place from 15,000 to 10,000 BCE. Using sharpened tools, iron and manganese oxides, and charcoal, Paleolithic humans recorded incidents from their daily lives for the edification of others. From 400 BCE to 1300 CE, people living in what is now the southwestern part of the United States also recorded the stories, events, beliefs, fears, and characters of their daily lives by carving their representations on stone surfaces of various kinds. Using the available means at their disposal (sharpened tools and stones), these First Americans composed stories that continue to speak to and intrigue us.

The contemporary rhetorical scene also offers many varieties of available means—from digital and printed to visual and spoken—for delivering as well as shaping potentially effective information for a specific audience. Let's review some of those means so that you can optimize your choices in order to succeed as a writer or speaker.

Cave painting in Lascaux, France.

© Martin Jenkinson/Alamy

Early stone carvings from the American Southwest.

© Steven Lunetta Photography, 2007

What are the available means?

When you successfully use language to address a problem, you've no doubt delivered a fitting response using the available means of persuasion. **Available means** can be defined as the physical material used for delivering the information, the place from which the writer creates and sends the information, and the elements of the presentation itself (elements that include persuasive strategies known as *rhetorical appeals*, the use of evidence or authority, the conventions of style, and the rhetorical methods of development).

We choose intuitively from among all of the means available. With experience and knowledge, each of us can make more conscious, strategic selections, based on the context, the audience, the **constraints** (obstacles) and **resources** (positive influences) of the rhetorical situation, and the consequences of our choices. Rhetorical consciousness (and success) comes with recognizing the vast array of options at our disposal, including those already in existence and those we can create as we attempt to negotiate the constraints of our rhetorical situation and reach our intended audience.

The available means deliver information

In the weeks following the September 11, 2001 attacks on the World Trade Center, many Americans responded to the rhetorical opportunity by extending their condolences, whether or not they knew any of the dead and missing personally. The range of fitting responses to the opportunity varied widely: for instance, those whose loved ones were missing contributed to memory walls, filling them with bouquets of flowers and photographs. Others wrote essays and newspaper columns, decrying the terrorists, mourning the victims, and extolling the rescue efforts. Some people presented television and radio programs focusing on what happened on that day and how the United States was responding. Still others created online memorial boards and chat rooms. And one inventive author went so far as to hire a skywriter, posting a message that spoke for and to millions of Americans: "We miss you." Each of these writers chose different physical means of delivering a message.

REUTERS/Kai Pfaffenbach/Landov

A visitor at a September 11 memory wall.

These writers worked within the constraints and resources of their individual rhetorical situations, whether those constraints and resources were physical ("What passerby or hospital worker may have seen my missing loved one?"), geographical ("How can I reach the survivors in New York City?"), or financial ("I'm going to spend money broadcasting my message in skywriting"). The means of delivery each writer used depended on the writer's expertise, intended audience, and contextual constraints and resources.

The available means are anchored to the writer's place

Every time a writer sends a message, he or she does so from a particular place. Whether that person is writing at a desk, talking on a telephone, preaching from a pulpit, speaking from a podium, or typing on a laptop, both the message itself and its means of delivery are influenced by the constraints and resources of that specific place.

Utah Valley University graduate Urangoo Baatarkhuyag was preparing to move to California to further her education when she learned she had cancer. The Mongolian native was stunned and scared. Hospital personnel told her that she would need a bone marrow transplant to survive, a procedure that costs $350,000. With no health insurance, no family nearby, and relatively poor international students for friends, Baatarkhuyag was not sure what to do, especially given her constraints. How could language possibly help her resolve her problem? She was living away from her home and her family, needing lots of money—and fast.

Fortunately, her friends identified an opportunity for change that could be resolved through language. Because their place (a university community in the United States) offered them easy access to electronic media, they could tap the resources of digital communication to reach a wide audience, rapidly and cheaply. They set up a Web site for their friend in the belief that an Internet request could travel faster than acute myeloid leukemia could progress. Together, the friends' digital know-how (they knew how blogs work as well as how to take advantage of online social networking sites) and the Internet became contextual resources. Providing background information, photos of a healthy Baatarkhuyag, and an easy-to-use PayPal account for donations, "Help us save her life from leukemia" brought in nearly $40,000 within the first month—not enough for chemotherapy, let alone a transplant, but a terrific start, nonetheless. Plus, as the Web site itself gained momentum, it sparked other kinds of donations: the Latter Day Saints Hospital (LDS) in Salt Lake City donated a month's worth of chemotherapy and launched an international search for a hospital that could treat her for less money; friends and supporters held silent auctions, fundraisers featuring live entertainment, concerts, and garage sales. They also

Friends of Urangoo Baatarkhuyag set up the Web site to help with fundraising for her leukemia treatments.

arranged for Baatarkhuyag's story to be featured on various televised news programs and in local newspapers.

As her friends worked to strengthen the resources of Baatarkhuyag's situation, they surveyed the various means available to them in terms of efficiency and appropriateness. For example, Artan Ismaili, a Brigham Young University student from Kosovo who had never met Baatarkhuyag, worked on her behalf because, like him and his wife, she was an international student with no insurance. Ismaili first learned about Baatarkhuyag's medical crisis when another student alerted members of a class Ismaili was taking, asking them to go to the Web site to donate whatever amount they could. After Ismaili and his wife donated, they wanted to do even more. He announced the situation and the Web site to the students in his other classes, arranged with a Mongolian restaurant to hold a fundraiser there, and posted information on Baatarkhuyag's status and how to donate to help her on all his social networking sites. And, since he and his wife planned to move to Boston, they pledged to sell everything they had and donate the money to Baatarkhuyag's medical fund.

Like the best of speakers and writers, then, Ismaili analyzed the resources and constraints of the rhetorical situation and took advantage of as many digital and oral available means as he could think of. Not only did he tap these resources and available means; he also used the appropriate rhetorical methods of development to fulfill his purpose: narration (the story of the uninsured international student and her dire illness), cause-and-effect analysis (what would happen if she did or did not receive the transplant), and process analysis (how to use PayPal, the U.S. postal service, or an electronic bank transfer to donate money to the fund) in order to reach his intended audience (people who could help by donating money). Ismaili's choices were practical ones, influenced by the various resources and constraints. They were also political ones, for in the United States today, every person (whether international visitor or U.S. citizen) has a right to speak and to speak publicly.

Unlike Ismaili, many speakers and writers in the United States have not enjoyed the right to speak, let alone been able to make use of the available means of persuasion. Many groups of people throughout American history have been denied the right to education, the right to speak publicly, and the right to civic participation on grounds of their gender, race, ethnicity, physical ability, or lack of property. For example, if you think of voting as an available means of persuasion—as a means of sending a message to a specific audience—you understand how punitive the lack of voting rights would be. In 1776, only white Protestant men who owned land had the right to vote. By 1847, all white men could vote, including Catholics and non-Christians. In 1870, black males were awarded the right to vote—but only under certain conditions, including the requirements that they furnish proof of their literacy and that they pay a poll tax. Women were not granted voting rights until 1920, and American Indians not until 1924. Thus, the means of persuasion available to all these groups were fewer than those available to white male landowners.

The available means include the rhetorical elements of the message itself

When a writer or speaker considers the available means for sending a purposeful message to a specific audience, he or she considers the rhetorical elements of the message. Because human beings are not persuaded to believe or act in a certain way based only on facts or only on what can be proved, writers and speakers use **rhetorical appeals**. These three persuasive strategies are **ethos**, the ethical appeal of the writer's credibility; **logos**, the logical appeal of a reasonable, well-supported argument; and **pathos**, the emotional appeal of language and examples that stir the audience's feelings (within a reasonable limit). The use of these appeals is balanced in most successful messages, for to exaggerate any one of the

Courtesy of Library of Congress

Sojourner Truth, whose 1851 speech survives as an example of the available means of persuasion skillfully used.

three is to risk losing the audience and thereby failing to achieve the rhetorical purpose.

Many successful messages emphasize each of these appeals separately, but doing so is not the same as exaggerating any one of them. Consider the following excerpts from a speech given at the 1851 Women's Rights Convention in Akron, Ohio. During a time when white women were rarely permitted to speak in public, especially to a "promiscuous assembly" of men and women, former slave Sojourner Truth (born Isabella Baumfree, 1787–1883) faced an audience of educated white Northerners, mostly women, to speak about the importance of women's rights for black women as well as white women. Truth negotiated the constraints and resources of her rhetorical situation to reach her audience.

According to tradition, Truth, the only black person in attendance, had been listening carefully to the various speeches, many of which denounced the rights of women. Truth was constrained by being illiterate, black, a Southerner, and a woman, and her spoken ideas (recorded and later published in multiple versions by white people) would be met with resistance if not outright objection. Some of her constraints, however, proved to be her richest resources. The minute she ascended the platform to address the audience, Truth transgressed all the social norms of the educated Northern white "lady."

In her opening paragraphs, Truth set out the circumference of the struggle for women's rights as she saw it, establishing her ethos. Notice how her first paragraph establishes common ground with the white women in her audience: both speaker and audience subscribe to the idea that both Northern and Southern women, white and black, share a concern over women's rights. Truth continues to burnish her ethos by demonstrating her goodwill toward her audience, her good sense and knowledge of the subject at hand, and her good character:

> Well, children, where there is so much racket there must be something out of kilter. I think that 'twixt the Negroes of the South and the women of the North, all talking about rights, the white men will be in a fix pretty soon. But what's all this here talking about?

That man over there says that women need to be helped into carriages and lifted over ditches, and to have the best place everywhere. Nobody ever helps me into carriages, or over mud puddles, or gives me any best place! And ain't I a woman? Look at me! Look at my arm! I could have ploughed and planted, and gathered into barns, and no man could head me! And ain't I a woman? I could work as much and eat as much as a man—when I could get it—and bear the lash as well! And ain't I a woman? I have borne thirteen children, and seen them most all sold off to slavery, and when I cried out with my mother's grief, none but Jesus heard me! And ain't I a woman?

A speaker in Truth's position had to devote most of her words to establishing her ethos; after all, she needed to be heard and believed as the black woman she was. But like many successful speakers, Truth spent the body of her speech emphasizing logos, the shape of her reasoning, particularly her response to arguments against women's rights:

Then they talk about this thing in the head; what's this they call it? ["Intellect," somebody whispers.] That's it, honey. What's that got to do with women's rights or Negros' rights? If my cup won't hold but a pint, and yours holds a quart, wouldn't you be mean not to let me have my little half measure-full?

Then that little man in black back there, he says women can't have as much rights as men, 'cause Christ wasn't a woman! Where did your Christ come from? Where did your Christ come from? From God and a woman! Man had nothing to do with Him.

If the first woman God ever made was strong enough to turn the world upside down all alone, these women together ought to be able to turn it back, and get it right side up again! And now they is asking to do it, the men better let them.

The closing of her speech emphasizes pathos in the form of her gratitude for being allowed to speak.

Obliged to you for hearing me, and now old Sojourner ain't got nothing more to say.

Ethos, logos, and pathos are often distributed among three sections of any piece of powerful writing in both separate and overlapping forms. Once you start looking for them, you'll discover that these rhetorical appeals appear in much of the reading and writing you do.

Within the message itself, the available means also include the writer's or speaker's use of evidence or authority. You can see for yourself how Truth used the example of her own hardworking life as evidence that women were just as suited for voting rights as men. In fact, her evidence might have been stronger than that offered by any of the well-educated white women who shared the speaker's platform with her. And for authority, Truth wisely went straight to the Bible, the ultimate authority for all her listeners, whether they were

Northern or Southern, black or white, male or female, educated or uneducated.

In addition to the rhetorical appeals and the use of evidence and authority, conventions of style constitute yet another feature of the available means. Truth's 1851 speech circulated in at least four versions, all of them recorded by white people, all of them resorting to some version of dialect. The most prominent instance of dialect is the use of the word *ain't*, but it's not the only one. Even allegedly cleaned-up versions of the speech include the expressions *out o' kilter*, *a-talking*, *be in a fix*, and *Aren't I a woman?* No version of her speech has appeared in **Standardized English**, the style of writing and speaking expected in most academic and business settings, which would dictate *Am I not a woman?* as the refrain. The use of dialect authenticates Truth as an uneducated former slave.

Finally, speakers and writers choose the most appropriate of the **rhetorical methods of development** (description, narration, exemplification, classification and division, comparison and contrast, process analysis, cause-and-effect analysis, and definition). In her speech, Truth used definition and narration in the second paragraph: she defined herself as a woman, just not the kind of woman that opponents of women's rights had in mind, and she narrated several incidents from her life that supported her self-definition. In the body of her speech, she used cause-and-effect analysis to bring home her point that women had already set a powerful precedent, one supported by scripture. (Chapter 9 discusses each of the rhetorical methods of development.)

Regardless of the version you examine, Truth's speech provides a useful textual context for examining the available means of persuasion.

> ANALYZING THE RHETORICAL SITUATION

For two or three of the following situations, identify available means of persuasion that take into consideration (1) the physical means of delivering the information, (2) the place from which the author creates and sends the information, and (3) the rhetorical elements (including the rhetorical appeals) of the message itself. Be prepared to share your answers with the rest of the class.

1. You want to support your favorite recording artist, who is under scrutiny for criticizing the current government of the United States.

2. Your family wants to help some neighbors, who have lost all of their worldly possessions in a house fire.

3. You want to change majors, from communications to international business, but your grade-point average is slightly below the necessary minimum for acceptance to the School of Business.

4. Your spouse wants to relocate in order to further his or her career, but you're making good progress on your undergraduate degree at the nearby college.

5. Your economics professor has assigned you a research project: you are to evaluate the kinds of jobs that are appropriate for high school students.

Recognizing Available Means

When Boston University's School of Public Health created Join Together to provide information to individuals and communities interested in fighting and preventing underage drinking and substance abuse, it needed to tap the available means for distributing that information. One of the available means chosen was a Web site. Under "About Us," the group mentions specific means: coalitions, leadership training for

This Web site is an available means of communication for the organization Join Together.

Courtesy of Join Together/www.jointogether.com

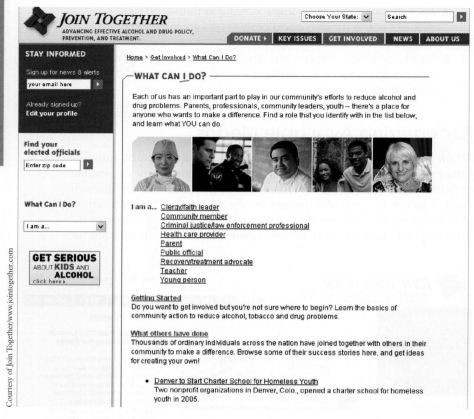

This Web page has links to additional available means of response.

community-based efforts, public education and media, and public policy initiatives—all of which can be realized through print, oral, visual, and electronic means of delivery.

In addition, Join Together's Web site contains links to many other available means. As you analyze Join Together's Web site, you'll see that it uses the rhetorical appeals, evidence and authority, a specific style, and various rhetorical methods of development. In fact, the site argues for the importance of its existence not only by recounting specific evidence and making use of the rhetorical appeals of pathos and logos, but also by sending the reader to relevant links to find out how to take further action.

No matter what document, Web site, or television program you're reading or viewing (and analyzing rhetorically), you need to keep in mind that the creators of those communications have tried to choose the best from among all means of communication available to them. As you read and view, then, you'll want to remain alert to the specific choices writers have made and to consider whether those choices are the most fruitful ones.

Rarely will two writers make identical choices in response to a rhetorical opportunity. Each writer's place of composing and status in terms of the situation often complicate those choices. Each writer must negotiate a unique set of rhetorical constraints and resources in order to determine the best available means.

>YOUR WRITING EXPERIENCES

1. Chances are you do not know very many people, if any, in your writing class. Your instructor may not know anyone either. Describe the available means you could use to remedy this situation. How exactly would you do so, and what would be the substance of your message?

2. What means are available to you for letting your writing instructor know what kind of person, student, and writer you are? Write for ten minutes, describing the available means in terms of three constituent parts: (a) the physical means of delivering the information, (b) the place from which you would create and send the information, and (c) the rhetorical elements of the message itself. How might you use the rhetorical appeals (ethos, pathos, and logos) to convey an impression of yourself to your instructor?

3. After you receive a marked and graded piece of writing from your instructor, what are the means available to you for responding? In terms of the three constituents of available means, describe how you usually respond. How might you more profitably respond? Write for five minutes and be prepared to share your answer with the rest of the class.

4. Reconsider the answers you wrote for questions 1, 2, and 3. Carefully translate your three answers into one that takes advantage of the available means of persuasion. Consider your rhetorical constraints and resources (including the rhetorical appeals) as you introduce yourself as a college writer to the rest of your class, including your instructor. Be prepared to share your fitting response with the rest of the class.

Reading an essay for available means

Acclaimed author Susan Orlean has established her career by writing about the ordinary things in life. In an interview at the University of Oregon, Orlean said that she's drawn to the extraordinary in the ordinary: "There's no question in my mind that being a writer is a moral occupation and one that requires an awareness all the time of what that means morally and philosophically." As you read the following excerpt from one of her essays, note the extraordinary features of this ten-year-old's daily existence that Orlean identifies.

Excerpt from

> The American Man, Age 10
Susan Orlean

Vince Bucci/Getty Images

If Colin Duffy and I were to get married, we would have matching superhero notebooks. We would wear shorts, big sneakers, and long, baggy T-shirts depicting famous athletes every single day, even in the winter. We would sleep in our clothes. We would both be good at Nintendo Street Fighter II, but Colin would be better than me. We would have some homework, but it would never be too hard and we would always have just finished it. We would eat pizza and candy for all of our meals. We wouldn't have sex, but we would have crushes on each other and, magically, babies would appear in our home. We would win the lottery and then buy land in Wyoming, where we would have one of every kind of cute animal. All the while, Colin would be working in law enforcement—probably the FBI. Our favorite movie star, Morgan Freeman, would visit us occasionally. We would listen to the same Eurythmics song ("Here Comes the Rain Again") over and over again and watch two hours of television every Friday night. We would both be good at football, have best friends, and know how to drive; we would cure AIDS and the garbage problem and everything that hurts animals. We would hang out a lot with Colin's dad. For fun, we would load a slingshot with dog food and shoot it at my butt. We would have a very good life. . . .

Here are the particulars about Colin Duffy: He is ten years old, on the nose. He is four feet eight inches high, weighs seventy-five pounds, and appears to be mostly leg and shoulder blade. He is a handsome kid. He has a broad forehead, dark eyes with dense lashes, and a sharp, dimply smile. I have rarely seen him without a baseball cap. He owns several, but favors a University of Michigan Wolverines model, on account of its pleasing colors. The hat styles his hair into wild disarray. If you ever managed to get the hat off his head, you would see a boy with a nimbus of golden-brown hair, dented in the back, where the hat hits him.

Colin lives with his mother, Elaine; his father, Jim; his older sister, Megan; and his little brother, Chris, in a pretty pale blue Victorian house on a bosky street in Glen Ridge, New Jersey. Glen Ridge is a serene and civilized old town twenty miles west of New York City. It does not have much of a commercial district, but it is a town of amazing lawns. Most of the houses were built around the turn of the century and are set back a gracious, green distance from the street. The rest of the town seems to consist of parks and playing fields and sidewalks and backyards—in other words, it is a far cry from South-Central Los Angeles and from Bedford-Stuyvesant and other, grimmer parts of the country where a very different ten-year-old American man is growing up today.

There is a fine school system in Glen Ridge, but Elaine and Jim, who are both schoolteachers, choose to send their children to a parents' cooperative elementary school in Montclair, a neighboring suburb. Currently Colin is in fifth grade. He is a good student. He plans to go to college, to a place he says is called Oklahoma City State College University. OCSCU satisfies his desire to live out west, to attend a small college, and to study law enforcement, which OCSCU apparently offers as a major. After four years at Oklahoma City State College University, he plans to work for the FBI. He says that getting to be a police officer involves tons of hard work, but working for the FBI will be a cinch, because all you have to do is fill out one form, which he has already gotten from the head FBI office. Colin is quiet in class but loud on the playground. He has a great throwing arm, significant foot speed, and a lot of physical confidence. He is also brave. Huge wild cats with rabies and gross stuff dripping from their teeth, which he says run rampant throughout his neighborhood, do not scare him. Otherwise, he is slightly bashful. This combination of athletic grace and valor and personal reserve accounts for considerable popularity. He has a fluid relationship to many social groups, including the super-bright nerds, the ultrajocks, the flashy kids who will someday become extremely popular and socially successful juvenile delinquents, and the kids who will be elected president of the student body. In his opinion, the most popular boy in his class is Christian, who happens to be black, and Colin's favorite television character is Steve Urkel on *Family Matters*, who is black, too, but otherwise he seems uninterested in or oblivious to race. Until this year, he was a Boy Scout. Now he is planning to begin karate lessons. His favorite schoolyard game is football, followed closely by prison dodgeball, blob tag, and bombardo. He's crazy about athletes, although sometimes it isn't clear if he is absolutely sure of the difference between human athletes and Marvel Comics action figures. His current best friend is named Japeth. He used to have another best friend named Ozzie. According to Colin, Ozzie was found on a door-step, then changed his name to Michael and moved to Massachusetts, and then Colin never saw him or heard from him again.

He has had other losses in his life. He is old enough to know people who have died and to know things about the world that are worrisome. When he dreams, he dreams about moving to Wyoming, which he has visited with his family. His plan is to buy land there and have some sort of ranch that would definitely include horses. Sometimes when he talks about this, it sounds as ordinary and hard-boiled as a real estate appraisal; other times it can sound fantastical and wifty and achingly

continued

"The American Man, Age 10" *(continued)*

naïve, informed by the last inklings of childhood—the musings of a balmy real estate appraiser assaying a wonderful and magical landscape that erodes from memory a little bit every day. The collision in his mind of what he understands, what he hears, what he figures out, what popular culture pours into him, what he knows, what he pretends to know, and what he imagines makes an interesting mess. The mess often has the form of what he will probably think like when he is a grown man, but the content of what he is like as a little boy.

He is old enough to begin imagining that he will someday get married, but at ten he is still convinced that the best thing about being married will be that he will be allowed to sleep in his clothes.

The physical means Orlean uses to deliver her information is print, for the most part, despite the fact that one of her books and one of her essays have been made into films (*The Orchid Thief* and *Blue Crush*) and that she's a regular on the lecture circuit. The place in which she composes and from which she sends her message is transitory: she travels to do research and conduct interviews; then she writes about what she learns and observes. All of her writing, however, tends to be tethered to other people, the ones she observes and interviews. The distinctive features of her prose are her clear style and her use of rhetorical appeals, evidence and authority, and rhetorical methods of development.

> ANALYZING THE RHETORICAL SITUATION

Based on the excerpt from Susan Orlean's essay, answer the following questions.

1. If Orlean's purpose is to find the extraordinary in the ordinary, what is her rhetorical opportunity?
2. How does she work to respond to that opportunity through her language? How does her language fit the problem?
3. What are the available means she taps to form her response? Where and how does she use the rhetorical appeals of ethos, pathos, and logos?
4. Who or what does she use as evidence or authority?
5. What stylistic choices does Orlean make that enhance her response as a fitting one?
6. Which of the rhetorical methods of development (see page 52) does she use to shape her response? Which passages in the excerpt are built on those identifiable rhetorical methods?
7. Who might be Orlean's audience? How does her choice of available means suit her intended audience?

COMMUNITY CONNECTIONS

1. Some feature of college life is no doubt a source of dissatisfaction to you: living conditions, roommates, the commute, lack of family time, cost, instructors, course offerings. Choose one feature that is problematic and identify the means available to you for resolving that problem. Make sure that the available means account for each of three features: (a) the physical means of delivering the information, (b) the place from which the information is created and sent, and (c) the rhetorical elements (including the rhetorical appeals) of the message itself. Be prepared to share your response with the rest of the class.

2. Consider a trial being held locally (a case involving irresponsible drinking, murder, embezzlement, theft, assault, or arson, for example). As you keep up with local news (in print or any other medium, even in the form of gossip), try to determine the available means of persuasion being used by the prosecution as well as by the defense. Also identify the means of persuasion that remain either unavailable to or untapped by either the defense or the prosecution. List possible reasons why those specific means are not being used. Be prepared to share your findings with the rest of the class.

Assignment: Writing a Rhetorical Analysis

Now that you are familiar with the features of the rhetorical situation and the ways those features can be employed to shape a fitting response, you can use your knowledge to analyze someone else's rhetoric.

Your task is to select and then analyze a written or visual text, one that appears to be a fitting response. You can choose from the texts in this or the previous chapter or find a text online or in print. You are looking for a piece of writing or a visual produced by a person or a group with a vested interest in the effect of the words or the image. The following two questions will help you determine if the selection you've chosen is appropriate for a rhetorical analysis:

1. Is the text responding to an opportunity to make a change through verbal (spoken or written) or visual language?
2. Is the response verbal or visual?

After you have selected a text, read it carefully, keeping in mind that *the ultimate goal of a rhetorical analysis is twofold: (1) to analyze how well the rhetorical elements work together to create a fitting response and (2) to assess the overall effectiveness of that response.* Then, write answers to the following questions, using textual or visual evidence to support each answer:

1. Who created the text? What credentials or expertise does that person or group have? What opinions or biases did the person or group bring to the text?

2. What is the rhetorical opportunity for change? How is it identified? Why is the creator of the text engaged with this opportunity? Is this an opportunity that can be modified through language?

3. Who is the audience for the message? What opinions or biases might the audience hold? How does the audience feel about this rhetorical opportunity? What relationship is the creator of the text trying to establish with the audience? And, most important, can this audience modify or help bring about a modification of the rhetorical opportunity? How?

4. Identify the rhetorical elements of the message itself. In other words, where and how does the person or group employ the rhetorical appeals of ethos, pathos, and logos? How are credentials, goodwill, or good sense evoked to establish ethos? How is evidence (examples, statistics, data, and so forth) used to establish logos? And how is an emotional connection created to establish pathos? Keep in mind that the rhetorical appeals can sometimes overlap.

5. What kind of language does the creator of the text use? Is it plain or specialized, slang or formal? How does the choice of language reveal how the person or group views the intended audience?

6. What is the place (physical, social, academic, economic, and so on) from which the creator of the text forms and sends the response? What are the resources of that place? What are its constraints (or limitations)?

7. What medium does the creator of the text use to send the response to the audience? How private or public, accessible or inaccessible is the medium? What are the resources and the constraints of that medium?

The next part of your job is to consider whether the response is a fitting and successful one. To achieve that goal, respond in writing to these questions:

1. Is the intended audience for the text a rhetorical audience? Draw on evidence from the text to support your answer.

2. If the audience is a rhetorical one, what can it do to resolve the problem?

3. Does the response address and fit the rhetorical opportunity? How exactly? If not, how might the response be reshaped so that it does fit?

4. Is the response delivered in an appropriate medium that reaches its intended audience? If so, describe why the medium is appropriate. If not, explain how it could be adjusted so that it would be appropriate.

5. Can you think of other responses to similar rhetorical situations? What genre is commonly used to respond to such situations? Does the creator of this text use that genre? If not, what is the effect of going against an audience's expectations?

Now that you have carefully read the text and answered all of the questions, you are ready to write your rhetorical analysis. As you begin, search your answers for an idea that can serve as the basis for your thesis statement. For example, you might focus on the declared goal—if there is one—of the creator of the text and whether it has been achieved. You might assess how successfully that person or group has identified the rhetorical audience, shaped a fitting response, or employed the best available means. Or you might focus on the use of the rhetorical appeals and the overall success of their use. Whether or not you agree with the text is beside the point. Your job is to analyze, in an essay built on a clear thesis statement, how and how well its creator has accomplished the purpose.

Rhetorical Situations for Composing

You already know how to engage in rhetorical situations that call for your response; after all, for most of your life, you've been observing the elements of such situations (opportunity for writing, audience, message, purpose, and context) in order to shape your messages purposefully into the most fitting responses. The following six chapters will help you become more familiar with types of writing you've likely already practiced, even if you don't know them by the names used here. You'll come to understand how memoirs, profiles, investigative reports, position arguments, proposals, and evaluations can serve as appropriate responses to rhetorical situations. As you work through the chapters, you'll recognize the everyday nature of rhetorical theory and practice. In addition, you'll understand how well you're already using rhetorical techniques, how you resort to these kinds of writing as your response, and how you can quickly become even more skilled in their use.

3 Sharing the Experience of Taste: Responding with Memoirs

Many college students—and former students—have had highly animated conversations about the cafeteria food at their schools. Legends have been passed down through the generations about the quality of the food and the havoc it could wreak on unsuspecting students. *Boston Globe* reporter Taryn Plumb interviewed University of New Hampshire students who "expressed unease about the long-standing rumor—common to many college campuses—that servers mix laxatives into recipes to safeguard against food poisoning or botulism." In his January 2000 article "Fond Memories of a Congenital Glutton," on the Web site epinions.com, Jonathan Kibera offered a different rumor, which circulated among the students at Harvard University: "We used to joke that there was one chicken dish at Harvard, the left-overs of which were reheated under different names throughout the week. General Wong's chicken on Monday had morphed into some greasy Kung Pao derivative by Wednesday, and could well have been the Soup du Jour by Friday."

© iStockphoto.com/Chris Schmidt

Chances are that more than once during your times in the college cafeteria you've longed for a home-cooked meal. Some alumni, on the other hand, have fond memories of the food they enjoyed while relaxing with their friends after a long day of classes. Readers of the food-related Web site Chowhound.com, which its creators describe as being "for those who live to eat," were asked to post stories about their college dining experiences in order to determine which college has the best food. Many contributors to the online discussion expressed longing for their school's unique delicacies. "Lidi B" of Penn State University opined, "Oh, to have a grilled sticky from the Ye Olde College Diner à la mode with Penn State Creamery ice cream . . . that would just about be heaven . . . ," and "Quick" from Cornell University admitted, "I still remember the great reuben and chicken salad sandwiches from Cascadeli, the Dijon burger and roast chicken from Ivy room, and the awesome breakfasts from Hughes." For each of these contributors, the thoughts of college food brought back pleasant memories—not only of the food itself but also of fun and relaxation with friends.

Memoirs are a kind of writing used to narrate and analyze significant experiences in our lives, including those concerning certain foods. Food-related memoirs, which are appearing in greater numbers on bookshelves around the world, present past experiences with food that resonate with a larger historical, psychological, or social meaning. For example, Diana Abu-Jaber's memoir of her childhood in upstate New York and Jordan, *The Language of Baklava*, centers on food but is also a reflection on living between two cultures. In other words, a good food-related memoir, like any memoir, is a kind of history that captures distinctive moments in the life of the writer and the larger society. Food memories are primarily sensory, starting with an aroma, a texture, or a visual delight but then encompassing an event, an occasion, or an interaction.

IDENTIFYING AN OPPORTUNITY

Throughout this chapter, you'll work to identify an opportunity for writing a memoir of an experience with food. You might focus on the food itself (how it's produced or prepared), or you might describe the sensory experience of eating it. Your memoir might capture a compelling food-related moment from your childhood or one from the more recent past. As you determine what you want to share, consider the most fitting means of delivery for your memoir:

▶ Print memoir, to be published in a community or campus newspaper or a local 'zine

▶ Audio memoir, to be recorded for a community or campus radio station

▶ Electronic memoir, to be presented as a blog entry or a contribution to a Web site

To begin, freewrite for five minutes in response to each of the following questions (or use any of the invention techniques presented on pages 306–320):

1. What kinds of food best represent your childhood? In other words, what foods did you eat at home and with your family? Of those foods, which ones were your personal favorites? If you are now living away from home at college, what kind of memories and emotions do thoughts of this food bring to mind?

2. What locations and foods make up the culture of food on your campus or in your community? Think about the restaurants, dining halls, convenience stores, snacks, take-out meals, and cafeteria offerings that make your school's or community's culture of food unique.

3. Select the location or food from the preceding questions that you find most significant, most memorable, or most satisfying. Write about the experiences you've had in this location or with this food or the memories that it brings to mind for you. Be as specific as possible when describing your experiences or memories.

Real Situations

Many food memories, like the ones the three alumni posted online at Chowhound.com, are positive. On a discussion forum for Roadfood's Web site, "Mosca" reminisced similarly about a food truck just off Cornell's campus: "After 30 years I can still taste the (great) heartburn from the Ithaca hot truck, which was the source of my personal 'freshman 15.'" That hot truck is just one of numerous food trucks serving college campuses today or in the past, such as the "Chinese Kitchen" at Harvard, the grease trucks at Rutgers, "Chuck's" at the University of Miami, and the enchilada trucks at the University of Arizona.

© Michael Newman / Photo Edit

This food truck at UCLA will no doubt become part of many students' memories.

Chocolate, perhaps more than any other food, provides delightful memories for people of all ages. Clotilde Dusoulier, the author of the blog "Chocolate & Zucchini," prefers to enjoy high-quality chocolate with fresh coffee—for her, that combination simply makes for happiness.

Memoirs

On a Sunday afternoon, after a copious lunch, wait for your next-door neighbor Patricia to knock on your window with a wooden spoon. Agree to come over to their place for coffee. From the special chocolate cabinet in your kitchen (surely you must have one) grab what's left of the excellent dark chocolate with fragments of roasted cocoa beans that your friend Marie-Laure brought you last time she came for dinner. Walk next door in your socks. Leave Maxence and Stéphan to chat about Mac OS-X and guitar tuners in the living room, while you watch Patricia brew coffee on their espresso machine. When asked, opt for the designer coffee cups. Bring the four cups to the table on a metal tray. Take a cup, break a square of the chocolate, sit down, relax. Have a bite of chocolate, then a sip of coffee.

—**Clotilde Dusoulier, "Happiness (A Recipe)"**

Some food memories are negative—yet still entertaining—as shown by the following excerpt from Ruth Reichl's food memoir:

This is a true story.

Imagine a New York City apartment at six in the morning. It is a modest apartment in Greenwich Village. Coffee is bubbling in an electric percolator. On the table is a basket of rye bread, an entire coffee cake, a few cheeses, a platter of cold cuts. My mother has been making breakfast—a major meal in our house, one where we sit down to fresh orange juice every morning, clink our glasses as if they held wine, and toast each other with "Cheerio. Have a nice day."

Right now she is the only one awake, but she is getting impatient for the day to begin and she cranks WQXR up a little louder on the radio, hoping that the noise will rouse everyone else. But Dad and I are good sleepers, and when the sounds of martial music have no effect she barges into the bedroom and shakes my father awake.

"Darling," she says, "I need you. Get up and come into the kitchen."

My father, a sweet and accommodating person, shuffles sleepily down the hall. He is wearing loose pajamas, and the strand of hair he combs over his bald spot stands straight up. He leans against the sink, holding on to it

a little, and obediently opens his mouth when my mother says, "Try this."

Later, when he told the story, he attempted to convey the awfulness of what she had given him. The first time he said that it tasted like cat toes and rotted barley, but over the years the description got better. Two years later it had turned into pigs' snouts and mud and five years later he had refined the flavor into a mixture of antique anchovies and moldy chocolate.

Whatever it tasted like, he said it was the worst thing he had ever had in his mouth, so terrible that it was impossible to swallow, so terrible that he leaned over and spit it into the sink and then grabbed the coffeepot, put the spout into his mouth, and tried to eradicate the flavor.

Ruth Reichl, formerly editor-in-chief of *Gourmet* magazine.

My mother stood there watching all this. When my father finally put the coffeepot down she smiled and said, "Just as I thought. Spoiled."

And then she threw the mess into the garbage can and sat down to drink her orange juice.

—**Ruth Reichl, "The Queen of Mold"**

As Reichl makes clear elsewhere in her memoir, Americans are not known for their appreciation of fine food. In fact, internationally, Americans are better known for their love of junk food and fast food. Eric Schlosser captures the fast food experience in the following excerpt:

Pull open the glass door, feel the rush of cool air, walk in, get in line, study the backlit color photographs above the counter, place your order, hand over a few dollars. Watch teenagers in uniforms pushing various buttons, and moments later take hold of a plastic tray full of food wrapped in colored paper and cardboard. The whole experience of buying fast food has become so routine, so thoroughly unexceptional and mundane, that it is now taken for granted, like brushing your teeth or stopping for a red light. It has become a social custom as American as a small, rectangular, hand-held, frozen and reheated apple pie.

—**Eric Schlosser, *Fast Food Nation***

In recent years, the American culture of food has been the focus of a good deal of criticism. You've no doubt seen articles about the obesity epidemic in the United States, an epidemic linked directly to overconsumption of fast food. With 65.4 percent of Americans either

Food, Inc. has reached international markets with its hard look at the American food industry.

Memoirs

overweight or obese, the detrimental effects of fast-food consumption have been well publicized in books, in movies such as *Fast Food Nation, Super Size Me*, and *Food, Inc.*, in public debates, and even in lawsuits.

In industrialized, developed nations like the United States, the culture of food is increasingly characterized by an overabundance of choices—from dozens of ethnic cuisines and hundreds of snack and frozen food products to fresh fruits, vegetables, and fish imported from around the globe and available twelve months a year. The once strong connection between eating and ritual, represented by Clotilde Dusoulier's chocolate-and-espresso routine, is weakening in the United States. On-the-go eating habits and reliance on fast food don't necessarily lend themselves to meaningful experiences with nourishment, but many people still have vivid and personally significant memories of their experiences with food.

DESCRIBING THE CULTURE OF FOOD

1. Identify a key moment when you were first introduced to an unfamiliar kind of food. How did that event affect you?

2. Our food experiences are often shaped just as much by our visual sense as by smell or taste. We might think a food looks disgusting and thus resist tasting it, or we might favor a particular restaurant as much for its hip décor as for its food. Choose one of the images in this chapter and write for five minutes about what it suggests to you.

3. Working with a classmate, make a list of ways in which the eating habits of current college students either differ from those of past generations of students or differ from how those students ate when they lived with their parents. Explain how, when, and where you learned about these differences.

4. Call up a memory about awaiting a particular food—something that had not yet come into season, something only available at your family's vacation spot, something you would seek out upon your return to your hometown, or something always served at a holiday meal. Now write a description of that food and the anticipation of it.

5. Recall a negative stereotype about food on your college campus or nearby neighborhood, the ill effects of a particular food, or the students who eat that specific food. Write for several minutes about how that stereotype is perpetuated—or how you came to hear of it.

Real Responses to Real Situations

Telling the stories of their kitchens

With the proliferation of cable television channels such as The Food Network and Fine Living, specialty magazines such as *Cooking Light* and *Everyday Food,* and smartphone apps such as Epicurious, Yelp, and Urban Spoon, food lovers now have more ways than ever to satisfy their appetite for new recipe ideas, reviews of local restaurants and bars, descriptions of how their favorite foods are made, and stories about food industry personalities.

One particularly noteworthy contribution of the cooking and dining community to the entertainment industry has been the food memoir. Many good family recipes have interesting stories behind them, from Grandma and Grandpa's ill-fated experimentation with prune-filled pierogies on Christmas Eve in 1953 to a father's tale of picking onions in the blazing hot Texas summers, the same kind of onions his children are now piling high on top of their chili. The food memoir brings those narratives from the realm of family folklore and the margins of cookbooks to the *New York Times* bestseller list. Steve Inskeep, host of National Public Radio's "Morning Edition," interviewed food memoirist Ruth Reichl, who helped him and his listeners understand this popular genre.

> Interview with Ruth Reichl: Favorite Food Memoirs

Steve Inskeep

STEVE INSKEEP: Okay. Some people love to eat, some people love to write about what they eat, and apparently many people love to read other people's writing about what they eat. Walk into a big bookstore and you may find an entire shelf devoted to food memoirs. So, this morning, we'll pull some books off that shelf to review them.

Our reviewer is Ruth Reichl, the editor of *Gourmet* magazine. She has written two food memoirs of her own, so she is the perfect person to answer this question. Would you explain what a food memoir is for somebody who's never read one?

RUTH REICHL: It's a sort of new genre where people are writing about their lives and food. I mean, they are actually looking at the world food first. . . .

INSKEEP: You begin with the meal that you prepare and go on from there. There's actually a quote from George Orwell in one of these books. . . . This book by Bill Buford, called *Heat*, included a quote from George Orwell, which begins, "A human being is primarily a bag for putting food into."

REICHL: Many of the other authors that we will meet today don't quite agree with that.

INSKEEP: They think that there's meaning in food itself, and they try to draw out that meaning and try to draw larger meanings, don't they?

REICHL: Exactly.

INSKEEP: Let's talk about one of these books that you have selected here, *Animal, Vegetable, Miracle* by Barbara Kingsolver. Maybe that's an example of someone drawing a larger meaning out of what they eat.

REICHL: Well, Barbara Kingsolver . . . is by anybody's measure just an extraordinary writer. I just sort of opened the book at random and picked out one sentence. This is just her description of cactuses. It says, "The tall, dehydrated saguaros stood around all teetery and sucked in like very prickly super models." So here's this extraordinary writer who decides that for a year she and her family are going to try and raise all their food or get it from neighbors.

INSKEEP: What do they have to do without, if anything?

REICHL: Citrus, because . . .

INSKEEP: [It's from Florida and] they're in Virginia.

REICHL: Exactly. They had to do without almost all processed foods. They each got to choose one thing that would be outside of this law. So her husband chose coffee because, of course, there would be no coffee if you were totally feeding yourself.

INSKEEP: Did you find yourself thinking about what would be the one thing that you would insist on not doing without if you were doing this?

REICHL: Oh, there were so many things. And there are actually moments where you find them cheating a little. They do a party for her fiftieth birthday and suddenly they're doing these Vietnamese rice rolls. And I'm thinking, wait a minute, these rice paper wrappers, I don't believe that they were grown in Virginia.

continued

Memoirs

INSKEEP: Now, how is a year of eating depicted differently, if at all, when we move to a book called *The Kitchen Diaries: A Year in the Kitchen with Nigel Slater*?

REICHL: I cannot tell you how much I love this book. Nigel Slater is an English writer and chef, and I don't think anybody has ever made food sound more delicious. When he describes a beet, for instance, it comes alive for you on the page and you suddenly want to run out and eat as many beets as you possibly can. . . . This is from late May. He says, "There were beets at the farmers market today. I buy six, each the size of a plum and the color of damson jam. The stalks are young and translucent, a vivid magenta purple, yet the beets have the coarse, curly whiskers of an old man. They need no washing, just a rub with a wet thumb and a while in a very hot oven. I cut off the stalks, leaving a short tuft behind, then put the beets in a roasting tin with a splash of water and cover the tin with foil. An hour in the oven and they are done. Their skin slides off effortlessly to reveal sweet, ruby flesh." And everything he talks about is like that, and I mean there's no "shoulds" in this. It's just sheer pleasure and sensuousness in food.

INSKEEP: How long has this sort of food memoir been around?

REICHL: I think that M. F. K. Fisher really, at least for us in the United States, is the person who first wrote a food memoir. And hers was written in the forties. She wrote a book called *The Gastronomical Me*. She says that when she's writing about food, what she's really writing about are larger things, about love and our need for it. And she has a wonderful quote when she says she believes that we would all be better people if we paid attention to our appetites.

INSKEEP: May I read a sentence or two from that very book? This is from—she's remembering something that happened in 1912. She says: "The first thing I remember tasting and then wanting to taste again is the grayish-pink fuzz my grandmother skimmed from a spitting kettle of strawberry jam. I suppose I was about four." That doesn't actually sound very delectable, but it's clearly about the relationship there, isn't it?

REICHL: It is about the relationship, and it's about the memory. And actually, Barbara Kingsolver has a wonderful quote where she talks about when she's cooking, all the people who taught her to cook are standing in the kitchen with her and that there's a sort of communion of the stove and that they're all there, you know, every time she cooks. And it's that same idea, that the act of cooking is sort of going down through the ages and it's, you know, passed on from mother to daughter, from grandmother to child, and that there's a kind of sacred place in the kitchen where your relatives come to join you when you cook.

Even though every bookstore offers at least a shelf's worth of food memoirs, and cable television features round-the-clock cooking shows, our appetite for food-related media has not yet been satisfied. The increasing popularity of cooking shows such as The Food Network's *Iron Chef America* and Bravo's *Top Chef* and of cookbooks such as Jamie Oliver's *Jamie's Food Revolution* and Renee Behnke and Cynthia Nims's *Memorable Recipes to Share with Family and Friends* is proof.

But books and television shows are not the only indications that we Americans have an insatiable hunger for food-related media. Food-focused blogs have become a cottage industry, with literally thousands appearing online daily. Some of these blogs are compelling, well-written, and photographically stunning; they focus on bacon, chocolate, finding the best tamale, cooking professionally or at home, and an array of other topics. One of the most successful of such blogs was The Julie/Julia Project, which attracted forty, fifty, sometimes even eighty comments a day from readers interested in Julie Powell's culinary and personal journey. In the blog, as in Powell's spin-off food memoir (*Julie & Julia: 365 Days, 524 Recipes, 1 Tiny Apartment Kitchen*) and the movie based on it (*Julie & Julia),* Powell narrates her year-long effort to pull herself out of a rut of living in a run-down New York apartment, working in dead-end secre-

tarial jobs, and approaching her thirtieth birthday without a clear direction in her life. Her recovery came in the form of her mother's battered copy of Julia Child's classic cookbook, *Mastering the Art of French Cooking.* Powell cooked every recipe in Child's influential cookbook—from Filets de Poisson Bercy aux Champignons and Poulet Rôti to Carottes à la Concierge and Crème Brûlée—and recorded her reflections on these cooking ventures on her blog. In Powell's blog and memoir (as well as in the movie), Julia Child becomes a model, not just for aspiring cooks, but for anyone who wants to keep learning while growing older.

© Ethan Hill/Contour by Getty Images

Julie Powell, author of *Julie & Julia* and The Julie/Julia Project blog.

Excerpt from

> The Julie/Julia Project

Julie Powell

Working with the book, one comes to know Julia as a teacher—a brilliant one, with a spark of humor, a passion for her subject, and an unfailing intuition for how to create a feeling of comfort in the midst of chaotic striving. But in her shows, and particularly her later ones, "Cooking with Master Chefs," . . . Julia proves an exemplary, and inspirational, student. She is endlessly curious—every time she sticks her big, curled paws into a pot of boiling water, or right under the flying knife of a chef forty years her junior, to pick up some bit of something to taste, the tiny bit of my soul that still harbors a belief in a higher power squeezes its eyes shut and crosses its fingers and prays as hard as it can that when I am her age, I'll be just like Julia. She asks endless questions—in the episode PBS is so obsessed with that they show it about once a week, it's the anti-flatulence properties of epazote that holds her attention, to a rather unseemly degree—and always seems glad to learn from the people she brings on to the show, often wet-eared young whipper-snappers who treat her like she's some dotty old biddy until I want to grab them by the shoulders and shake them—"Show some respect, kid, this is *Julia,* and you wouldn't be here if it wasn't for her!!!" But she never seems to feel slighted or disrespected—really, in the end, how could she? She is Julia—always changing, but always, utterly, herself. As a student, on these shows, she's teaching us all how to learn.

She has a wonderful aside in [the] endlessly repeated episode about lard—when she gets off the epazote for a minute. "We should talk about this," she warbles, as Rick dumps a nice big scoop of lard into a frying pan, "because everyone's so *afraid* of lard." They discuss the pros and cons of the stuff—less cholesterol than butter, but more saturated fats, the authenticity lard lends to Latin American dishes, etc. . . ., and Julia says, "The point is, if you don't want to make something right, *don't make it.* Choose something else. Like making tamales with olive oil, it's *TERRIBLE!*" And her voice swoops briefly up into the stratosphere, and you feel this passion in her, and yes, she's probably had a glass or two of wine, which God love her she deserves, but to me the wonderful thing is the hint that there's yet another Julia, another face. I've learned from the teacher and I've learned again from the student, but when she talks of lard, Julia hints that there is another, wilder, Julia beneath it all, a rebellious, passionate, dare I say *dangerous* individual. Was it this Julia who joined [the] OSS and created shark repellent? Or maybe just this Julia who walked into a cooking school in France—no longer a spring chicken herself, but with an unquenchable fire in her that she herself didn't quite understand. That's the Julia I'm striving toward, the Julia that I hope someday to be like.

> ANALYZING THE RHETORICAL SITUATION

The texts in this section suggest that food memoirs have great appeal for many people in the United States. The following questions ask you to consider this kind of writing in terms of the elements of the rhetorical situation. You'll want to reread the excerpts in this section carefully before answering.

1. Who might be the intended audience of Julie Powell's food blog The Julie/Julia Project? What textual evidence can you provide for your answer? Be prepared to share your answers with the rest of the class.

2. To what rhetorical opportunity is Steve Inskeep responding? How does his interview address that opportunity?

3. Who might be the intended audience for Inskeep's interview with Ruth Reichl on food memoirs? How does Inskeep's audience differ from Powell's? What textual evidence supports your conclusions?

4. Is the purpose of each excerpt in this section evident? If so, what is the purpose of each one? What are the differences among the excerpts in terms of purpose? And how does each purpose relate to the writer's or speaker's intended audience? Again, be prepared to share your answers with the rest of the class.

5. The publication or recording of each of the pieces in this section occurred in the past. Keeping that in mind, suggest a rhetorical opportunity for change to which each piece might be a response. How does the piece work to resolve or address that opportunity?

6. How does each writer and speaker demonstrate his or her use of the rhetorical appeals of ethos, logos, and pathos to fulfill the purpose? Cite passages from the texts to support your answer.

The changing significance of food

Some food memoirists share their experience of tasting the fresh winter-into-spring salad or their first failed attempt at flipping omelets; others have focused their attention on better understanding people's relationship to food and the consequences of that relationship. Indeed, the growing popularity of food writing and programming within the entertainment industry suggests that Americans connect food more with pleasure and fun than with nourishment and sustenance. Newspaper headlines over the past few years have begun to warn readers about scientific findings that link growing health epidemics to problematic obsessions with food. However, this evolving relationship with food has been a topic that some anthropologists and sociologists have been writing and speaking about for decades.

AP Photo

Margaret Mead holds a baby on Admiralty Island, Papua New Guinea, in 1954.

Margaret Mead (1901–1978) was the most influential and the most persistent explorer of the American culture of food. A graduate of Barnard College with a degree in psychology, Mead went on to earn a PhD in anthropology at Columbia University. After graduate school, believing that understanding human behavior held great promise for the future, Mead conducted research among adolescents in Samoa, which culminated in the 1928 publication of the now classic *Coming of Age in Samoa*. In another of her studies, Mead argued that the biological differences between men and women should not preclude women's full participation in the world. All of Mead's anthropological work—whether on indigenous cultures, social roles, or family structure—advanced the idea that human traits are primarily social, not biological.

Mead's observations on the social influences on human traits were continued in her sociological studies of Americans' eating habits. During World War II (1939–1945), for instance, she focused her research on the culture of food in the United States. At that time, she was one of the scientists and social scientists recruited by the U.S. government to conduct various "national character" studies and then to give public policy advice. As an anthropologist already versed in the interconnectedness of all aspects of human life, Mead understood the connections among the elements of national character, including ritual, belief, and identity—and the ways those elements linked up with the culture of food.

Mead remained interested in food and nutrition throughout the tremendous social and cultural changes of the 1960s in the United States. As a skilled writer and observer of human behavior and social structures, she continued to study both domestic and international changes in the availability of food and the consequences of the increased efficiency, automation, and industrialization of the food industry. She had good reason to be concerned with such issues: famine struck India and Pakistan in the late 1960s. And despite the great progress of U.S. agriculture during that same time, hunger was a major American problem as well, as Marion Nestle, author of *Food Politics,* points out. Even today, despite agricultural advances, hunger affects 50 million Americans, or one-sixth of the nation's population, with children and the elderly at the greatest risk, according to the organization Food First.

When President Lyndon Baines Johnson took office in 1963, poverty and hunger affected one-fifth of all Americans. He declared a war on poverty and established food assistance programs, some of which still remain. Around that same time, Margaret Mead dedicated herself to updating the World War II–era findings of the National Research Council's Committee for the Study of Food Habits, believing that social and technological developments had significantly altered the way people ate in the United States. In a section of her update, Mead observes the following:

> In the United States, within the lifetime of one generation, there has been a dramatic shift from malnutrition as a significant nutritional state on a national scale, to over-nutrition as one of the principal dangers to the nation's health. Over-nutrition, in the United States, may be attributed to food habits carried over from a situation of relative scarcity to one of plenty and to the development of food vending methods which continually expose people to an extreme amount and variety of foods. . . . Today we may distinguish an increasing number of affluent industrialized countries in which it is essential to develop an educational system within which children can

© Bubbles Photolibrary / Alamy

Prepackaged and highly processed foods are often consumed along with entertainment today.

learn self-regulation in the face of tremendous variety. Conditions in these countries contrast sharply with those which prevail—and may be expected to continue to prevail—in the underdeveloped areas of the world, where children must still be taught a rather rigid adherence to a diet that is only just sufficient for survival.

—**Margaret Mead**, *Food Habits Research: Problems of the 1960s*

Mead's observations about Americans' eating habits led her to consider the changing significance of food in people's lives. No longer was food being used to commemorate special events or traditions; instead, it was used for easy consumption or quick entertainment, with little thought for its nutritional value. In her update, Mead also noted dramatic alterations in the way food was produced (mass production), prepared (breaded and fried), and distributed (frozen and canned). Given the current debates over American diets, eating habits, and agricultural practices—as well as the presence of widespread hunger—Mead's writing now seems prophetic. She brought national attention to the split between food as nourishment and food as a commercial commodity as well as to the profound postwar changes in the foods produced by industrialized nations and their distribution (or lack thereof).

In 1970, Mead published what would become one of her most famous essays, "The Changing Significance of Food," which appeared in the magazine *American Scientist*. Mead argued that despite all the national attention, the United States remained dangerously ignorant of its food-related challenges and capabilities. "Today, for the first time in the history of mankind," she asserts, "we have the productive capacity to feed everyone in the world." But the United States was not feeding every American, let alone everyone else in the world. World hunger and food scarcity simply had not yet been properly addressed. Mead used this essay, then, to single out conditions that had contributed to this refusal or inability to recognize the severity of the situation. In the following passage, Mead describes one such condition—"the increase in the diseases of affluence."

Excerpt from

> # The Changing Significance of Food

Margaret Mead

In a country pronounced only twenty years before to be one-third ill-fed, we suddenly began to have pronouncements from nutritional specialists that the major nutritional disease of the American people was over-nutrition. If this had simply meant overeating, the old puritan ethics might have been more easily invoked, but it was over-nutrition that was at stake. And this in a country where our ideas of nutrition had been dominated by a dichotomy which distinguished food that was "good for you, but not good" from food that was "good, but not good for you." This split in man's needs, into our cultural conception of the need for nourishment and the search for pleasure, originally symbolized [by] the rewards for eating spinach or finishing what was on one's plate if one wanted to have dessert, lay back of the movement to produce, commercially, nonnourishing foods. Beverages and snacks came in particularly for this demand, as it was the addition of between-meal eating to the three square, nutritionally adequate meals a day that was responsible for much of the trouble.

We began manufacturing, on a terrifying scale, foods and beverages that were guaranteed not to nourish. The resources and the ingenuity of industry were diverted from the preparation of foods necessary for life and growth to foods non-expensive to prepare, expensive to buy. And every label reassuring the buyer that the product was not nourishing increased our sense that the trouble with Americans was that they were too well nourished. The diseases of affluence, represented by new forms of death in middle-age, had appeared before we had . . . conquered the diseases of poverty—the ill-fed pregnant women and lactating women, sometimes resulting in irreversible damage to the ill-weaned children, the school children so poorly fed that they could not learn. . . .

It was hard for the average American to believe that while he struggled, and paid, so as not to be overnourished, other people, several millions, right in this country, were hungry and near starvation. The contradiction was too great. . . . How can the country be overnourished and undernourished at the same time?

For Mead, the increased availability of highly processed snack foods and drinks and American businesses' focus on these products was proof that the United States had a problem with over-nutrition and food abundance. The boom in consumer goods and prepared foods—from TV dinners to baby formula—rendered nearly invisible the millions of Americans who were not benefiting from food surpluses. Mead warned that once food became an international commodity, a product separated entirely from its cultural and nutritional significance, its production, distribution, and consumption would become a huge international problem.

Margaret Mead warned about the trend toward easy-to-make, prepackaged foods that were believed to be a solution to the world's nutrition problems because they seemed easier to distribute and consume. You likely have experienced the end results of this trend in the

In a cafeteria at Kenyon University in Ohio, the word *Local* on the salad bar sneeze guard tells diners that the food came from a nearby family farm.

school cafeterias where you went to grade school, high school, and college. These facilities have long struggled to balance the need to provide students with nourishing foods with the constraint of a limited budget, while keeping students happy that they're eating something that tastes good. If you're like many college students, you may be more than a little skeptical about or resistant to some of the culinary offerings in your college cafeteria, and you may even buy into the rumors about what the cooks may be stirring into your dinner. Indeed, for many college graduates, the memories they have of their college dining experiences have more to do with the people they were with and the stories that were told than with the food they happened to be eating.

Many college dining facilities are seeking to change students' negative impressions and to assume nutritional responsibility for their students and ecological responsibility for their communities at the same time. And while they're at it, these new-and-improved cafeterias are having an influence on the college recruiting process. The following excerpt from an article in the *Atlantic Monthly* describes efforts by Yale University to provide students with delicious foods while also teaching them the value of producing foods in locally sustainable ways.

> Good-bye Cryovac
Corby Kummer

I recently washed up after a supper consisting of four kinds of veg-etables from the farmers' market—all four of them vegetables I usually buy at the local right-minded supermarket. As I considered the vivid, distinctive flavor of every bite, I thought, What is that stuff I've been eating the rest of the year?

One of the twelve residential colleges at Yale University is trying to give students that kind of summertime epiphany at every meal, by serving dishes made from produce raised as close to New Haven as possible. In just two years the Yale Sustainable Food Project has launched two ambitious initiatives to bridge the distance from farm to table: the complete revamping of menus in Berkeley College's din-ing hall to respect seasonality and simplicity, and the conversion of an overgrown lot near campus to an Edenic organic garden. The garden does not supply the dining hall—it couldn't. Rather, it serves as a kind of Greenwich Mean Time, suggesting what is best to serve, and when, by illustrating what grows in the southern New England climate in any given week. The goal of the project is to sell students on the superior flavor of food raised locally in environmentally responsible (but not always organic) ways, so that they will seek it the rest of their lives.

A few dishes I tasted last summer during a pre-term recipe-testing marathon in Berkeley's kitchen convinced me that this goal is within reach for any college meals program willing to make an initial outlay for staff training and an ongoing investment in fewer but better ingre-dients. I would be happy to eat pasta with parsnips once a week, for example, the candy-sweet roots sharpened by fresh parsley and Parme-san. In fact, I demanded the recipe. Any restaurant would be pleased to serve fresh asparagus roasted with a subtle seasoning of balsamic vin-egar and olive oil alongside, say, filet of beef. Even the chicken breasts, coated with black pepper, grilled, and served with a shallot, garlic, and white-wine sauce, tasted like chicken.

Not long ago a college would never have thought to mention food in a brochure or on a school tour—except, perhaps, in a deprecating aside. Now food is a competitive marketing tool, and by the second or third stop on the college circuit parents and students practically expect to be shown the organic salad bar and told about the vegan options and the menus resulting directly from student surveys. Yale has gone these colleges what I consider to be a giant step further, showing stu-dents what they should want and making them want it.

As caring about food has become interwoven with caring about the environment, enjoying good food has lost some of the elitist, hedonistic

continued

Memoirs

taint that long barred gourmets from the ranks of the politically correct. The challenge, as with any political movement, is to bring about practical institutional change that incorporates ideals.

It's a very big challenge with college food, almost all of which is provided by enormous catering companies like Sodexho, Chartwells, and Aramark, the company that has run Yale's dining services since 1998. These companies have long offered vegetarian, organic, and vegan choices. But none of those options—not even, sadly, going organic—necessarily supports local farmers and local economies, or shows students how much better food tastes when it's made from scratch with what's fresh. Vegetarian, organic, and vegan foods can all be processed, overseasoned, and generally gunked up, and in the hands of institutional food-service providers they usually are. . . .

Whatever the argument for spending more money on food . . . , the practical successes at Yale should encourage other schools to consider similar changes. [Associate Director of the Yale Sustainable Food Project Josh] Viertel gives the example of granola, a simple seduction tool. At the beginning of this year the Food Project's formula of organic oats, almonds, and raisins, a local honey, and New England maple syrup was so popular that Commons had to take over making it for every college. And the project's recipe is actually cheaper than buying pre-made granola in bulk. Viertel recently began a composting program; the first step is asking students to scrape their own plates, which shows close up the waste involved when they take, say, just one bite of cheese lasagne. Other schools ought to take that same step, even if they stop there. . . .

Kummer's description of this food project at Yale University illustrates the kinds of efforts going on at some colleges to combat the disturbing trend toward "over-nourishment" that Mead saw four decades ago. While Mead emphasized the social and, elsewhere in her writings, the environmental benefits that would follow from producing more local-based diets, Kummer adds the element of economic gain that colleges and universities would achieve by enticing more students to their schools. Indeed, we can all imagine that such locally oriented dining experiences might someday leave all of us longing for the days in college cafeterias, not only because we experienced such great times relaxing and telling stories with friends, but also because we were eating such delicious, inventive foods.

> ANALYZING THE RHETORICAL SITUATION

1. What is "over-nutrition," and how does Mead argue that it came to be a problem?

2. What evidence does Mead provide to demonstrate that diseases of affluence result not just from biological traits but

also from social traits? Who is the audience for this argument? What is her purpose?

3. What problems (or rhetorical opportunities) does Mead address? What arguments does she make about the roots of these problems? What evidence does she provide to support these claims about the sources of the problems?

4. What is Mead's purpose, given her audience? Provide textual evidence for your answer.

5. What are Mead's proposals for solving the problems she identifies? Referring to your answer to question 4, suggest how her intended audience might help her resolve or address the problem she's investigating.

6. How does Mead use the rhetorical appeals of ethos, pathos, and logos to build the arguments in her two pieces? Provide textual evidence to support your answer. Which of the rhetorical appeals does she rely on most? Be prepared to share your answer with the rest of the class.

7. What rhetorical opportunities prompted Kummer's piece on the Sustainable Food Project at Yale University? How would you characterize the relationship between his work and Mead's theories? In what ways is he helping to develop the conversation about the culture of food in the United States?

COMMUNITY CONNECTIONS

1. How do Julie Powell's reflections and descriptions coincide with or diverge from your experiences with cooking and with food? Take about ten minutes to write your response.

2. Now do the same for the pieces by Mead and Kummer: how do their analyses coincide with or diverge from your experiences or observations about the culture of food in the United States?

3. Do you agree with Mead's argument that "ideas of nutrition [in the United States have] been dominated by a dichotomy which distinguished food that was 'good for you, but not good' from food that was 'good, but not good for you'"? Draw on your experiences in childhood or in college to support your answer.

4. Now that you have considered various arguments made about humans and their relationships with food, how would you describe the

culture of food on your campus or in your community? What food options or eating habits seem most significant to you? What economic, political, social, cultural, or biological forces have shaped the culture of food?

Memoirs: A Fitting Response

A memoir on food and culture

Food triggers vivid memories for all of us—some joyous or satisfying, others painful or awkward. Food can also serve to define our relationships with family, friends, and even complete strangers. Many writers have discussed their experiences with food in their memoirs precisely to trigger reflections on defining moments in their lives or to crystallize their own perceptions of people and cultures. Pooja Makhijani provides one such reflective memoir in her essay "School Lunch." As you read, notice the rich details that Makhijani provides to help readers visualize, smell, taste, and even feel the food that her mother packed for her each day before she left for school. As you take pleasure in these descriptions, though, see how Makhijani uses her descriptions of food to illustrate a larger point about her relationship with her mother and with the American culture in which she wants to immerse herself.

School Lunch

Pooja Makhijani

The writer provides examples with details to help readers visualize the contents of the lunches she totes to school. She also introduces the main characters of her memoir, including herself as the narrator.

Mom says she is being "sensible" about what I eat and she likes to pack "sensible" lunches. Plastic sandwich bags filled with blood-red pomegranate seeds. Fresh raisin bread wrapped in foil. Homemade vegetable biryani made with brown rice and lima beans. Yellow pressed rice with potatoes and onions. A silver thermos full of warm tamarind-infused lentil soup. Blue and white Tupperware containers that can be reused. Lunch sacks that have to be brought home every day. Silverware. •

With the short first sentence of the second paragraph, the writer creates tension between her and her mother, tension that will give momentum to the rest of the memoir.

I don't want her lunches. I want to touch a cold, red Coca-Cola can that will hiss when I open it. I want to pull out a yellow Lunchables box so I can assemble bite-size sandwiches with Ritz crackers and smoked turkey. I want to smell tuna salad with mayonnaise and pickles. I want bologna on white bread, Capri Sun Fruit Punch, and Cool Ranch Doritos in a brown paper bag. I want plastic forks that I can throw away when I am done eating. But I am too scared to ask her. I know she will say, "No."

"Why don't you invite Chrissy over this Friday after school?" Mom ladles a spoonful of sweetened, homemade yogurt into a white ceramic bowl. "You've already been to her house twice." I hoist myself onto one of the high chairs at my kitchen table and pull my breakfast toward me. I tear the hot masala roti into eight irregular pieces and dip the largest one into the cold yogurt.

"I will, I will." I rub my fingers on the paper towel in my lap. The last time I went to Chrissy's house, Mrs. Pizarro gave us mini–hot dogs wrapped in pastry topped with a squirt of mustard, and tall glasses of Hawaiian Punch as an after-school snack. I can't imagine Chrissy coming to our house and munching on cauliflower and broccoli florets while gulping down chilled milk. I don't want to think about all the questions she will ask. When she sees the bronze Ganesh idol on the wooden stool near the sofa, she will inquire, *What is that elephant-headed statue in your living room?* When she sniffs the odor of spices that permeates the bedrooms, she will question, *What's the smell?* And when she accidentally touches my mother's henna colored sari, she will query, *What's your mom wearing?*

"I will," I say between bites so Mom won't ask me again. "Just not this week."

She glances at the clock on the oven. "Hurry up with your food, beti. Nishaat Aunty will be here any second." She grabs the rest of the roti, dunks it into the yogurt, and shovels it into my mouth. Thick globs of yogurt slide in rivulets down her palms and she licks it off once I am done eating. She wipes her hands on her red gingham apron and hands me a bulging brown paper bag. "Your lunch," she says.

"What did you pack today?" I ask as I shove the bag into my purple canvas backpack alongside my spelling and math textbooks.

"Aloo tikkis. Left over from last night."

"Oh." I part the curtains of the kitchen window and look for Nishaat Aunty's midnight-blue station wagon. "Chrissy brought Coke with her to school yesterday." I look into her eyes, hoping she will understand.

"Coca-Cola! During school?" she says. "Of course, that's what those American parents do. That's why their children are so hyper and don't concentrate on their studies." I am not allowed to drink soda, except on Saturdays when Mom makes fried fish. Recently, I've been drinking lots of apple juice because she is worried that there is too much acidity in orange juice.

"Okay, class, time for lunch." Miss Brown, my fifth-grade teacher, puts down the piece of chalk and rubs her hands on her chocolate-brown pleated pants, leaving behind ghostly prints. She grabs her cardigan off her chair and heads to the teachers' lounge near the gym.

The writer also introduces dialogue, which reveals the first-person point of view. The essay moves from scene to scene during a pivotal period of the author's life.

The writer provides a vivid description of the snacks served at Chrissy's house and her own house in order to help readers visualize the cultural differences she believes are keeping her distanced from friends at school.

As she uses flashforward to describe what will happen in the future, the writer concentrates on events, detailed descriptions, characters, setting, and a sequence of events.

Memoirs

Our lunch aide, Ms. Bauer, walks into the classroom. Her long silver hair cascades over her shoulders and down her back, hiding her ears.

"Row One, you can go to the closets and get your money or your food," Ms. Bauer's raspy voice instructs the five students in the front of the room. I wait for her to call "Row Four" so I can run to the back of the classroom and yank my sack off the top shelf of the closet. Every day, I take my food out of my sack and slide it into my desk. I leave it there until the end of the day so I can throw it away in the large garbage bin next to Principal Ward's office before I head home.

"Row Two." I look out the window. I see the rusty swing set in the front of Washington School. Before Christmas, there were three wooden planks attached to the bar. This spring, only one remains and it sways, lonely, in an early April breeze.

"Row Three." By now, several of my classmates have lined up near the globes in front of the room. They will wait there until everyone whose parents gave them a dollar and two quarters this morning have lined up. Ms. Bauer will walk them down the hall to the temporary lunch stations and they will bring back compartmentalized Styrofoam trays loaded with food.

"Row Four." I bolt. As I reach for my sack, I feel someone tug on my pink turtleneck. I turn around to see who tapped me on the shoulder.

"Aisha." She reintroduces herself.

It's the new girl. Mr. Ward brought her to our classroom on Monday, right after we had finished the Pledge of Allegiance. "Aisha's family just came from Pakistan two days ago," he said. "Please make her feel welcome."

Miss Brown rearranged our desks a bit, and put Aisha in the center of the room. Then she pulled down the world map and gave everyone a quick geography lesson. "Now, who can find Pakistan?" she asked. Even though I knew, I didn't raise my hand. Months before, we'd studied India and Pakistan and Bangladesh in our South Asia unit in social studies. As we took turns reading aloud paragraphs, Miss Brown asked me to read the longest section on topography of the subcontinent. "And in the northeast, Nepal is separated from Tibet by the mighty Himalayan Mountains," I concluded as I heard snickers behind me.

"Hima-aa-layan," Eddie whispered to no one in particular.

"It's Him-a-lay-an." Miss Brown corrected me at the same time. An accent of the first syllable. Short 'a' sounds. Four quick strokes and not the drawn-out vowels that had rolled off my tongue.

I wasn't going to pronounce "Pakistan" the way I knew how to—with a hissing "st" sound not heard in the English language.

"Will you have lunch at my desk today?" she asks. Today, just like yesterday, she wears her fanciest salwaar khameez to school. Yesterday, she wore a blue kurta over a satin white churidaar, and today she wears a shimmery lavender top decorated with clusters of pearls along the edges. She slings her dupatta over her left shoulder. It is longer in the front than in the back and the end gets caught in the heel of her white chappal.

The inclusion of undefined cultural terms demonstrates Pooja's fluency with the terms and enhances her sense of not fitting in.

I look down at my cuffed jeans and wonder if she wants to wear sneakers. Will everyone ask Aisha questions about what she is wearing, why she has an accent, or where she comes from? I have always said "No, thank you" when Chrissy or Heather have asked me to eat with them because I don't want to explain anything that makes me different from them. Will I have to explain things about Aisha too? I don't know whether to say yes and be nice, or say no, and read a book while waiting for recess.

"Sure, I'll eat with you," I say finally. I know she has asked me to sit at her desk because I am the only person in the classroom who looks somewhat like her.

She looks relieved. "I have to go buy some food." She rummages through her fleece-lined jacket and takes out $1.50. "Pull your chair up to my desk. I will be back in ten minutes." I watch her get into the lunch line that Ms. Bauer directs out the door.

I drag my chair over to the front of the room. I haven't had a chance to stuff my lunch into my desk, so I peer inside my bag.

I see Mom's aloo tikkis. She's stuffed the leftover potato patties inside a hard roll from La Bonbonniere bakery. The deep-fried flattened ball of potato is spiked with garam masala and shoved into a bun slathered with fresh coriander chutney, which Mom makes with coarsely ground almonds that crunch in my mouth when I least expect it. Below the sandwich are a bunch of grapes in a Ziplock bag. No dripping-wet can of Sprite. No Little Debbie apple pie. No Hostess chocolate cupcakes filled with vanilla cream. No strawberry Pop-Tarts.

The writer doesn't stop at describing the food that is in her lunch bag; she also describes the food that is not there. In this way, she sets up a comparison and contrast that leads into the following scene comparing Pooja's and Aisha's comfort levels with American culture.

I zip up my bag again and wait for Aisha to return. She brings back her tray and places it on her desk. Today's lunch is six chicken nuggets, a spoonful of corn, sticky peach halves floating in sugar syrup, and a tough dinner roll.

"I thought you would have started eating by now." Aisha pierces her chocolate milk carton with a straw.

"I am not that hungry." My stomach growls. I am used to ignoring the sounds. I can usually get through the day on the normal, easily-explainable-if-anyone-sees food. Carrot sticks, apple slices, or Saltines.

"But you brought your lunch. I saw you take something out of the bag. What is it?" she insists.

I reach inside my bag and feel the crusty bread. I draw it out, pressing it between my fingers and thumb, flattening it into a tiny Frisbee, mashing the roll into the soft potatoes.

"See, it is just bread." The disk is so flat that you can't see the tikki inside.

"No, there's something inside it." Aisha peers at the sandwich. "Is that an aloo tikki in a bun? I wish my mother would pack them in my lunch for me. Yesterday, I bought peanut-butter-and-jelly sandwiches. I've never had peanut butter before. It's such a funny food. It stuck to the back of my teeth and I could taste it for the rest of the day."

I look at the flattened mess in my hands and think about licking peanut butter from the crevices in my mouth. I gaze at Aisha's chicken nuggets.

"Wanna trade?" I ask.

"Are you sure? If I were you, I'd keep my food." She cocks her head and her eyes dart between the multicolored array in front of her and the earth-tone concoction just a few inches away from her.

"If you want it, you can have it." My fingers inch over to her side of the desk.

"You can have everything except the corn. I like that." She passes her plate to me and I hand my lunch to her.

"How long have you been here?" I devour all the chicken nuggets before Aisha changes her mind.

"We just got here last weekend. We are living in Edison Village, right near the train station." She nibbles her way around the entire circumference of the bun. "You've probably been here longer than that. You sound American."

I realize she is commenting on the way I pronounce words. Her accent sounds like my mother's. "I was born in New York. I've lived in Edison as long as I can remember."

"Then why don't you eat the school lunch?" Aisha spoons the corn into her mouth.

All good memoir writers pause in their narration of events to reflect on the significance of those events to their personal development and worldview.

I don't have an answer for Aisha. I know it's not because it's too expensive or that Styrofoam trays are environmentally unsound. It's because Mom thinks her deep-fried aloo tikkis and freshly ground masalas are what good Indian parents give their daughters. She doesn't understand that good Indian daughters just want to become American.

It's too complicated an issue to explain. Like my mother, Aisha won't understand it.

"Time for recess." Ms. Bauer claps her hands three times. I throw the tray and the plastic utensils in the garbage can in the front of the room, and Aisha walks with me back to the closets to put my lunch sack back on the shelf. I race back towards the front of the line that is heading out the door, a few steps behind Chrissy and Heather, following them to the asphalt playground. The boys bolt off to play kickball, their four bases taking up most of the space on the grounds. The girls congregate near the fence around Ms. Bauer as she pulls multicolored jump ropes out of her tote bags.

"Cookies, candies in a dish. How many pieces do you wish?" Chrissy and Heather both jump into the twirling rope. "One, two, three, four," twenty-five girls chant. "Twelve, thirteen. . . ." The rope gets caught under Heather's sneaker.

"Aisha, would you like to try?" Ms. Bauer turns to Aisha and me, who both watch intently.

"Okay." She kicks off her chappals and ties her dupatta round her waist. "But I don't know any of the songs."

"Don't worry. I will pick one for you." Aisha stands between the two lunch ladies, the rope swaying in the wind against her bare feet. I collapse down onto the ground and sit, legs crossed, as I usually do, singing along, but never joining in. "Cinderella, dressed in yella. Went upstairs to see her fella. How many kisses did she get?" Aisha is jumping furiously in time with the music. "Twenty-eight, twenty-nine, thirty, thirty …" Aisha missteps and stumbles.

"That was fun." She sits down next to me.

I smile. "You are very good."

"There is a new girl in our class," I tell Mom after school as I peel the tangerine she's given me. "She's from Pakistan." I pull the segments apart and arrange them in a circle on the napkin.

"When did they come?"

"Last weekend." I tell her all the stories Aisha told me at lunch—about her all-girls school in Islamabad, her two younger brothers, and how busy her parents are trying to find a job in New Jersey. I pick up a single slice of the tangerine and glide it between my teeth. "She even wore Indian—I mean, Pakistani—clothes to school every day this week."

"You should do that too." She sweeps the discarded peel with her hands.

I sink my incisors into the fruit. A burst of juice fills my mouth. "She just came from there. That's why she does it," I rationalize to her. "She doesn't have American clothes. And she eats the school lunch." I hope that she picks up on my second subtle hint of the day.

"I am sure once they are all settled in, Aisha's mother will be giving her biryani as well." She wipes the tangerine juice that's dribbled out of my mouth onto my chin, and I lower myself from the chair. "They'll want to hold onto that in this country. Don't you want your banana today?"

Again, the writer uses dialogue to good effect—this line succinctly captures the mother's perspective on the importance of continuing to cook Indian food in their adopted homeland and to pass on such cultural touchstones to her children.

"No, I am not hungry. I ate lunch."

Aisha and I continue to exchange meals for the rest of the school year. I give her more of my mom's aloo tikkis, and she hands over her pizza bagels. I demolish her macaroni and cheese, and she inhales my masala rice. Aisha starts to wear jeans by June. She always takes off her sneakers and socks before jumping rope, though; she says it's easier that way.

Every day, at 3:15, as I jump into our ice-blue Dodge Caravan, Mom asks me, "Did you finish the lunch I packed you for today?"

"Yes, Mom," I lie. I am not about to spoil my arrangement.

■ GUIDE TO RESPONDING TO THE RHETORICAL SITUATION

Understanding the Rhetorical Situation

When you want to narrate and analyze a significant experience in your life, consider composing a memoir. Memoirs share the following characteristics:

- Memoirs focus on a particularly significant experience or series of experiences in the writer's life. Rather than narrating from birth to adulthood, the way an autobiography does, a memoir focuses on those experiences or events that carry the most significance for shaping who the writer is and his or her perspective on the world.
- Memoirs contain ample sensory details to help readers visualize, hear, smell, taste, or feel key events, characters, experiences, and objects.
- Memoirs include dialogue or quoted speech that reveals something unique about or central to a character or the character's relationship with other people, events, or objects in the story.
- Memoirs include clear transitional phrases to show how events relate to one another in time and how the action of the narrative unfolds.
- Memoirs provide reflection on or analysis of the key narrative events to help readers understand their significance for the writer's development and his or her perspective on everyday life.

The following sections will help you compose a memoir about an experience with food. To work with an online guide to the elements of the rhetorical situation, access your English CourseMate through CengageBrain.com.

Identifying an opportunity

Consider the foods, the recipes, and the dining spots that you find most familiar and most comforting—or, conversely, most alien and most unpleasant—so that you can begin the process of thinking about how the culture of food has shaped who you are. You might, for example, think back to a time when a parent or other relative calmed your anxieties about a bad result on an exam or your distress following a devastating break-up with a comforting meal. Or you might remember the specific details of a meal at your favorite diner or coffee shop in your hometown, the one where you and your friends still congregate when you are all home for semester break. What you are searching for is an experience or event or relationship within which food has played a vital

Memoirs

role—and helped you to understand something about life that you want other people to know.

1. Make a list of the foods that are most pleasurable, most memorable, or most meaningful to you, including those you might have written about in response to the questions on page 66. Describe at least one experience involving each food. Explain why the experiences were positive or negative, providing as many details as possible. If anything could have made the bad experiences better, explain what and how. For each experience, include as many contributing factors as you can: the people you were with when you were eating the food, the place where you were eating the food, the occasion, the events that led up to the moment or that followed immediately after it, and so forth.

2. Choosing one or two foods, make sketches or take photos of the food or the location where you enjoyed it from different vantage points, paying particular attention to the details and features that you find most intriguing about the experience of eating the food.

3. Choose the food you want to write about and compose four or five descriptions of the significance that food has for you. Vary your descriptions by emphasizing different features of the situation in which you have eaten or most often eat the food. For example, one description might emphasize your pleasant or unpleasant memories of the first time you ate the food. Another description might emphasize a particular person the food reminds you of, and yet another might deal with the sense of belonging or alienation that eating this food has created in you.

Locating an audience

The following questions will help you locate your rhetorical audience as well as identify their relationship to the food-related experience you've decided to write about. Having identified your audience, you'll be able to choose the most descriptive details to include and the best way to deliver the message you want that audience to receive, whether that message is informative, entertaining, argumentative, analytical, or explanatory.

1. List the names of the persons or groups who might be most interested in hearing about your experiences with this particular food or who might be most resistant to your story but need to hear about it anyway.

2. Next to the name of each potential audience, write reasons that audience could have for acknowledging the significance of your experience. In other words, what would convince these audiences

that you have a unique and interesting story to tell—a story they need to hear more about in order to think more deeply about the food experiences in their own lives?

3. What kinds of responses to your writing could you reasonably expect from each of these audiences? In other words, what would you like your audience to do with the information you're providing? Think here about similar experiences that the audience might have had, as well as the audience's openness to new perspectives or desire for familiar experiences.

4. With your audience's interests, experiences, and perspectives in mind, look again at the descriptions and visual illustrations of food experiences and their significance that you composed in the preceding section on identifying an opportunity. Decide which descriptions will most likely engage your audience and help your audience connect your food-related experience with their own. At this point, it is probably necessary to revise your best descriptions to tailor them to your audience.

Identifying a fitting response

Because different purposes and different audiences require different kinds of texts—different media—you'll want to consider all of the options available to you. For example, the desire to recount your inability to resist the temptations of the college cafeteria's dessert table might prompt you to write a humorous column for the school's alumni magazine. Your narrative describing how your grandfather taught you to cook his delicious stir-fry recipe might find a place in your family's scrapbook or be preserved in an audio recording as part of your family's oral history. The point is that once you identify your opportunity, audience, and purpose, you need to determine what kind of format will best respond to the rhetorical situation.

Use the following questions to help you narrow your purpose and shape your response:

1. What specific message do you want to convey about your food-related experience? What is the purpose of your message?

2. What kind of reaction do you want from your audience? Are you asking the audience to be more thoughtful about the experiences that have shaped their own lives? Are you asking the audience to reconsider foods that they tend to think of as "different" or "bad"? Or are you asking the audience to perform a particular action?

3. What is the best way to connect with your audience? That is, what kind of text is this audience most likely to have access to and most likely to respond to? (Chapter 10 can help you explore options for media and design.)

Writing a Memoir: Working with Your Available Means

Shaping your memoir

As you have probably figured out by now, a memoir is a genre arranged much like a fictional work such as a novel or a short story. The **introduction** hooks readers by dropping them right in the middle of an interesting situation or by presenting them with an especially vivid page 310 description (see Chapter 9). This introduction announces the focal point of your memoir, whether that is a specific food, a significant culinary experience, or a particular aspect of your present personality that was shaped by an earlier experience with a food or eating. Pooja Makhijani, for example, opens her memoir with descriptions of what her mother packs in her lunch bag and what she yearns for instead—what would be on her classmates' lunch trays that day. In so doing, she introduces the tension between herself and her mother, which manifests itself in their different ideas about what is appropriate or desirable food. But Makhijani also begins to build a conflict for the rest of her memoir by leaving this tension unspoken. Rather than being open about her desire to eat bologna on white bread and Cool Ranch Doritos like her classmates, she says nothing. In short, Makhijani, like all good memoir writers, creates effective pathos appeals through the introduction of her piece—she describes the characters and their actions in such a way as to get readers emotionally invested in her topic.

The **body** of a memoir presents the narrative, the plot or the major sequence of events. As you've learned in this chapter, a memoir focuses on a specific event or series of events that is significant, rather than narrating each and every event in a person's life. The events or experiences that you choose to include should be those that have proven to be most meaningful for you, that best illustrate the point you want to make, or that best convey the message you want to send. As you describe the specific events, choose concrete, precise verbs that reveal the actions taken by the different characters and use transitional phrases such as *by that time* and *later in the day* to show the sequence of events and help readers see how the events relate to one another in time.

In addition, the body of a memoir provides specific sensory details. You'll want to describe the food you ate, the place where you ate it, and the people you were with (the characters in your memoir). Makhijani helps readers to understand the care with which her mother made those school lunches by describing each piece of food in mouth-watering de- pages 310–312 tail; she contrasts these homemade lunches with the bland, mass-produced foods on her classmates' lunch trays. Such sensory details are important for helping readers to imagine the events, the foods, and the characters at the heart of your memoir; they also help you to deliver the specific message you want to convey to readers. Vivid descriptions invite readers to connect emotionally with and invest themselves in the lives and activities of the major characters. In Makhijani's memoir, her vivid details help readers feel just how strong her desire to assimilate is, so strong that she would rather eat peaches from a can than her mother's deep-fried potato patties "spiked with garam masala" and "slathered with fresh coriander chutney."

The body of a memoir also develops the various characters. You'll certainly want to use sensory details to help readers visualize the key features and actions of each character. Equally important, you'll want to create dialogue between the characters to reveal important aspects about their personalities and relationship to one another. For example, Makhijani never directly asks her mother if she can buy school lunches. Instead, because she fears what her mother will say, she speaks indirectly about what her classmates do and eat ("Chrissy brought Coke with her to school yesterday") in the hope that her mother will get her point. It's important to use dialogue or quoted speech purposefully, to give readers deeper insight into the thoughts and emotions of your characters.

One more element to incorporate into the body of your memoir is reflection on or analysis of the events that you're narrating. Reflection and analysis encourage readers to notice particular details or help them understand the significance of a particular experience for a character's self-development. Drawing on the methods of critical analysis allows you to craft compelling rhetorical appeals. In the case of logos, you may try to convince readers that your analysis is the best way to interpret the significance of certain events in the memoir. In terms of ethos, you may present an analysis that seems to consider the perspectives of all characters involved in order to cast yourself as an open-minded, well-reasoned observer of events. For example, look again at the paragraph that comes immediately after Aisha asks, "Then why don't you eat the school lunch?" Makhijani's reflection not only gives dramatic pause but also reveals her perception of herself: "I know it's not because it's too expensive or that Styrofoam trays are environmentally unsound. It's because Mom thinks her deep-fried aloo tikkis and freshly ground masalas are what good Indian parents give their daughters. She doesn't understand that good Indian daughters just want to become American." This allows readers to see how Makhijani's relationship to her mother's food was directly connected to her desire to identify herself as an "American." As you narrate the events in your memoir, look for places where you can help readers understand the significance of specific details or events by stopping the action and providing a few sentences of reflection or analysis.

The **conclusion** of a memoir reinforces the message, or the point of the story. The important consideration here is to be sure the events you've narrated, the details you've provided, and the reflection or analysis you've composed all work together to deliver a clear,

pages 317–318

Introduction	Body	Conclusion
▶ Announces focal point ▶ Gets readers emotionally invested	▶ Presents the main narrative ▶ Provides specific sensory details ▶ Develops characters ▶ Reflects and analyzes	▶ Reinforces message ▶ Leaves readers with an understanding of events' significance for writer and reader

coherent message. You might, as Makhijani does, conclude your memoir with a scene that captures precisely the mood you want readers to experience or the image you want them to remember. Or you might decide to conclude your memoir with a more traditional paragraph that, like your reflective components, speaks fairly explicitly about the point of the events that you've described. Either way, your readers will respond favorably to your conclusion if it helps them to see how the events have significance both for you as the writer and for them as your readers.

Revision and peer review

After you've drafted your memoir, ask one of your classmates to read it. You'll want your classmate to respond to your work in a way that helps you revise it into the strongest memoir it can be, one that addresses your intended audience, helps you fulfill your purpose, and is delivered in the most appropriate means available to you.

Questions for a peer reviewer

1. To what opportunity for change is the writer responding?
2. Who might be the writer's intended audience?
3. What might be the writer's purpose? How does purpose connect with audience?
4. What information did you receive from the introduction? What suggestions do you have for the writer for enhancing the effectiveness of the introduction?
5. Note the key narrative events in the memoir. Are transitions used in a way that helps the reader keep track of the narrative? If not, identify places that could use transitional words or phrases.
6. Note passages in which the writer reflects on or analyzes the key narrative events. What seems to be the significance of these events for the writer?
7. How does the writer establish ethos? How can the writer strengthen this appeal?

8. What material does the writer use to establish logos? How might the writer strengthen this appeal?

9. How does the writer make use of pathos? Does the writer rely on pathos too much or too little? How might the writer strike a balance?

10. What did you learn from the conclusion that you didn't already know after reading the introduction and the body? What information does the writer want you to take away from the memoir? Does the writer attempt to change your attitude, action, or opinion?

11. What section of the memoir did you most enjoy? Why?

Memoirs

Audio Memoir

This audio memoir about an Italian-American family restaurant was recorded for StoryCorps. To listen, find *Memoirs in Three Media* in your English CourseMate, accessed through CengageBrain.com.

© *Image: Courtesy of StoryCorps, a national nonprofit dedicated to recording and collecting stories of everyday people: www.storycorps.org*

Blog Entry

This blog entry by Ree Drummond, also known as "Pioneer Woman," presents an illustrated memoir about the writer's first encounter with Nova salmon. To read the blog, find *Memoirs in Three Media* in your English CourseMate, accessed through CengageBrain.com.

© *Image: copyright barbaradudzinska, 2009. Used under license from Shutterstock.com*

Print Memoir

In the following memoir, student writer Anna Seitz remembers her first experience "processing" a chicken.

© *Image copyright Anton Novik, 2009. Used under license from Shutterstock.com.*

pages 318–320

Anna's lesson in chicken killing could have been relayed in any of several genres or media. If her purpose had been to inform other novices, she could have posted a how-to guide on YouTube. If she wanted her somewhat gory descriptions to make a direct argument against eating meat, she could have written a position argument. A letter tucked inside a birthday card to her cousin would have conveyed a funny anecdote about the perils of animal husbandry. Instead, Anna wanted her readers to feel the conflict she experienced, and she knew that to replicate those feelings, she would need to appeal to her readers' physical senses and to pay particular attention to the ethos she was creating for herself. She also knew that her experience was about more than just chickens—and that she could describe it in a way that made clear its larger significance. Thus, Anna knew a memoir was appropriate for her rhetorical situation. She chose the print format because it fit the requirements of her class assignment.

Anna Seitz

English 260

Professor Lundin

April 22, 2010

Herb's Chicken

Last year, my husband Bill and I, fueled by farmers' market

fantasies, decided we wanted to keep some backyard chickens. Since we

had to wait until spring to order birds, we spent the winter getting our

coop, and ourselves, ready. We read stacks of books and magazines on

raising chickens, and we decided to ask our friend Herb to teach us to

"process" them. •

When we pulled into Herb's driveway on the big day, he was already

hanging out the back door, gesturing to the cane at the bottom of the

steps. He's 87 years old and has been a poultry farmer since he got back

from the war. He shuffles slowly, hunched over. He can't hear much of

what we say. When he can hear, he usually just rolls his eyes. Bill handed

him the cane, and Herb led us to the last of his coops that still has

chickens. His farm of 6,000 birds is down to 75. "Well, how many you

want?" Herb asks.

"I don't know," said my husband. "Got one that's not layin'?" •

"Get that one there," said Herb. He pointed his finger in the

direction of a group of three birds, and my husband, appearing to know

which one Herb meant, took a couple of steps toward them. They

immediately dispersed.

Herb grabbed a long handle with a hook at the end, resembling the

sort of wand I've used to roast weenies over a campfire, and handed it to

Bill. He pointed again. "There," he said. Bill grabbed the tool and

Margin notes:

Anna's memoir uses the narrative form, which includes a setting, characters, dialogue, and a sequence of events.

The significant experience related in this memoir arose from Anna's "farmers' market fantasy" of raising chickens.

Anna includes many sensory details to help her readers visualize the setting and Herb's character.

The dialogue reveals the characters' relationships to one another as well as to the raising of chickens.

Side tab: Memoirs

managed to at least tangle up the bird's feet. Herb snapped up the bird with the efficient movement of someone who has snapped up tens of thousands of birds, and handed the bird, upside-down, to me.

I held it carefully by the ankles and got a little shiver. It flapped its wings a few times, but it didn't really try to fight me. It actually looked pretty pitiful hanging there. Herb was already walking back to the house.

"Pull up that bird feeder, Billy," barked Herb, in his thin voice.

My husband had worked digging graves with Herb since he was fifteen, and he was used to taking orders. "Yup," he said. He walked up to a bird feeder on a stake and pulled it up from the ground.

Herb unhooked a metal cone which he'd been using on the stake as a squirrel deterrent and slid it off the bottom. "For the chicken," he told me as I caught up to them. "I'll open the cellar."

Bill and I waited outside the bulkhead for Herb. He opened it up, still holding the metal cone in his hand. "Come on," he instructed. We made our way down into the dark. The chicken tried to arch its head up, to peck me. I handed it over to Bill.

In the cellar, Herb hooked the cone to a beam. "Give me that," he said to me, gesturing at a dusty bucket on the floor next to me. I pushed it with my foot until it was under the cone.

"All right!" said my husband brightly. I stiffened. He pushed the chicken head-first into the cone, until her head poked through the opening at the bottom and her feet stuck out the top. The chicken got one wing free, but my husband put a rubber band around her feet and hooked it on the nail that held the cone. She was stuck.

Herb fished through his pocket for his knife, and my eyelids started to wrinkle. I held my lips tightly closed. "You just need to go through the

Memoirs

This paragraph works as a transition between the present series of events and the past relationship of the characters.

roof of the mouth and get them right in the brain," said Herb. "It's better than chopping the head off because they don't tense up. Makes it easier to get the feathers off." •

This series of five short paragraphs includes graphic details and purposeful dialogue.

"Won't it bite you?" I asked.

"So what if it does?" answered Herb. "Last thing it'll ever do." Herb easily pried the mouth open with his left hand, and with his right, he pushed the knife into its brain and turned it. It was over. I furrowed my brow.

"Then you gotta bleed it," he said. Herb pulled the knife down, and in one quick motion, cut the chicken's throat from the inside. Blood spilled from its open beak into the bucket. My husband watched with interest, offering the same occasional "Yup" or "Uh-huh" that he uses when listening to any good story. I watched with my eyes squinted and my face half turned away.

Herb rinsed the knife in the washbasin and announced, "Gotta get the water. Anna, it's on the stove. Hot but not boiling." I went up to the kitchen and fiddled with the temperature under a big soup pot. It looked about right, I guessed.

•By the time I got the water down to the cellar, Herb and Bill had already pulled the chicken out of the cone and tossed the head into the bloody bucket. It looked more like food when I couldn't see the eyes. Herb told my husband to dip the bird in the hot water a few times, and he did, holding it by the rubber-banded legs. When he pulled it out, some of the feathers on its chest started to drop off.

This is another strong transitional sentence.

From under the stairs, Herb pulled out a large plastic drum, the sides dotted with rubber fingers. He put the chicken inside and switched it on. After a few minutes, he pulled out a mostly featherless chicken. The

Memoirs

feathers stuck to the sides of the drum. "Get that," he said to Bill. While Bill pulled feathers out of the plucker, Herb held the chicken by the feet and pulled off the remaining feathers—mostly large wing and tail feathers, and a few small pin feathers. By now there really wasn't any blood left, and the chicken looked pretty close to what you might get in the store, except skinnier.

Bill brought the chicken and the bucket up to the kitchen, and Herb and I followed. Herb took the bird and dropped it down into the sink with a smack. "Now, you cut out the crop," Herb said. He pointed to something I couldn't see, then cut into the throat and showed us a little sack full of stones and grain. "It's how they chew, I guess," he added. He tugged on it, and it brought with it a large section of the windpipe. "To get the rest of the guts out, you gotta cut in the back."

Herb made an incision and stuck in his hand, making a squishy sound. He pulled out a handful of guts and dropped most of it into the bucket. He cut off one section and held it toward Bill. "You got the wrong bird," he said. The slimy tube was sort of transparent, and through it we could see a string of about eight little eggs of increasing size, beginning with a tiny yolk, and ending with an almost full-sized egg.

"Can you eat 'em?" I asked.

"Guess you could," said Herb, throwing the whole mess into the bucket, "but I got eggs." He turned the chicken, lopped off the feet, and tossed them into the bucket. They landed toes up, like a grotesque garnish. "Well, want a plastic bag?"

I accepted the grocery bag and some plastic wrap and wrapped the carcass up while Herb and Bill took the bucket outside. They talked for a while, and then Herb directed Bill up onto a ladder to check a gutter.

I stood with my back to the carcass, examining Herb's wife's display of whimsical salt and pepper shakers.

When my husband and I got back in the car, I put the carcass at my feet. "That was great!" said my husband. "Think we can do it on our own?"

I thought through the steps in my mind. "I think I can," I chirped. I thought of the bucket and the toe garnish. "But I'm not eating it."•·········

Anna reflects on the narrative events, helping her readers understand their significance to her changing perspective.

Alternatives to the Memoir

Fitting responses come in many forms, not just memoirs. Your instructor might call upon you to consider one of the following opportunities for writing.

1. Have you recently had a satisfying experience dining out that you want your friends and classmates to enjoy as well? Or have you suffered through a restaurant meal that you would not wish on your worst enemy? What aspects of your experience made it satisfying and enjoyable or unfulfilling and unpleasant? Write a critical review of that dining experience. Be sure to specify the criteria on which you're basing your evaluation and to provide specific examples that show how the food, the service, and the atmosphere contributed to the overall dining experience.

2. In *Fast Food Nation*, Eric Schlosser notes a disturbing trend in the culture of food in industrialized nations, and he investigates this trend (particularly in terms of its consequences). In an investigative report, analyze a positive or negative feature of food culture on your campus or in your community. Be sure to provide concrete evidence and details to support your analysis.

3. Margaret Mead identified a particular problem in the American culture of food and offered a difficult solution for that problem. Identify a problem concerning the culture of food on your campus or in your community and write a proposal in which you outline a plan for solving that problem. Be sure to identify the rhetorical audience for your proposal (that is, some person or group in a position to act on it) and to describe the problem in a way that emphasizes the importance of addressing the problem right away. Present your solution in specific detail and include analysis that shows its appropriateness and feasibility.

Memoirs

4 Portraying Successful Speakers and Writers: Responding with Profiles

What thoughts come to your mind when you see the famous image of the Reverend Dr. Martin Luther King, Jr., speaking at the March on Washington for Jobs and Freedom, on August 28, 1963? Perhaps you think about the values in which King believed and the civil rights for which he fought. Perhaps you think of his nonviolent resistance to the oppression faced by African Americans in the 1950s and 1960s. Perhaps you remember other images from the civil rights movement—marchers beaten back by powerful streams of water or sit-ins at once-segregated lunch counters. Chances are, though, that this image brings to your mind the famous words spoken on that day in 1963 on the steps of the Lincoln Memorial:

> So even though we face the difficulties of today and tomorrow, I still have a dream. I have a dream that one day this nation will rise up and live out the true meaning of its creed … that all men are created equal. I have a dream that one day even the state of Mississippi, a state sweltering with the heat of oppression, will be transformed into an oasis of freedom and justice. I have a dream that my four little children will one day live in a nation where they will not be judged by the color of their skin but by the content of their character. I have a dream to-day. And if America is to be a great nation, this must become true.
>
> —**Martin Luther King, Jr.,**
> **"I Have a Dream"**

AP Photo

King's legacy in U.S. history centers on his great victories in the civil rights movement. This legacy was shaped, in part, by his enviable ability to put his message into words. He could create moving narratives, vivid images, and logical arguments.

He employed a host of rhetorical tools to persuade Americans of the need to act to ensure universal civil rights.

There have been times in all of our lives when we have been moved to tears or to action or have been angered by the words of a public figure. What makes language move us in this way? How does the speaker or the writer craft language that can move us? As curious human beings, we often want to learn about what motivates a person to say or write the things that he or she does or to learn when, where, and how the person learned to use language as effectively and as powerfully as he or she does. In pursuing answers to these questions, we often learn that how a person comes to craft a speech or a piece of writing is just as interesting as what any particular passage might say.

Every bit as important as how a person crafts the message is how those words are delivered. Given our highly digital world, you may already have a great deal of experience—maybe even expertise—in delivering your ideas electronically, whether you're using words, visuals, video, audio, or some combination of these. You are also likely an experienced and good speaker when the situation calls for it, even if you don't feel like an expert when giving a formal oral presentation. If you're not already, you can become a more confident writer and speaker.

Successful speakers and writers know the importance of gauging the relationship between the content of their message and the expectations of their intended audience. Therefore, they spend a good deal of time preparing their message to fit the context. They adjust their assertions, examples, choice of words, and the delivery of those words at the same time that they weigh the decision whether to deliver their message orally, in writing, or in images—or to combine these forms. Most of the successful speakers and writers profiled in this chapter, like Martin Luther King, Jr., say good things—and say those good things very well.

Writers have used profiles—biographical sketches—to help others better understand how the most eloquent writers and speakers have honed their skills and how they have deployed them to effective ends. As readers of a **profile**, we gain glimpses into a person's private life and see how personal experiences affect the often very visible work that the person does. A profile of Dr. Martin Luther King, Jr., for example, might help us to better understand how his daily life experiences as a black man and as a father affected his ideas about the value of words in public life. A profile might also help us to better understand how King viewed his public speaking in relation to his actions, whether boycotting, marching, or conducting acts of civil disobedience such as those that landed him in the Birmingham Jail.

Writers create profiles to help readers gain a deeper understanding of a public figure—or of a person their readers might not otherwise have heard of. Often, writers create profiles to analyze the individuals who have shaped history. In profiles, writers paint portraits with words, to describe a person in detail and to show how the pieces fit together to form the whole person.

Profiles

Throughout this chapter, you'll work to identify an opportunity to profile a person who is successful with words. This person might be someone you're related to, work with, know, or admire from afar: a grandparent, minister, counselor, group leader, politician, public figure, artist, author, or celebrity. As you work to determine the person who most interests you, consider the most fitting means of delivery for your profile:

▶ Printed article, to be published in a community or campus newspaper or local 'zine

▶ Audio profile, to be recorded for a community or campus radio station

▶ Electronic profile, to be presented as a blog entry or a PowerPoint presentation

To begin, freewrite for five minutes in response to each of the following questions (or use any of the invention techniques presented on pages 306–320):

1. When have you listened to, read the writing of, or watched a performance by someone whom you consider successful with words?

2. Did reading, hearing, or watching the delivery of this person's words make you think or act differently in response? If so, how did your thinking or behavior change?

3. What qualities or characteristics did this person possess that made him or her an effective speaker or writer? What made his or her words effective?

Real Situations

Your college or university may require you to take a public speaking course. Such a requirement, like the requirement that all students take at least one writing course, is grounded in the belief that professionals need to possess more than the technical knowledge at the heart of their field or discipline—they need to be able to communicate this knowledge to others, as well. Moreover, your experiences in your public speaking course are meant to instill in you the ability to appreciate and engage in informed discussions in your other courses and in your community. Many colleges and universities also give their students extracurricular opportunities to improve their abilities in public speaking through participation in debate teams. Students on these teams learn to generate arguments in response to challenging ethical, legal, and political questions and to present their positions in a logically reasoned and stylistically polished way. Many students use their experiences on college debate teams as preparation for future careers in the law, business, or politics.

Public speaking is such an important skill in professional life that many organizations hire coaches to help their executives improve. Carmine Gallo is one such speaking coach. Some of Gallo's advice comes directly from what he has noticed about the presentations of Apple CEO

A student speaks at the YMCA Youth and Government mock trial competition.

Steve Jobs. Here are the five elements every Jobs presentation includes (Gallo's observations are reprinted in full on pages 121–123):

1. **A headline.** Steve Jobs positions every product with a headline that fits well within a 140-character Twitter post.
2. **A villain.** In every classic story, the hero fights the villain. This idea of conquering a shared enemy is a powerful motivator and turns customers into evangelists.
3. **A simple slide.** Apple products are easy to use because of the elimination of clutter. The same approach applies to the slides in a Steve Jobs presentation.
4. **A demo.** Neuroscientists have discovered that the brain gets bored easily. Steve Jobs doesn't give you time to lose interest. In most of his presentations he's demonstrating a new product or feature and having fun doing it.
5. **A holy smokes moment.** Every Steve Jobs presentation has one moment that neuroscientists call an "emotionally charged event." The emotionally charged event is the equivalent of a mental post-it note that tells the brain, Remember this!

College public speaking courses and the work of professional coaches like Carmine Gallo are premised on the belief that anyone can become a more effective wielder of words by learning to apply some basic skills and keeping in mind some valuable advice. Most people, however, are somewhat awed by public figures who, like King, possess a powerful ability to move people through words. Where did they gain this ability? Were they born with it? Did they learn it? What motivates their work, and how do they approach their tasks?

In this chapter, you'll gain insight into some successful and effective speakers and writers. Just as important, you'll learn about the profile, a kind of writing that can give readers a fuller understanding of how public figures have come to their lives' work, how they have learned to use words effectively, and what motivates them to wield this power in their professional lives.

Profiles

DESCRIBING SUCCESSFUL SPEAKERS

1. What do you know about Dr. Martin Luther King, Jr.'s abilities with words? What skills did he use most effectively or most often? Where did he acquire those skills? What motivated him to use words in the ways that he did? After freewriting in response to these questions for several minutes, conduct online research to learn what others have said about King's ability to achieve things with words.

2. Conduct online research on the topic of effective public speaking. What do your searches reveal about common beliefs and attitudes concerning the importance of wielding the spoken word effectively?

3. What do the images in this chapter suggest to you about successful speakers and writers?

Real Responses to Real Situations

Persuasion from the presidential podium

When President Barack Obama ran for president in 2008, he had a modest political résumé: eight years in the Illinois state senate and only three as a U.S. senator. To get himself elected, he had to marshal all the means of persuasion available to him, both verbal and visual. Even if you don't remember the words he used, you may remember his widely circulated campaign poster (designed by Shepard Fairey), which presented in visual form his biracial, forward-looking character, his red-white-and-blue patriotism, and his campaign theme of "hope."

The campaign poster was just one of the available means of persuasion that Obama and his team employed to rally supporters and publicize his plans and policies. Obama's campaign was distinguished by its integrated use of technology, employing both digital and analog means and profiting from the efficiency of the Internet in bringing about real-time distribution of his messages. As many of you already know, Obama's team targeted the under-30 age group by employing online forums and social networking Web sites (such as MySpace, Facebook, and Neighbor-to-Neighbor) to engage this specific group in discussing the issues most important to them. In addition, the YouTube videos that "mashed up" Obama's speeches into songs (will.i.am's "Yes We Can," Ruwanga Samth and Maxwell D's "Make It to the Sun," JFC's "Barack Obama," and Misa/Misa's "Unite the Nation") generated support for Obama among the young (and young in spirit). And the YouTube versions of "They Said This Day Would Never Come" functioned as oral profiles of Obama the candidate and Obama the man.

By circulating his policies, ideas, and speeches digitally (through email, text messages, and online), Obama set himself apart from the other candidates, especially from his toughest political foes, the ones with more political experience (Hillary Clinton and John McCain, for

AP Photo/Damian Dovarganes, File

Shepard Fairey standing in front of the campaign posters he designed.

instance). His use of technology to engage in continual dialogue with his supporters transformed this conventional liberal Democratic senator into a "techno-cool" presidential candidate.

Obama's use of communication technology was a boon to his campaign, to be sure, but his messages ("Change We Can Believe In" and "Yes, We Can") were every bit as crucial to his ultimate success. He had plenty of ideas about health care, social security, immigration, and banking—some of them controversial—so he needed to avail himself of the best staff possible, people who could assist him in successfully transforming his ideas of "hope," "change," and "progress" into actual votes. This first black man to be a strong contender for president needed to be more than an inspirational, charismatic speaker. Because his opponents were using his eloquence against him, he had to demonstrate both style and substance, not either/or. The man who was promising change and unity needed to win. And he needed help to do so.

Obama turned to speechwriting genius Jon Favreau. Only twenty-six years old, Favreau was nonetheless an experienced speechwriter who could help Obama craft the words to express his substantial and concrete ideas in ethical, and ultimately persuasive, language. Ashley Parker's January 2008 profile of Favreau in the *New York Times* introduces readers to someone they likely don't know, giving information about his background and outlining his impressive accomplishments in specific ways.

> What Would Obama Say?

Ashley Parker

At the Radisson Hotel in Nashua, N.H., Jon Favreau sipped Diet Coke and munched on carrot sticks and crackers to pass the time. His boss, Senator Barack Obama wandered in and out of the room.

Finally, results from the New Hampshire Democratic primary started coming in, surprising everyone. Hilary Clinton was pulling past Senator Obama, who had won the Iowa caucuses only five days earlier.

Mr. Favreau, the campaign's 26-year-old head speechwriter, found himself in the hotel lounge with less than three hours to revise what was to have been a victory speech. What made it particularly strange was that his words were being challenged. Mrs. Clinton had helped

continued

Profiles

turn her campaign around by discounting Mr. Obama's elegant oratory, saying, "You campaign in poetry, but you govern in prose."

"To be honest," Mr. Favreau said, "the first time I really stopped to think about how it felt was when he started giving the speech. I looked around at the senior staff, and they were all smiling. And I looked around the room and thought, 'This is going to be O.K.' "

Mr. Favreau, or Favs, as everyone calls him, looks every bit his age, with a baby face and closely shorn stubble. And he leads a team of two other young speechwriters: 26-year-old Adam Frankel, who worked with John Kennedy's adviser and speechwriter Theodore C. Sorensen on his memoirs, and Ben Rhodes, who, at 30, calls himself the "elder statesman" of the group and who helped write the Iraq Study Group report as an assistant to Lee H. Hamilton.

Together they are working for a politician who not only is known for his speaking ability but also wrote two best-selling books and gave the much-lauded keynote speech at the 2004 Democratic National Convention.

"You're like Ted Williams's batting coach," Mr. Favreau said.

But even Ted Williams needed a little help with his swing.

"Barack trusts him," said David Axelrod, Mr. Obama's chief campaign strategist. "And Barack doesn't trust too many folks with that— the notion of surrendering that much authority over his own words."

When he first met Mr. Obama, Mr. Favreau was 23, a recent graduate of the College of the Holy Cross in Worcester, Mass., near where he grew up. Mr. Obama was rehearsing his 2004 convention speech backstage, when Mr. Favreau, then a member of John Kerry's staff, interrupted him: the senator needed to rewrite a line from his speech to avoid an overlap.

"He kind of looked at me, kind of confused—like, 'Who is this kid?' " Mr. Favreau recalled.

Mr. Obama became his boss the following year. Mr. Favreau had risen to a job as a speechwriter on the Kerry campaign, but by then was unemployed. He was, he said, "broke, taking advantage of all the happy-hour specials I could find in Washington."

Robert Gibbs, Mr. Obama's communications director, had known Mr. Favreau during the Kerry campaign, and recommended him as a writer.

Life was relatively quiet then, and Mr. Obama and Mr. Favreau had some time to hang out. When Mr. Obama's White Sox swept Mr. Favreau's beloved Red Sox three games to none in their American League 2005 division series, the senator walked over to his speechwriter's desk with a little broom and started sweeping it off.

Mr. Favreau also used this time to master Mr. Obama's voice. He took down almost

Speechwriter Jon Favreau on the Obama campaign trail.

Jacob Silberberg for The New York Times

everything the senator said and absorbed it. Now, he said, when he sits down to write, he just channels Mr. Obama—his ideas, his sentences, his phrases.

"The trick of speechwriting, if you will, is making the client say your brilliant words while somehow managing to make it sound as though they issued straight from their own soul," said the writer Christopher Buckley, who was a speechwriter for the first President Bush. "Imagine putting the words 'Ask not what your country can do for you' into the mouth of Ron Paul, and you can see the problem."

Many Democratic candidates have attempted to evoke both John and Robert Kennedy, but Senator Obama seems to have had more success than most. It helps that Mr. Obama seems to have the élan that John Kennedy had, not to mention a photogenic family.

For his inspiration, Mr. Favreau said, "I actually read a lot of Bobby" Kennedy.

"I see shades of J.F.K., R.F.K.," he said, and then added, "King."

Not everyone is so enamored. Mr. Obama excels at inspirational speeches read from a teleprompter before television cameras, critics have noted, but many of his other speeches on the campaign trail have failed to electrify.

Ted Widmer, a historian at Brown University, said that Mr. Obama's speeches "were perfect for getting to where he was early in the race, but I think now that we're in a serious campaign, it would be helpful to hear more concrete proposals."

"There's more to governing, there's more to being president, than speechwriting," he added.

Mr. Favreau said that when he is writing, he stays up until 3 a.m. and gets up as early as 5. He hasn't slept for more than six hours in as long as he can remember, he said.

Coffee helped him through the Iowa caucuses. Two days before the victory there, he walked across the street from the campaign's Des Moines headquarters and cloistered himself inside a local cafe.

He and Mr. Obama had talked about the post-caucus speech for about 30 minutes, settling on a theme of unity and an opening line: "They said this day would never come."

"I knew that it would have multiple meanings to multiple people," Mr. Favreau said. "Barack and I talked about it, and it was one that worked for the campaign. There were many months during the campaign when they said he'd never win. And of course there was the day that would never come, when an African-American would be winning the first primary in a white state."

In discussions about the speech, the issue of race never came up, Mr. Favreau said. But, he added, "I know I thought about it."

As Senator Obama's star has risen, so has Mr. Favreau's. In New Hampshire, Mr. Favreau stood in the back of a gym watching his boss campaign when Michael Gerson, a former speechwriter to the current President Bush, introduced himself. He complimented him on the Iowa victory speech.

continued

CHAPTER 4 PORTRAYING SUCCESSFUL SPEAKERS AND WRITERS **111**

Profiles

The campaign staff has started teasing Mr. Favreau about his new-found celebrity. Not that it's any great pickup line. Mr. Favreau, who said he doesn't have a girlfriend, observed somewhat dryly that "the rigors of this campaign have prevented any sort of serious relationship."

"There's been a few times when people have said, 'I don't believe you, that you're Barack Obama's speechwriter,' " he went on. "To which I reply, 'If I really wanted to hit on you, don't you think I'd make up something more outlandish?' "

He does have other things to worry about. "Can you get through this process and keep the core of yourself?" Mr. Favreau asked. "You know, we're finding out. I'm confident he can. And I think I can, too."

This profile gives you a sense of the speechwriter-candidate relationship, the ways they collaborated and took advantage of one another's strengths all through the presidential campaign, and some of the reasons that Obama eventually won the Iowa caucuses and then the presidency itself. The profile also mentioned Obama's idea for opening a post-caucus speech: "They said this day would never come." That speech follows.

> Caucus Speech
Barack Obama

You know, they said this day would never come.

They said our sights were set too high. They said this country was too divided, too disillusioned to ever come together around a common purpose.

But on this January night, at this defining moment in history, you have done what the cynics said we couldn't do. You have done what the state of New Hampshire can do in five days. You have done what America can do in this new year, 2008. In lines that stretched around schools and churches, in small towns and in big cities, you came together as Democrats, Republicans and independents, to stand up and say that we are one nation. We are one people. And our time for change has come.

You said the time has come to move beyond the bitterness and pettiness and anger that's consumed Washington. To end the political strategy that's been all about division, and instead make it about addition. To build a coalition for change that stretches through red states and blue states.

Because that's how we'll win in November, and that's how we'll finally meet the challenges that we face as a nation.

We are choosing hope over fear. We're choosing unity over division, and sending a powerful message that change is coming to America.

You said the time has come to tell the lobbyists who think their money and their influence speak louder than our voices that they don't own this government—we do. And we are here to take it back. The time has come for a president who will be honest about the choices and the challenges we face, who will listen to you and learn from you, even when we disagree, who won't just tell you what you want to hear, but what you need to know.

And in New Hampshire, if you give me the same chance that Iowa did tonight, I will be that president for America. I'll be a president who finally makes health care affordable and available to every single American, the same way I expanded health care in Illinois, by bringing Democrats and Republicans together to get the job done. I'll be a president who ends the tax breaks for companies that ship our jobs overseas and put a middle-class tax cut into the pockets of working Americans who deserve it. I'll be a president who harnesses the ingenuity of farmers and scientists and entrepreneurs to free this nation from the tyranny of oil once and for all. And I'll be a president who ends this war in Iraq and finally brings our troops home, who restores our moral standing, who understands that 9/11 is not a way to scare up votes but a challenge that should unite America and the world against the common threats of the 21st century. Common threats of terrorism and nuclear weapons, climate change and poverty, genocide and disease.

Tonight, we are one step closer to that vision of America because of what you did here in Iowa.

And so I'd especially like to thank the organizers and the precinct captains, the volunteers and the staff who made this all possible. And while I'm at it on thank yous, I think it makes sense for me to thank the love of my life, the rock of the Obama family, the closer on the campaign trail. Give it up for Michelle Obama.

I know you didn't do this for me. You did this—you did this because you believed so deeply in the most American of ideas—that in the face of impossible odds, people who love this country can change it.

I know this. I know this because while I may be standing here tonight, I'll never forget that my journey began on the streets of Chicago doing what so many of you have done for this campaign and all the campaigns here in Iowa, organizing and working and fighting to make people's lives just a little bit better.

I know how hard it is. It comes with little sleep, little pay and a lot of sacrifice. There are days of disappointment. But sometimes, just sometimes, there are nights like this; a night that, years from now, when we've made the changes we believe in, when more families can afford to see a doctor, when our children—when Malia and Sasha and your children inherit a planet that's a little cleaner and safer, when the world sees America differently, and America sees itself as a nation less divided and more united, you'll be able to look back with pride and say that this was the moment when it all began. This was the moment when

continued

the improbable beat what Washington always said was inevitable. This was the moment when we tore down barriers that have divided us for too long; when we rallied people of all parties and ages to a common cause; when we finally gave Americans who have never participated in politics a reason to stand up and to do so. This was the moment when we finally beat back the [politics] of fear and doubts and cynicism, the politics where we tear each other down instead of lifting this country up. This was the moment.

Years from now, you'll look back and you'll say that this was the moment, this was the place where America remembered what it means to hope. For many months, we've been teased, even derided for talking about hope. But we always knew that hope is not blind optimism. It's not ignoring the enormity of the tasks ahead or the roadblocks that stand in our path. It's not sitting on the sidelines or shirking from a fight. Hope is that thing inside us that insists, despite all the evidence to the contrary, that something better awaits us if we have the courage to reach for it and to work for it and to fight for it.

Hope is what I saw in the eyes of the young woman in Cedar Rapids who works the night shift after a full day of college and still can't afford health care for a sister who's ill. A young woman who still believes that this country will give her the chance to live out her dreams.

Hope is what I heard in the voice of the New Hampshire woman who told me that she hasn't been able to breathe since her nephew left for Iraq. Who still goes to bed each night praying for his safe return.

Hope is what led a band of colonists to rise up against an empire. What led the greatest of generations to free a continent and heal a nation. What led young women and young men to sit at lunch counters and brave fire hoses and march through Selma and Montgomery for freedom's cause.

Hope—hope is what led me here today. With a father from Kenya, a mother from Kansas and a story that could only happen in the United States of America.

Hope is the bedrock of this nation. The belief that our destiny will not be written for us, but by us, by all those men and women who are not content to settle for the world as it is, who have the courage to remake the world as it should be.

That is what we started here in Iowa and that is the message we can now carry to New Hampshire and beyond. The same message we had when we were up and when we were down; the one that can save this country, brick by brick, block by block, callused hand by callused hand, that together, ordinary people can do extraordinary things.

Because we are not a collection of red states and blue states. We are the United States of America. And in this moment, in this election, we are ready to believe again.

Profiles

Peggy Noonan worked as a speechwriter for Presidents Ronald Reagan and George H. W. Bush. She also authored *What I Saw at the Revolution: A Political Life in the Reagan Era*. In the following excerpt from that book, Noonan gives readers a glimpse into the process of crafting presidential rhetoric and helps them to evaluate how it works and achieves—or fails to achieve—its desired ends. Her reflections on her own writing process also help readers understand the ways all good communicators envision their audiences so they can connect with them through the spoken or written word.

Excerpt from

> What I Saw at the Revolution: A Political Life in the Reagan Era

Peggy Noonan

All speechwriters have things they think of when they write. I think of being a child in my family at the dinner table, with seven kids and hubbub and parents distracted by worries and responsibilities. Before I would say anything at the table, before I would approach my parents, I would plan what I would say. I would map out the narrative, sharpen the details, add color, plan momentum. This way I could hold their attention. This way I became a writer.

The American people too are distracted by worries and responsibilities and the demands of daily life, and you have to know that and respect it—and plan the narrative, sharpen the details, add color and momentum.

I work with an image: the child in the mall. When candidates for president are on the campaign trail they always go by a mall and walk through followed by a pack of minicams and reporters. They go by Colonel Sanders and have their picture taken eating a piece of chicken, they josh around with the lady in the mall information booth, they shake hands with the shoppers. But watch: Always there is a child, a ten-year-old girl, perhaps, in an inexpensive, tired-looking jacket. Perhaps she is by herself, perhaps with a friend. But she stands back, afraid of the lights, and as the candidate

Courtesy of Ronald Reagan Presidential Library

Peggy Noonan with President Ronald Reagan.

continued

Profiles

comes she runs away. She is afraid of his fame, afraid of the way the lights make his wire-rim glasses shine, afraid of dramatic moments, dense moments. When you are a speechwriter you should think of her when you write, and of her parents. They are Americans. They are good people for whom life has not been easy. Show them respect and be honest and logical in your approach and they will understand every word you say and hear—and know that you thought of them.

The irony of modern speeches is that as our ability to disseminate them has exploded (an American president can speak live not only to America but to Europe, to most of the world), their quality has declined.

Why? Lots of reasons, including that we as a nation no longer learn the rhythms of public utterance from Shakespeare and the Bible. When young Lincoln was sprawled in front of the fireplace reading *Julius Caesar*—"Th' abuse of greatness is, when it disjoins remorse from power"—he was, unconsciously, learning to be a poet. You say, "That was Lincoln, not the common man." But the common man was flocking to the docks to get the latest installment of Dickens off the ship from England.

The modern egalitarian impulse has made politicians leery of flaunting high rhetoric; attempts to reach, to find the right if sometimes esoteric quote or allusion seem pretentious. They don't really know what "the common man" knows anymore; they forget that we've all had at least some education and a number of us read on our own and read certain classics in junior high and high school. The guy at the gas station read *Call of the Wild* when he was fourteen, and sometimes thinks about it. Moreover, he has imagination. Politicians forget. They go in for the lowest common denominator—like a newscaster.

People say the problem is soundbites. But no it isn't. …

Soundbites in themselves are not bad. "We have nothing to fear…" is a soundbite. "Ask not …" is a soundbite. So are "You shall not crucify mankind upon a cross of gold," and "With malice toward none; with charity for all …."

Great speeches have always had great soundbites. The problem is that the young technicians who put together speeches are paying attention only to the soundbite, not to the text as a whole, not realizing that all great soundbites happen by accident, which is to say, all great soundbites are yielded up inevitably, as part of the natural expression of the text. They are part of the tapestry, they aren't a little flower somebody sewed on.

They sum up a point, or make a point in language that is pithy or profound. They are what the politician is saying! They are not separate and discrete little one-liners that a bright young speechwriter just promoted out of the press office and two years out of business school slaps on.

But that is what they've become. Young speechwriters forget the speech and write the soundbite, plop down a hunk of porridge and stick on what they think is a raisin. (In the Dukakis campaign they underlined them in the text.)

The problem is not the soundbitization of rhetoric, it's the Where's-the-beefization. The good news: Everyone in America is catching on to the game, and it's beginning not to work anymore. A modest hope: Politicians will stop hiring communications majors to write their speeches and go to history majors, literature majors, writers—people who can translate the candidate's impulses into literature that is alive, and true.

>ANALYZING THE RHETORICAL SITUATION

1. Who do you think might be the intended audience of Peggy Noonan's book? In what ways might Noonan's book-reading audience differ from Ashley Parker's newspaper-reading audience? What textual evidence have you analyzed that leads you to these conclusions? Be prepared to share your answers with the rest of the class.

2. Given their intended audiences, what purpose do Noonan and Parker each want to fulfill with their writing? What opinions does each writer want readers to leave with? What are the specific differences in the purposes of these two pieces? How does the purpose of each intersect with the writer's intended audience? Again, be prepared to share your answers with the rest of the class.

3. To what opportunity for writing might Noonan and Parker be responding? How does each piece of writing work to address that opportunity?

4. How do Noonan and Parker mobilize the rhetorical appeals of ethos, logos, and pathos to support an opinion on presidential rhetoric? Draw on passages from the texts to support your answer.

5. Parker's profile reveals that Favreau and then–presidential candidate Obama understood the import of opening the post-caucus speech with "They said this day would never come." Such an opening "would have multiple meanings to multiple people." Which people (audiences) were Favreau and Obama trying to reach? How might those audiences interpret that opening?

6. In their original forms, the three pieces of writing were delivered through three different means: a printed book (Noonan), a newspaper article (Parker), and a speech (Obama). Choose one of these pieces and examine how the choice of delivery was fitting for the particular rhetorical situation.

Rhetorical success in a digital world

Writer Virginia Heffernan writes a weekly article for the *New York Times Magazine*. "The Medium" focuses on the convergence of television and the Internet, analyzing the wide variety of online images and stories (from political rants to celebrity exposés) and the ever-expanding on-line means of visual and oral delivery (including, as Heffernan reports in her description of the column, "Web video, viral video, user-driven video, custom interactive video, embedded video ads, Web-based VOD [video on demand], broadband television, diavlogs [video blogs in-volving at least two people], vcasts, vlogs, video podcasts, mobisodes, Webisodes, mashups, and more"). In the following column, Heffernan analyzes the TED talks to which she's so addicted. As she informs her readers about the TED world, TEDsters, and their various personalities and agendas, she entertains her readers with her TED experience.

> Confessions of a TED Addict
Virginia Heffernan

Help. Here I go. My pulse is racing. I'm completely manic.

Oh why oh why have I been bingeing on TED talks again? I prom-ised myself I would quit watching the ecstatic series of head-rush disquisitions, available online, from violinists, political prisoners, brain scientists, novelists and Bill Clinton. But I can't. Each hortatory TED talk starts with a bang and keeps banging till it explodes in fire-works. How can I shut it off? The speakers seem fevered, possessed, Pentecostal. No wonder I am, too, now.

Richard Termine/The New York Times

A TED talk begins as an audi-torium speech given at the multi-disciplinary, invitation-only annual TED conference.... TED then creates videos of the speeches and puts them online so they can find a broader audience—and usurp my life. There are around 370 speeches and counting on Ted.com. A new one is added every weekday.

TED (which stands for "Tech-nology, Entertainment, Design") was founded in 1984 by the ar-chitect Richard Saul Wurman and his partners. Their first con-ference included one of the first demonstrations of the Macintosh

Singer-songwriter Nellie McKay is one of those who have presented TED talks.

computer. In 2001, TED was acquired and is now run by Chris Anderson, the new-media entrepreneur who started Business 2.0, among other magazines and Web sites. Giving a TED talk has become an opportunity for name-in-lights speakers to throw down, set forth "ideas worth spreading" and prove their intellectual heroism.

According to June Cohen, the executive producer of TED Media, the speeches were once filmed and cut for a TV pilot. ("The idea of a 'lecture series' wasn't exactly greeted with enthusiasm by the networks," she says.) But she had another idea when she brought on Jason Wishnow, an online-video virtuoso. Together, they made the TED talks streamable on the Web in 2006. In less than three years, the talks have become a huge hit, attracting sponsorship from BMW and others. Karen Armstrong, Jeff Bezos, Jared Diamond, Helen Fisher, Peter Gabriel, Jane Goodall, Stephen Hawking, Maira Kalman, Nellie McKay, Isaac Mizrahi, Jimmy Wales and Rick Warren have all given TED talks. As of this month, the talks have been viewed more than 90 million times.

I have seen about 40. Let me say straight up that one of my favorites is "Simplicity Patterns," by the designer John Maeda. His talk made clear to me the uncanny resemblance between a block of tofu (the kind Maeda grew up making in his family's business in Seattle) and the I. M. Pei building that houses the M.I.T. Media Lab (where Maeda, who is now the president of the Rhode Island School of Design, used to work). Almost haphazardly associative, Maeda's talk expresses respect for the mandate of the talks—to change the world—without becoming sententious. You get rapid, straight-to-the-bloodstream access to his mental life.

The other talk that does this poetically is Jill Bolte Taylor's "My Stroke of Insight." A brain scientist who studied the way she lost her own faculties during and after she suffered a stroke, Taylor urges the audience to pay attention to the sybaritic, present-tense right brain. Repeatedly, she recalls the pleasurable aspects of her stroke with such sensory precision that she seems to enter a rapturous trance. Not only do I buy her case for unfettered right-brain experience, but I began scheming to unfetter my right brain then and there.

While looking for your perfect TED talk, don't make the mistake I first did. I started with the 10 most popular. If you do that, you could form the impression that TED talkers are nutcase bullies like the self-help entrepreneur Tony Robbins, who gave a menacing, abrasive performance in "Why We Do What We Do, and How We Can Do It Better." Boasting about his renegade ways, he gunned through a series of piggish sophistries, only to fault fellow TEDster Al Gore—who was sitting in the front row, no less—for not making an emotional connection with the American electorate. (This was 2006.)

Once you start watching TED talks, ordinary life falls away. The corridor from Silicon Alley to Valley seems to crackle, and a new

continued

in-crowd emerges: the one that loves Linux, organic produce, behavioral economics, transhistorical theories and "An Inconvenient Truth." Even though there are certain TED poses that I don't warm to—the dour atheist, the environmental scold—the crowd as a whole glows with charisma. I love their greed for hope, their confidence in ingenuity, their organized but goofy ways of talking and thinking.

TED supplies its speakers with strict guidelines. "Start strong" is the most obvious one, and there is virtually no throat clearing or contrived thanking. Instead, speakers blaze onto the stage like stand-up comics, hellbent on room domination. Some consult notes and stay close by their audiovisual equipment—PowerPoint is used for emphasis, but it never directs the talks—while others pace, spread their arms wide and take up space. No one apologizes for himself. No one fails to make jokes. The appreciative room roars at humor, when they're not literally oohing and aahing at insight.

It's not easy to admit, then, that no single idea put forth in the TED talks seized me with its specifics. The necessary fiction at TED is that matters of substance—policy, practice, code—will emerge from the talks. But it's unlikely that a plan to disarm Iran or treat autism will surface; there's too much razzle-dazzle for brass tacks. What's really on display is much more right brain, and that's what I've come to be addicted to: the exposure to vigorous minds whirring as they work hard.

Right now I'm holed up on TED.com, sampling the talks. The TEDsters bellow their ideas at me, and I try to brook more stimulation. These are the people of the brain, after all, the understanders. They have only to chant some nostrums and cast rhetorical spells and I'm suddenly thinking some combination of *It's all going to be all right* and *The heck it is—but only I can stop it!* Thanks, TED. I'm clearly inspired out of my mind.

Communications coach Carmine Gallo helps big businesses do business better. Whether he's training CEOs and executives in crisis management and running successful meetings or talking with managers and sales professionals about commitment to customers or persuasive presentations, he talks about motivation and engagement. An Emmy award–winning television anchor (he has worked for CNN, CNET, and CBS) and popular media consultant for major industries (such as Intel, Toshiba, SanDisk, and Clorox), Gallo has written a number of motivational books for business leaders. He also contributes a weekly column to BusinessWeek.com. "Uncovering Steve Jobs' Presentation Secrets" is one such column.

> Uncovering Steve Jobs' Presentation Secrets

Carmine Gallo

The Apple music event of Sept. 9, 2009, marked the return of the world's greatest corporate storyteller. For more than three decades, Apple co-founder and CEO Steve Jobs has raised product launches to an art form. In my new book, *The Presentation Secrets of Steve Jobs: How to Be Insanely Great in Front of Any Audience,* I reveal the techniques that Jobs uses to create and deliver mind-blowing keynote presentations.

Steve Jobs does not sell computers; he sells an experience. The same holds true for his presentations that are meant to inform, educate, and entertain. An Apple presentation has all the elements of a great theatrical production—a great script, heroes and villains, stage props, breathtaking visuals, and one moment that makes the price of admission well worth it. Here are the five elements of every Steve Jobs presentation. Incorporate these elements into your own presentations to sell your product or ideas the Steve Jobs way.

1. **A headline.** Steve Jobs positions every product with a headline that fits well within a 140-character Twitter post. For example, Jobs described the MacBook Air as "the world's thinnest notebook." That phrase appeared on his presentation slides, the Apple Web site, and Apple's press releases at the same time. What is the one thing you want people to know about your product? This headline must be consistent in all of your marketing and presentation material.

2. **A villain.** In every classic story, the hero fights the villain. In 1984, the villain, according to Apple, was IBM. Before Jobs introduced the famous 1984 television ad to the Apple sales team for the first time, he told a story of how IBM was bent on dominating the computer industry. "IBM wants it all and is aiming its guns on its last obstacle to industry control: Apple." Today, the "villain" in Apple's narrative is played by Microsoft. One can argue that the popular "I'm a Mac" television ads are hero/villain vignettes. This idea of conquering a shared enemy is a powerful motivator and turns customers into evangelists.

3. **A simple slide.** Apple products are easy to use because of the elimination of clutter. The same approach applies to the slides in a Steve Jobs presentation. They are strikingly simple, visual, and yes, devoid of bullet points. Pictures are dominant. When Jobs introduced the MacBook Air, no words could replace a photo of a hand pulling the notebook computer out of an interoffice manila envelope. Think about it this way—the average PowerPoint

continued

Profiles

slide has 40 words. In some presentations, Steve Jobs has a total of seven words in 10 slides. And why are you cluttering up your slides with too many words?

4. **A demo.** Neuroscientists have discovered that the brain gets bored easily. Steve Jobs doesn't give you time to lose interest. Ten minutes into a presentation he's often demonstrating a new product or feature and having fun doing it. When he introduced the iPhone at Macworld 2007, Jobs demonstrated how Google Maps worked on the device. He pulled up a list of Starbucks stores in the local area and said, "Let's call one." When someone answered, Jobs said: "I'd like to order 4,000 lattes to go, please. No, just kidding."

5. **A holy smokes moment.** Every Steve Jobs presentation has one moment that neuroscientists call an "emotionally charged event." The emotionally charged event is the equivalent of a mental post-it note that tells the brain, Remember this! For example, at Macworld 2007, Jobs could have opened the presentation by telling the audience that Apple was unveiling a new mobile phone that also played music, games, and video. Instead he built up the drama. "Today, we are introducing three revolutionary products. The first one is

a widescreen iPod with touch controls. The second is a revolutionary mobile phone. And the third is a breakthrough Internet communications device ... an iPod, a phone, an Internet communicator ... an iPod, a phone, are you getting it? These are not three devices. This is one device!" The audience erupted in cheers because it was so unexpected, and very entertaining. By the way, the holy smokes moment on Sept. 9 had nothing to do with a product. It was Steve Jobs himself appearing onstage for the first time after undergoing a liver transplant.

One more thing ... sell dreams. Charismatic speakers like Steve Jobs are driven by a nearly messianic zeal to create new experiences. When he launched the iPod in 2001, Jobs said, "In our own small way we're going to make the world a

AP Photo/Paul Sakuma

Profiles

better place." Where most people saw the iPod as a music player, Jobs recognized its potential as a tool to enrich people's lives. Cultivate a sense of mission. Passion, emotion, and enthusiasm are grossly underestimated ingredients in professional business communications, and yet, passion and emotion will motivate others. Steve Jobs once said that his goal was not to die the richest man in the cemetery. It was to go to bed at night thinking that he and his team had done something wonderful. Do something wonderful. Make your brand stand for something meaningful.

Profiles

>ANALYZING THE RHETORICAL SITUATION

1. What opportunity might Heffernan be responding to by writing a weekly column on new media? How does her column respond to that opportunity for change? What are the constraints and resources of her rhetorical situation?
2. Who might be Heffernan's intended audience? What might be the audience's concerns, values, or knowledge?
3. Who is Gallo's intended audience? How does Gallo use the rhetorical appeals (ethos, logos, pathos) to connect with that audience? What is his rhetorical purpose?
4. How does Gallo deliver his message? What media and genre does he choose?
5. How does the arrangement of Gallo's text match what is being said? What effect does the form have? How does he use style and tone purposefully?

COMMUNITY CONNECTIONS

1. Spend several minutes freewriting about your response to President Obama's speech. Why was this speech important? Next, spend several minutes freewriting about whether Peggy Noonan's description of speechwriting made you think differently about the effectiveness, purpose, or value of Obama's speech. Why or why not? Refer to specific passages from the text as you compose your response.

2. What reasons does Noonan offer for the importance of political speeches? What is your opinion of each of these reasons? In what ways have technological innovations since 1990, when Noonan presented her ideas, affected political speeches?

3. Ashley Parker writes "[Hillary] Clinton had helped turn her campaign around by discounting Mr. Obama's elegant oratory, saying, 'You campaign in poetry, but you govern in prose.'" What did Clinton mean by such a statement? How might her ranking in the polls have influenced her statement?

4. Think of a time when you believed that someone's actions did not or could not live up to his or her words. What was the rhetorical situation? What was the outcome? What features of the rhetorical situation led to the outcome that proved you right—or maybe even wrong?

5. Perhaps you hadn't considered that public figures (political candidates, university presidents and administrators, CEOs, and so on) often rely on professional speechwriters. As you reconsider the Favreau piece, can you imagine any people you know or listen to who might be using speechwriters? What makes you think so? What are the results of using—or not using—a trustworthy speechwriter?

6. Identify two or three speeches or presentations—formal or informal—that you've heard in the past year. Of these, choose one that you consider a success, and explain what made it successful.

Profiles: A Fitting Response

A profile of a professional who shapes his world with words

We seem to be fascinated by people who have demonstrated unique abilities to establish a character, connect with our emotions, and move others to action through words. Profiles serve as a means through which readers can understand what motivates these writers and speakers and what experiences have helped them develop their abilities with words.

In the following profile, Marisa Lagos examines Tommie Lindsey's efforts to help students at Logan High School in California improve their abilities in public speaking and debate.

Profiles

Successes Speak Well
for Debate Coach

Marisa Lagos

Logan High School forensics coach Tommie Lindsey's classroom says a thing or two about his success: It's crowded with banners, trophies and kids. On this morning, Lindsey is just minutes from loading 38 high school students into buses and heading to Long Beach, where they will compete in the Jack Howe Invitational. More than 60 schools from across the nation would participate in the three-day forensics challenge, competing in public speaking, presentation and debate. The Logan High team would take the grand sweepstakes award as well as six individual first-place awards. •

The writer shows that she not only interviewed her subject but spent time with him engaged in the activity that has made him newsworthy.

Lindsey, a 15-year teacher at the Bay Area school, was recently named one of 23 recipients of the MacArthur Foundation's annual $500,000 award—a so-called "genius grant" the foundation disburses over a five-year period with no strings attached.•Meant to underscore "the importance of a creative individual in society," according to the foundation, "fellows are selected for their originality, creativity, and the potential to do more in the future."

The writer explains why the subject is interesting and important—he's a prestigious award winner (a "genius," no less).

Recipients of the grants are nominated anonymously, but Lindsey's qualifications are obvious. Logan High, a public school in a middle- to low-income area, has claimed four state forensics titles and many other awards in a type of academic competition usually more suited for prep schools than public schools.•Typically, the 16 forensic categories include speech, interpretation and acting.

This paragraph gives details about how the subject is making a difference in his community.

Lindsey, 53, a Mississippi transplant, is known for his dedication. He usually works seven days and up to 150 hours a week. If he's not practicing with the 300-plus-member team—most schools have about 40 members and as many as eight coaches—he's attending weekend tournaments from 6 A.M. to 11 P.M.•"I think every teacher does a lot," said Alphonso Thompson, Lindsey's substitute teacher and former student, "but what Lindsey does goes above and beyond the call of duty a million times over. I don't know where I would be if it wasn't for Mr. Lindsey." He has had numerous offers, mostly from private schools, to bring his expertise, and his assistant coach, Tim Campbell, elsewhere, and says he has entertained some of those offers seriously, especially since learning that the program's funding for next year is threatened. For now, Lindsey is still at Logan, where he has taught public speaking and debate to about 3,000 students, many of them from poor and/or single-parent homes.

This paragraph gives readers a sense of the specific types of work that the subject does as well as the attitude with which the subject approaches his job.

When Lindsey started at Logan in 1989 there were many skeptics. "Even the principal didn't think we would be able to do forensics at Logan," he said. So Lindsey began recruiting athletes, whom he believed would take to competition. "I went out and started getting

Profiles

athletes and putting them to the challenge. I would say, 'I don't think you can do this.' ... Finally, they would come out and find that they love it."

It's that mix of tough love, confidence and intuition that makes Lindsey both a friend and a foe. But most of all, it's what sparks his students. Varun Mitra, a senior at Logan, started on the team as a freshman. "Mr. Lindsey sacrifices a lot," Mitra said. "He never gives up on you if you say no to him.... He'll keep going after you to the point where you realize he was right, until he molds you into a better life." Before forensics, Mitra had planned to go to a University of California campus because his parents encouraged it. Now, he has even grander plans: after a bachelor's degree, law school. "Four years ago when I came in, I wasn't able to speak in front of anyone.... This program made me want to pursue a career in public speaking—as a lawyer, in politics," he said. "This program has helped me decide what I want to do in life." •

The writer doesn't simply tell readers that Lindsey "sparks his students"; she lets one student's experiences serve as an example to show how Lindsey motivates students.

Not all of Logan's students fit the typical mold for a forensics team, however. Many have been diagnosed with learning disabilities; others have never made academics their focus. And half the team members are female, still somewhat unusual in forensics.

But what really sets Lindsey's program apart is that its popularity has made being smart cool, mainly because the students see each other getting good grades. "When you join the program it creates expectations that you're going to further your education in college," said Mike Joshi, a senior. He plans to apply to several Ivy League colleges this year. "There are kids in honors classes that need the intellectual outlet," Lindsey said, "but many of the kids may not fit into standard academics. Some have been labeled special ed, and they come in and we find a place for them.... It's a matter of believing in a kid and finding a special something the kid does." •

The writer has consulted more than one source in putting together this profile: the subject himself and several students.

It's also about pushing students to do what they never thought possible: More than 90% of them go on to attend college. "I presently have a kid living in a two-bedroom apartment with five people. He sleeps on the couch.... But he wants to be able to do forensics, because it's an outlet," Lindsey said. "Once you're involved in this group, you start thinking about four-year colleges. Not if, but when." Lindsey moved to west Oakland as a child and graduated from Castelmont High School. He received a bachelor of arts degree from the University of San Francisco—where he was the school's first African American valedictorian—and went on to get a bachelor of science degree and secondary teaching certificate there.•Lindsey then went to law school for a year and simultaneously began teaching to "pay the bills." He was hooked, and after five years teaching at Alameda County's Juvenile Hall, Lindsey landed a full-time teaching job at El Rancho Verde High School, where he stayed until moving to Logan.

The profile turns to Lindsey's past to show how his experiences have informed his present-day efforts to motivate students to attend college.

Profiles

He is the father of two Logan students—Terrence, a junior at the school, and Erica, 21, now a student at UCLA. It was his children he thought of first when he was awarded the grant last month, he said. "With this money, we're finally going to get some relief here. Most important is my daughter and son's educations.". That help is well-deserved, say Lindsey's colleagues and students, who are pleased that the money is for him alone.

Lindsey said he was surprised and happy when he got the call. "It's great, not just because I was honored, but because teachers are not respected as they should be. Teaching changes lives and builds kids up.... They should be given more recognition than they receive," he said. "I was so happy the MacArthur Foundation is now looking at public school teachers, because it's very different. You have to be loyal to work in a public setting. I was shocked, and very appreciative."

Lindsey said he ended up in forensics because he was always fascinated by oration—including listening as a child to sermons at the Baptist churches he attended and to civil rights speeches by the Rev. Martin Luther King, Jr. While in high school, Lindsey decided he wanted to speak at the graduation ceremony. Though his teacher doubted him, she said he could try, then handed him his topic: "Investing in Learning to Cultivate the Intellect." After his initial frustration melted away, Lindsey sat down with a neighbor and hashed out a speech—one that got him a standing ovation at the ceremony. "I took that negative energy and propelled it," he said, adding that he still looks after that neighbor, who is now 102. The students at Logan are not the only ones to gain something, however. Logan journalism teacher Patrick Hannigan said: "At the end of my career, what I will remember is that I worked with Tommie Lindsey."

> The writer shows readers how the concerns Lindsey has for his family also shape his encouraging of his students.

> The writer helps readers see what motivates the subject.

> The anecdote reveals how the subject's own experiences showed him the power and possibilities of effective public speaking; it also helps to bring the subject to life.

■ GUIDE TO RESPONDING TO THE RHETORICAL SITUATION

Understanding the Rhetorical Situation

When you want to share your understanding of somebody with an audience, consider composing a profile. Profiles commonly have the following features:

- Profiles have as their subject someone readers will find compelling or interesting.
- Profiles provide descriptive details to help readers imagine how the subject looks, sounds, or acts.
- Profiles includes several direct quotations from the subject or others that help readers understand the person's opinions and perspectives.
- Profiles draw on evidence and insights from a variety of sources, such as personal observations, interviews, and research.
- Profiles present several anecdotes about the subject that show readers the background and experiences that have shaped the subject.
- Profiles lead readers to a particular emotional response or logical conclusion about the subject.

The following sections will help you compose a profile about someone who is successful with words. To work with an online guide to the elements of the rhetorical situation, access your English CourseMate through CengageBrain.com.

Identifying an opportunity

Consider the people who work or study in the community around you. You might listen to those individuals on campus whose voices have shaped the dialogue about pressing concerns. Or you might listen to others whose voices influence the people in your community, such as the preachers who craft their messages with deft rhetorical style or the teachers and debate coaches who create learning opportunities for students to develop writing and speaking skills they can put to use as active civic participants.

1.   Make a list of the interesting writers you've read or the inspiring speakers you've heard over the past few weeks or months, including the one you wrote about in response to the questions on page 106. Have any of your fellow students inspired others to action through their words? Do you know of any teachers who

have inspired students to develop their own voices in their writing and add these voices to the important conversations on campus? Are there any poets, rappers, or writers pushing the boundaries of how words are used in our everyday lives? For each one, write a few sentences describing your initial impressions of the speaker or writer. To help explain your impressions, write down as many details about the writer's presentation or the speaker's performance as you can.

2. For one or two of the writers or speakers whom you wrote about in response to question 1, locate images—or, if the opportunity presents itself, take photos—that capture some aspects of the individual's personality. Then spend several minutes writing about what the visuals convey about the person's ability to inject life and energy into his or her words.

3. Choose the writer or speaker you would like to profile and compose four or five sentences that describe the ways in which that person has succeeded. page 310 Then spend several minutes freewriting about the contexts in which this person's words have had influence and the specific ways in which they move people: What is the purpose of the person's writing or speeches? When and where do this person's words have the most influence, and who has been the audience for these words? Describe what you know about the person's background and analyze how this background might be influencing the person's public success with words. If your profile will feature a particular text or speech, describe how you interpreted it when you initially encountered it and after you thought about it.

Locating an audience

The following questions will help you identify your rhetorical audience for your profile. Your answers will also help you describe and analyze your subject's effective way with words.

1. List the names of the persons or groups (students, faculty, administrators, community members, or alumni) likely to be engaged—positively or negatively—by your subject's words.

2. Next to the name of each potential audience, write reasons that audience could have for appreciating the subject's rhetorical prowess. In other words, what would persuade these audiences that they need to learn about this person's experiences, perspectives, and motivations in greater detail?

3. How could each of these audiences be influenced by a profile of this individual? In other words, what emotional responses or logical conclusions could you expect your profile of this successful speaker to lead to? Consider the implications of these emo-

tional responses or logical conclusions for each audience and the motivations each audience might have for learning more about the personal experiences, values, and worldview that have affected your subject.

4. With these different audiences' interests and motivations in mind, return to the descriptions of the subject's speaking or writing that you composed in the preceding section. Add descriptive details, images, and compelling quotes or audio snippets (you may need to conduct some interviews or do other kinds of research) that will enable your readers to feel invested in exploring the life of this person who has shaped the campus or the local or broader community with his or her words. A good description will help your audience more clearly visualize the person at work, hear how he or she has moved people to action through speeches or writing, and understand how this individual has affected the school or the local or broader community. Tailor your best description to connect closely to your audience's needs and interests.

Identifying a fitting response

As you've been learning throughout this book, different purposes and different audiences require different kinds of texts—delivered through different media. For example, if you're writing about a student leader on campus, you might want to compose a feature article to appear in the student newspaper, the alumni magazine, or on the Web site of the Office of Student Life. If you're writing about a community activist, your profile could take the form of a creative piece for a local 'zine. Your profile of a community business or political leader could be the PowerPoint centerpiece of a program for an awards banquet honoring that person. You could record an audio profile of an inspiring professor for your campus radio station or for a podcast, encouraging other students to take this professor's course next semester. The point is that once you identify your opportunity, locate your audience, and find your purpose, you will want to determine what kind of text will best respond to the rhetorical situation.

Use the following questions to help you narrow your purpose and shape your response:

1. What kinds of facts and details do you need to provide in order to create a vivid picture of your subject and his or her success?
2. What past experiences or current activities and actions make your subject compelling to your audience?
3. What do your readers need to know in order to understand what motivates this speaker or writer and to appreciate the significance of this person's words for the school or community?
4. Are you asking the audience to adopt a new perspective on this individual? Or do you want to prompt the audience to take a specific action in response to your message?

5. What is the best way to reach this audience? That is, to what kind of text will this audience most likely respond? (Chapter 10 can help you explore options for media and design.)

Writing a Profile: Working with Your Available Means

Shaping your profile

One major reason writers create profiles is to let others know more about the people who are important to them or who shape the world in which we live. A writer using this genre often uses the rhetorical appeal of pathos in the introduction to connect the subject to the readers' emotions and values. In short, the introduction to a profile needs to show readers that the subject is someone they need to know more about— right now. Marisa Lagos, for example, immediately offers evidence of Tommie Lindsey's success: banners and trophies won by his students and his own "genius grant." Writers also use the introduction of a profile to highlight some key feature of the subject's personality, character, or values; by noting that genius grants are given to original and creative individuals, Lagos draws attention to these characteristics of Lindsey.

After capturing readers' attention with a brief image of the subject, the writer may begin the body of the profile by presenting a fuller description of the subject and his or her life's work. Marisa Lagos, for example, lets readers know that Tommie Lindsey possesses "obvious" credentials for the MacArthur Foundation's grant because of his work in helping students from a middle- to low-income area win several state titles "in a type of academic competition usually more suited for prep schools than public schools." Lagos uses the rhetorical appeal of pathos

Introduction	Body	Conclusion
▶ Shows readers that the subject is someone they need to know more about ▶ Highlights some key feature of the subject's personality, character, or values	▶ Presents a fuller description of the subject and his or her life's work ▶ Includes details that help readers to visualize the subject's actions and hear the subject's words ▶ Provides logical appeals in the form of examples that show how the individual's work affects the lives of people like the readers themselves	▶ Often contains one final quote or anecdote that nicely captures the essence of the individual ▶ May bring readers into the present day, if the profile has had a historical scope

as she describes Lindsey as a "genius." This appeal to the emotions of the readers—who's not fascinated by geniuses and interested in learning how they see the world?—helps convince them that Lindsey is worth learning more about.

The body of a profile also includes descriptive details that help readers visualize the subject's actions and hear the subject's words. Readers of Lagos's profile, for example, learn that Lindsey "usually works seven days and up to 150 hours a week. If he's not practicing with the 300-plus-member team . . . he's attending weekend tournaments from 6 A.M. to 11 P.M." Lagos incorporates these and other details into her profile in order to draw readers closer to the subject and to let them feel they're learning about aspects of Lindsey's personality that make him unique and influence the ways in which he works with words.

Writers also use the body of a profile to provide logical appeals in the form of numerous examples that show that the subject is indeed making a difference in the community. The crux of the logical appeal, in fact, is the explanation of how the individual's work affects the lives of people like the readers themselves. Lagos, for example, presents the story of Varun Mitra, a senior at Logan High School whose participation on Lindsey's forensics team has inspired him to work toward a

pages
309–310 law degree. Readers see from exemplification that Lindsey has indeed helped to inspire many students to continue their education. Through details supporting Lindsey's success in improving the lives of students often ignored and marginalized in public education, Lagos connects his achievements with a value her readers no doubt hold: the importance of all students having equal access to quality education and equal opportunities to succeed in life.

Lagos strengthens this logical appeal by providing quotations from Varun Mitra and Lindsey's colleague Patrick Hannigan. These quotations lend support to Lagos's assertions about Lindsey's significance to his community. The strength of Lagos's logical appeal ultimately rests on the assumption that her readers value people who expend the energy and effort necessary to make contributions to their communities. The quotations from Lindsey's students and colleague, as well as quotations from Lindsey himself, also help Lagos create an ethical appeal. That Lagos talked directly with several people before composing the profile strengthens the credibility of her claims about Lindsey's abilities to motivate his students as well as to inspire his fellow teachers. If Lagos had created an audio profile, the quotations could have been incorporated as audio snippets from her interviews, thereby literally bringing new voices into the profile.

Finally, the conclusion of a profile often contains one final quote or anecdote that nicely captures the essence of the individual. Lagos, for example, leaves readers with a quotation conveying high praise from one of Lindsey's colleagues: "At the end of my career, what I will remember is that I worked with Tommie Lindsey."

Revision and peer review

After you've drafted a strong version of your profile, ask one of your classmates to read through or look over it. You'll want your classmate to respond to your work in a way that helps you revise it into the strongest profile it can be, one that addresses your intended audience, helps you fulfill your purpose, and is delivered in the most appropriate means available to you.

Questions for a peer reviewer

1. To what opportunity for change is the writer responding?
2. Who might be the writer's intended audience?
3. What might be the writer's purpose?
4. What information did you receive from the introduction? How effective is the introduction in terms of establishing an emotional connection between the subject and the audience? What suggestions do you have for the writer regarding the introduction?
5. Note the facts and details the writer provides in order to create a vivid picture of the subject and his or her success.
6. What past experiences or current activities and actions does the writer point out to make the subject compelling to you? How could the writer help you better understand what motivates his or her subject?
7. How does the writer establish ethos? How could the writer strengthen this appeal?
8. What material does the writer use to establish logos? How might the writer strengthen this appeal (see questions 5 and 6)?
9. Other than in the introduction, how does the writer make use of pathos?
10. What did you learn from the conclusion that you didn't already know after reading the introduction and body? What information does the writer want you to take away from the profile? Does the writer attempt to change your attitude, action, or opinion?
11. What section of the profile did you most enjoy? Why?

Profiles

Audio Profile

The audio profile of Bill McKibben was written and recorded by Alena Martin and produced at WBYX at the University of Oregon. To listen, find *Profiles in Three Media* in your English CourseMate, accessed through CengageBrain.com.

Image: AP Photo/Toby Talbot

Online Profile

The online profile of Beverly Wright of the Deep South Center for Environmental Justice was composed by Faiza Elmasry. To read it, find *Profiles in Three Media* in your English Course-Mate, accessed through CengageBrain.com.

Image: Lori Waselchuk/The New York Times

Print Profile

In the following profile, student writer Matthew Glasgow addresses the rhetorical opportunity of capturing a classroom experience.

Image: Photo by Richie Wireman, Courtesy of the University of Kentucky.

pages 318–320

Matthew could have worked in various genres or media to present his professor's skills. If his purpose had been to persuade his fellow education majors of the power of particular teaching practices, he could have written a position argument for their newsletter. If he had wanted to nominate his professor for a teaching award, he could have drafted a formal letter to the nominating committee. Or, if he had wanted to share his musings on why some people are so good with words, he could have composed a blog entry. Matthew knew that his subject was someone that his audience—his college classmates—didn't know well but would find compelling. He also knew that he had several anecdotes based on experiences in and out of the classsroom that he could combine with observations and direct quotations to provide a well-rounded picture of his subject—in a word, a profile. He chose the printed form because the piece was turned in as a class assignment.

Profiles

Matthew Glasgow

Professor Goldthwaite

English 215

November 20, 2009

The Liberating Mind

Colloquially speaking, he's rad. He entered the lecture hall donning his sleek black-rimmed glasses, in one hand a notebook and a text, our first reading, Plato's *Five Dialogues*. Bookmarks jutted out on all sides, drawing attention to the annotated pages within, which he had no doubt read upwards of twenty times throughout his relatively young lifetime. In the other hand he carried a cup of coffee, envied by most students, particularly myself, at 8:30 A.M. on that first Tuesday of the fall semester at Saint Joseph's University. After placing each item on the table, Dr. Arnold Farr began to read off the names listed on his roster, thus launching his course The Human Person, which, for many of us, served as our first experience in the realm of philosophy.

Though quickly impressed with the subtleties of Dr. Farr's professional mien, I soon came to increasingly respect the process behind his work and the way he successfully communicated with his students and colleagues. Throughout the course he was able to identify with his students by relating the texts to topics that a college student might be more prone to understand. The first of these many connections occurred during our studies of Sigmund Freud and Herbert Marcuse.

When discussing Marcuse's interpretation of the Freudian Performance Principle, Dr. Farr informed us that he does not carry a cell

The writer's first sentence aims to establish a connection between the subject and college-age readers.

Not only is the professor "rad," but he's teaching a course that college-age students would be interested in. Thus, a connection is made.

The writer identifies a key feature of the subject's ability to successfully communicate: relating texts to topics a college student would likely understand.

Profiles

phone. The principle refers to how socially and historically created

structures serve as guidelines for what societies should desire. Marcuse believed that such a standard of behavior functioned as a subtle form of oppression, isolating those who differed from the societal norm.

"If you don't have a cell phone, people look at you funny," Farr explained, yet he found his life simplified by using only his office and home phones when necessary. This example shows not only how he explains philosophy in more readily understood terms, but also the way in which he himself manifests his philosophical beliefs in his own life.

Another clarifying example came from the music industry. During our study of Marcuse's "Dialectic of Civilization," we considered culture's influence on communities. Marcuse identified Eros as a pleasure-seeking and creative principle, which finds itself in conflict with the death instinct. This death instinct also seeks pleasure; however, its qualities are more destructive and produce aggression. To help us understand the relationship between Eros and the death instinct, Dr. Farr explained that the history of music and the music industry have a similar

relationship. Originally musicians wrote songs and melodies as a means of personal, social, and cultural expression, but as record labels emerged as major corporations seeking greater profits, artists' music became increasingly formulaic. By repressing musicians' freedom of expression, the music industry destroyed what the art of music was meant to achieve.

Farr's explanations in his course lectures provided guidance for his students; however, in several functions on campus, Dr. Farr also identified with people of various walks of life. "In a way I am still the same kid from years ago, while a part of me has also matured as well," Farr said of this ability to speak several forms of English, which proved vital when he lectured to students, fellow professors, and members of the local community simultaneously.

Fig. 1. Dr. Arnold Farr in his office (photograph courtesy of Richie Wireman and the University of Kentucky).

As part of the celebration of Black History in February, he organized multiple events, including an African-American Read-In and a campus visit by actress Ruby Dee Davis. Farr spoke at both events, sharing a passage by Dr. Cornel West at the read-in and providing an introduction for Ms. Davis, to audiences of students, professors, and many residents of the Philadelphia area. With such a range of people, most of whom spoke to Farr prior to or following the festivities, it was not hard to notice the appreciation and respect he had earned over the years through his cordial nature and stimulating intellectual activities.

In yet another significant contribution to the community, Dr. Farr organized the Alain Locke Conference, an event celebrating and discussing the work of the praised African-American philosopher.

Through Farr's efforts, several of the top Lockeian experts from across the country joined together to present their own essays interpreting and expanding upon Locke's philosophies. In addition to hosting and organizing the conference, Dr. Farr presented his essay entitled "Beyond Repressive Tolerance: Alain Locke's Hermeneutics of

Democracy as a Response to Herbert Marcuse's Deconstruction of
the Same."

Though the extensive title of his work appeared to be slightly
intimidating, Dr. Farr provided a clear lecture to ensure clarity for all
persons present. He examined the extent to which tolerance serves as a
democratic value, specifically questioning the tolerance of harmful views
and ideas. When misunderstood by a colleague, Farr clarified his thesis
by explaining the need for a struggle and potential for change.
Interpreting values as contingent rather than dogmatic, Farr stated that
one's ability to change or legitimate his views over time allowed for a
greater chance for true tolerance.

After Dr. Farr's thoughts on "the problem of tolerance as a
democratic value" were clarified, the man replied, "if that is what you
are saying, then I understand and I agree with you." Once again,
Farr's communication through his essay and his words following its
presentation revealed the ease with which he can educate both young
and old, scholar and student.

As the semester progressed, we reached one of the more sensitive
subjects—race and its prevalence in the philosophical realm. Race, in
itself, arose as an intriguing medium through which to consider the
philosophies of liberation, criminalization, and dialectics of past and
present human relations.

For this subject we turned to the writings of Angela Davis, who had
made a much publicized visit to the campus the previous year, tainted by
unfair assaults on her character. Prior to her visit, flyers produced by a
select group of students and faculty were posted labeling Davis as a
"lesbian, communist, and black panther" among other things. As a friend

of Davis and the administrator who had invited her to speak, Dr. Farr quickly came to her defense and even emailed a colleague who had been involved with the flyers and negative articles in the newspapers. He simply asked his co-worker if he had ever taken the time to read any of Davis's work, which his colleague had not.

A student later posted on a Web site created to rate professors that Dr. Farr's class was aimed at making white people feel bad about slavery and the oppression of African Americans. Upon discovering this accusation, Farr decided to incorporate a question on his final exam asking his students to agree with or deny this statement based upon the readings and class focus. The responses overwhelmingly disproved the allegation, primarily discussing the calls by Davis for change and liberation in the future, rather than sympathy for slavery.

Strangely enough, the attacks were manifestations of many of the philosophies in Davis's texts and discussed by Farr during course lectures. Due to the events surrounding his friend's visit and the need for greater understanding of the role of race in philosophy, Dr. Farr committed himself to teaching Davis's texts in every semester of The Human Person. His professional and humorous responses to these unfortunate claims emphasize his clever use of language to resolve conflict and succeed at his position as teacher, philosopher, and friend.

"I have always advocated the ability to think critically," Farr has said, careful to differentiate between critique and criticism. Farr referred to social critique in philosophy as a means of improving injustices and liberating individuals in the future, while criticism offers only negative responses without any means of progress.

Profiles

What keeps this profile believable (thereby enhancing the ethos of the writer) is that Dr. Farr is portrayed authentically. Many students admire him, but at least one does not. Being a human being (with feelings), Farr not only checks out his ratings but tries to resolve the criticism he finds on the ratings Web site.

"I also take into account the historical context which gave birth to all these ideas. It is important to understand how language has come to be in itself," Farr said of his appreciation of the history of both the philosophical ideologies and the language by which they are communicated.

At the conclusion of the semester, I interviewed Dr. Farr concerning a documentary I had been crafting entitled "War and Peace." Hundreds of texts lined the walls of his office, all surely consolidated in the man before me who spoke of Immanuel Kant's "Perpetual Peace" and mankind's current inability to reconcile differences without violence.

"We have to be careful to not always assume we are the 'good guy'," he told me. "You cannot force democracy on people, and we have not yet completed our democratic experiment here." These words were not spoken with spite, like many in the political realm, but rather were grounded in reason and conscientious thought.

These words were a product of his extensive studies at Carson-Newman College and the University of Kentucky, where he received his master's and doctoral degrees. He remembers those years at the University of Kentucky as ones that changed and matured his way of thinking, providing a constant value for education.

The writer closes with a moving quotation by Farr that captures the essence of the professor's key characteristic.

And now, as the educator, Dr. Arnold Farr recognizes himself as one person attempting to inspire many young people, but realizes his students have the same opportunities he once did. "Teaching is difficult when students have no interest," he says, "but I hope that by the end of the semester some lights go on." And though those lights may be sparse in a world where philosophy seems to be fading, each new gleam sheds hope on the future. •

The final sentence brings readers to the present and leads them into a hopeful future.

Alternatives to the Profile

Fitting responses come in many forms, not just profiles. Your instructor might call on you to consider one of the following opportunities for writing.

1. What have you accomplished through the persuasive or inventive use of language? What specific events exemplify your ability to get things done or to move people to action through words? What life experiences propelled you to this success? Write a memoir that describes how you succeeded with spoken or written words. Be sure to include details and quotations to help your readers imagine what that experience must have been like, as well as a concise analysis of the insights you gained through that experience.

pages 309–310

2. How effective are eloquent, rhetorically powerful speeches? What political, cultural, or social consequences have followed from them? In an analytical essay, trace the effects of one public address that many people claim is historically significant or even timeless. As you conduct this analysis, consider the extent to which this speech contributed to actions that followed it.

pages 312–314

3. Write a critical review of a speech or a public document that addressed an issue of particular importance to your campus or your community. Identify the criteria that you will use to evaluate the effectiveness of the speech or text and then evaluate the extent to which it does or does not meet those criteria. Be sure to provide specific evidence and details from the speech or public document in order to support your conclusion.

Profiles

5 Investigating Corporations on Campus: Responding with Reports

Chances are that you have witnessed something like the scene shown in the photo on your own college campus—a table set up by a credit card company in the student union or another high-traffic location to solicit new customers. Like the University of Michigan grad student seen here, students can sign up for a card in a few short minutes. After providing their names, addresses, and average yearly incomes, they often walk away with promotional T-shirts, frisbees, or tote bags emblazoned with the school's logo and the credit card company's name.

Some colleges and universities have signed marketing deals with credit card companies, giving a company exclusive rights to sell credit cards decorated with the school's logo or some image associated with the school (such as the University of Colorado at Boulder's buffalo logo or a photo of Penn State's football coach Joe Paterno) to alumni, students, and employees. In exchange for these rights and the names and addresses of alumni, employees, and students, the cooperating colleges and universities often receive millions of dollars in revenue.

Credit card companies have also established a presence on college and university campuses through purchasing the naming rights to buildings. MBNA donated $25 million to finance the MBNA Student Center at Columbia University and $7 million for the MBNA Performing Arts Center at Georgetown University. At Penn State, MBNA's funding of the Career Services Center enabled the school to build the facility and pay for the balance of its cost with public funds. In exchange for its funding, MBNA gained public recognition and marketed its brand name to a large student body.

Investigations into the cozy relationship between credit card companies and universities are part of what led to the Credit Card Accountability, Responsibility, and Disclosure (CARD) Act of 2009. CARD specifies that you must be 21 years old to obtain a credit card, unless you can prove that you have independent means of paying the bills. This may not stop credit card companies from targeting college students, but it makes doing so far less profitable.

The presence of credit card companies on campuses reflects a larger trend of corporations in general becoming involved in the day-to-day operations of universities and colleges and, in some instances, shaping schools' teaching and research missions. Yet it's not always clear to students and faculty—or to the larger community—what the exact nature of corporate involvement on a campus is. This lack of knowledge provided a rhetorical opportunity for Robert Cwiklik, who published an investigative report, "Ivory Tower Inc: When Research and Lobbying Mesh," in the *Wall Street Journal*. In researching the attempt of UPS to endow a professorship (called an academic chair) at the University of Washington, Cwiklik discovered the benefits of such a professorship: an impressive amount of research and travel funding as well as a reduced teaching load. In the process of his research, Cwiklik also uncovered the considerable amount of influence UPS would have on the university if the university accepted the funding. **Investigative reports** like Cwiklik's are commonly used when a writer wants to present the results of research.

IDENTIFYING AN OPPORTUNITY

Throughout this chapter, you will work to identify an opportunity to investigate the influence of corporations on your campus and then write about it. If you haven't already noticed the corporate presence, take some time to look at the names of buildings and various facilities and to note the companies that provide food, janitorial, vending machine, laundry, computer, and groundskeeping services, that run the bookstore, and that provide supplies. Just staying alert for an entire day to these kinds of details will expand your understanding of the corporate presence on your campus, whether the corporations advertise explicitly or not. In fact, the presence may be so prevalent that you barely notice it (think of the brand of soda sold in your school's cafeterias. As you work to determine what most interests you, consider the most fitting means of delivery for your investigative report:

- ▶ Article or editiorial, to be published in a community or campus newspaper or local 'zine
- ▶ Audio or video report, to be recorded for a campus news station
- ▶ Short documentary film for YouTube or your online campus newspaper

To spark your thinking about this issue, freewrite for five minutes in response to each of the following questions (or use any of the invention techniques presented on pages 306–320):

1. Which forms of the corporate presence on campus have you had experience with—in the dorm (who owns the contract to supply paper products in the bathrooms?), in the student union (which franchises serve food and coffee there?), in the bookstore (who owns it?), in the classroom or at sports events? Describe a specific experience in as much detail as possible.

2. What corporations have established the most visible presence on your campus? How have they made their presence known? Where and when have they done so?

3. Which of these types of corporate presence would be most likely to affect your day-to-day life on campus? How?

4. What would you like to know about how a particular corporation influences the activities on your campus? How might you find out exactly what kind of influence it wields? Be as specific as possible.

Real Situations

Whether you attend a small, liberal arts college; a two-year college; a large public university; a private, church affiliated school; or any other, you likely encounter corporations on campus in some form. Corporate advertisements might line bulletin boards in your student union or fill the pages of your student newspaper. They might be featured prominently in sports arenas or stadiums, as on the scoreboard at the University of Arizona. Or you might note that corporations provide services on your campus, running operations from food and hospitality services to the bookstore. For example, Sodexho-Marriott Services has been awarded contracts to supply food services for more than 500 campuses. Coke and Pepsi routinely battle for campus "pouring rights," a battle that began when Pepsi and Penn State entered a ten-year, $14 million agreement in 1992, according to which "The University agrees during the term of the Agreement to purchase its total requirements of soft drink products from Pepsi." Meanwhile, at the University of Pennsylvania and more than 340 other universities and colleges, Barnes & Noble manages the campus bookstore.

A scoreboard at the University of Arizona advertises for a number of corporate sponsors.

Furthermore, some prominent media outlets, from MTV and ESPN to the *New York Times,* have extended their reach onto campuses by producing cable television channels and readership programs specifically for college students. Both the *New York Times* and *USA Today,* for example, donate free newspapers five days a week as part of the Newspaper Readership Program, a program that provides daily newspapers to college students in both digital and paper versions. These newspapers are highly visible on campus, with dispensers located in the student union, in high-traffic areas of academic buildings, and along the campus bus route. Although the program is touted as providing students with broader perspectives on world and national affairs and as a way to spur civic awareness and engagement, the newspapers know they'll receive something in return for their donation: they'll have life-long readers of their newspapers.

The practice of enmeshing itself in daily campus life helps a corporation create customers who will continue to show brand loyalty long after graduation. One advertising agency, Alloy Media + Marketing, has explained the demographic appeal of college students for corporations: "Away from the influence of home, college students make hundreds of first-time, independent buying decisions . . . decisions

A Newspaper Readership Program on campus offers a variety of free newspapers.

that will influence their preferences and purchasing habits for years to come."

At several institutions of higher education, however, students, faculty, and staff members have resisted this encroachment of corporations onto campuses. Student newspapers and groups have investigated the business practices of the corporations with which schools have made agreements and, in several instances, have found that the business practices of specific corporations have run counter to the schools' educational and social missions.

Barnes & Noble's bookstore at Georgia Institute of Technology is one of hundreds of campus bookstores run by that chain.

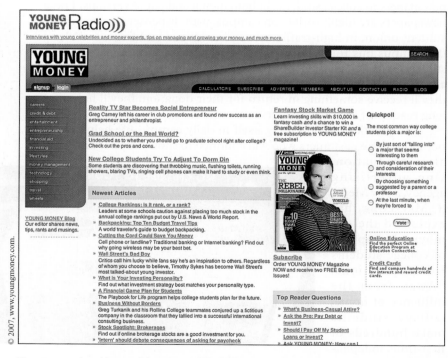

The magazine *Young Money* and its Web site directly target college students and recent graduates.

In 1998, the Union of Needletrades, Industrial and Textile Employees (UNITE) published a report on the BJ&B factory in the Dominican Republic, which made the baseball hats for at least nine large American universities, including Cornell, Duke, Georgetown, Harvard, and the University of Michigan. As Naomi Klein explains in her book *No Logo: No Space, No Choice, No Jobs,* UNITE's report showed that workers at the BJ&B factory were subjected to "long hours of forced overtime, fierce union busting (including layoffs of organizers), short-term contracts, paychecks insufficient to feed a family, pregnancy tests, sexual harassment, abusive management, unsafe drinking water and huge markups (while the hats sold, on average, for $19.95, workers saw only 8 cents of that)."

The UNITE report and Klein's book spurred several student groups into action, calling for university administrators to award clothing licenses only to businesses that use fair labor practices. Students at Duke University, for example, a school that sells approximately $25 million worth of clothing associated with its men's basketball team each year, pressured university administrators to review the university's 700 licensees that contract production work to hundreds of plants. In March 1998, public arguments by student groups led Duke University to create a policy requiring that every university licensee agree to follow clear labor standards in the production of Duke apparel. As Klein explains, "The code required that contractors pay the legal minimum wage, maintain safe working conditions and allow workers to form unions, no matter where the factories were located." Two months later, Brown University passed a similar licensing code, and the following September students at Georgetown, Wisconsin, North Carolina, Arizona, Michigan, Princeton, Harvard, Cornell, and University of California at Berkeley held conferences, teach-ins, protests, and sit-ins to draw attention to the labor practices that their schools were tacitly approving through their licensing arrangements with athletic apparel producers. At many of these schools and others, administrators have developed policies requiring that all of their licensees agree to higher labor standards in

AP Photo/Sara D. Davis

Wanisha Smith of the Duke University women's basketball team, which has a licensing agreement with Nike.

the production of clothing bearing the school's name and logo.

Students' investigative reports on colleges' and universities' corporate partners have extended to other types of goods and services as well. As Liza Featherstone explains in her May 2000 article in the *Nation*, students on ten college campuses that year launched a boycott against Sodexho-Marriott, trying to draw attention to the facts that the company was the nation's largest investor in U.S. private prisons and had been censured by the National Labor Relations Board. Three years earlier, students and faculty took action in response to the California State University (CSU) system's planned partnership with four corporations—Microsoft, Fujitsu, GET, and Hughes Electronics—which was to provide a telecommunications infrastructure for CSU in exchange for the right to provide related services to the state schools at a profit. Several investigative reports in student newspapers, such as San Francisco State University's *Golden Gater,* explored the implications of the partnership for the CSU system's academic and financial integrity, focusing particularly on how the partnership would enable the four corporations to create a new generation of students familiar with their technological products and thus more likely to buy them after graduation. By April 1997, Microsoft and Hughes Electronics had pulled out of the partnership under pressure from faculty and student groups; two months later, the other two corporations withdrew as well.

United Students Against Sweatshops protest at the Niketown store in New York City.

AP Photo/Tina Fineberg

DESCRIBING THE CORPORATE PRESENCE ON CAMPUS

1. How do you define a corporation? Make a list of all the things you think define a corporation. How do you define a college or university? Make a list of all the things you think define a college or university. In what ways do these definitions overlap? Where do they diverge?

2. Working on your own or with a classmate or two, describe when and where you have seen or experienced any corporate presence on your college or university campus. Describe these experiences in as much detail as you can and explain how they affect your private or personal life.

3. What kinds of questions about corporations' presence on campuses might an investigator hope to answer? How would someone go about trying to find answers to these questions?

4. What information about your college or university's corporate connections is available in your library? What information might your college or university's Central Development Office make available on its Web site or in the office itself? Does your college have an Office of Corporate and Foundation Relations? Does the Career Services office of your college (Liberal Arts, Science, Business, etc.) publish guidelines for local and national corporations looking to establish a presence on campus? Are any relevant meeting minutes made public through the library or online?

5. What groups, both on campus and off campus, might have a stake in the findings of investigative reports on relationships between corporations and colleges or universities? Make a list of the kinds of things an investigative report about corporations' presence on campus might uncover.

Real Responses to Real Situations

In the pages that follow, writers use their available means to respond to rhetorical opportunities they have identified related to the investment of corporations on university and college campuses. As you explore their responses to situations that may be unfamiliar to you, ask yourself if what they have to say relates in any way to the corporate presence on your campus.

Investigating corporations in student unions and classrooms

Perhaps the most obvious ways in which corporations create a presence in any particular demographic group are through marketing their brands and advertising their services. Corporations and other businesses place print ads in newspapers, run commercials on radio and television, and sponsor special events both on campus and off. Nevertheless, corporations historically have had a difficult time reaching college students through traditional media outlets such as national newspapers and magazines. They have therefore researched and tested methods of marketing and advertising more implicitly by having their products available for students to use. For instance, marketers for computer companies have come to realize that whatever brand of computer students learn on is most often the kind they eventually buy. Therefore, computer corporations often outfit entire labs for free.

Businesses and corporations increasingly seek to target college students with their advertising messages, seeing this group as possessing a largely untapped buying power, especially in light of their new independence often combined with generous parental support. However, there are some difficulties inherent in targeting college students, given that they come and go so frequently. To meet these challenges, advertising and marketing agencies have developed some innovative practices to effectively market corporations' brands to college students.

One company that has developed new approaches to help corporations target college students is EdVenture Partners. EdVenture Partners runs a variety of marketing programs that bring corporations' advertising into the college classroom. The various programs that EdVenture Partners offers to corporations and universities tap into corporations' need to market their products as efficiently and effectively as possible, as well as college students' desire for real-world work experiences to supplement their classroom learning. In the following article from the *Pittsburgh Post-Gazette,* journalist Don Hammonds describes the participation of a group of University of Pittsburgh marketing students in one such marketing program.

> Honda Challenges Students to Market Its Latest Car to Younger Buyers

Don Hammonds

Honda is counting on a group of University of Pittsburgh students to size up the Fit, its all-new entry-level subcompact. Pros in Motion, a student organization within the College of Business Administration, is developing a marketing campaign aimed at buyers just like themselves—both on and off campus. The students' project is part of the Honda Fit Marketing Challenge, a competition among 18 universities. Honda supplied students at each of the schools an operating budget of $2,500. The Fit goes on sale at the end of April [2006], with prices starting at around $14,500.

"It's a really definite win-win-win for us," said Tom Peyton, senior manager–marketing support for Honda. "First and foremost, we love the energy and ideas that the students come up with in regard to marketing our products. There's only so many ideas in this world and taking this to the campuses is a big help with that."

The students recognize the campaign is a rare opportunity for them, too. "It's significant for us because in class, it's a lot of theory and not a lot of practice. It's almost like having an internship because you are arguing a campaign that affects a company and the new products they are coming [up] with," said Lindsay Livorio, a senior marketing major who is working on the public relations segment of the Fit campaign. "And in job searching, in some of the interviews I've gone on, our campaign has been a huge topic of conversation because it's doing something that not a lot of students get to do," she added.

The students are competing for a top prize of $5,000, a second place prize of $3,000 and a third place prize of $1,000. The top three teams will be flown, all-expenses paid, to Honda headquarters in Torrance, Calif., on June 1 to present their campaigns to top executives from Honda and RPA, Honda's advertising agency. Teams from Honda and RPA will visit the Pitt campus on April 21 for a presentation on the campaign, and the finalists will be selected based on both quantitative factors—such as the number of hits on Web sites, results from surveys and other items—and qualitative factors, Ms. Livorio said. She expects to find out whether Pitt made the final cut in early May.

The sky's the limit on how the ideas generated by the students could be used by Honda, Ms. Livorio said. "For all we know, Honda could totally love the whole campaign and use all of it, or they could use a certain part of our campaign, or perhaps a slogan. Or they could use something from our campaign and something from the other schools' campaigns, too," Ms. Livorio said. "If they like what they see when we get to California it's definitely possible it could be used in a national Fit campaign."

Regardless of the outcome of the national competition, Pros in Motion's ideas will be used for the promotion of the Fit in Pittsburgh through early May when Pitt's classes and the advertising campaign end. "Our campaign is based solely on a new product that has not been seen here yet," said Lauren Feintuch, coordinator of Pros in Motion's project. "It's all up to us. There's nothing on television about it yet. It's just our little class that's introducing it to the school and to Pittsburgh. Better us to market it than some corporate person who doesn't really know us. We know what we want. Who better to market to our peers than us because we know what they want," Ms. Feintuch said.

"We also are at the age where we want new things, including new cars, not old, used ones—and the Honda Fit is priced just right for us," said Erin Conlon, senior marketing major, who heads the public relations group of the campaign.

As part of the campaign, the students already have come up with a number of ads that will be published in the *Pitt News* and have been distributed as fliers in the South Side and Oakland. Each calls attention to

continued

"Honda Challenges Students to Market Its Latest Car to Younger Buyers" *(continued)*

the Bigelow Bash from 10 a.m. to 6 p.m. tomorrow at the William Pitt Union, which will be the main marketing event for the car to the students. The event will include break dancers, inflatable jousting, food and prizes for participants, including a contest to see how many people can fit into the Honda Fit in 30 seconds. One advertisement features a kindergarten-style picture of the Fit in which color is scribbled all over the surface. The ad says, "You couldn't stay in the lines then. Why change now?" Another is a play on words for the well-known game show "The Price is Right"—"It's a new car! Come on down!" A third calls attention to the Fit's many features and calls them a "Blueprint for fun."

In a contest handbook, Honda urges students to do something the automaker would not ordinarily do in its ad campaigns—to push the envelope. "Since they're looking for something different, we can do whatever we want. They're looking for people who think a little different, and that makes it easy for us," said Mike Jack, a senior marketing student who is working on the ad campaign. Other students are working on public relations events and market research.

Regardless of how the student group finishes in the contest, the experience that they are getting is invaluable, said Bob Gilbert, an associate professor at Katz Graduate School of Management. The campaign contest is sponsored by EdVenture Partners, a company that specializes in industry-education partnerships. Shadyside Honda also is assisting. "We're really committed to this program. It gives them real-world experience and it looks great on the resume. The research that we are doing here is first-class research and the advertising is quite well done, too," he added.

And the students are learning the ins and outs of the advertising industry. Just listen to how Ms. Feintuch, the coordinator of the project, talks about the Fit: "First, it doesn't look like any other car out there. And it's small and very well built. And I was really surprised how many of us could actually fit into it. It's really ingenious." Spoken like a seasoned advertising executive.

Another significant feature of the corporate presence on campus has been the formal agreements that corporations—particularly those in the fields of science, engineering, and business—have created with various institutions to fund research projects. In the following excerpt from an investigative report that appeared in the *Atlantic Monthly,* Eyal Press and Jennifer Washburn define what they see as a new category among institutions of higher education: the kept university. This category, they explain, consists of schools where corporations exert significant control over the direction of research, teaching, and service. Press and Washburn see the kept university illustrated most clearly in a November 1998 business agreement between the University of California at Berkeley's College of Natural Resources and Novartis, a Swiss pharmaceutical company and producer of genetically engineered crops. Through this agreement, Novartis agreed to pay $25 million to fund basic research in the college's Department of Plant and Microbial Biology. In

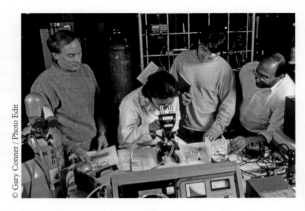

Graduate students at work in a plant and microbial lab at Berkeley.

exchange, the college granted the Novartis Agricultural Discovery Institute (NADI) the licensing rights to a portion of the discoveries made by the department as well as two-fifths representation on the department's research committee, which makes decisions about how research money will be allocated. Several faculty members and student groups argued that this business deal threatened to undermine the college's mission to serve the public interest; others maintained that the agreement provided the money and technology necessary to fulfill this mission. Press and Washburn explored such corporate sponsorships of academic research in order to better understand their implications for the future of higher education and the nation's social, political, and economic vitality.

Investigative Reports

Excerpt from

> # The Kept University
Eyal Press and Jennifer Washburn

Gordon Rausser, the chief architect of the Novartis deal, believes that faculty concerns about the alliance reflect ignorance about both the Novartis deal and the changing economic realities of higher education. When we met with Rausser last year, in his spacious office in the ornate neoclassical Giannini Hall, he insisted that the deal, far from violating Berkeley's public mission, would help to perpetuate the university's status as a top-flight research institution. An economist who served on the President's Council of Economic Advisors in the 1980s and now operates a sideline consulting business, Rausser contends that Berkeley's value is "enhanced, not diminished, when we work creatively in collaboration with other institutions, including private companies."

continued

In a recent article in the Berkeley alumni magazine Rausser argues, "Without modern laboratory facilities and access to commercially developed proprietary databases . . . we can neither provide first-rate graduate education nor perform the fundamental research that is part of the University's mission."

Rausser's view is more and more the norm, as academic administrators throughout the country turn to the private sector for an increasing percentage of their research dollars, in part because public support for education has been dropping. Although the federal government still supplies most of the funding for academic research (it provided $14.3 billion, or 60 percent, in 1997, the latest year for which figures are available), the rate of growth in federal support has fallen steadily over the past twelve years, as the cost of doing research, particularly in the cutting-edge fields of computer engineering and molecular biology, has risen sharply. State spending has also declined. Berkeley Chancellor Robert Berdahl says that California now supplies just 34 percent of Berkeley's overall budget, as compared with 50 percent twelve years ago, and he claims that other state universities have suffered similar cuts.

Meanwhile, corporate giving is on the rise, growing from $850 million in 1985 to $4.25 billion less than a decade later—and increasingly the money comes with strings attached. One marked trend is a boom in industry-endowed chairs. Kmart has endowed a chair in the management school at West Virginia University which requires its holder to spend up to thirty days a year training assistant store managers. Freeport-McMoRan, a mining company embroiled in allegations of environmental misconduct in Indonesia, has created a chair in environmental studies at Tulane. In its series on privatization at Berkeley, *The Daily Californian* noted that buildings throughout the Haas School of Business were "plastered with corporate logos." One major contributor to the school is Don Fisher, the owner of The Gap, whose company also happens to be featured as a case study in an introductory business-administration course. Laura D'Andrea Tyson, formerly one of President Clinton's top economic advisers, is now officially known as the BankAmerica Dean of Haas. . . .

In an age when ideas are central to the economy, universities will inevitably play a role in fostering growth. But should we allow commercial forces to determine the university's educational mission and academic ideals? In higher education today corporations not only sponsor a growing amount of research—they frequently dictate the terms under which it is conducted. Professors, their image as unbiased truth-seekers notwithstanding, often own stock in the companies that fund their work. And universities themselves are exhibiting a markedly more commercial bent. Most now operate technology-licensing offices to manage their patent portfolios, often guarding their intellectual property as aggressively as any business would. Schools with limited budgets are pouring money into commercially oriented fields of research, while downsizing humanities departments and curbing expenditures on teaching. Occasional reports on these developments, including a recent *60 Minutes* segment on corporate-sponsored research, have begun to surface beyond the university. But the larger picture has yet to be filled out. It is this: universities, once wary beneficiaries of corporate largesse, have become eager co-capitalists, embracing market values as never before.

Investigative Reports

Their investigation of the agreement between Novartis and the University of California at Berkeley led Press and Washburn to conclude that opportunities for free intellectual exploration were in danger. They called for university administrators and academic researchers to disclose their connections to sponsoring corporations, and they called for scholars and teachers to follow their own instincts about the types of topics that should be explored in the public interest.

Several corporations have bypassed marketing courses and research labs and directly hired undergraduate students to market their products and imprint their brand in the minds of the student body. Like the Ed-Venture Partners' programs, these corporate initiatives seek to tap into college students' general openness to messages that come from their peers. In the following article, which first appeared in the *Boston Globe*, Sarah Schweitzer investigates corporations' use of student "ambassadors" on college campuses.

Excerpt from

> Building a Buzz on Campus

Sarah Schweitzer

During lunch at Boston University, five girls ogled a 6-foot-7 blond senior with a winning smile and high cool-quotient as he approached their table. He was cute, they agreed. But equally intriguing was his pitch.

"I heard this is amazing!" Pam Spuehler, a sophomore in general studies, said as she read a postcard touting the OneNote software program that Cody Gossett had handed her.

"It is," Gossett said. "You should check it out!"

"I will!" Spuehler said, adding as she eyed the phrase "Save Trees. Use OneNote" on his chest, "How do I get one of those T-shirts?"

The exchange was a corporate marketer's dream—and one, in this case, come true for Microsoft, which hired Gossett to peddle its

continued

notes-organizing software on campus. Microsoft is among a growing number of companies seeking to reach the elusive but critical college market by hiring students to be ambassadors—or, in more traditional terms, door-to-door salesmen. In an age when the college demographic is no longer easily reached via television, radio, or newspapers—as TiVo, satellite radio, iPods, and the Internet crowd out the traditional advertising venues—a microindustry of campus marketing has emerged. Niche firms have sprung [up] to act as recruiters of students, who then market products on campus for companies such as Microsoft, JetBlue Airways, The Cartoon Network, and Victoria's Secret. "There is a paradigm shift in the way that corporations are marketing to college students," said Matt Britton, a managing partner of Mr. Youth, a New York-based firm that specializes in college student marketing. "The student ambassador tactic embraces all the elements that corporations find most effective: It's peer-to-peer, it's word of mouth, it's flexible, and it breaks through the clutter of other media. For all that, it's growing very quickly."

By the estimate of leading youth marketing firms, tens of thousands of students work as campus ambassadors nationwide, with many in the college-rich Boston region. The students selected tend to be campus leaders with large social networks that can be tapped for marketing. Good looks and charm tend to follow. Many are specially trained, sometimes at corporate headquarters, Gossett said, as in the case with Microsoft. They are expected to devote about 10 to 15 hours a week talking up the products to friends, securing corporate sponsorship of campus events, and lobbying student newspaper reporters to mention products in articles. They also must plaster bulletin boards with posters and chalk sidewalks—tactics known as "guerilla marketing," which, marketing firms acknowledge, intentionally skirt the boundaries of campus rules.

Students are compensated with the products they hawk, and some are paid a small stipend. The bigger attraction appears to be the resume-worthy experience and a possible inside track for a job with a company after graduation. The companies generally track the work through self-reporting: Mr. Youth maintains an online portal where students log their numbers of fliers posted, e-mail addresses collected, and the like. Microsoft, Gossett said, monitors the work by counting the number of student downloads by school.

Colleges and universities say they have little say over student marketers on campus and are often unaware they exist. While many schools bar companies from setting up shop or sending nonstudent representatives to approach students on campus property, administrators say many campus spaces are difficult to restrict to students. "We are not in a position to tell people that they can't talk to people," said Bruce Reitman, dean of student affairs at Tufts University. . . .

College students are, however, a tough crowd for marketers. Wired as the generation may be, its members not only tend to ignore traditional media—television, radio, and newspapers—but, studies show, they are no more likely to click open an Internet ad than older adults are. They do, however, listen to one another. Gary Colen, an executive vice president of marketing at Alloy, said telecommunication companies were early users of campus ambassadors, but, increasingly, retail and consumer goods firms are relying on them to counter the cacophony of corporate messages.

The method is a blend of other emerging tactics: buzz marketing, in which people talk up a product to friends and family without necessarily revealing corporate representation; and street teams, young people who hand out stickers, fliers, and products. But the use of campus ambassadors differs, specialists say, in that it is not cold-call salesmanship, used by street groups, and it is more forthcoming than buzz marketing. Campus ambassadors generally are not required to state their corporate affiliation, but most companies instruct them not to try to obscure it.

At BU, Gossett, 22, and his co-worker, Trevor Guthrie, 21, also a senior majoring in advertising, did not announce their corporate ties—allowing their logo-bearing T-shirts to do the work. Students they approached said, in interviews after listening to the pitch, they did not understand the students' relationship with Microsoft, but that it mattered little. "I probably listened to Trevor more because he's a friend," said Kelsey Henager, a sophomore studying public relations. "Students come from your level, and you don't feel like they are just pushing a product on you—it's more like they're sharing their opinion." Youth marketing firms say that sentiment is echoed in their research, which indicates that students have a growing mistrust of corporate messages—both because of the number of them and [because of] the recent string of corporate scandals. . . .

[Josh] Velasquez, who heard about the JetBlue job though the career services center at [MIT's] Sloan School of Management, said his marketing methods have focused on filling campus bulletin boards with company posters, placing flight schedule booklets on computer consoles at the campus computing center, and securing corporate sponsorship of MIT's fall festival. The website for the festival now includes the JetBlue logo. Velasquez said he is continually brainstorming new

continued

Investigative Reports

ways of getting his message out. His latest: preprinted Post-it notes, the better for sticking to computing center monitors. "We're supposed to break the rules a little bit," he said. "Traditional media doesn't work, so you have to go out and be creative."

Student ambassadors have proved effective at helping corporations strengthen their brand identity and market new products and services to the college market; the ambassadors' already established and ever expanding connections with friends and classmates enable corporations to tap directly into college social networks. The ambassador positions have also proved attractive to college students because they offer income, sales experience, and potential postgraduate employment. As some colleges and universities establish policies and rules that limit corporations' advertising on campus, use of student ambassadors gives companies access to the college market through more informal—and, they hope, more authentic—means.

>ANALYZING THE RHETORICAL SITUATION

1. What specific feature of the corporate presence on college campuses does each report in this section investigate?
2. Who is the specific audience for each of the three reports? For what purpose was each report written? How does that purpose affect the audience for each report?
3. What kinds of facts and evidence does each report present to help readers better understand corporations' presence and activity on college campuses? What kinds of research did the writers likely do to find those facts and that evidence?
4. What rhetorical opportunities or problems prompted the reports in this section? How would you characterize the authors' responses to the corporate presence on college and university campuses?
5. How do the writers of these reports draw on the rhetorical appeals of ethos, logos, and pathos to support their opinions on corporations' proper role on college campuses? Cite passages from the texts to support your answer.

Investigating corporations' involvement in collegiate athletics

On many college and university campuses in the United States, the corporate presence is most visible on the football field, basketball court, and soccer pitch. Major college athletic programs have signed multimillion-dollar deals in which an athletic apparel company such as Nike, Adidas, or Reebok produces the athletes' uniforms and the fans' T-shirts, hats, and sweatshirts—all of which are emblazoned with the corporation's logo. Corporate leaders have also made large financial contributions to the athletic departments of their alma maters, such as former Nike CEO Phil Knight's donations to upgrade the athletic facilities at the University of Oregon, where he competed in cross-country running and track and field as an undergraduate, and T. Boone Pickens's $165 million donation to the

© Sol Neelman/Icon SMI/Corbis

The University of Oregon's football uniforms clearly display the school's Nike affiliation.

Investigative Reports

athletic program at Oklahoma State University. Sponsorship deals and alumni donations like these have served as another advertising medium for corporations, and several corporate executives have wielded significant influence in athletic departments at colleges and universities. As investigative journalist Mike Fish explains in the story that he filed for ESPN.com, it's not only CEOs' alma maters that profit from an affinity for college athletics.

Excerpt from

> Riding the Trojan Horse
Mike Fish

Not all boosters run around town singing their school's fight song. Or dressing like colorful clowns on football Saturdays. Some, like Joe Malugen, current sugar daddy to Troy University's upstart Division I-A squad, never set foot in a class on campus. His roots, in fact, trace to the University of Missouri (Class of '73). So here, in a rural southeast Alabama town of about 15,000, boosterism has nothing to do with emotional ties and everything to do with smart business.

continued

And let it be noted the dough isn't coming out of Malugen's pocket, but the coffers of his video rental company, Movie Gallery—No. 2 in the business behind only Blockbuster. Two years ago, Malugen signed a $5 million marketing deal with Troy to name its freshly renovated stadium Movie Gallery Veterans Stadium. Malugen fancied it as a way to tie the company's name to a sports team—a Trojan program flush with a pair of NCAA Division II national titles that aspired to tee it up with the big boys—and also curry favor in the local community, where Movie Gallery is headquartered just an hour down Highway 231 in Dothan.

Years ago, Syracuse kicked off the football naming rights deals with the Carrier Dome, followed by Louisville and Papa John's Stadium and Texas Tech's SBC Stadium. And now comes Troy. "We sort of rolled the dice and did the deal, and what we found was the impact was greater than we anticipated," says Malugen, the Movie Gallery chairman and CEO. "And I think that is probably due to the TV coverage we have gotten of the stadium. And, of course, one of the good things is we picked a good horse to ride. Troy University is kind of a Cinderella-type team. They have had some great successes beating Marshall and beating Missouri [in 2004]. They sort of delivered in doing what they said they were going to try and do. Obviously if they'd gotten blown out in every game I probably would be less excited about it. They've been on national and regional TV quite often, so that Movie Gallery Stadium, logos and all, has certainly gotten around the southeast."

This fall's 4-7 Troy squad didn't prove quite the entertainment buy, yet Malugen can't say much after a steeper-than-anticipated downturn in the movie rental business resulted in $12.5 million third-quarter losses for Movie Gallery. Both sides are in this for the long haul anyway, thanks to the 20-year naming rights deal.

So what does Movie Gallery get for Malugen signing on? For starters, Suite 509, a 20-seat skybox perched squarely above the 50-yard line, outfitted with movie theater seats and posters from "Radio" and "Remember the Titans" hanging on the walls. The company this fall leased a larger, 40-seat skybox that's near the 25-yard line. Malugen also sits on the Troy University Foundation's Board of Directors, the major fundraising arm of the university. According to the most recent IRS Form 990 filed last year, the foundation has $32 million in net assets after having issued cash grants of almost $5.5 million—$3.4 million of it going to the athletic department. When Troy went looking for an athletic director last fall, Malugen was called to serve on the eight-person search committee . . . .

Malugen says he doesn't meddle in the day-to-day affairs of the athletic department, and by all accounts that's true. When he does offer an occasional thought, it's usually about scheduling—Troy has an ambitious, if not downright silly nonconference road stretch next season at Florida State, Georgia Tech and Nebraska—and down the road perhaps upgrading its Sun Belt Conference affiliation. "He gives money, offers his opinions, but doesn't dictate," [Troy's Senior Associate Athletic Director Scott] Farmer explains.

Troy chancellor Jack Hawkins Jr. says the university has no trepidation dealing with outside corporate types such as Malugen and Richard Scrushy, former HealthSouth founder and CEO. Hawkins buys into the grander sports profile as a vehicle to bring name recognition and push his vision for a global campus; Troy currently has a physical presence in 13 countries.

Perhaps even more pressing is the necessity to find and attract diverse revenue streams to keep the university running, which is true of most universities not named Harvard or Yale. When Hawkins came to Troy almost two decades ago, he says 43 percent of his budget was derived from the state. Today, the number is only 23 percent. So there'd be no big-time athletics if not for corporate checks signed by Malugen and Scrushy. And, as an acknowledgement, displayed prominently on a wall in the athletic department offices are enlargements of the original checks they wrote.

Scrushy—who still faces civil claims after a June acquittal on federal fraud charges in the $2.7 billion overstatement of earnings at Health-South, the chain of rehabilitation hospitals he helped found—provided the seed money spawning Troy's move to I-A. Hawkins had personally lobbied Alabama Gov. Fob James for Scrushy's appointment to the Troy board of trustees. And you find the football field still bears his name, if you look hard enough. It was at a 1998 meeting at the HealthSouth headquarters in Birmingham that Scrushy pushed Troy trustees to take the sports teams to the next level. "We were wrestling with, 'Do we go I-A?'" Hawkins recalls. "Right in the middle of the meeting, Richard slapped the table and he said, 'I'm good for a million dollars.' And the hands went up and we went I-A."

In Scrushy's case, there was an emotional attachment because his wife and an uncle graduated from Troy. For Malugen, at least initially, it was bottom-line business. "I see the athletic programs as really the marketing department for the university," Malugen offers. "I feel like

continued

these universities are really a brand. Just like a Movie Gallery brand or the Hollywood Video brand. Just like the ESPN brand. Like I tell them at Missouri, 'People don't sit around on any given day very often and talk about what is happening at the University of Missouri's School of Business. They sit around and talk about what is happening with the Mizzou football team.' It is just branding." With rare exceptions, more and more schools are happy to play the game.

Joe Malugen understands that athletic teams are often what give a college or university visibility in the mass media. Tapping into the marketing potential of this visibility just makes good business sense to Malugen, and administrators at Troy University and other schools seem willing to accept the financial windfall that comes from such corporate support.

> ANALYZING THE RHETORICAL SITUATION

1. What specific problem does Mike Fish explore in his investigative article?
2. What specific argument does Fish appear to be making in his article? What do you think he sees as the ideal relationship between corporations and universities?
3. What specific conclusions does Fish want his audience to reach? What rhetorical appeals of ethos, logos, and pathos does he use to try to produce this response?

COMMUNITY CONNECTIONS

1. Write for ten minutes responding to one of the articles you've just read about the corporate presence on campus. How do the various activities described by these writers coincide with or diverge from your experiences on your campus?

2. What specific corporate advertising and marketing activities can you identify on your campus? List several examples. Who likely made the various decisions leading to these instances of corporate presence on your campus?

3. Write for ten minutes about the causes or the consequences of one specific instance of corporate presence on your college or university

Investigative Reports

campus. You may want to conduct research at your library or in your campus's Office of Development.

4. Based on your experiences on your campus, what is your definition of the ideal relationship between corporations and institutions of higher education? Write for ten minutes and be prepared to share your answer.

Investigative Reports: A Fitting Response

As the readings in this chapter illustrate, corporations have created a presence on many college and university campuses. Some corporations advertise their products and services in the campus newspaper; others use less conventional means such as Oscar-Meyer's Weinermobile. Some corporations sponsor classroom projects and athletic programs; still others provide financial resources to fuel—and, in some cases, shape the direction of—academic research. Each of the investigative reports precisely defines the nature of a corporate-academic partnership, clarifies the various perspectives and motivations that gave rise to this partnership, and illustrates how this partnership affects various stakeholders.

A report investigating the corporate presence on campus

In her investigative report, which appeared as an editorial in the *Los Angeles Times*, Jennifer Washburn explores what she sees as the negative ramifications of a new partnership between British Petroleum (BP) and two public universities: the University of California at Berkeley and the University of Illinois at Urbana-Champaign.

Courtesy of the author

The Oscar-Meyer Weinermobile occasionally cruises around Penn State's Campus.

Big Oil Buys Berkeley: The BP-UC Berkeley Research Deal Pushes Academic Integrity Aside for Profit

Jennifer Washburn

Washburn encourages readers to rethink the "good deals" that corporations are making with universities, deals that influence the direction and shape of university research, which has traditionally been an objective, "open knowledge exchange."

On Feb. 1, [2007], the oil giant BP announced that it had chosen UC Berkeley, in partnership with the Lawrence Berkeley National Laboratory and the University of Illinois at Urbana-Champaign, to lead the largest academic-industrial research alliance in U.S. history. If the deal is approved, BP will give $500 million over 10 years to fund a new multidisciplinary Energy Biosciences Institute devoted principally to biofuels research.

Gov. Arnold Schwarzenegger, UC administrators and BP executives immediately proclaimed the alliance—which is not yet a done deal—a victory for higher education and for the environment. But here's another way to see it. For a mere $50 million a year, an oil company worth $250 billion would buy a chunk of America's premier public research institutions, all but turning them into its own profit-making subsidiary.

This is shameful. The core mission of Berkeley is education, open knowledge exchange and objective research, not making money or furthering the interests of a private firm. In the last two decades, however, Cal and other universities—increasingly desperate for research dollars—have signed agreements that fail to protect their essential independence, allowing corporations excessive control over their research.

Early in her report, Washburn establishes her ethos: she opens with the results of her careful investigation.

The BP deal magnifies this trend. Most corporations sponsor university research one study and one lab at a time. With the Energy Biosciences Institute, BP would exert influence over an entire academic research center (spanning 25 labs at its three public partners), bankrolling and setting the agenda for projects that cut across many departments.

What's more, BP would set up shop on campus: 50 scientists employed by the company would work on joint projects with academic scientists at Berkeley and the University of Illinois. BP also would set up private labs on these campuses, where all the research would be proprietary and confidential.

Robert Reich, former secretary of labor and now a professor of public policy at Berkeley, has warned that—because of its size and commercial scope—the BP alliance could be either "a huge feather in Berkeley's cap or a huge noose around Berkeley's neck." The question is, do rules and practices set up to safeguard academic integrity and independence stand up to a corporate deal of this magnitude?

The fine print of the plan, which UC made public only after it was leaked, doesn't create much confidence. Californians need to know that their public university is dedicated to pursuing the best science, not just science that generates profits for BP. Unfortunately, the plan indicates that narrow commercial criteria could guide much of the Energy Biosciences Institute's research.

Normally, even when university research is corporate sponsored, professors alone direct and shape it. Often, funds are assigned and research proposals are accepted through an independent, peer-review process. In the BP deal, however, the institute—with a director to be "proposed" by BP and other high-level positions to be filled by BP employees or appointees—would play a major role in setting research agendas and controlling purse strings. The plan touts the company's role: BP's "business industry leadership will strongly differentiate the EBI from other primarily academic research enterprises." •·······

Washburn's citations and quotations help build the logos of her argument, as she provides support for her thesis.

The plan also would hand unusual control to BP in other areas. A bedrock principle of academia is that campus-based research should be published. That's why Berkeley bans classified military research from campus; the open exchange of information is fundamental to the advancement of science and education. But those 50 BP scientists on campus would, according to the plan, have "no obligation to publish."

Universities also, as a rule, hold the intellectual property rights in their research, no matter how it's funded. In order to foster competition and innovation, they generally allow more than one company to use their discoveries for commercial purposes. This plan allows BP to co-own intellectual property in some instances and to receive exclusive (albeit time-limited) commercial licenses as well. The plan itself notes that such terms "deviate from standard policy" and "require exceptions to policy in order to be implemented."

Ultimately, there is an even more basic question to consider. Would the institutionalization of BP at Berkeley call into question the essential objectivity of the research generated by the collaboration? BP is clearly investing its $500 million not just in public-good research; it's hoping to advance an energy source it's already committed to commercially. Given that there is nothing in the plan that calls for truly independent selection of research proposals, can the Energy Biosciences Institute be trusted to pursue research that might prove that biofuels are the wrong alternative-energy choice? Would its social sciences arm freely investigate potential ecological and economic downsides?

UC President Robert Dynes has characterized the BP deal in telling words. "It is my belief," he said, "that we are reinventing the research university in this public-private partnership."

Five hundred million dollars is a nice chunk of change, but does any amount of money justify "reinventing" UC Berkeley's academic integrity? That's what UC officials should ask themselves before they sign this deal.

■ GUIDE TO RESPONDING TO THE RHETORICAL SITUATION

Understanding the Rhetorical Situation

When you want to present results of research you have done, consider composing an investigative report. Reports commonly have the following features:

- A report defines the issue in precise terms.
- A report makes clear why the issue is one that needs to be investigated.
- A report provides convincing facts and details to help readers understand how the issue affects different groups that have some stake in the situation.
- A report uses direct quotations to vividly convey the perspectives of various groups with a stake in the issue.
- A report clearly identifies the conclusion readers should reach about the issue.

 The following sections will help you compose an investigative report about corporations on campus. To work with an online guide to the elements of the rhetorical situation, access your English CourseMate through CengageBrain.com.

Identifying an Opportunity

Are there any corporations with a highly visible presence on your campus? Are there any corporations that have a less visible presence but some significant relationship to your college or university? Is any aspect of this corporate presence a source of contention among groups at your school? Do any features of this corporate presence seem positive, harmless, or even unclear to you? Are some features of this corporate presence more acceptable, even welcome, than others to you or other students? Can you imagine some unrealized opportunities for advantageous corporate-academic partnerships on your campus?

You might survey the walls in your student union, the pages of your campus newspaper, the walkways outside stadiums or arenas on game days, or the list of investments that fund the school's endowment (which can be found in the Office of Development on your campus). Maybe there are few visible signs of corporate advertising and marketing on your campus. Or perhaps your campus seems to be permeated by corporate presence, with corporations determining what soft drinks you can buy in the vending machines, your food choices in the student union, the availability of textbooks and trade books in your bookstore, and even the curricula in your business courses or science labs.

1. Make a list of experiences you have had that were either directly or indirectly shaped by a corporate presence on campus, including those you wrote about in response to the questions on page 144. If the experiences were positive, explain why, providing as many details as possible. If the experiences were negative, identify the factors that contributed to that outcome. Write down details about the factors that shaped your experiences: where and when (both time of day and when in the semester) the experiences occurred, the number of people involved in or affected by the experiences, the school policies affecting this corporate presence on campus, and so forth.

2. Take photos documenting the corporate presence on your campus. Pay particular attention to documenting how this corporate presence shapes students' activities.

3. Choose which corporate presence on campus you would like to write about and compose four or five sentences that describe the various groups that seem to be affected by this presence. Describe what you understand to be the college or university's mission and its obligation to the student body, to its employees, to the citizens of surrounding communities, to its corporate partners, and to the public at large. Describe policies that you think the school might have established or should establish to determine the particular activities that corporations are able to pursue on campus.

Locating an audience

The following questions will help you identify the rhetorical audience for your investigative report on the corporate presence on your campus. Having identified your audience, you'll be able to choose the best way to deliver your message about corporate-academic relationships.

1. List the names of the persons or groups who are affected by or have a stake in the particular corporate-academic relationship you're going to explore. This step may require some research.

2. Next to the name of each potential audience, write possible reasons that audience could have for acknowledging the importance of this corporate presence. In other words, what would convince them that this particular corporate-academic relationship needs to be investigated in more detail?

3. How could these audiences reasonably be influenced by an investigative report? In other words, what emotional responses or logical conclusions could they be expected to reach through reading your investigative report? What actions could these audiences reasonably be expected to take in response to your report? Consider what motivations each audience might have for learning more about the particular corporate-academic relationship.

4. With these different audiences' interests and motivations in mind, look again at the descriptions of the corporate presence on campus that you composed in the preceding section. Decide which descriptions will enable your audiences to feel invested in exploring this particular corporate presence in greater depth and will help them understand why and how it affects them. At this point, it will probably be necessary to revise your best descriptions to tailor them to the audiences.

Identifying a fitting response

As you know, different purposes and different audiences require different kinds of texts in different media. For example, your discovery of university investments in corporations that have questionable labor or environmental practices might prompt you to write a pamphlet you could distribute in the student union to raise awareness of those practices and their implications for university life. On the other hand, an interest in having more real-world experiences in the classroom might prompt you to draft a letter to your faculty advisor or compose a multimedia presentation for the faculty curriculum committee, in which you describe corporate involvement in business and marketing classes at colleges and universities. The point here is that once you identify your opportunity, audience, and purpose, you need to determine what kind of text will best respond to the rhetorical situation.

Use the following questions to help you narrow your purpose and shape your response:

1. What kind of facts and details do you need to provide in order to precisely define the nature of this corporate presence on campus?
2. What perspectives on this corporate presence do you need to acknowledge?
3. Are you asking the audience to adopt a new perspective, or do you want the audience to perform a particular action in response to your writing?
4. What is the best way to reach this audience? That is, to what kind of text is this audience most likely to respond? (Chapter 10 can help you explore options for media and design.)

Writing an Investigative Report: Working with Your Available Means

Shaping your investigative report

Like many other genres, investigative reports take advantage of the power of the rhetorical appeals. At the same time as it establishes the writer's ethos, the introduction of an investigative report provides readers with a specific description or definition of the issue to be explored as well as the writer's stance vis-à-vis that issue. Jennifer Washburn, for example, opens her investigative report by pointing out a problem that most (if not all) corporate donations to universities share: they buy corporate influence. She also states her thesis that universities are increasingly signing over their independence in exchange for huge corporate donations that allow "excessive control over their research." page 310 / pages 306–308

The body of an investigative report provides many facts, details, and direct quotations in order to further clarify the issue under question while shaping the logic (and thus the persuasiveness) of the writer's argument. A successful investigative report is one in which the writer displays good sense in the presentation and analysis of evidence. At every turn, the writer uses attributive tags to show where each piece of evidence came from and how each source of information is credible and possesses authority to speak to this issue, thereby enhancing the writer's ethos as well as the logos for the piece. For example, Washburn quotes from the "fine print" of the agreement, which "indicates that narrow commercial criteria could guide much of the Energy Biosciences Institute's research." She also quotes from Robert Reich, former Secretary of Labor and now a professor of public policy, who says the agreement pages 318–320

Investigative Reports

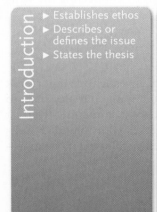

Introduction
- Establishes ethos
- Describes or defines the issue
- States the thesis

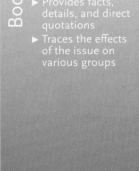

Body
- Establishes logos
- Provides facts, details, and direct quotations
- Traces the effects of the issue on various groups

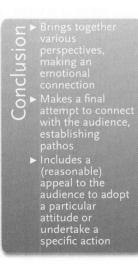

Conclusion
- Brings together various perspectives, making an emotional connection
- Makes a final attempt to connect with the audience, establishing pathos
- Includes a (reasonable) appeal to the audience to adopt a particular attitude or undertake a specific action

could be either wonderful or terrible. University of California president Robert Dynes declares that his university is "reinventing the research university in this public-private partnership." Washburn's citations and quotations help build the logos of her argument, as she provides support for her thesis, thereby helping her readers understand the complex nature of such an agreement. If Washburn had used video to deliver her report (in the form of a short documentary, for example, or a segment on the news), she could have shown clips from actual interviews along with on-screen captioning to support the credibility of her sources.

The body of an investigative report also traces the effects of the issue on various groups, particularly those groups that are not in a position of power. Every use of examples, statistics, and other data accentuates the good sense or ethos of the writer at the same time that it establishes the appeal of logos.

In addition, the body of an investigative report works to characterize fairly the positions and motivations of the various stakeholders in the issue, another way for the writer to establish ethos and logos simultaneously. As you can see, all the rhetorical appeals must continually overlap, even if one appeal is emphasized over others at certain points. In a successful investigative report, the writer presents different perspectives in a fair, even-handed way, balancing the ethical appeal of good sense with the logical appeal of supporting information. The writer attends carefully to the connotations of words used to describe the different perspectives of groups involved in the issue and gives voice to members of these different groups by quoting them directly.

Finally, the conclusion of an investigative report brings together the various perspectives on the issue and sometimes makes a final appeal for readers to adopt a specific attitude or opinion or take a specific action, using the emotional appeal (of pathos) by connecting the writer's cause with the interests of the readers.

Revision and peer review

After you've drafted a strong version of your investigative report, ask one of your classmates to read through it. You'll want your classmate to respond to your work in a way that helps you revise it into the strongest investigative report it can be, one that addresses your intended audience, helps you fulfill your purpose, and is delivered in the most appropriate means available to you.

Questions for a peer reviewer

1. To what opportunity for change is the writer responding?
2. Who might be the writer's intended audience? What might be the writer's purpose?
3. What information did you receive from the introduction? Does the writer define the issue in terms that will make sense to the audience of the report? What suggestions do you have for the writer regarding the introduction?
4. Note the writer's thesis statement. If you cannot locate a thesis statement, what thesis statement might work for this report?
5. Note the assertions the writer makes to support the thesis of the report. Are the assertions presented in chronological or emphatic order? Does the writer use the order that seems most effective? Would you re-order some of the assertions?
6. If you cannot locate a series of assertions, what assertions could be made to support the thesis statement?
7. Note the supporting ideas (presented using narration, cause and effect, description, exemplification, analysis, or definition) that the writer uses to support his or her assertions.
8. What reasons are given for investigating the issue immediately?
9. What facts and details are given to explain how the issue affects different groups that might have an interest in or connection to the issue?
10. Whom does the writer quote? Whose perspectives are represented in direct quotations? Whose perspectives are not represented through the use of quotations?
11. How does the writer establish ethos? How could the writer strengthen this appeal?
12. How does the writer make use of pathos?
13. What specific conclusion do you reach about the issue as a result of reading the report?
14. What section of the report did you most enjoy? Why?

Newspaper Editorial

This editorial by Barry Bergman of the UC Berkeley News examines the controversial agreement between that university and British Petroleum (BP). To read it, find *Reports in Three Media* in your English CourseMate, accessed through CengageBrain.com.

Image: Justin Sullivan/Getty Images

Audio Report

Free Speech Radio News, which describes itself as part of the "global alternative media," created this report about the BP-Berkeley partnership. To read it, find *Reports in Three Media* in your English CourseMate, accessed through CengageBrain.com.

Image: Willee Cole/Big Stock Photo

Print Report

In the following report, West Virginia University student Kelly McNeil investigates the presence of a corporation on her campus.

Image: Glen Argov/Landov

- Kelly's findings could have been conveyed through various genres and media. A letter to the editor of the campus newspaper would have been an appropriate genre if Kelly's main purpose had been to urge fellow students or the administration to take a particular action. She also could have written a case study if her rhetorical context had been a business course. But she knew that her extensive research and her surprising finding—that Red Bull is somehow able to maintain a presence on campuses where Coca-Cola products are the drinks "officially" sold—lent themselves to a genre she had encountered in journalism classes, the investigative report. Kelly chose the printed form because the piece was to be turned in as a class assignment. Her plans are to translate her print paper into a script that can be easily read (and heard) when she delivers her report on her college radio station.

Kelly McNeil

Professor Harmon

English 210

October 23, 2009

Red Bull:

Out-Marketing the Campus Competition One Energy Drinker at a Time

"Red Bull gives you wings," according to its tagline. It's no mystery why: each 8.3-ounce can of Red Bull contains 80 milligrams of caffeine, about the same amount as a cup of coffee and more than twice as much as a 12-ounce can of Coke, giving consumers a feeling of immediate alertness and an energy high. What is more mystifying, at a Coca-Cola campus such as West Virginia University (WVU), is how Red Bull has become the preferred study buddy, chosen by eleven out of twelve students over Coke-distributed Full Throttle, RockStar, Tab Energy, and Vault, according to the results of a focus group study conducted by my advertising class. After all, Coke products are the only drinks sold in campus stores. What makes Red Bull such a presence on a campus limited to Coke is a relatively new kind of marketing strategy that is well suited to its college-aged audience, a strategy that relies on grass-roots, or person-to-person, marketing.

> The author defines the subject of her report in precise terms. She also points out the specific feature of a corporate presence on campus that she wants to investigate, using specific details to help establish her ethos as a good investigator.

College students born in or around the 1980s are known as the Echo Boomers, the Millennium Generation, and, more formidably, Generation Y. Typically considered a more diverse and socially conscious group than their predecessors, Generation Y has grown up in a media-saturated and brand-conscious world, consequently keeping advertisers on their toes. This age group tends to be increasingly skeptical of traditional advertising, such as commercials and print ads, and more receptive to nontraditional marketing methods, including grassroots

> The author identifies her specific audience.

marketing. Unfortunately for Coca-Cola, Red Bull's grassroots marketing tactics are truly some of the most innovative and successful around.

The author makes clear why her audience should be interested in this issue.

Unlike Coca-Cola with its classic multimillion-dollar advertising campaigns, Red Bull focuses its time on saturating the everyday lives of the Generation Y consumers aged eighteen to twenty-four. In addition to the company's popular sponsorship of extreme sporting events and

After opening her essay with facts and evidence to help her readers better understand the corporate presence on campus, the author extends her evidence into this paragraph.

video games, Red Bull has a significant presence on college and university campuses nationwide. The company employs Student Brand Managers (SBMs) for its Wiiings Team. These SBMs are the face of the brand on campuses. Driving around in specially designed Red Bull "Racers" topped with an oversized can of Red Bull, the SBMs, in Red Bull logoed shirts, complete daily missions that include bringing energy where it is needed (*Red Bull University*).

From an advertising perspective, the Red Bull company is ingenious. Not only is the company reaching the Generation Y population, its target audience, but it is doing so on their turf—the college campus. This allows the company to build a trusting relationship with the consumers. Red Bull hopes that this relationship will be long term and will carry over into their adult, post-graduation lives.

In this paragraph, the author is supplying information that her readers may be surprised to learn. Again, she's working to establish her logos.

The Coca-Cola Company may have had the same long-term goals in mind in 2002, when it signed a marketing and sponsorship agreement with WVU. Under this ten-year contract, only Coke products are available in on-campus vending machines, eateries, convenience stores, and athletic concessions. Product logos also appear on the front of WVU vending machines, at athletic promotions, and in other university-oriented retail sites. In exchange, WVU receives "significant annual revenues for academic initiatives targeted by the University-wide budget committee," according to Chief Procurement Officer Ed Ames in a May 2002 press release ("Life Tastes Good").

Not surprisingly, the SBMs are not always welcomed at campus events. Recently, the SBMs were kicked out of a study abroad fair in the Mountainlair, the WVU student union, by the school administrators. This was not the first time something like this happened. Much to the chagrin of the student population, the SBMs have often been banned from on-campus activities. Many students, including two student body leaders who wish to remain anonymous, presume that the reason is simply because WVU is a Coke campus; therefore, the administration will not condone solicitation for any competitors' products for fear of retaliation by The Coca-Cola Company, which extensively contributes products and funding to the school.

WVU administrators have also been working hard to relieve the campus of Red Bull Energy Drink due to the negative press surrounding the substance on an international level. In Europe, a number of young people have died after consuming the beverage after exercise or after mixing the drink with alcohol, a popular combination for the party crowd, despite company warnings. However, there has been no finding that directly correlates the product with these deaths. The Austrian-made product is now banned in France and has been considered a medicine in other European countries (Rodgers).

While a Red Bull cooler filled with the energy drink is prominently displayed in bars up and down High Street, Morgantown's bar-lined district, the SBMs discourage students from making, ordering, or drinking Red Bull cocktails and advise them to drink a lot of water in addition to the beverage to prevent dehydration. Thus, Generation Y still considers Red Bull to be a consumer-friendly and socially conscious company.

On the other hand, it seems that The Coca-Cola Company has far worse social troubles to combat. Between 1990 and 2002 thousands of Coke workers lost jobs and many communities were forced to give up land and water resources to the corporate giant (Wendland). An international campaign, the Campaign to Stop Killer Coke (killercoke. org), was created to reduce the Coca-Cola market share and to punish the company for its ongoing involvement in environmental, human, and workers' rights abuses in several South American countries. According to a June 2006 article in *Political Affairs Magazine*, the major organizer of this campaign is working with students from universities around the country, including Harvard, Yale, and, yes, West Virginia University, to block Coke's access to college campuses and other venues (Wendland). The WVU administration has not commented on this campaign. Five months after the article was published, WVU is still a Coke campus, and the continued partnership prompts some students to wonder whether WVU values money more than social responsibility.

Despite some negative viewpoints on the company's campus presence, Red Bull is not deterred. On a daily basis, the friendly SBM is seen zooming around campus in the Red Bull Racer, a moving advertisement in its own right, and handing out chilled cans of the syrupy energy-boosting substance to its unsuspecting audience. The company could not have dreamed up a more effective or affordable marketing method. While it might not taste as good as a mouth-watering Coca-Cola beverage, the student enthusiasts at WVU will continue to choose Red Bull, over its competitors, for an energy jolt. Thus, the corporate presence of Red Bull on the West Virginia University campus, welcome or not, seems to be there to stay.

Throughout the body of her report, the author uses carefully researched facts to support her thesis. As she builds the logos of her argument, she's also sustaining her strong ethos.

Because she doesn't guilt-trip her readers or ask them to try to overthrow a practice they have little cause or ability to change, she makes an emotional appeal to them to accept the status quo. In these final paragraphs, she establishes effective pathos.

Works Cited

"Life Tastes Good: WVU and Coca-Cola Launch Partnership."

  WVU News & Information Services News Release. 22 May 2002.

  Web. 8 Feb. 2010.

Red Bull University: What Does a Student Brand Manager Do? Red Bull

  North America, n.d. Web. 30 Jan. 2010.

Rodgers, Anni L. "It's a (Red) Bull Market After All." *Fast Company*.

  Mansueto Ventures LLC, Sept. 2001. Web. 2 Feb. 2010.

Wendland, Joel. "Coca-Cola: Classic Union Buster." *Political Affairs*

  Magazine. Communist Party, USA, 26 June 2006. Web. 9 Feb. 2010.

Alternatives to the Investigative Report

Fitting responses come in many forms, not just reports. Your instructor might call upon you to consider one of the following opportunities for writing.

1. What forms does the corporate presence take on your college campus? How does this presence affect students' daily lives? Write a narrative of a day in the life of a fellow student that describes in vivid detail how the corporate presence shapes his or her personal and academic activities.

2. As you saw throughout this chapter, the corporate presence on a college or university campus can take various forms. Compose an essay that uses classification and division to help students, teachers, or administrators understand the different ways in which corporations have assumed either a visible or an invisible presence on your campus. pages 308–309

3. Identify a particular problem on your campus that either results from the presence of a corporation or could be resolved by inviting some corporation onto campus. Write a proposal that describes the problem and argues for a specific solution. As you write, make sure that you consider your audience (who should be in a position to act on your solution) and the feasibility of your proposal (its cost and how it might negatively affect the institution's research, teaching, and service missions).

6 Persuading in a Multilingual Context: Responding with Position Arguments

According to the latest census figures, over 50 million people in the United States speak a language other than English in their homes. Of the more than 200 million other inhabitants who do speak English in their homes, very few claim knowledge of the rules and conventions that govern what they might call "correct" English. This is another term for **Standardized English**, the English used in schools, businesses, government, textbooks, standardized tests, entrance examinations, and other kinds of official places and documents.

WORD COURT

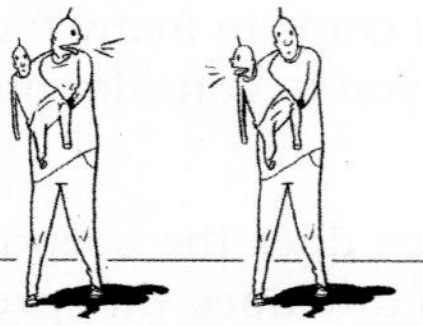

BY BARBARA WALLRAFF

CAROLYN SIMON, of Tucson, Ariz., writes: "I am seeking evidence to present to the activities committee here at my retirement center. Each evening on our closed-circuit TV channel a feature film is broadcast. In the past we've had variety. Now we have a new activities director. I suggested *Babel*, and one of our members said, 'No, it has the F word!' I said that the F word is part of today's accepted vernacular and often simply means 'Omigosh!' or 'Oops!' or 'Look what I did!' Our activities director has been swayed by the puritan wing of our committee. What do you think?"

I think saying the F word, like doing the F thing, is appropriate behavior for consenting adults in private. Newspapers and many magazines are concerned mainly with the public sphere, so they (we) tend to shy away from the word unless it's part of a quotation that was uttered in public. Saying the word in public demonstrates recklessness, crassness, or both. But movies almost inevitably portray private life. Here the word, like the deed, tends to come up. Anyone who is truly shocked when he

word *dubious* where I'm certain the writer means *doubtful*. I see this error in newspapers and in books by respected writers. It upsets me every time I see it. Is *dubious* now synonymous with *doubtful*?"

Even worse: *Dubious* has been synonymous with *doubtful* for centuries. The two main definitions for *dubious* in the *Oxford English Dictionary* begin "objectively *doubtful*; fraught with doubt or uncertainty" (the supporting citations include this one, from 1548: "To abide the fortune of battayle,

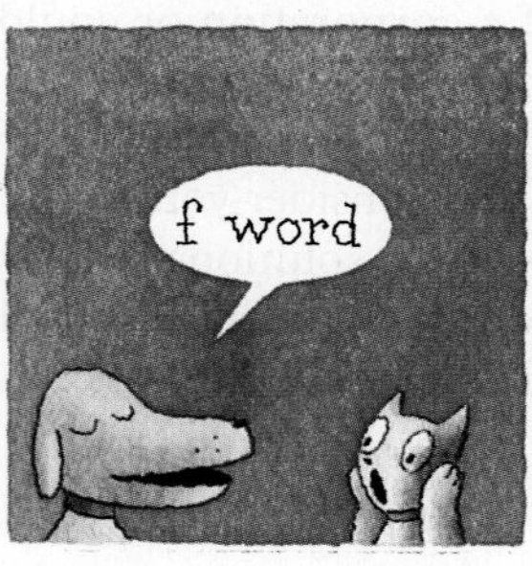

indifferent musical performance, *sure* of a *sure* thing. Granted, this imprecision could give rise to misunderstandings. But it hardly ever does: Does the chair feel *comfortable* or does it make us feel that way? You say that when you read *dubious*, sometimes you're "certain the writer means *doubtful*." That's about as much clarity as you can reasonably expect.

HAROLD SIMON, of Camarillo, Calif., writes: "An article in *Time* magazine, a very positive one about a popular TV personality, called her 'antisnob and utterly *nonaspirational*.' My medical background complained. *Aspiration*, medically, is the oral ingestion of a substance into the trachea instead of the esophagus, and it may have serious consequences. Am I being picky or reasonable?"

Aspiration in medical lingo is one thing; in common parlance it's something else. Though the word comes from the Latin for *breathe*, its meaning is often more nearly "desire." As for *aspirational*, time was it tended to have to do with lofty spiritual desires. In recent

In "Word Court," a feature in the *Atlantic Monthly*, Barbara Wallraff regularly settles disputes for people who concern themselves with the rules and conventions of English grammar and usage. For instance, Frederick G. Rodgers wrote asking Wallraff about the trend of "people using the word *do* as an alternative to a more fitting verb": "When I hear statements such [as] 'I often *do* French bread twice a week' and 'The mayor is not planning to *do* an investigation yet,' I automatically wonder why *bake* in the first statement and *order* in the second were not used." After pointing her finger at Nike for its successful "Just do it" campaign, Wallraff maintains that beyond the world of advertising, this overuse of *do* "sabotages communication," allowing us to "express ourselves in ways that can mean anything listeners want." For many American readers, "Word Court" would feed anxieties about their use of spoken and written English, about their inability to use English "right"—either in English class or outside of it. Even those of us who speak English fluently freeze up the minute we have to speak or write something that other people will be judging for correctness. Paradoxically, these are the kinds of experiences that lead so many Americans to believe in the importance of Standardized English for maintaining civility and precise communication in U.S. public life.

A **position argument**—the delivery of a point of view and the use of logical, emotional, and ethical appeals to help an audience understand that point of view—is one means of asserting how and why Americans ought to use English. Given the increasing linguistic and cultural diversity of the United States, however, questions about "correctness" are complicated to address. Whether the overuse of *do* signals the decline of the English language or any similar issue is overshadowed by the larger concern of whether English is the national (i.e., official) language of the United States, especially given the public presence of Spanish, Mandarin Chinese, and Tagalog. Position arguments can serve as individuals' and groups' means for participating in debates concerning speaking and writing in this increasingly multilingual context.

IDENTIFYING AN OPPORTUNITY

Throughout this chapter, you'll work to identify an opportunity to compose a position argument. You might want to consider your home dialect or language, particularly if you're comfortable with it and it contrasts with Standardized American English. You might want to explore an issue of discrimination—or advantage—based on language. Or perhaps you'll want to reflect on how some particular feature of your language has changed as you've become more educated. As you work to determine the language issue you want to argue, consider the most fitting means of delivery:

▶ Visual argument, such as a cartoon or an advertisement

▶ Online argument, such as a blog entry or a contribution to a Web site

▶ Print argument, such as an academic essay (with or without visuals for illustration)

To begin, freewrite for five minutes in response to each of the following questions (or use any of the invention techniques presented on pages 306–320):

1. Look at the images in this chapter. What specific argument does each visual make about the relationship between language and diversity in the United States? What details in the image lead you to your conclusions?

2. Select the particular image that resonates most strongly for you as you think about the language differences in the United States. What seems most familiar—or disorienting—in this image? What interests you the most about it?

3. In what ways does this particular image seem to support or oppose a viewpoint you have about language differences?

Real Situations

The last page of the *Atlantic Monthly* provides a space for people to police the boundaries of "correct" English, but one hundred years ago, the magazine featured a series of articles critiquing an educational policy aimed at eradicating the languages and cultural ways of Native American tribes. In three successive issues, autobiographical essays by Zitkala-Ša argued for the end of that educational policy. Zitkala-Ša, born in 1876 on the Yankton Reservation in South Dakota and later a student and teacher at the off-reservation Indian School in Carlisle, Pennsylvania, published "Impressions of an Indian Childhood," "The School Days of an Indian Girl," and "An Indian Teacher among Indians" in 1900. She criticized the school's policy of forbidding students to use their tribal languages to communicate with teachers or to converse with fellow students. While directors at the school claimed to be freeing the students from their "savage ways" by teaching them English, Zitkala-Ša declared in "Impressions of an Indian Childhood" that, as she lost her native

Book cover from DO YOU SPEAK AMERICAN? By Robert MacNeil and William Cran. Copyright © 2005 by Neely Productions, Inc. and William Cran. Reproduced by permission of Harcourt, Inc.

language, "I no longer felt free to be myself, or to voice my own feelings." She argued, in effect, that rather than dictating students' language choices and deciding what constitutes "correct" and "proper" language use, U.S. schools should give students opportunities to learn English while also maintaining the language of their cultural heritage.

Zitkala-Ša's arguments speak to the difficulties faced by thousands of Native American students at off-reservation boarding schools at the turn of the twentieth century. But those difficulties remain for many students in the twenty-first century. As you will read later in this chapter, students from language minority groups continue to experience cultural tensions in their formal schooling, often being forced to leave behind the language of their friends, families, and relatives. Other groups of non-English speakers in the United States, however, live in tightly knit communities where they can thrive without using English at all, conducting their domestic life and daily business in the language with which they feel most comfortable. In still other settings, speakers of several languages encounter situations that require them to mix their languages. Such mixing sometimes helps a person express exactly something a single language could not convey; it can also, however, make a person feel uncertain about issues of identity. Puerto Rican poet Sandra Mariá Esteves uses Spanglish in her poem "Not Neither," in which she identifies herself as both "Puertorriqueña" and "Americana" but shows that

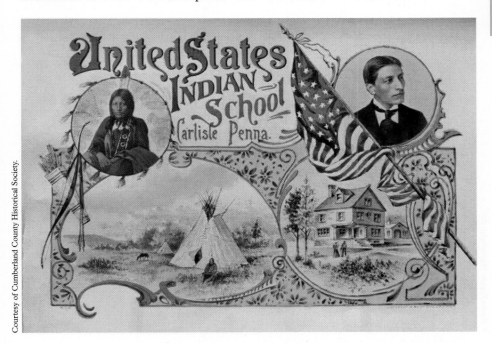

Courtesy of Cumberland County Historical Society.

Cover of the 1895 catalogue for the federal Indian School in Carlisle, Pennsylvania, one of many off-reservation boarding schools.

she does not feel a full member of either community: "Pero ni portorra, pero sí portorra too / Pero ni que what am I?" The billboard shown here attests to one business's "strategic" mixing of Spanish and English to tap into patrons' linguistic preferences—and to make profits.

During the past forty years, arguments echoing those by Zitkala-Ša and others have helped to make the use of languages other than English more evident in American political, educational, journalistic, and legal arenas. According to the Voting Rights Act of 1965, when 5 percent of the voting-age citizens in any state or political subdivision are members of a single language minority group, local election boards must print ballots and other relevant materials in that language. The Federal Bilingual Education Act of 1968 allowed languages other than English to be used in schools across the nation. (That practice has since been at the center of public debate on educational policies, most notably concerning California's Proposition 227, whose adoption meant that all public school instruction in California had to be conducted in English only.) In 2010, there were nearly twenty Spanish-language television networks in the United States, with Univision reaching 95 percent of Hispanic households with televisions and Telemundo reaching 86 percent. Annually, nearly 200,000 federal court proceedings required the work of qualified translators and interpreters. Close to 95 percent of these cases involve Spanish, with the remainder involving over 100 other languages.

© Steven Lunetta Photography, 2007

In parts of the United States where Spanish speakers are numerous, advertisers often use that language to appeal to consumers.

The prevalence of Spanish and other languages in the U.S. political, educational, journalistic, and legal arenas gives added layers of meaning to the question Robert MacNeil and William Cran pose in the title of their book, *Do You Speak American?*

As the linguistic and ethnic demographics of the U.S. population continue to change, local, state, and federal agencies have explored ways of making public services and public communications more accessible to language minority groups. For example, the city government of Minneapolis, Minnesota, posted a sign printed in four languages: English, Hmong, Spanish, and Somali. Medical service providers similarly have sought to make printed and online materials available in multiple languages in order to communicate essential health information to all the language groups in a community. The National Institutes of Health, for example, published a booklet on cholesterol levels in a side-by-side, English-Spanish format.

¡Conozca su nivel de colesterol!

Learn Your Cholesterol Number!

NATIONAL INSTITUTES OF HEALTH
NATIONAL HEART, LUNG, AND BLOOD INSTITUTE
AND OFFICE OF RESEARCH ON MINORITY HEALTH

Courtesy of The National Institutes of Health

Public notices and government publications are increasingly multilingual or bilingual.

Some people in the United States, however, consider the visible presence of non-English languages as a threat to the English language's prominence in the nation's public affairs. These people want to halt the use of languages other than English in the public sphere. Joey Vento, a third-generation Italian American and owner of Geno's Steaks in Philadelphia, Pennsylvania, went so far as to post a sign at the counter where restaurant patrons place their orders instructing them to do so in English. This sign sparked an intense month-long debate in the

© Peter Tobia/The Philadelphia Inquirer.

Joey Vento with his controversial "Speak English" sign.

Members of the Dominican vocal group Voz a Voz get ready to sing in an ensemble performance of "Nuestro Himno" at Ellis Island in New York.

local newspapers and on radio and television talk shows. The Philadelphia Commission on Human Relations even filed a discrimination complaint, arguing that the sign violates the city's Fair Practices Ordinance, which prohibits discrimination in public accommodation. In several interviews, including one conducted by Neil Cavuto of Fox News, Vento responded that he simply wants all Americans to learn English the way his ancestors did when they arrived in the United States.

A similar debate centers on a Spanish-language version of the U.S. national anthem. British music producer Adam Kidron created the song in 2006 as a response to the immigration debate in the United States. The recording, entitled "Nuestro Himno" ("Our Anthem"), features Puerto Rican singers Carlos Ponce and Olga Tanon and hip-hop artists including Wyclef Jean and Pitbull singing Spanish lyrics based on those of "The Star-Spangled Banner." At certain points, however, the song switches to English and directs sharp criticism at U.S. immigration policy; for example:

> These kids have no parents
> 'cause all of these mean laws . . .
> let's not start a war with all these hard workers
> they can't help where they were born.

Pitbull suggested that "the American dream is in that record: struggle, freedom, opportunity, everything they are trying to shut down on us."

Despite such appeals to Americans' democratic values, countless numbers of critics have expressed outrage that the U.S. national anthem might be sung in anything but English. U.S. Senator Lamar Alexander, a Republican from Tennessee, went so far as to propose a resolution:

> . . . giving senators an opportunity to remind the country why we sing our National Anthem in English . . . . We Americans are a unique nation of immigrants united by a common language and a belief in principles expressed in our Declaration of Independence and our Constitution, not by our race, ancestry or country of origin. We are proud of the countries we have come from, but we are prouder to be Americans.

In expressing his pride in the common culture and political ideals of the United States, Alexander argues for a specific view of how citizens can and should reaffirm the nation's democratic principles.

Ironically, as calls for using only English to reaffirm the nation's political and cultural values have multiplied, the U.S. Defense Department has argued that language education plays a key role in strengthening U.S. security capabilities. The Defense Department came to see language education as a national security concern shortly after September 11, 2001, when it realized that it did not have enough linguists and translators to read the covert documents (written in Arabic, Chinese, Korean, Russian, and other less frequently taught languages) warning of the terrorists' attack. Concluding that language education is important to the military, Defense Department officials now believe that schools—and, in particular, language arts classrooms—are valuable resources for securing the nation against terrorist threats.

And while the U.S. government is striving to build the nation's resources in certain foreign languages, scholars and community activists have launched campaigns to draw attention to and revitalize the nation's heritage languages (Native American, Alaska Native, and Native Hawaiian languages), many of which have died out or are threatened with extinction as a result of monolingual educational policies and the use of English in the mass media. In effect, these language revitalization projects are attempting to reverse the effects of the educational legacy Zitkala-Ša warned *Atlantic*

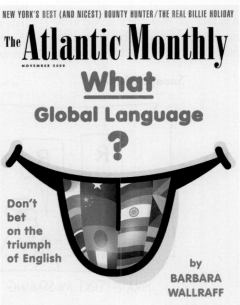

NEW YORK'S BEST (AND NICEST) BOUNTY HUNTER / THE REAL BILLIE HOLIDAY

The **Atlantic Monthly**
NOVEMBER 2000

What
Global Language
?

Don't
bet
on the
triumph
of English

by
BARBARA
WALLRAFF

© Atlantic Monthly, 2000.

Cover of *Atlantic Monthly*, questioning the status of English as the global language.

Waihona ▶ Hoʻololi	Mʟ
Mea Hou	⌘N
Wehe...	⌘O
Pani	⌘W
Mālama	⌘S
Hoʻouka...	⌘T
Hoʻoili...	
Holoi	⌘D
Kiʻi ʻIke	⌘I
Huli...	⌘F
Huli Hou Aʻe	⌘G
Hoʻokuene ʻAoʻao...	
Paʻi...	⌘P
Haʻalele	⌘Q

A pull-down menu translated into Hawaiian increases the perception of that language as a living one.

Savage Chickens   by Doug Savage

PIRATE TEXT MESSAGING

www.savagechickens.com

What effects do technological advances such as text messaging have on language?

Monthly readers about in 1900. The projects bring communities together physically or virtually in order to create a meaningful context for learning and using their heritage languages. Scholars and community leaders in Hawaiʻi, for instance, have successfully adapted Apple software to meet the needs of their language revitalization project by translating computer commands into the Hawaiian language. Most recently, Hawaiian language scholars have worked with Google to make its search page available in Hawaiian. This adaptation of literacy tools helps students to see Hawaiian as a living language they can use to communicate with others across the Hawaiian island chain.

While revitalization advocates try to breathe life into languages that have declined because of educational, political, and technological trends that have established English's prominence in the world, others have turned their attention to what English might be like in the United States in the years to come, given immigration, the growth of the Spanish-speaking population, and technological advances that abridge the language. One thing is certain: within the next fifty years in the United States, native speakers of English will be outnumbered by nonnative speakers of English, and all Americans will use English in a multilingual context. Consequently, while some readers of the *Atlantic Monthly* hold fast to the seemingly fixed rules of Standardized English and bring cases before the "Word Court," the notion of plural "Englishes" may prove to be a more useful way of characterizing the language usage of the future.

DESCRIBING LANGUAGE USE IN THE UNITED STATES

1. Write for five to ten minutes about your experiences using, listening to, or reading languages other than English in the United States. Is your reaction to the use of these languages in public spaces positive, negative, or neutral?

2. Write for five minutes about the experiences your parents (or children) have had with languages other than English in the United States. Are their experiences like yours or different? What is their level of frustration or acceptance?

3. Finally, take five minutes to consider your viewpoint on language diversity in the United States by composing a claim (or assertion). What reason can you provide for your claim? What evidence supports that reason?

4. Does your viewpoint match that of your family members, or is it different from theirs? How do you account for the similarity or difference?

Real Responses to Real Situations

Should we make English the official language of the United States?

There would be no United States were it not for immigration. In fact, the history of this country is directly linked to a sequence of immigrants. The dominant image for the assimilation of the various national and ethnic groups has long been the melting pot. Although many people see the melting pot as a symbol of Americans' openness to immigrants, each new wave of immigrants—Irish, Italians, Eastern Europeans, Asians, or Mexicans—became an object of scorn for those who were already citizens. Throughout U.S. history, immigrants have come to this country to escape danger, poverty, or persecution and to improve their lives. Those who had the easiest time assimilating had Northern European backgrounds, which made it easier for them to blend into the mainstream.

When huge numbers of Latin Americans and Asians arrived in the United States between 1970 and 1990, many joined ever-growing linguistic communities of Chinese, Korean, Japanese, and Spanish speakers who live out their entire lives without learning, let alone using, English. Perceiving these non–English-speaking communities as a threat to English as the dominant U.S. language, some citizens began rallying to make English the official language of the United States. Supporters of this position argue that Americans—regardless of native language—should all speak the same language in order to work toward common national goals and participate fully in public life.

S. I. Hayakawa (1906–1992) served California as a Republican Senator from 1977 to 1983. In 1981, he introduced the first English language amendment to the Constitution. After serving his state and nation, Hayakawa, the son of immigrants and a speaker of English as a second language, helped to found the organization U.S. English, whose dual missions are generating public support for an English language amendment to the Constitution and lobbying congressional representatives to enact such legislation. Subcommittees of the Senate Judiciary Committee, in 1984, and the House Judiciary Committee, in 1988, conducted public hearings on Hayakawa's proposed amendment. Although the U.S Congress has taken no action to add an English language amendment to the Constitution, thirty states have now adopted English as the state's official language in some way, such as an amendment to the state constitution or a legislative statute. Hayakawa outlined the vision guiding English-only supporters in his 1985 policy paper "One Nation . . . Indivisible? The English Language Amendment." According to Hayakawa, an English language amendment to the U.S. Constitution would reinforce the nation's political and cultural values.

Excerpt from

> One Nation . . . Indivisible? The English Language Amendment

S. I. Hayakawa

What is it that has made a society out of the hodgepodge of nationalities, races, and colors represented in the immigrant hordes that people our nation? It is language, of course, that has made communication among all these elements possible. It is with a common language that we have dissolved distrust and fear. It is with language that we have drawn up the understandings and agreements and social contracts that make a society possible. . . .

One need not speak faultless American English to become an American. Indeed, one may continue to speak English with an appalling foreign accent. This is true of some of my friends, but they are seen as fully American because of the warmth and enthusiasm with which they enter into the life of the communities in which they live. . . .

In the past several years, strong resistance to the "melting pot" idea has arisen, especially for those who claim to speak for the Hispanic peoples. Instead of a melting pot, they say, the national ideal should be a "salad bowl," in which different elements are thrown together but not "melted," so that the original ingredients retain their distinctive character. . . .

I welcome the Hispanic—and as a Californian, I especially welcome the Mexican—influence on our culture. My wife was wise enough to insist that both our son and daughter learn Spanish as children and to keep reading Spanish as they were growing up. Consequently, my son, a newspaperman, was able to work for six months as an exchange writer for a newspaper in Costa Rica, while a Costa Rican reporter took my son's place in Oregon. My daughter, a graduate of the University of California at Santa Cruz, speaks Spanish, French, and after a year in Monterey Language School, Japanese.

The ethnic chauvinism of the present Hispanic leadership is an unhealthy trend in present-day America. It threatens a division perhaps more ominous in the long run than the division between blacks and whites. Blacks and whites have problems enough with each other, to be sure, but they quarrel with each other in one language. Even Malcolm X, in his fiery denunciation of the racial situation in America, wrote excellent and eloquent English. But the present politically ambitious "Hispanic Caucus" looks forward to a destiny for Spanish-speaking Americans separate from that of Anglo-, Italian-, Polish-, Greek-, Lebanese-, Chinese-, and Afro-Americans, and all the rest of us who rejoice in our ethnic diversity, which gives us our richness as a culture, and the English language, which keeps us in communication with each other to create a unique and vibrant culture.

The advocates of Spanish language and Hispanic culture are not at all unhappy about the fact that "bilingual education," originally instituted as the best way to teach English, often results in no English being taught at all. Nor does Hispanic leadership seem to be alarmed that large populations of Mexican Americans, Cubans, and Puerto Ricans do not speak English and have no intention of learning. Hispanic spokesmen rejoice when still another concession is made to the Spanish-speaking public, such as the Spanish-language Yellow Pages telephone directory now available in Los Angeles.

"Let's face it. We're not going to be a totally English-speaking country any more," says Aurora Helton of the governor of Oklahoma's Hispanic Advisory Committee. "Spanish should be included in commercials shown throughout America. Every American child ought to be taught both English and Spanish," says Mario Obledo, president

continued

of the League of United Latin American Citizens, which was founded more than a half-century ago to help Hispanics learn English and enter the American mainstream. "Citizenship is what makes us all American. Nowhere does the Constitution say that English is our language," says Maurice Ferré, mayor of Miami, Florida.

"Nowhere does the Constitution say that English is our language." It was to correct this omission that I introduced in April 1981 a constitutional amendment which read as follows: "The English language shall be the official language of the United States." Although there were ten cosponsors to this resolution, and some speeches were given on the Senate floor, it died without being acted upon in the 97th Congress.

But the movement to make English the official language of the nation is clearly gaining momentum. It is likely to suffer an occasional setback in state legislatures because of the doctrinaire liberals' assumption that every demand made by an ethnic minority must be yielded to. But whenever the question of English as the official language has been submitted to a popular referendum or ballot initiative, it has won by a majority of 70 percent or better.

It is not without significance that pressure against English language legislation does not come from any immigrant group other than the Hispanic: not from the Chinese or Koreans or Filipinos or Vietnamese; nor from immigrant Iranians, Turks, Greeks, East Indians, Ghanians, Ethiopians, Italians, or Swedes. The only people who have any quarrel with the English language are the Hispanics—at least the Hispanic politicians and "bilingual" teachers and lobbying organizations. One wonders about the Hispanic rank and file. Are they all in agreement with their leadership? And what does it profit the Hispanic leadership if it gains power and fame, while 50 percent of the boys and girls of their communities, speaking little or no English, cannot make it through high school?

While the U.S. Congress has yet to ratify an English language amendment to the Constitution, English-only legislation is periodically introduced in both houses. On May 6, 2009, for example, Oklahoma Republican Senator James Inhofe introduced a bill to declare English the "national language of the Government of the United States" in order "to promote the patriotic integration of prospective U.S. citizens," further declaring that "no person has a right, entitlement, or claim to have the Government of the United States or any of its officials or representatives act, communicate, perform or provide services, or provide materials in any language other than English" (U.S. Senate, Bill 992).

From the first time an English language amendment was introduced in the U.S. Congress in 1981, the idea has met significant opposition from people who argue that negative legal, social, and cultural consequences would follow passage of such a constitutional amendment. In 1988, a diverse collection of groups (American Civil Liberties Union, American Jewish Congress, Chinese for Affirmative Action, Haitian Refugee Center, Mexican American Legal Defense and Educational Fund, Organization of Chinese Americans, and Teachers of English to Speakers of Other Languages) rallied to counter the English-only movement by forming the English Plus Information Clearinghouse (EPIC). EPIC called on the federal government to expand access to comprehensive English-language instruction and social services in order "to ensure all persons the ability to exercise the rights and responsibilities of full participation in society," a policy EPIC referred to as "English Plus." In addition, EPIC encouraged the federal government to foster multilingualism for all people in order to advance the national interest economically and politically as well as to strengthen the nation's commitment to democratic and cultural pluralism.

The various ethnic groups represented in EPIC reflect a broad-based concern over official English legislation. Some critics (including Juan F. Perea, who is featured later in this chapter) have labeled the ideas of Hayakawa, U.S. English, and the entire English-only movement as anti-immigrant, even nativist; others have questioned the assumptions about language, culture, and politics on which the English-only movement builds its case.

Linguist Geoffrey Nunberg, a researcher at Stanford University's Center for the Study of Language and Information, has attempted to understand the motivations of official English proponents, who continue to push for an English language amendment to the U.S. Constitution. His findings indicate that Hayakawa, U.S. English, and other English-only advocates concern themselves far more with the symbolic importance of the English language—that is, what an individual's competency in English seems to signal about his or her commitment to American ideals and values—than with the practical matters affecting bilingual education and social services.

Excerpt from

> # The Official English Movement: Reimagining America

Geoffrey Nunberg

[L]inguistic diversity is more conspicuous than it was a century ago. To be aware of the large numbers of non-English speakers in 1900, it was necessary to live in or near one of their communities, whereas today it is only necessary to flip through a cable television dial, drive past a Spanish-language billboard, or (in many states) apply for a driver's

continued

"The Official English Movement: Reimagining America" *(continued)*

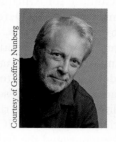

Courtesy of Geoffrey Nunberg

license. As a best guess, there are fewer speakers of foreign languages in America now than there were then, in both absolute and relative numbers. But what matter symbolically [are] the widespread impressions of linguistic diversity, particularly among people who have no actual contact with speakers of languages other than English. . . .

[T]he debate is no longer concerned with the content or effect of particular programs, but the symbolic importance that people have come to attach to these matters. Official English advocates admit as much when they emphasize that their real goal is to "send a message" about the role of English in American life. From this point of view, it is immaterial whether the provision of interpreters for workers' compensation hearings or of foreign-language nutrition information actually constitute a "disincentive" to learning English, or whether their discontinuation would work a hardship on recent immigrants. Programs like these merely happen to be high-visibility examples of government's apparent willingness to allow the public use of languages other than English for any purpose whatsoever. In fact, one suspects that most Official English advocates are not especially concerned about specific programs per se, since they will be able to achieve their symbolic goals even if bilingual services are protected by judicial intervention or legislative inaction (as has generally been the case where Official English measures have passed). The real objective of the campaign is the "message" that it intends to send.

What actually is the message? . . . Proponents of Official English claim that they seek merely to recognize a state of affairs that has existed since the founding of the nation. After two hundred years of common-law cohabitation with English, we have simply decided to make an honest woman of her, for the sake of the children. To make the English language "official," however, is not merely to acknowledge it as the language commonly used in commerce, mass communications, and public affairs. Rather, it is to invest English with a symbolic role in national life and to endorse a cultural conception of American identity as the basis for political unity.

Nunberg sees the official English movement granting a symbolic power to language that previous generations of Americans did not. He explains that the nation's founders believed "the free institutions of the new nation would naturally lead to the formation of a new and independent culture," symbolized by an American variety of English increasingly distinct from the British variety, but today's advocates for official English legislation consider a common language to be a guarantee of the cultural sameness they believe is necessary for political unity.

Every ten years, the U.S. Census Bureau collects, distributes, and analyzes information concerning the demographics of the population, including data on race, age, sex, ancestry, income, and household types. Beginning in 1890, one hundred years after the first census, the Census Bureau started inquiring about language use. The following excerpt discusses some of the most recent findings on the daily language practices of the U.S. public.

Position Arguments

Excerpt from

> Language Use and English-Speaking Ability: Census 2000 Brief

Hyon B. Shin with Rosalind Bruno

The ability to communicate with government and private service providers, schools, businesses, emergency personnel, and many other people in the United States depends on the ability to speak English. In Census 2000, as in the two previous censuses, the U.S. Census Bureau asked people aged 5 and over if they spoke a language other than English at home. Among the 262.4 million people aged 5 and over, 47.0 million (18 percent) spoke a language other than English at home. . . .

These figures were up from 14 percent (31.8 million) in 1990 and 11 percent (23.1 million) in 1980. The number of people who spoke a language other than English at home grew by 38 percent in the 1980s and by 47 percent in the 1990s. While the population aged 5 and over grew by one-fourth from 1980 to 2000, the number who spoke a language other than English at home more than doubled.

In 2000, more people who spoke a language other than English at home reported they spoke English "Very well" (55 percent, or 25.6 million people). When they are combined with those who spoke only English at home, 92 percent of the population aged 5 and over had no difficulty speaking English. The proportion of the population aged 5 and over who spoke English less than "Very well" grew from 4.8 percent in 1980, to 6.1 percent in 1990, and to 8.1 percent in 2000.

continued

. . . Spanish was the largest of the four major language groups (Spanish, Other Indo-European language, Asian and Pacific Island languages, and All other languages), and just over half of the 28.1 million Spanish speakers spoke English "Very well."

Other Indo-European language speakers composed the second largest group, with 10.0 million speakers, almost two-thirds of whom spoke English "Very well." Slightly less than half of the 7.0 million Asian and Pacific Island language speakers spoke English "Very well" (3.4 million). Of the 1.9 million people who composed the All other languages category, 1.3 million spoke English "Very well."

After English and Spanish, Chinese was the most commonly spoken at home (2.0 million speakers), followed by French (1.6 million speakers) and German (1.4 million speakers . . .). Reflecting historical patterns of immigration, the numbers of Italian, Polish, and German speakers fell between 1990 and 2000, while the number of speakers of many other languages increased.

Spanish speakers grew by about 60 percent and Spanish continued to be the non-English language most frequently spoken at home in the United States. The Chinese language, however, jumped from the fifth to the second most widely spoken non-English language, as the number of Chinese speakers rose from 1.2 million to 2.0 million people. . . . The number of Vietnamese speakers doubled over the decade, from about 507,000 speakers to just over 1 million speakers.

Of the 20 non-English languages most frequently spoken at home . . . , the largest proportional increase was for Russian speakers, who nearly tripled from 242,000 to 706,000. The second largest increase was for French Creole speakers (the language group that includes Haitian Creoles), whose numbers more than doubled from 188,000 to 453,000. . . .

In the United States, the ability to speak English plays a large role in how well people can perform daily activities. How well a person speaks English may indicate how well he or she communicates with public officials, medical personnel, and other service providers. It could also affect other activities outside the home, such as grocery shopping or banking. People who do not have a strong command of English and who do not have someone in their household to help them on a regular basis are at even more of a disadvantage. They are defined here as "linguistically isolated."

In 2000, 4.4 million households encompassing 11.9 million people were linguistically isolated. These numbers were significantly higher than in 1990, when 2.9 million households and 7.7 million people lived in [linguistically isolated] households.

The texts you have just read demonstrate that the issue of making English the official U.S. language is a complex one, not easily settled on the basis of a few examples or statistics. The following questions ask you to consider the writings of S. I. Hayakawa and Geoffrey Nunberg in terms of the elements of their respective rhetorical situations. Be sure to reread each excerpt carefully before answering.

1. Who might be the intended audience of each of the two excerpts? How do the audiences for the two excerpts differ? What textual evidence can you provide for your answers?
2. Is the purpose of each excerpt evident? If so, what is it? What are the differences between the excerpts in terms of purpose? How does each purpose relate to the intended audience?
3. To what rhetorical opportunity might each writer be responding? How does the piece of writing work to resolve the problem? Who holds the power to resolve or affect the resolution of the problem?
4. How does each writer deploy the rhetorical appeals of ethos, pathos, and logos to support an opinion of the official English movement? Use passages from each excerpt to support your answer.

© Steven Lunetta Photography, 2007

Living on the margins of English-speaking America

The official English movement has been opposed by a number of professional and public advocacy groups in addition to EPIC. Bilingual educators have argued about the cultural perspective and the sense of cultural identity that nonnative English speakers gain from having their native languages valued in school. And legal scholars have criticized the legal viability of English-only laws, arguing that they constitute national-origin discrimination, which was made illegal by the Civil Rights Act of 1964.

Legal scholar Juan F. Perea may be best known for his analyses of the social consequences of English language amendments, but he has long worked to confront anti-immigration laws and attitudes, as well as national-origin

You can find newspapers in many languages at newsstands in any major U.S. city.

discrimination, in the United States. In the following excerpt, Perea writes of the social and legal situations that prevent ethnic and linguistic minorities from participating fully in U.S. society. For Perea, English language amendments give nonnative English speakers no incentive to learn English or to enter the melting pot. Perea's argument encourages his readers to think more carefully about how the language of Spanish-speaking U.S. citizens affects their public identity.

Excerpt from

> Los Olvidados: On the Making of Invisible People

Juan F. Perea

In his recent book, *Latinos*, Earl Shorris poignantly describes Bienvenida Pation, a Jewish Latino immigrant, who clings to her language and culture "as if they were life itself." When Bienvenida dies, it is "not of illness, but of English." Bienvenida dies of English when she is confined to a nursing home where no one speaks Spanish, an environment in which she cannot communicate and in which no one cares about her language and culture.

"Death by English" is a death of the spirit, the slow death that occurs when one's own identity is replaced, reconfigured, overwhelmed, or rejected by a more powerful, dominant identity. For Latinos, illness by English of varying degree, even death by English, is a common affliction, without known cure. It may be identified, however, by some of its symptoms.

The mere sound of Spanish offends and frightens many English-only speakers, who sense in the language a loss of control over what they regard as "their" country. Spanish also frightens many Latinos, for it proclaims their identity as Latinos, for all to hear. The Latino's fear is rational. Spanish may subject Latinos to the harsh price of difference in the United States: the loss of a job, instant scapegoating, and identification as an outsider. Giving in to this fear and denying one's own identity as a Latino is, perhaps, to begin to die of English.

Latino invisibility is the principal cause of illness by English. When I write of Latino invisibility, I mean a relative lack of positive public identity and legitimacy. Invisibility in this sense is created in several ways. Sometimes we are rendered invisible through the absence of public recognition and portrayal. Sometimes we are silenced through prohibitions on the use of Spanish. Sometimes we are rendered politically invisible, or nearly so, through the attribution of foreignness, what I shall call "symbolic deportation." I do not maintain that Latinos are the only people rendered invisible in America. In many respects the processes of invisibility have more general application. In this chapter, however, I shall discuss only the invisibility I know best: How American culture, history, and laws make "invisible people" out of American Latinos who arrived before the English. . . .

According to its English conquerors, America was always meant to belong to white Englishmen. In 1788, John Jay, writing in the *Federalist* Number 2, declared, "Providence has been pleased to give this one connected country to one united people—a people descended from the same ancestors, speaking the same language, professing the same religion, attached to the same principles of government, very similar in their manner and customs." Although Jay's statement was wrong—early American society was remarkably diverse—his wish that America be a homogeneous, white, English-speaking Anglo society was widely shared by the Framers of the Constitution and other prominent leaders. . . .

The Framers' white America also had to be a predominantly English-speaking America in the words of John Jay and later echoes by Thomas Jefferson. Benjamin Franklin's dislike of the German language was palpable. I will use two examples to illustrate the perceived need for a white and English-speaking America.

In 1807, Jefferson proposed the resettlement, at government expense, of thirty thousand presumably English-speaking Americans in Louisiana in order to "make the majority American, [and] make it an American instead of French State." The first governor of Louisiana, William Claiborne, unsuccessfully attempted to require that all the laws of Louisiana be published in English.

The saga of New Mexico's admission to statehood also illustrates the perceived need for a white and English-speaking America. Despite repeated attempts beginning in 1850, New Mexico did not become a state until 1912, when a majority of its population was English-speaking for the first time. Statehood was withheld from New Mexico for over sixty years because of Congress's unwillingness to grant statehood to a predominantly Spanish-speaking territory populated by Mexican people.

A tremendous disparity, of course, separated the country the Framers desired and the one they came to possess. The country was composed of many groups, of different hues and speaking different languages. Several examples of governmental recognition of American multilingualism illustrate my point. The Continental Congress, hoping to communicate with and win the allegiance of American peoples whose language was different from English, published many significant documents in German and French. After the Revolutionary War, the Articles of Confederation were published in official English, German, and French editions.

continued

Position Arguments

Particularly during much of the nineteenth century, several states had rich legal histories of official bilingualism, by which I mean statutory or constitutional recognitions of languages other than English: Pennsylvania was officially bilingual in German and English; California and New Mexico were officially bilingual in Spanish and English; and Louisiana was officially bilingual in French and English. The implementation of official bilingualism in these several states shared common features. All of the laws of those states were required to be published in more than one language. Although this state-sponsored bilingualism mostly died out during the nineteenth century, New Mexico's official bilingualism was remarkably long-lived. New Mexico was officially bilingual between 1846 and early 1953, over one hundred years.

Most people are not aware of the existence and the extent of American multilingualism and its official, state-sponsored character. I am not aware of any United States history texts that include this material. Nor will you find it in any legal history text. . . .

Latinos are made invisible and foreign . . . despite our longtime presence, substance, and citizenship. Latinos must be recognized as full and equal members of our community. This equality I describe is an equality of respect and of dignity for the full identity and personhood of Latino people. It is an equality and respect for the similarities we share with our fellow Americans. It is also an equality and respect for the differences we contribute to American identity. In 1883, Walt Whitman complained that the states "showed too much of the British and German influence." . . . "To that composite American identity of the future," Whitman wrote, "Spanish character will supply some of the most needed parts." Our Mexican and Latino character continues to supply some of our most needed parts.

In *Hunger of Memory,* Richard Rodriguez reflects on his educational experiences, particularly how his Spanish-language identity at home conflicted with the English-speaking identity he felt that he needed to succeed in public school. For him, learning the English of the classroom offered the public identity necessary for participating in American civic life. In the following excerpt from his book, Rodriguez describes how he came to believe that English should be his "public language" and Spanish his home language. He argues from his own experience that immigrants to the United States remain invisible until they learn the public language of English.

Excerpt from

> Hunger of Memory

Richard Rodriguez

Supporters of bilingual education today imply that students like me miss a great deal by not being taught in their family's language. What they seem not to recognize is that, as a socially disadvantaged child, I considered Spanish to be a private language. What I needed to learn in school was that I had the right—and the obligation—to speak the public language of los gringos. The odd truth is that my first-grade classmates could have become bilingual, in the conventional sense of that word, more easily than I. Had they been taught (as upper-middle-class children are often taught early) a second language like Spanish or French, they could have regarded it simply as that: another public language. In my case such bilingualism could not have been so quickly achieved. What I did not believe was that I could speak a single public language.

Without question, it would have pleased me to hear my teachers address me in Spanish when I entered the classroom. I would have felt much less afraid. I would have trusted them and responded with ease. But I would have delayed—for how long postponed?—having to learn the language of public society. I would have evaded—and for how long could I have afforded to delay?—learning the great lesson of school, that I had a public identity.

Fortunately, my teachers were unsentimental about their responsibility. What they understood was that I needed to speak a public language. So their voices would search me out, asking me questions. Each time I'd hear them, I'd look up in surprise to see a nun's face frowning at me. I'd mumble, not really meaning to answer. The nun would persist, "Richard, stand up. Don't look at the floor. Speak up. Speak to the entire class, not just to me!" But I couldn't believe that the English language was mine to use. (In part, I did not want to believe it.) I continued to mumble. I resisted the teacher's demands. (Did I somehow suspect that once I learned public language my pleasing family life would be

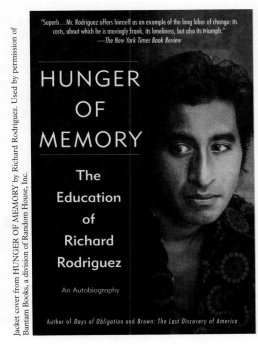

Jacket cover from HUNGER OF MEMORY by Richard Rodriguez. Used by permission of Bantam Books, a division of Random House, Inc.

"Superb...Mr. Rodriguez offers himself as an example of the long labor of change: its costs, about which he is movingly frank, its loneliness, but also its triumph."
—The New York Times Book Review

HUNGER OF MEMORY

The Education of Richard Rodriguez

An Autobiography

Author of *Days of Obligation* and *Brown: The Last Discovery of America*

continued

changed?) Silent, waiting for the bell to sound, I remained dazed, diffident, afraid. . . .

Today I hear bilingual educators say that children lose a degree of "individuality" by becoming assimilated into public society. (Bilingual schooling was popularized in the seventies, that decade when middle-class ethnics began to resist the process of assimilation—the American melting pot.) But the bilingualists simplistically scorn the value and necessity of assimilation. They do not seem to realize that there are two ways a person is individualized. So they do not realize that while one suffers a diminished sense of private individuality by becoming assimilated into public society, such assimilation makes possible the achievement of public individuality.

>ANALYZING THE RHETORICAL SITUATION

1. Compare the excerpts from the writings of Juan F. Perea and Richard Rodriguez. How does each writer explain the invisibility of some people in the United States? What claim does each writer make about this invisibility?
2. What reasons does each writer give for the invisibility? What evidence does each author provide to support his claim?
3. What do the two writers say about resisting or embracing assimilation into the melting pot? How does each writer evaluate the importance of public language?
4. Identify the opportunity, audience, purpose, and context of Perea's and Rodriguez's rhetorical situations. What are the resources and constraints of their contexts? Be prepared to share your answers with the class.

COMMUNITY CONNECTIONS

1. Write for ten minutes about your own perspective on the English-only movement. What do you think about Hayakawa's aim of adding an English language amendment to the U.S. Constitution or about the arguments of U.S. English? What statement, or claim, can you make to summarize your position?

2. Write for five minutes about the vision of public life that Hayakawa believes an English language amendment will reflect. What positive

consequences does he see arising from making English the official language of the United States? What claim might you make about such positive effects?

3. Write for another five minutes about the negative consequences that might follow from making English the official language of the United States. What claim can you make? What reasons can you provide to back up your claim? What evidence can you provide?

4. Perea writes, "Most people are not aware of the existence and the extent of American multilingualism and its official, state-sponsored character." Were you aware of the multilingual history of the United States? If so, where and when did you learn about it? If not, why do you suppose you never heard of it? Write for ten minutes about your response to Perea's historical overview, including how you knew—or why you didn't know—about the history of American multilingualism. At the end of the ten minutes, write one sentence that captures your opinion on multilingualism. If possible, make a claim about multilingualism.

5. Both Perea and Rodriguez talk about how language shapes both public and private identities. How would you characterize the language-based differences between these two identities? What are the roots of these differences? Using your own experiences or those of someone you know well, write for five to ten minutes on how a person can use language to distinguish his or her public and private selves.

6. Rodriguez argues that Latinos who push for public bilingualism think they can "have it both ways"—that is, can participate in public life while retaining their cultural and ethnic identities. Drawing on your observations of life in the United States and within your community, do you think it is possible for people to "have it both ways"? On what evidence do you base your conclusion?

7. Perea and Rodriguez have different views of the emphasis the mainstream culture in the United States should place on the cultural and linguistic heritages of minority communities. After writing a sentence that captures the view of each of these writers, write for ten minutes about whether each view has crucial implications for education, focusing on your own campus community or hometown. Provide specific evidence from both excerpts to support your claim.

Position Arguments: A Fitting Response

An argument about language diversity in the United States

As you have learned in this chapter, many people—from politicians and scholars to activist groups and individuals—have made arguments about the political, economic, social, and cultural consequences of the use of non-English languages in the United States. Some of these arguments (Hayakawa's and Perea's, for instance) attempt to present objective analyses of how particular laws or policies will or will not bring about certain ends. Equally compelling are the narratives of writers such as Rodriguez who argue for or against official recognition of language diversity in the United States by describing personal experiences.

Let's consider another example of an argument from personal experience. In an editorial, Gabriela Kuntz, a retired elementary-school teacher living in Cape Girardeau, Missouri, tells why her own painful experiences of ethnic and linguistic discrimination have led her to decide not to teach her children Spanish.

My Spanish Standoff

Gabriela Kuntz

Kuntz indirectly presents her position in the introduction. She alludes to the counterarguments, too.

Once again my 17-year-old daughter comes home from a foreign-language fair at her high school and accusingly tells me about the pluses of being able to speak two languages. Speaker after speaker has extolled the virtues of becoming fluent in another language. My daughter is frustrated by the fact that I'm bilingual and have purposely declined to teach her to speak Spanish, my native tongue. She is not the only one who has wondered why my children don't speak Spanish. Over the years friends, acquaintances and family have asked me the same question. Teachers have asked my children. My family, of course, has been more judgmental.

This final sentence creates the impression that the writer has thought hard about her decision and has strong reasons to support her argument.

I was born in Lima, Peru, and came to the United States for the first time in the early '50s, when I was 6 years old. At the parochial school my sister and I attended in Hollywood, Calif., there were only three Hispanic families at the time. I don't know when or how I learned English. I guess it was a matter of survival. My teacher spoke no Spanish. Neither did my classmates. All I can say is that at some point I no longer needed to translate. When I spoke in English I thought in English, and when I spoke in Spanish I thought in Spanish. I also learned about peanut-butter-and-jelly sandwiches, Halloween and Girl Scouts.

By saying that she "also learned about peanut-butter-and-jelly sandwiches, Halloween and Girl Scouts," Kuntz implicitly argues that learning English marks an important part of the process of becoming "American."

We went to a high school in Burbank. Again, there were few Hispanic students at the time. My sister and I spoke English without an "accent." This pleased my father to no end. He would beam with pleasure when teachers, meeting him and my mother for the first time and hearing their labored English, would comment that they had no idea English was not our native tongue.

My brother was born in Los Angeles in 1959, and we would speak both English and Spanish to him. When he began to talk, he would point to an object and say its name in both languages. He was, in effect, a walking, talking English-Spanish dictionary. I have often wondered how his English would have turned out, but circumstances beyond our control prevented it. Because of political changes in Peru in the early '60s (my father being a diplomat), we had to return to Peru. Although we had no formal schooling in Spanish, we were able to communicate in the language. I was thankful my parents had insisted that we speak Spanish at home. At first our relatives said that we spoke Spanish with a slight accent. But over time the accent disappeared, and we became immersed in the culture, our culture. My brother began his schooling in Peru, and even though he attended a school in which English was taught, he speaks the language with an accent. I find that ironic because he was the one born in the United States, and my sister and I are the naturalized citizens.

In 1972 I fell in love and married an American who had been living in Peru for a number of years. Our first son was born there, but when he was 6 months old, we came back to the States. My husband was going to get his doctorate at a university in Texas.

It was in Texas that, for the first time, I lived in a community with many Hispanics in the United States. I encountered them at the grocery store, the laundry, the mall, church. I also began to see how the Anglos in the community treated them. Of course, I don't mean all, but enough to make me feel uncomfortable. Because I'm dark and have dark eyes and hair, I personally experienced that look, that unspoken and spoken word expressing prejudice. If I entered a department store, one of two things was likely to happen. Either I was ignored, or I was followed closely by the salesperson. The garments I took into the changing room were carefully counted. My check at the grocery store took more scrutiny than an Anglo's. My children were complimented on how "clean" they were instead of how cute. Somehow, all Hispanics seemed to be lumped into the category of illegal immigrants, notwithstanding that many Hispanic families have lived for generations in Texas and other Southwestern states.

To be fair, I also noticed that the Latinos lived in their own enclaves, attended their own churches, and many of them spoke English with an accent. And with their roots firmly established in the United States, their Spanish was not perfect either.

It was the fact that they spoke neither language well and the prejudice I experienced that prompted my husband and me to decide that English, and English only, would be spoken in our house. By this time my second dark-haired, dark-eyed son had been born, and we did not want to take a chance that if I spoke Spanish to them, somehow their English would be compromised. In other words, they would have an accent. I had learned to speak English without one, but I wasn't sure they would.

When our eldest daughter was born in 1980, we were living in southeast Missouri. Again, we decided on an English-only policy. If our children were going to live in the United States, then their English

Kuntz juxtaposes the uncontrollable circumstances that influenced her brother's language development and those surrounding her daughter, which Kuntz has controlled as much as possible.

Kuntz concedes a point to those who disagree with her position. She has yet to reveal her reasons for not teaching her child Spanish.

The writer signals that she is shifting to the reasons supporting her argument. Yet this paragraph does not mention the Spanish language.

Kuntz uses the phrase "to be fair" to anticipate readers' objections.

Kuntz presents the major reasons supporting her argument that she's doing her daughter a service by not teaching her Spanish.

Position Arguments

Kuntz anticipates readers' counterarguments with this question and then answers them in the next sentences.

Kuntz begins to situate her personal decision within the context of larger public events.

Kuntz ties together earlier strands of her argument in which she juxtaposed racial discrimination and linguistic discrimination.

should be beyond reproach. Of course, by eliminating Spanish we have also eliminated part of their heritage. Am I sorry? About the culture, yes; about the language, no. In the Missouri Legislature, there are bills pending for some sort of English-only law. I recently read an article in a national magazine about the Ozarks where some of the townspeople are concerned about the numbers of Hispanics who have come to work in poultry plants there. It seemed to me that their "concerns" were actually prejudice. There is a definite creeping in of anti-Hispanic sentiment in this country. Even my daughter, yes, the one who is upset over not being bilingual, admits to hearing "Hispanic jokes" said in front of her at school. You see, many don't realize, despite her looks, that she's a minority. I want to believe that her flawless English is a contributing factor.

Last summer I took my 10-year-old daughter to visit my brother, who is working in Mexico City. She picked up a few phrases and words with the facility that only the very young can. I just might teach her Spanish. You see, she is fair with light brown hair and blue eyes.

■ GUIDE TO RESPONDING TO THE RHETORICAL SITUATION

Understanding the Rhetorical Situation

When you want to help an audience understand your point of view—and you're prepared to use logical, emotional, and ethical appeals to deliver that point—you want to consider composing a position argument. Arguments commonly have the following features:

- Arguments vividly describe a problem or issue.
- Arguments are directed toward an audience with a clear connection to or investment in the problem being addressed.
- Arguments include a concise statement of the writer's point of view.
- Arguments provide reasons in support of the writer's position, and each supporting reason takes into account the audience's beliefs, attitudes, and values.
- Arguments contain specific evidence—details, examples, and direct quotations—to back each supporting reason.
- Arguments describe the benefits that will be achieved by responding to the writer's position in the intended way or the negative situation that will result from ignoring it.

The following sections will help you compose a position argument about language diversity. To work with an online guide to the elements of the rhetorical situation, access your English CourseMate through CengageBrain.com.

Identifying an opportunity

Consider the communities you are part of—academic, activist, artistic, athletic, professional, civic, ethnic, national, political, or religious. What language practices or attitudes toward language have shaped your experiences within each group? You might, for example, think about how your soccer team developed a shared vocabulary for cheering each other on, one not shared by family members or friends on the sidelines. Or perhaps you've noticed that your ability to communicate in more than one language has been seen as a positive thing in many of your communities but not, strangely, in others. Maybe you're a member of an online community in which certain rules have been established about language use. The point is to reflect on the unique role that language plays within a particular group so that you can identify a rhetorical opportunity.

1. Make a list of the communities with which you identify most strongly. For each group, list several significant or unique language

experiences that have marked your participation in that group. If the experiences were positive, explain why, providing as many details as possible. If the experiences were negative, describe the factors that made them difficult or unpleasant. Also, write down any rules—whether written or unwritten—that influence the ways in which you or other group members use language to participate in the community.

2. Choosing one or two of your communities, take photos or sketch pictures of group members speaking, writing, texting, posting updates to Facebook or Twitter, or engaging in some other use of language. Or download a screenshot illustrating a relevant example of the group's online communication. Whatever visual you choose should illustrate details or features that make the community's language use compelling to examine.

3. Choose the community whose language practices or rules you want to write about and compose four or five descriptions of a problem related to language use in that community. Vary the ways you describe the problem. For example, one description might emphasize how some people are marginalized by an online community member's language practice, and another might emphasize the ways in which others in the community respond to or ignore this language practice. Another description might focus on the process by which rules for language use are communicated to new group members, and yet another might describe what ideal seems to guide the online community's language use.

Locating an audience

The following questions can help you locate your rhetorical audience as well as identify the audience's relationship to the problem you're addressing. Then, you'll be able to choose the best way to describe that problem.

1. List the names of the persons or groups who are affected directly or indirectly by the problem you're addressing.

2. Next to the name of each potential audience, write reasons that audience could have for acknowledging the existence of your problem. In other words, what would persuade these audiences that something needs to change or that they need to view the situation in a new way?

3. What actions could these audiences reasonably be persuaded to perform? What new perspectives could they be expected to adopt? In other words, consider what each audience would be able to do to resolve this problem.

4. With your audience's interests and capabilities in mind, look again at the descriptions of the problem that you composed in the preceding section. Decide which description will best help your audience feel connected to the situation as you've described

it. Be open to revising your best description in order to tailor it to the audience's attitudes, beliefs, experiences, and values.

Identifying a fitting response

Different purposes and different audiences require different kinds of texts. For example, a lack of local resources for people who speak languages other than English might prompt you to create a newsletter that draws attention to the daily challenges these people face and argues for a greater public commitment to addressing this problem. Community debate over an English-only policy or a bilingual education program might lead you to write a letter to the county commissioners or the school board to highlight an important aspect of the issue they may be overlooking. As these two examples suggest, once you identify your problem, audience, and purpose, you need to determine what kind of text will best respond to the rhetorical situation.

Use the following questions to help you narrow your purpose and shape your response:

1. What reasons support the argument you want to make? What evidence or examples can you provide to persuade readers that each supporting reason is valid?
2. Which supporting reasons are most likely to resonate with your audience? What are the audience's beliefs, attitudes, or experiences that lead you to this conclusion?
3. What specific response are you hoping to draw from your audience? Do you want the audience to feel more confident in its current position? Do you want the audience to listen to and consider an overlooked position? Or do you want the audience to take some specific action to address the problem you're trying to resolve?
4. What is the best way to present your argument to your audience? That is, what kind of text is this audience most likely to respond to? (Chapter 10 can help you explore options for media and design.)

Writing a Position Argument: Working with Your Available Means

Shaping your position argument

You are likely familiar with the form and arrangement of position arguments because you come across examples of this genre in your daily life. The introduction of an argumentative essay grabs an audience's attention as it describes the problem in a way that helps readers page 310 see how it concerns them as well as why the situation needs their atten-

Introduction	Body	Conclusion
▶ Establishes ethos ▶ Describes the problem ▶ Makes clear how the problem concerns the audience ▶ Emphasizes why the time to address the problem is now ▶ States the thesis	▶ Outlines the major reasons supporting the argument ▶ Connects the reasons to the thesis ▶ Presents evidence and examples in the form of facts and figures, direct quotations, brief narratives ▶ In other words, establishes logos	▶ Reinforces the benefits for an audience of responding to the writer's argument in the intended way ▶ May illustrate the negative situation that will result if the writer's argument is ignored

tion right now. The introduction also states the thesis, which presents the writer's argument in a single sentence or short string of sentences; supporting reasons might also be presented in the introduction in a cluster of concise sentences following the thesis statement.

The body of an argumentative essay provides the major reasons supporting the argument. Here the writer not only presents the supporting reasons but also explains how each reason strengthens his or her larger argument. And, as you have already learned, the stronger supporting reasons are those that connect to readers' beliefs, values, and attitudes. For example, Gabriela Kuntz grounds much of her argument in support of English-only education on two interrelated supporting reasons: learning to speak and write only in English improves one's ability to speak the language "without an accent"; speaking "without an accent" improves one's ability to live in the United States without facing discrimination and to fully assimilate into mainstream culture. The first of Kuntz's supporting reasons projects a logical appeal, as it reinforces readers' commonsense understanding of how language learning works (although many bilingual educators would refute this claim). Kuntz's second supporting reason creates an emotional appeal, as it connects with readers' belief that all people should have an equal opportunity to succeed in life. Ultimately, the success of most arguments depends on how well the writer has identified the audience's core beliefs and values and how successfully the writer has supported her or his argument with reasons that speak to those beliefs and values.

pages 309–310 In addition, writers use the body of an argumentative essay to present evidence and examples that create stronger logos and ethos appeals. Writers present facts and figures, direct quotations, and brief narratives to persuade readers that each supporting reason does strengthen the larger argument. Any of these supports may be presented through words (written or spoken) or images. For example, Juan F. Perea uses historical evidence to show that the belief that the United States should have English as its official language is long-standing. By quoting John Jay and Thomas Jefferson, Perea supports his analysis of the ways in which Latinos have been made to seem invisible in the language of government documents. Perea presents historical evidence to advance both a logical and an ethical appeal, demonstrating that he has the good sense to draw on a documented, shared history to support his argument.

The body of an argumentative essay also acknowledges and responds to counterarguments and opposing viewpoints. This rhetorical move helps writers not only to create stronger logical appeals, as they address possible gaps in their arguments, but also to project more convincing ethical appeals, as they show readers that they are open to considering alternative perspectives on the issue. Kuntz, for example, acknowledges that "by eliminating Spanish" from her children's education, she and her husband "have also eliminated part of their heritage." She presents herself as being open to the views of English-only opponents who lament the loss of people's culture and who perceive "a definite creeping in of anti-Hispanic sentiment in this country." At the same time, though, Kuntz asserts that she's not sorry her daughter has lost the language of her heritage because, Kuntz explains, her daughter's "flawless English" has helped her to assimilate into mainstream U.S. culture. Ultimately, Kuntz shows readers she has weighed her argument against compelling counterarguments.

Finally, the conclusion of an argumentative essay reinforces the benefits that will be realized if the audience responds to the writer's argument in the intended way. Or, conversely, the conclusion may illustrate the negative situation that will result if the writer's argument is ignored.

Avoiding rhetorical fallacies

As you develop information that advances your thesis and supports specific points in your argument, you'll want to take care that your reasoning is logical, that you're enhancing the overall effectiveness of your argument as well as your own ethos. Constructing your argument logically requires avoiding **rhetorical fallacies**, which are errors in reasoning or logic.

Sloppy reasoning, snap judgments, quickly drawn conclusions, missing data, one-sided opinions—all of these signal that a writer's or speaker's thinking is not trustworthy and that the argument is not well reasoned. When we encounter problems in someone else's argument, we respond with "That's simply not so," "That's an unfair tactic," "Just because X happened doesn't mean Y will," or "What does that have to do with anything?" Because it's often easier to detect the flaws in someone else's argument than in our own, even the most experienced writers inadvertently make these errors in arguments.

pages 312–314

Non sequitur The phrase *non sequitur* is Latin for "it does not follow." The non sequitur rhetorical fallacy serves as the basis for many
other fallacies, for it is an error in cause-and-effect analysis, a faulty
conclusion about consequences. "Helen loves the stars; she'll major in
astronomy." "My client is not guilty of speeding because he did not see
the posted speed limit." "I need a raise because of my child support
payments." "The war in Vietnam was a disaster for the United States;
therefore, U.S. troops should not be in Iraq." Each of these statements
is based on the faulty claim that there's a logical connection between
the parts of the statement.

Ad hominem The Latin phrase *ad hominem* translates as "toward the
man himself." The ad hominem fallacy is an attack on a person, which
draws attention away from the actual issue under consideration. So, for
example, rather than discussing the problem of fidelity in your relationship, you criticize your partner's weight. You attack the person rather
than the opinion that person holds: "I don't want golfing tips from my
neighbor, even if she is a professional golfer—that woman believes in
X." Whether the belief relates to a woman's right to abortion, the value
of plastic surgery, the importance of a war in Iraq, gay marriage, a comprehensive health plan, or lower taxes, the speaker is refusing the golf
tips for the wrong reason.

Appeal to tradition Many people resist change—it unsettles their routines and makes them uncomfortable. Such people often invoke an appeal to tradition; in other words, "That's how we've always done it, so
you should, too" or, to put it another way, "That's how it's always been
done, so it should continue." This appeal is often used in political campaigns ("Four more years"), by social groups ("We've never invited
X or Y to Thanksgiving; why would we start?"), and in many other situations ("My family always fills the gas tank before getting on the highway, so you should fill up now"; "My mother always uses Crisco in her
pie crust, so I should, too").

Bandwagon The bandwagon argument is "Everyone's doing or thinking it, so you should, too." Highway patrol officers often hear "Everyone else was speeding, so I was merely keeping up with the traffic."
Parents hear from their children that everyone else is getting to go to
that concert, everyone else has a certain kind of cell phone, and everyone else text-messages during the night.

Begging the question Often referred to as a "circular argument" and
similar to equivocation, begging the question involves simply restating
the initial arguable claim as though it were a conclusion or a good rea-

son. In other words, that arguable claim has not been supported in any way. "O. J. Simpson did not kill his wife because he is a world-class football player, not a murderer." "I can talk to my parents any way I choose because of freedom of speech." "We must test students more in order to improve their test scores." In each of these examples, the initial claim needs to be established and argued, whether it's Simpson's innocence, your right to speak to your parents as you choose, or that low test scores can be blamed on too little testing.

False analogy Effective writers and speakers often use analogies to equate two unlike things, explaining one in terms of the other—for example, comparing a generous grandma with an ATM machine or a diamond ring with eternal love. False analogies, however, stretch beyond the valid resemblance to create an invalid comparison. "Vietnam War veterans were greeted by the animosity of an antiwar U.S. populace; Iraqi war veterans will surely return to the same antipathy." "Like the beautiful and talented Elizabeth Taylor, Jennifer Lopez will also be married at least eight times."

False authority One of the most prevalent rhetorical fallacies, false authority assumes that an expert in one field is credible in another field. Just think of all the professional athletes and celebrities who argue that a particular brand of car, coffee, undershorts, or soft drink or a particular vacation, charge card, or political candidate is the best one, and you'll understand immediately how false authority works—and why it's often undetected. When celebrity Jenny McCarthy discovered that her son presented the symptoms of autism, she set to work, investigating the biomedical reasons for his symptoms and drastically changing his diet and her family's cleaning, eating, and living habits. She also helped launch Generation Rescue, a coalition of doctors, parents, and children who believe that autism and related neurological disorders "are environmental illnesses caused by an overload of heavy metals, live viruses, and bacteria. Proper treatment . . . is leading to recovery for thousands." In her role as spokeswoman for the organization, McCarthy writes, "I want to offer you the same hope that Generation Rescue offered me. Many children can and do recover from autism. Recovery is real!" McCarthy's words have encouraged many families to follow her lead. But where does her authority lie? She's an actress, an activist, and a mom, but not a physician.

AP Photo/Jose Luis Magana

False cause Also referred to by the Latin phrase *post hoc, ergo propter hoc*, the fallacy of false cause is the assumption that because A occurs before B, A is therefore the *cause* of B. We all know that events that follow each other do not necessarily have a causal relationship—although I sneezed right before the lights went out, my sneeze did not cause the electrical outage. The false-cause fallacy, however, occurs when there might actually be some relationship between the two events but not a direct one: "Jim got fired from his job, and his wife divorced him; therefore, his job loss caused his divorce." Jim's job loss might have been the last of several job losses he suffered in the past three years, and his wife, tired of depending on him to hold a job, filed for divorce.

False dilemma Also referred to as the "either/or fallacy," the false-dilemma fallacy sets up only two choices in a complex situation, when in fact there are more than two choices. In addition, the false dilemma offers the writer's or speaker's choice as the only good choice, presenting the only other choice as unthinkable. "If we don't spank our children, they will run wild." "If you don't get straight A's, you won't be able to get a job." These examples offer only one right choice and no analysis of a complex situation.

Guilt by association An unfair attempt to make someone responsible for the beliefs or actions of others, guilt by association is one of the reasons so many Arabs living in the United States were brutally beaten and persecuted in other ways after the September 11th attacks. Many innocent Arabs suffered for the deeds of the Arab terrorists. Social tensions in the United States often stem from this fallacy and are passed on for the same reason: "those people" are bad—whether they are members of a racial, ethnic, or religious group, a particular profession, or a certain family.

Hasty generalization A conclusion based on too little evidence or on exceptional or biased evidence, the hasty generalization results in statements such as "Fred will never get into law school when he didn't even pass his poli sci exam" or "Mexican food is fattening." The otherwise very intelligent Fred may have a good reason for failing one exam, and although beef and cheese burritos may well be high in calories, many Mexican dishes rely on the healthy staples of black beans and rice.

Oversimplification Closely related to hasty generalization, oversimplification occurs when a speaker or writer jumps to conclusions by omitting relevant considerations. "Just say 'No'" was the anti-drug battle cry of the 1980s, but avoiding drug use can be much more complicated than just saying no. The "virginity pledge" is an oversimplified solution to the

Position Arguments

problem of unwanted teenage pregnancy, as it ignores the fact that many teenagers need to become educated about human sexuality, safe sex practices, sexually transmitted disease, and aspects of teen social and sexual behavior.

"Decoy ducks on the lake, scapegoats in the paddock, and red herrings on the fishing line. If this is a cover-up, it's big..."

Red herring A false clue or an assertion intended to divert attention from the real issue under consideration, the red herring is intended to mislead, whether it appears in a mystery novel or in an argument. "Why go to the doctor for a mammogram when I haven't been able to stop smoking, and smoking is known to cause cancer?" "We cannot defeat the piracy in Somalia when we're involved in the Israeli-Palestinian conflict." The real issues in the preceding statements (the importance of getting a mammogram and defeating piracy) are blurred by other issues that, while important, are not the primary ones under consideration.

Slippery slope In order to show that an initial claim is unacceptable, the slippery slope fallacy presents a sequence of increasingly unacceptable events that are said to be sure to follow from that initial claim: "Confidential letters of recommendation allow for damning comments." "If I accept your late paper, I'll have to let anyone else who asks turn in late papers." "Marijuana is the gateway drug to crack cocaine and then heroin." "A national health plan will lead to 'death panels.'" We hear these kinds of slippery slope arguments every day, in contexts from weight loss ("You're losing too much weight; you'll end up anorexic") to taste in music ("Once you start listening to gansta rap, you'll become violent").

Revision and peer review

After you've drafted your argument, ask one of your classmates to read it. You'll want your classmate to respond to your work in a way that helps you revise it into the strongest argument it can be, one that addresses your intended audience, helps you fulfill your purpose, and is delivered in the most appropriate means available to you.

Questions for a peer reviewer

1. To what opportunity for change is the writer responding?
2. Who might be the writer's intended audience?
3. What might be the writer's purpose?
4. What information did you receive from the introduction? How effective is the introduction? What suggestions do you have for the writer for improving the introduction?
5. Note the writer's thesis statement. If you cannot locate a thesis statement, what thesis statement might work for this argument?
6. Note the assertions the writer makes to support the thesis. Are they presented in chronological or emphatic order? Does the writer use the order that seems most effective? Would you re-order some of the assertions?
7. If you cannot locate a series of assertions, what assertions could be made to support the thesis statement?
8. Note the supporting ideas (presented through narration, cause-and-effect analysis, description, exemplification, process analysis, or definition) that the writer uses to support his or her assertions.
9. How does the writer establish ethos? How could the writer strengthen this appeal?
10. What material does the writer use to establish logos? How might the writer strengthen this appeal (see questions 6–8)?
11. How does the writer make use of pathos?
12. What did you learn from the conclusion that you didn't already know after reading the introduction and the body? What information does the writer want you to take away from the argument? Does the writer attempt to change your attitude, action, or opinion?
13. What section of the argument did you most enjoy? Why?

Visual Argument

This visual argument is in the form of an editorial cartoon by John Darkow. To view the cartoon, find *Arguments in Three Media* in your English Course-Mate, accessed through CengageBrain.com.

Image: John Darkow, Columbia Daily Tribune, Missouri/Cagle Cartoons

Online Argument

Anand Giridharadas of the *New York Times* has written an argument about language in the digital age. To read the article, find *Arguments in Three Media* in your English Course-Mate, accessed through CengageBrain.com.

Image: Photo by Priya Parker

Print Argument

In the following essay, student Alicia Williams develops her position on American Sign Language (ASL), which she believes is an authentic, live, and vibrant language with a rich history and vital present. ----------

Image: Courtesy of the author of the student paper.

Position Arguments

Alicia Williams has strong opinions about the status of ASL as a language and became interested in how the English-only movement might affect it. Alicia knew that, as a deaf person, she could have written a personal narrative such as a memoir or autobiography that would shed light on her experiences and beliefs. She could also have joined forces with others concerned about English-only education and started a letter-writing campaign to influence the local school board. But Alicia decided that a good first step would be to further understand how ASL, like Spanish, Tagalog, or Mandarin Chinese, is a language affected by English-only policies. She could then use a position argument to help her develop and present her thoughts for others to consider. Notice that she includes photographs that she has taken herself to support her argument and aid readers who do not know ASL.

Alicia Williams

Professor Glenn

English 275

November 20, 2009

The Ethos of American Sign Language

The termination of the Bilingual Education Act was followed by the
No Child Left Behind Act (2001), thus removing a bilingual approach
from the education tracks of non-English native speakers. The loss of

Alicia
identifies a
problem and
establishes her
character as
an informed,
engaged,
reasonable
writer (ethos).
At the end of
this paragraph
she directs
her readers to
her thesis, a
statement that
includes her
point of view
with regard to
the problem.

bilingual education has caused the political group English First to lobby
hard for an English-only education that purports to produce truly
American citizens. This, in turn, produces more momentum for the
group's side project: making English the official language of the United
States of America. Not only does this negate the melting pot of languages
in America, but it diminishes the impact of a truly unique language—
American Sign Language (ASL). The drive for English-only education
treats the manifestations of language through a purely verbal platform,
thereby perpetuating long-held prejudices and the common mistaken
assumption that ASL is not, in fact, a language.

Only fifty years ago did ASL receive its long overdue recognition as

Alicia provides
a historical
overview of
the problem
as well as
reasons for her
point of view.
She includes
specific details
and a direct
quotation
(logos).

a distinct language, rather than being perceived as a "hindrance to
English," a "bastardization of English," or even a "communication
disorder." By the end of the nineteenth century, during the rise of formal
educational instruction in ASL for the Deaf, an oppositional camp
known as Oralists had fervently portrayed signing by the Deaf
community as a pathological version of spoken language.[1] A few even
preposterously correlated deafness with low intelligence. Ironically, the
husband of a Deaf woman, Alexander Graham Bell, who was the inventor

of the telephone and hearing aids, was a supporter of the Oralists'
philosophy. He endorsed "genetic counseling for the deaf, outlawing
intermarriages between deaf persons, suppression of sign language,
elimination of residential schools for the deaf, and the prohibition of deaf
teachers of the deaf " (Stewart and Akamatsu 242).

Oralism faced counteractions by the numerous, though less famous,
people who were working for the needs of the Deaf community as its
educators. They understood that ASL is requisite for a deaf person's
social, cultural, and lingual needs. The Deaf community managed to keep
its educational programs intact without losing ASL, though not without
struggle. It was not until a half-century later, in the 1960s, that William
Stokoe's linguistic analysis of ASL produced the much-needed
equilibrium between the Deaf and hearing communities concerning the
legitimacy of ASL. Even so, when most people talk about language, their
thinking assumes communication through speaking: most classify as
unconventional forms of language outside of a verbal modality. Native
signers such as myself understand that our minority language must
coexist with a dominant majority language, but the practice of reducing
ASL to a type of communication disorder or, worse, obliterating it for the
spoken English-only movement, ignores the historical presence of Deaf
culture in America, as well as the key characteristics ASL shares with the
evolution of languages.

ASL was derived from French Sign Language (FSL) in the early
nineteenth century. Harlan Lane and François Grosjean, prominent ASL
linguists, found supporting evidence for this date from "the establishment
of the first American school for the deaf in 1817 at Hartford,
Connecticut. . . . Its founders, Thomas Gallaudet and Laurent Clerc,

In sentence 2, Alicia launches an assertion for her thesis, which is followed by specific narrative details, arranged in chronological order (logos). She ends this paragraph with an emotional connection with her audience (pathos).

Alicia continues to shape her argument with additional specific details and facts (logos).

Position Arguments

were both educated in the use of FSL prior to 1817" (Stewart and Akamatsu 237). Historically speaking, David Stewart and C. Tane Akamatsu have determined that "approximately 60% of the signs in present-day ASL had their origin in FSL" (237). The modification of a parent language, such as FSL for the birth of ASL, is part of the process spoken language has undergone in its evolution throughout history, producing our contemporary languages. For instance, the English spoken in England during Shakespeare's lifetime is not the same English spoken in America today; nonetheless, they are both of English tradition.

Another characteristic that ASL has in common with other languages is that it changes from one generation to another. Undoubtedly, spoken languages continue to change. For instance, slang words used now may not be the same when the toddlers of today are in college. ASL also experiences these changes, which is contrary to a common misconception that the signs in ASL are concrete in nature, meaning there are no changes. For example, an obsolete sign for "will/ future" is conveyed by holding your right arm bent in a ninety-degree angle with your fingertips parallel to the ground. Then you move your entire forearm upward to a forty-five-degree angle in one swift movement. The modern sign starts with an open palm touching the right jawline, underneath the ear; then the forearm moves forward until the arm is in a ninety-degree position, equivalent to the starting position of the arm in the old form. The evolution of signs is comparable to the changing connotations of various words found in the history of languages.

In the process of its shift to physical hand gestures and appropriate facial expressions, ASL does not discard the traditional syntax of language, maintaining its legitimacy as a distinct language. The rich

She opens this paragraph with another assertion that supports her thesis (logos), using process-analysis information arranged chronologically for support.

Another assertion is supported with a detailed comparison and contrast analysis and direct quotations for support (logos).

complexity of ASL's syntax conveys itself through designated facial expressions and specific sign constructions, demonstrating that "ASL is governed by the same organizational principles as spoken languages . . . [despite] essential differences based on the fact that ASL is produced in three-dimensional space" (Neidle et al. 30). As every language has a syntactical structure, so does ASL.

Despite its similarities to languages such as English, it is a mistake to think of ASL as pathology of spoken English. Perpetuating this myth is the misconception that ASL signs are direct translations of English. ASL has rules of its own, which are not identical to those of English syntax. In English, for instance, one says, "Who hates Smitty?" but in ASL, it is signed "Hate Smitty who?" The photos in Fig. 1 show another example of how signs in ASL are not a direct translation of English, but also show how differing hand placements denote different pronouns used with the verb *give*.

Her assertion is supported with a specific example, which she brings to life with visuals (logos).

Stokoe's work establishing the legitimacy of ASL spurred a movement for a bilingual approach in educating the deaf. The teaching of

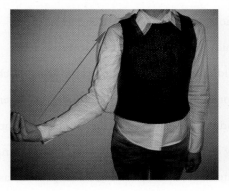

Fig. 1. The photograph on the left shows the signing of "Me give to him or her," and the photograph on the right shows that of "Me give to you." (Photographs by the author.)

Position Arguments

ASL was a top priority because of the hardship of expecting the Deaf

community to acquire English as our native language, which carries a disadvantage by working on a modality inaccessible to us—hearing. In the bilingual approach, after the deaf child has attained a solid working background in ASL, some parents elect to have oral English taught as a second language. The success of English as a second language is largely subject to the individual's capabilities, which are dependent on numerous factors. My parents chose the bilingual approach in my education track at Rufus Putnam Elementary School (for the Deaf). While I maintained my fluency in ASL, I developed an efficacy at speech reading (informally known as lip reading). For instance, when I speak, I am able to convince hearing persons that I am not deaf. In my Deaf community, I always resort to my first language—ASL. All this would not be possible if Oralism or English First were successful in a push for *spoken* English only.

My bilingual background has been met with fierce opposition from hearing people who believe ASL is a crutch language and that it is an

antiquated solution for the Deaf community. In other words, they believe the advances of medical technology will enable researchers to develop revolutionary digital hearing aids, while aggressively diagnosing deaf children at younger ages should cause a decreasing need for ASL, which they assume is a diminished form of English. But if ASL meets all other criteria of what linguists consider a language—with the exception of the use of a vocal apparatus—how can it be called a "crutch language"? And hearing aids only amplify whatever remaining hearing a deaf person has, if any at all; they do not compensate for hearing loss. Even if a doctor diagnoses a deaf child at birth, the child's sensorineural hearing loss may be so severe that spoken language will be impractical to acquire, whereas ASL will be a better approach for the child.[2] In rare cases, adults who become deaf later in their lives find comfort in ASL, rather than English. The naturalization associated with the visual-spatial lingual framework of ASL is uniquely characteristic of the Deaf community because it operates to their advantage, bypassing the confines of oral-aural languages. The use of a verbal apparatus in spoken languages is a natural reaction from the body possessing a functional audio-physiological system. Often this is not the case within the Deaf community; hence that is why ASL is deeply embedded in its culture and will remain the staple of its community, regardless of technology's novelty or the hearing community's desire to push for English-only education.

The most primeval function of language is to create a medium for people's desire to outwardly express themselves to others. Whatever form language may take—visual or verbal—it lays the foundation for humanity's collective identity as great storytellers. Through language we have been able to pass on stories of past heroes and enemies, warn future generations of failed philosophies, create new ideals for better living, share our aspirations and fears, even express our wonder at all that remains unknown to us. Language binds us as humans, and its diverse forms are reflected in the embodiments of its heterogeneous natives. ASL is but another paintbrush of language, and yet proof of humanity's palette of mutability.

Her final paragraph establishes a strong emotional connection with her audience (pathos) and lays out the benefits of her position.

Position Arguments

Notes

[1]I realize the use of the term *Deaf* might seem archaic, but for the purpose of this paper, it is representative of all members who psychologically or linguistically identify themselves as members of the Deaf community through ASL as their common language, regardless of their physiological hearing capacity.

[2]There are three basic types of hearing loss: conductive hearing loss, sensorineural hearing loss, and mixed hearing loss, which is any combination of the first two. All three types can make speech hard to acquire.

Works Cited

Neidle, Carol, et al. *The Syntax of American Sign Language: Functional Categories and Hierarchical Structures.* Cambridge: MIT P, 2000. Print.

Stewart, David A., and C. Tane Akamatsu. "The Coming of Age of American Sign Language." *Anthropology & Educational Quarterly* 19.3 (Sept. 1988): 235-52. Web. 7 Nov. 2009.

Fitting responses come in many forms, not just position arguments. Your instructor might call upon you to consider one of the following opportunities for writing.

Alternatives to the Position Argument

1. Compose a three- to four-page critical essay analyzing the consequences of legislation making English the official language. To fully understand the political, social, and cultural context in which the legislation was passed, conduct research to find print materials (newspaper articles, editorials and letters to the editor, transcripts of legislative hearings and testimony) from the time when the legislation was being considered. Use these materials to try to discern the stated and unstated goals of the advocates of the English language legislation. You also will want to conduct interviews with community leaders and local citizens, as well as other primary research, to determine what effects, if any, such legislation has had at the local level, such as restrictions on access to social services or implicit or explicit policies and practices in local workplaces.

2. Many supporters of English-only legislation draw attention to the costs of providing public services in languages other than English. Several opponents of English-only legislation suggest that these costs are not as significant as activists such as S. I. Hayakawa argue; others emphasize the costs of failing to provide such services. Respond to this debate by composing a four-page, double-spaced investigative report that explores the specific costs associated with multilingualism in your community. Conduct research on local, state, and federal government resources in order to create strong logical and ethical appeals in your report; you might also consider interviewing local policymakers as part of your research process.

3. How do English-as-a-second-language speakers experience life on your campus or in your community? What atmosphere of linguistic diversity or homogeneity do they perceive in their daily lives, and how does this atmosphere manifest itself in their academic, professional, and extracurricular activities? Interview a student or community member who speaks English as his or her second language, and write a profile of that person that helps readers better understand how multilingual people move between languages in their daily lives and what motivates them either to maintain their abilities in their first language or to let these abilities erode.

7 Taking Up (Public) Space: Responding with Proposals

Proposals

At Pioneer Courthouse Square, you can meet friends, buy a cup of coffee, sit and enjoy the weather, or catch the light rail. This square, in downtown Portland, Oregon, exemplifies the best kind of public space: it's centrally located, safe, beautiful, and free and open to the public. Twelve months a year, the square serves as a venue for various events, from the Senior Prom (for people 65 years and older) and Fashion Week (which previews local designers' collections) to a summer concert series and the annual Festival of Flowers. All year long, residents and visitors stand around the coffee shop, shop at the florist stand, and watch young people playing hacky sack or listen to them playing music.

AP Photo/Don Ryan

Portland's Pioneer Courthouse Square is hugely successful—and it was purposefully designed to encourage the specific kinds of activities that take place there. In fact, you could even say that the design was a top-down approach to organizing human interaction in a public space. Before the city acquired the property, it had been a department store parking lot (shown in the photo below), which served only the people shopping at a particular store and willing to pay to park their cars. In large cities such as Portland, open space like this is a precious commodity, a rarity among the tall buildings and busy streets. When such space is used to serve only a small percentage of a large population, many may wish it could be turned into something more people could use.

To transform a parking lot that served few people into a public square that serves many people, developers and city leaders first had to explain why the use of the space was somehow problematic for the city and its residents. Then, they had to propose a better use for the space, one that residents would approve. In so doing, they had to address the kinds of questions residents would be sure to ask: Who will pay for the transformation and subsequent upkeep? How will the new use of the space improve our lives? How long will the project take to complete? Where else will people be able to park? The developers and politicians had to create proposals that explained the rhetorical opportunity, defined the situation as a problem, offered various solutions, and explained which of those solutions were the most feasible and effective.

City of Portland Archives, A2005-005.438.3

Proposals are a common response to this question: How can something be improved? But that simple question leads to a number of other questions: Why is something a problem in the first place? What are viable solutions to the problem? Why is one solution better than others? What will it take to enact the best solution? Who will be affected by this solution? This chapter will challenge you to respond to these questions rhetorically as you identify or create opportunities in your own surroundings.

IDENTIFYING AN OPPORTUNITY

Throughout this chapter, you will work to identify an opportunity to propose a solution about a public space you know well. This space might be outdoors or indoors, near your campus or hometown, used by many or by few. As you work to determine the public space in need of attention, consider the most fitting means of delivery for your proposal:

▶ Print proposal, to be published in a community or campus newspaper or sent directly to the rhetorical audience

▶ Proposal with an image gallery to illustrate the problem and/or solution

▶ Spoken proposal to be delivered to the rhetorical audience as a short film or video podcast

To begin, freewrite for five minutes in response to each of the following questions (or use any of the invention techniques presented on pages 306–320):

1. Make a list of the public spaces you encounter over the course of a week. Consider parks, malls, streets, sidewalks, fairgrounds, stadiums, forests, game lands, beaches, river fronts, and any other places people gather and interact.

2. Which of these spaces you've listed do you use the most? How much time do you spend there, and what do you do?

3. If you could change just one thing about that space, what would it be? How could that space better accommodate your needs and desires? (Consider, too, the other people whose needs and desires would be accommodated as well.) Be as specific as you can about your proposal for improvement as well as the potential audience for it.

Real Situations

You do not have to be from Portland to understand the concept of public space. Even if you are not familiar with the term, you are familiar with such places. Whether you are from a large city, a small town, or a rural environment, you are conscious of the way public space is used. You know how to use the parks, malls, streets, sidewalks, fairgrounds, stadiums, forests, game lands, beaches, river fronts, and other public spaces. You understand how human interaction is organized at those places, whether people gather to watch the sights (passersby or a scenic attraction) or experience the space individually (noon-time churchgoers, for instance, who sit quietly in a pew). Whether you use public transportation, drive your car, or walk, you know how to get to and from those public spaces using means of public access: highways, streets, sidewalks, or trails.

Ever since you were a little child, you have inhabited public space. Whether you were taking turns on the playground equipment, waiting in line at the bus stop, or walking to school, you knew how to use the space, sometimes choosing to do so according to the rules for that space, sometimes not. By now, you are well accustomed to using public space of all kinds.

But not all uses of public space are planned for; no doubt, you are also aware of the ways uses emerge. From the bicycle messengers who dart between parked and moving cars and the kids who take shortcuts across a school lawn to the hunters who blaze a trail through a state game land—people cause systems of use to emerge rather than being created according to plans.

Take a look at the photographs on this page. Like many small college towns in the Midwest, Wooster, Ohio, has both rural and urban features. The first photograph shows a winding road through a residential section of town. The fairly narrow road provides access to driveways and a place for children to play, as the "Watch Children" sign indicates.

The photograph of downtown Wooster shows more direct planning than in the residential neighborhood. Main Street is a well-paved, two-lane street with on-street parking. It has stoplights and streetlights. Notice, too, how much taller and closer together the buildings are.

The College of Wooster is another kind of public space in Wooster, Ohio. Notice the shapes and heights of the various campus buildings. Notice, too, the pathways among the buildings.

Residential section of Wooster, Ohio.

Downtown Wooster, Ohio.

College of Wooster, Wooster, Ohio.

The photograph below was taken on the corner of Bleecker and Sullivan Streets in New York City's Greenwich Village, which is the hometown of many people. You can see signs, traffic lights, store fronts, and parallel parking spots, all of which indicate planning for how people are supposed to use the public space. Notice that the buildings allow for higher-density living than those in downtown Wooster.

In city suburbs, public spaces have been made to look as nonurban as possible. In the photo of an apartment complex on the next page, notice how a greenbelt takes the place of asphalt. Trees line the walkway, and bushes surround the buildings. The landscaping gives the complex a peaceful, tranquil look—far different from the action seen on the New York City street. Yet this space could be considered high density, since it houses multiple families in a relatively small area. In some ways, the occupants live as close together here as their counterparts do in Greenwich Village.

Corner in Greenwich Village, New York City.

Suburban apartment complex with greenbelt.

Many of us live or have lived in a suburban development, which offers yet another type of public space. The photograph below shows a well-paved street with single-family houses, a series of curbside mailboxes, and two sidewalks that end abruptly. You might notice, too, the garages, the stop signs, and the small trees—details that provide specific information about the way public space is used in the suburbs.

Suburban street with single-family residences.

DESCRIBING PUBLIC SPACES

1. Working with a classmate or two, choose two of the photographs in this section and make a list of specific details about the public space. What details can you discern that have not been mentioned in the text? Be prepared to share your answers with the rest of the class.

2. How many and what types of people use each of the spaces you chose? At what times of the day (and night) do they use that space? How long are they in that space? How do they get there? Where can they go to from that space?

3. How is each of these public spaces defined? What physical or geo-graphical boundaries define each of them? Be prepared to share your answers with the rest of the class.

4. Make a list of the things people can do in each of the spaces. Which of these uses of space seem to be encouraged by the way the space is planned?

5. What are the physical limitations on people's use of each of these spaces? What limitations are placed on children who want to play, people who want to walk for pleasure or to a destination, families who need a carton of milk and a loaf of bread, automobile driv-ers, people without automobiles, bicyclists, and parents with small children?

6. Translate one or more of these limitations into a one-sentence problem.

7. What solution can you imagine for the problem you stated? What specific action could be taken to resolve the problem? What money, time, or cooperative effort is necessary for the success of such an action?

Real Responses to Real Situations

This section features responses from four writers who used their avail-able means to try to resolve a rhetorical problem surrounding the use of public space. As you explore their responses to situations that may be unfamiliar to you, ask yourself if what they have to say relates in any way to the public spaces you know well.

Planning the spaces where we live

One of the most powerful people of the twentieth century was Robert Moses (1888–1981), who single-handedly reshaped New York City. Son of German-Jewish parents, both of whom had fulfilled their own aspirations, Moses grew up in New Haven, Connecticut, and graduated with honors from Yale University, received a master's degree from Oxford University, and finally earned a PhD in political science from Columbia in 1914. He developed his own theory of public service, one based on merit, not croneyism, a theory that helped propel his meteoric rise in a city that had tired of Boss Tweed and the Tammany Hall corruption. (William Marcy Tweed chaired the Democratic Party of New York County and headed the Tammany Society, an organization that controlled New York City politics for nearly a century.)

New York City provided Moses with a venue for pairing his strong work ethic with his aggressive progressivism, a social reform philosophy that aimed to reinstate political democracy and economic individualism and to eradicate slums and alleviate poverty. Before long, he was City Parks Commissioner, City Construction Coordinator, and a member of the City Planning Commission, three powerful public service positions that would allow him to fulfill his dream of reshaping the city through a system of integrated planning. Besides creating a highway system to crisscross all five boroughs of New York City, Moses reinvigorated the city's park system, transforming rundown parks and overgrown open spaces into inviting, often beautiful spaces for families to spend time in. He and his team of engineers and architects took control of abandoned industrialized areas and trash-laden oceanfront stretches as well, replacing them with affordable housing, public parks, and decent beaches. In many ways, Moses made the city of New York accessible to people of all social ranks and ethnic backgrounds. In *Working for the People*, his first-person account of public service, Moses described the city he helped to build.

Excerpt from

> Working for the People

Robert Moses

Here are a few examples of progress in the field of municipal construction which some visitors may overlook: They should note the emerging new neighborhood patterns along the East and Harlem rivers in Manhattan—parks, parkways, housing, the United Nations headquarters, on what was until recently a shambles, revising adjacent real estate values; the rebuilding of Astoria, across the river; the Triborough Bridge system, the Brooklyn Civic Center; Flushing Meadow Park and its burgeoning environment, with the corridors beyond it extending through Kissena and Cunningham parks to Alley Pond in Queens Borough.

continued

Working for the People *(continued)*

Arnold Newman/Getty Images

Those interested in the new city that is emerging should note the vast reclamation areas in Queens, Brooklyn and Staten Island, the West Side and Henry Hudson [Parkway] renovations with their widespread repercussions and influences; the gradual reduction of slums in every borough; the salvaging of all of Jamaica Bay and its frontage; the great Soundview, Ferry Point, Whitestone, Rockaway and Clearview park projects; the many constructive achievements of the Port of New York Authority; the reconstruction of our museums; new schools and hospitals and health centers; the many modern city buildings housing courts, libraries and countless other services.

We would not expect visitors to appreciate our prodigious sewage disposal systems, the pure Delaware upland water supply flowing down by gravity. Our own citizens do not fully appreciate these things or what they represent in the way of hard work on the part of little-known people in the public service. What business, industry, trade, and the arts and professions have done within this framework of municipal improvements is most impressive of all.

Local critics who refer mournfully to the exodus of industry from the city talk nonsense. They never see the new plants in the southeast Bronx, trucking in Williamsburgh, and the amazing waterborne commerce of Newtown Creek and the Gowanus Canal. We have had something of a waterfront mess, but it is being cleared up and I doubt if other ambitious ports will draw away our shipping.

We are rebuilding New York, not dispersing and abandoning it. The city spreads into the suburbs, to be sure, and that, within bounds, is what should happen. The process, however, needs no speeding up. It requires no compulsion. It demands no metropolitan supergovernment by ambitious regional planners.

The material, psychological, sociological, and political ramifications of planning public space are many. Robert Moses was not hesitant to make decisions and live with the consequences of those decisions. He identified a problem and offered himself and his ideas as the proposed solution. One such problem was the difficulty many New York City residents had in traveling among the city's boroughs, several of which are separated by water. In the 1930s, residents in Queens who wanted to travel to The Bronx had to cross over to Manhattan first, adding to traffic congestion in the city streets. In 1932, Moses resurrected plans for the Triborough Bridge, which is actually three bridges connecting The Bronx, Manhattan, and Queens. When it opened in 1936, the Triborough Bridge ushered in a new age, making travel to the suburban parks and southern shorelines much easier for many city residents. Today, it remains a vital artery for New York City commerce.

Moses's reputation as a civic force was chronicled daily in the *New York Times* from the 1930s throughout the 1960s, but some other accounts of his career have not been celebratory. In particular, Robert A. Caro's *The Power Broker* describes Moses as a man whose system of integrated planning overpowered the interests of the working poor, destroying their neighborhoods in order to serve the interests of upper-class people and their automobiles. Although Moses repeatedly espoused uncompromising devotion in order to the lower classes, Caro writes that Moses "never forgot that the lower classes were lower."

One of Moses's most impressive accomplishments, the West Side Improvement Project (the Hudson River Parkway and Riverside Park), serves as a case in point. According to various newspaper reports cited by Caro, the project "gives the island not only a new major highway and a new shore line along part of its length but park and . . . playgrounds" and "all that has been unsightly along the Hudson—the railroad, the ash dumps, the coal yards—has been swept away or completely disguised." These reports were true—as far as they went. Like all of Moses's projects, the West Side Improvement Project benefited many people, but not the most vulnerable residents of the city.

Courtesy of Library of Congress

Triborough Bridge from Manhattan, one of Robert Moses's projects.

Excerpt from

> The Power Broker
Robert A. Caro

"The railroad tracks are covered at last," an editorial said.

Not exactly.

The railroad tracks were covered until they reached 125th Street—the beginning of Harlem.

AP Photo/Jennifer Graylock

Moses had decided to economize on the section of the West Side Improvement, between 125th and 155th streets, that bordered the city's Negro community, and one of the economies was dispensing with the track covering in that section. Uncovered tracks meant a never-ending clanking, from the couplings of railroad cars, and periodic bawling, from the cows and other animals being transported south to the slaughterhouses, unless the people who lived in the apartments above kept their windows closed. And in the summer, when it was too hot to keep the windows closed, uncovered tracks meant not only noise but odors, the stench of the animals, and they meant soot and smoke that spread a coat of gritty grime, confined to window sills in winter, over walls and furniture. Now, thanks to the genius of Robert Moses, the white people who lived along Riverside Drive were freed from these annoyances.

But the black people weren't.

Robert Moses spent millions of dollars enlarging Riverside Park through landfill, but he did not spend a dime for that purpose between 125th and 155th streets. He added 132 acres to the parts of the park most likely to be used by white people—but not one acre to the part of the park most likely to be used by black people.

Robert Moses ruthlessly removed all commercial enterprises from the waterfront along the entire six-mile length of Riverside Park—except for those commercial enterprises (wharves, small warehouses, coal pockets, junk yards and the like) that were located in the Harlem section of Riverside Park. Those he allowed to remain—to occupy what otherwise would have been park land for Harlem.

Because he did not enlarge Riverside Park in the Harlem section, there was, really, for two-thirds of the Harlem section, the stretch between 125th and 145th streets, no Riverside Park at all. The green of lawns and trees that he laid out with such a lavish hand south of Harlem ends abruptly at 125th Street and the only green that remains is a very narrow, very steep treed slope, too steep for anything except slipping and sliding down it, that, for some of those twenty blocks, climbs from the uncovered tracks to Riverside Drive above. Except for that little ribbon of trees, pathetic when compared to the lush lawns and lavish plantings downtown, the "park" is, for these twenty blocks, only the grim steel of the tracks and the gray concrete of the parkway.

Robert Moses devoted endless ingenuity to making the Henry Hudson Parkway beautiful in and of itself. From Seventy-second to 125th Street, for example, he lined the roadway with trees and shrubs and faced the walls along its sides with granite and marble and expensive masonry. But between 125th and 145th streets, he lifted the roadway into the air—on a gaunt steel viaduct. There is not a tree or shrub on the viaduct. There is not a foot of granite or marble or masonry. The only ornamentation whatsoever on the starkly ugly steel is the starkly ugly cheap concrete aggregate with which it is paved.

And the viaduct is not only unlovely in and of itself. It makes the waterfront over which it runs even uglier than it was before, filling its streets with its shadows and the never-ending rumble of the cars that travel along it. And its presence insures that even should New York City one day decide to give those twenty blocks of Harlem what it has given most of the other residential neighborhoods along the Hudson River, a park below Riverside Drive, the park will have to be one filled with shadow and noise.

There is at least one spot in this twenty-block stretch at which it would have been easy to create a park even without landfill operations.

At the foot of 125th and 126th streets, these mean and narrow thoroughfares slope down and, after running under Moses' viaduct, run right out into a broad wharf that juts out into the river, so that turning it into a park would have made the riverfront a part of Harlem. Of the whole Hudson River waterfront, no area was more intimately a part of the adjoining community and more suitable to be a park for it.

Moses might not have wanted to spend much money on the Harlem section of the West Side Improvement but a park here would not have cost much money. Condemning the wharf would have been cheap, as would also have been placing playground facilities on it to give the children of the neighborhood a chance to play right on the river or laying earth and sod on it to bring a touch of brightness to a neighborhood without brightness. And seeing the park possibilities of the wharf was easy; in fact, it would have been hard not to, for on every sunny day it was crowded with people fishing, staring out over the water or washing their cars in the sun.

But somehow Moses didn't see. He never made a move to turn the 125th Street wharf into a park, and in 1974 it would still be standing vacant, a monument to a city's indifference to the needs of its poorest people.

Harlem does, of course, have a section of Riverside Park, the section between 145th Street, where the Henry Hudson Parkway swings down off the viaduct, and 155th Street—a stretch of land ten blocks long,

continued

plenty long enough to provide the playgrounds, ball fields and other facilities that a recreation-starved community so desperately needed.

Robert Moses built seventeen playgrounds as part of the West Side Improvement. He built one playground in the Harlem section of the Improvement. He built five football fields as part of the Improvement. He built one in the Harlem section. He built eighteen horseshoe courts, twenty-two tennis courts, half a mile of roller-skating paths and a mile of bicycle paths in the rest of the Improvement. He did not build a single horseshoe or tennis court or a foot of roller-skating or bicycle path in the Harlem portion.

When the Improvement first opened, in fact, there was not a single recreational facility of any type in the entire "Harlem section"—not so much as a stanchion with a basketball hoop attached. The initial plans Moses had distributed to newspapers when he was persuading La Guardia to approve the Improvement had shown a recreational area between 146th and 148th streets on the river side of the parkway, but while most of the recreational areas above and below Harlem were completed when the Improvement opened, the 146th Street–148th Street area was not even begun. He did move thereafter to build it— hurriedly, because, according to one report, La Guardia suddenly realized the omission and insisted it be rectified and Moses was afraid the Mayor would make it public. But its pitifully inadequate and cheaply built facilities proved remarkably difficult to reach from the community it was supposed to serve. The only way to reach it on foot from Harlem, in fact, was by walking to Riverside Drive, walking down an incredibly long flight of steps to the New York Central tracks, crossing the tracks on a footbridge (which meant climbing up another flight of steps to get on it and climbing down a flight to get off) and then walking down another flight of steps to an underpass under the parkway which led to the recreational area. And reaching it was downhill. Getting back up to Riverside Drive was uphill. On even pleasant summer afternoons, the recreational area Moses had so generously bestowed upon Harlem would be almost empty—except for motorists from other areas who found it remarkably accessible (just pull off the parkway and there you were) by car.

Robert Moses had always displayed a genius for adorning his creations with little details that made them fit in with their setting, that made the people who used them feel at home in them. There was a little detail on the playhouse–comfort station in the Harlem section of Riverside Park that is found nowhere else in the park. The wrought-iron trellises of the park's other playhouses and comfort stations are decorated with designs like curling waves.

The wrought-iron trellises on the Harlem playhouse–comfort station are decorated with monkeys.

> ANALYZING THE RHETORICAL SITUATION

As the excerpts in this section demonstrate, Robert Moses was a complex man. The following questions ask you to consider Moses and his work in terms of the elements of the rhetorical situation. You'll want to reread the excerpts carefully before answering.

1. Who might be the intended audience for each excerpt? How do the audiences for the excerpts differ? What textual evidence can you provide to support your answers? Be prepared to share your answers with the rest of the class.

2. Is the purpose of each excerpt evident? If so, what is it? How do the excerpts differ in terms of purpose? And how does each purpose correspond to the intended audience? Again, be prepared to share your answers with the rest of the class.

3. To what rhetorical opportunity might each writer be responding? (Keep in mind that these works were published in 1960 and 1975.) How does each piece of writing work to resolve the problem? Who holds the power to resolve or affect the resolution of that problem?

4. How does each writer draw on the rhetorical appeals of ethos, logos, and pathos? Cite passages from the text in order to support your answer.

Public space as emerging space

As you realize by now, Robert Moses's reputation as a city shaper ebbed and flowed. He held sway over New York City's planning for nearly thirty years, but by the middle of the twentieth century, his plans were being met with opposition, from the very people whose neighborhoods he wanted to "improve." Moses's belief that cities were created by and for traffic infuriated those who believed that cities should be planned to facilitate the intricate networks of contact, support, and diversity that neighborhoods provided. The turning point of Moses's power may have been the showdown he had with the residents of Greenwich Village in the 1960s; the opposition was led by Jane Jacobs (1916–2006), whose own theory of public space—that the city itself is more important than "moving traffic"—struck at the heart of Moses's basic theory.

In *Working for the People*, Moses wrote that "New York is too big for village intimacies, small-town fellowship and cracker-barrel town meetings." In contrast, Jacobs argued that those "village intimacies" are exactly what keep a city alive. In her response to what she considered to be short-sighted city planning, *The Death and Life of Great American Cities*, she claimed that observing how cities really function "is the only way to learn what principles of planning and what practices in rebuilding can promote social and economic vitality in cities, and what practices and principles will deaden these attributes." In what was to become a classic text of city planning, Jacobs recounted some costly and tragic decisions that were made in the name of progress, alluding to all the public works that Moses had supervised.

Excerpt from

> The Death and Life of Great American Cities

Jane Jacobs

There is a wistful myth that if only we had enough money to spend—the figure is usually put at a hundred billion dollars—we could wipe out all our slums in ten years, reverse decay in the great, dull, gray belts that were yesterday's and day-before-yesterday's suburbs, anchor the wandering middle class and its wandering tax money, and perhaps even solve traffic problems.

But look what we have built with the first several billions: Low-income projects that become worse centers of delinquency, vandalism and general social hopelessness than the slums they were supposed to replace. Middle-income housing projects which are truly marvels of dullness and regimentation, sealed against any buoyancy or vitality of city life. Luxury housing projects that mitigate their inanity, or try to, with a vapid vulgarity. Cultural centers that are unable to support a good bookstore. Civic centers that are avoided by everyone but bums, who have fewer choices of loitering places than others. Commercial centers that are lack-luster imitations of standardized suburban chain-store shopping. Promenades that go from no place to nowhere and have no promenaders. Expressways that eviscerate great cities. This is not the rebuilding of cities. This is the sacking of cities. . . .

© Cheryl Rondeau. Courtesy of Toronto Arts Council.

. . . [T]o become a specialized sidewalk character[, one need have only] a pertinent specialty of some sort. It is easy. I am a specialized public character of sorts along our street, owing of course to the fundamental presence of the basic, anchored public characters. The way I became one started with the fact that Greenwich Village, where I live, was waging an interminable and horrendous battle to save its main park from being bisected by a highway. During the course of battle I undertook, at the behest of a committee organizer away over on the other side of Greenwich Village, to deposit in stores on a few blocks of our street supplies of petition cards protesting the proposed roadway. Customers would sign the cards while in the stores, and from time to time I would make my pickups. As a result of engaging in this messenger work, I have since become automatically the sidewalk public character on petition strategy. Before long, for instance, Mr. Fox at the liquor store was consulting me, as he wrapped up my bottle, on how we could get the city to remove a long abandoned and dangerous eyesore, a closed-up comfort station near his corner. If I would undertake to compose the petitions and find the effective way of presenting them to City Hall, he proposed, he and his partners would undertake to have them printed, circulated and picked up. Soon the stores round about had comfort station removal petitions. Our street by now has many public experts on petition tactics, including the children.

Not only do public characters spread the news and learn the news at retail, so to speak. They connect with each other and thus spread word wholesale, in effect.

Jacobs detested the so-called improvements that Moses and other planners and developers made to New York City, as well as Boston, Seattle, and other big cities. (Later in her life, however, she praised Portland, Oregon's city center, with its balance of residents, retailers, sidewalks, and public transportation.) In her response to the short-sighted, traffic-oriented city planning of New York, she wrote at length about the importance of sidewalk public contact, which carries inestimable power in counteracting segregation and racial discrimination. A well-used street, according to Jacobs, is apt to be a safe street, where people meet and greet one another, quickly send important information over an extraordinary web of contacts, assimilate children into their daily lives (and therefore protect them), and naturally sustain a system of community surveillance. Wide sidewalks, city parks, small blocks, a mix of old and new buildings (which allows both commercial use and a socioeconomic diversity of tenants), and a concentration of people—including public characters—are the ingredients for a healthy city. Diversity of every kind—not replicable parks, monotonous highways, and a sweep of new buildings—is what continually nourishes city life.

Believing that cities should bring people and buildings together, not drive them apart, Jacobs galvanized the inhabitants of several neighborhoods, leading a successful opposition to Moses's proposed expressway through Washington Square in Greenwich Village. In doing so, Jacobs became the "public character" that she argued was so crucial to the life of any city. She used the sidewalk, storefronts, and other public spaces to become familiar to all Village residents as well as a conduit of information among them. Thus, Jacobs's theory of public space highlights a bottom-up, emergent system, which evolves from the ways inhabitants already use the space. Moses's system, on the other hand, is a top-down, planned system that requires people to rethink the ways they use public space.

> Ants and Jane Jacobs
Adina Levin

In "Death and Life of American Cities," Jacobs writes about the lively, crowded, haphazard streets of her Greenwich Village neighborhood, and compares them to the planned high-rise developments and efficient elevated highways of her nemesis, developer Robert Moses.

In the 50s and 60s, developers like Moses swept into run-down urban neighborhoods bearing a vision of "cities of the future," demolished the houses and stores, and replaced them with sterile projects that turned into slums worse than the neighborhoods they replaced.

Jacobs explains why the organically grown neighborhoods are better than the planned developments. The variety of newer and older structures [helps] the neighborhood support a diverse population—elderly folks on pensions, young folks starting out, families with children. The mix of commercial and residential properties helps keep the neighborhood safe, since the neighborhood is populated day and night, weekdays and weekends. The sidewalks and front porches enable people to stroll, chat, and look out for each other. By contrast, the uninviting plazas and parking lots surrounding high-rise buildings are often deserts where the ill-intentioned can prey on the unwary without being observed.

Simply by observing local norms, people extend the neighborhood by inviting their elderly parents to move in, buying and upgrading a ramshackle storefront, and sweeping their walk. These activities aren't centrally planned, individuals don't get permission to do them, and, in sum, they add up to pleasant and safe neighborhoods.

But looking at Greenwich Village as an example of ant-like emergent behavior misses a lot of the story.

There is a large substrate of social and cultural structures that enable these unplanned activities to create a pleasing and diverse order. The neighborhood has sewers and clean running water. Without these, the city neighborhood would harbor endemic infectious diseases. There is a fire department which protects the block if a single house catches fire. There are people with the technical and project-management skills required to design and repair plumbing, heating, and electrical systems.

A colony of ants couldn't create Greenwich Village. Neither could a tribe of hunter-gatherers. There are underlying levels of infrastructure—some of which require planning—in order to enable the higher-level decentralized behavior.

In order to facilitate decentralized, unplanned human systems that work, it's important to think about the ordered infrastructure patterns—like sewer systems—and ordered nodal activities—like designing an electrical system—that are needed to enable the larger unplanned pattern to emerge.

>ANALYZING THE RHETORICAL SITUATION

1. What is an emergent system, and how does it relate to the development of a city, town, or neighborhood? You may want to draw on your own hometown or neighborhood for examples.

2. What evidence do Robert Moses and Jane Jacobs provide that emergent systems are good or bad? Who is the audience for each of these excerpts?

3. What problem or opportunity does Jacobs address? Who can resolve or affect the resolution of that problem?

4. What is Jacobs's proposal for resolving the problem? What action does she want her audience to take?

5. How does Jacobs use ethos, pathos, and logos to build the argument in her proposal? (Provide textual evidence to support your answer.) On which of the rhetorical appeals does she most rely? Be prepared to share your answer with the rest of the class.

6. How does Jacobs evaluate the feasibility of her proposal in terms of the necessary time, money, and people? Provide textual evidence to support your answer.

7. What rhetorical opportunity prompted Adina Levin's response to Jacobs's theories? In what ways is Levin helping to develop the conversation about city planning?

COMMUNITY CONNECTIONS

1. Write for ten minutes about your response to Jacobs's opinions. How do her arguments coincide with or diverge from your experiences in a town or city you know well?

2. Now do the same for Moses. How do his arguments coincide with or diverge from your experiences in a town or city you know well?

3. Is it true that cities are built for traffic? To support your answer, draw on your experience (as a driver or pedestrian) in cities you have inhabited or visited.

4. What infrastructure can you identify in a town or city where you have lived? Who do you think planned it, or was it unplanned?

5. Write for ten minutes about the causes or the consequences of the infrastructure you identified in question 4. Be prepared to share your response with the rest of the class.

6. Given your experiences, what is your definition of a livable city? What elements constitute that sort of city? What are the sources of those elements? Write for ten minutes and be prepared to share your answers.

Proposals: A Fitting Response

As the readings in this chapter illustrate, public spaces, by their very nature, are of concern to more than just the individuals involved in designing them. What the spaces allow or don't allow and whom they serve or exclude are issues that create a need for conversation. To consider such issues and set forth their own visions, many writers offer proposals, which can be distributed to the intended audience in a variety of ways.

A proposal for Ground Zero

After the terrorist attacks of September 11, 2001, Ground Zero became one of the most famous public spaces in the world. The gaping hole, former site of the World Trade Center, was an eyesore, to be sure. Worse than that, it was a constant reminder of horror, not only on the day both towers collapsed but also on the day of the bombings some eight years earlier. Private citizens and civic leaders quickly agreed that the crater in lower Manhattan was a problem calling for a solution. In other words, Ground Zero presented an opportunity for change.

Agreeing that the site provided a problem was easy; agreeing on exactly what to do about that problem took longer. After extensive deliberation, the people of New York City decided to take specific action, to erect a memorial on the site that would meet four basic requirements: recognize each individual who was a victim of the attacks, provide space for contemplation, create a unique and powerful setting, and convey historic authenticity. In addition to honoring the dead (in lower Manhattan, Washington DC, and Shanksville, Pennsylvania) and the grieving, the memorial was also to celebrate heroism, international compassion, and the enduring values of democracy—"without establishing any hierarchies." The memorial's design would be chosen from proposals submitted to judges who would decide which was most appropriate.

Artist's rendering of World Trade Center Memorial.

Michael Arad and Peter Walker's proposal, "Reflecting Absence," was one of eight finalists, ultimately winning the competition. As you read their proposal, notice the ways in which they address each element of their rhetorical situation: opportunity for change, audience, purpose, fitting response, and available means. Notice, too, how they meet the requirements of any proposal: they (1) define the problem and the solution; (2) supply convincing arguments to support their design; (3) account for the feasibility of their design (a more detailed feasibility report accompanies the final plan); and (4) defend their proposal from potential objections.

Reflecting Absence
Michael Arad and Peter Walker

This memorial proposes a space that resonates with the feelings of loss and absence that were generated by the destruction of the World Trade Center and the taking of thousands of lives on September 11, 2001 and February 26, 1993. It is located in a field of trees that is interrupted by two large voids containing recessed pools. The pools and the ramps that surround them encompass the footprints of the twin towers. A cascade of water that describes the perimeter of each square feeds the pools with a continuous stream. They are large voids, open and visible reminders of the absence.

The surface of the memorial plaza is punctuated by the linear rhythms of rows of deciduous trees, forming informal clusters, clearings and groves. This surface consists of a composition of stone pavers, plantings, and low ground cover. Through its annual cycle of rebirth, the living park extends and deepens the experience of the memorial.

Bordering each pool is a pair of ramps that lead down to the memorial spaces. Descending into the memorial, visitors are removed from the sights and sounds of the city and immersed in a cool darkness. As they proceed, the sound of water falling grows louder, and more daylight filters in from below. At the bottom of their descent, they find themselves behind a thin curtain of water, staring out at an enormous pool. Surrounding this pool is a continuous ribbon of names. The enormity of this space and the multitude of names that form this endless ribbon underscore the vast scope of

The problem: how to honor the grief surrounding the loss of life on these two historic days.

Arad and Walker are aware of multiple audiences: the people who will visit and interact with the World Trade Center Memorial and the panel of judges.

the destruction. Standing there at the water's edge, looking at a pool of water that is flowing away into an abyss, a visitor to the site can sense that what is beyond this curtain of water and ribbon of names is inaccessible. •

The names of the deceased will be arranged in no particular order around the pools. After carefully considering different arrangements, [we] have found that any arrangement that tries to impose meaning through physical adjacency will cause grief and anguish to people who might be excluded from that process, furthering the sense of loss that they are already suffering.•

The haphazard brutality of the attacks is reflected in the arrangement of names, and no attempt is made to impose order upon this suffering. The selfless sacrifices of rescue workers could be acknowledged with their agency's insignia next to their names. Visitors to the site, including family members and friends of the deceased, would be guided by on-site staff or a printed directory to the specific location of each name. For those whose deceased were never physically identified, the location of the name marks a spot that is their own.

In between the two pools is a short passageway that links them at this lower level. A single alcove is located along this passageway, containing a small dais where visitors can light a candle or leave an artifact in memory of loved ones. Across from it, in a small chamber, visitors might pause and contemplate. This space provides for gatherings, quiet reflection, and memorial services.

Along the western edge of the site, a deep fissure exposes the slurry wall from plaza level to bedrock and provides access via a stairway. Descending alongside its battered surfaces, visitors will witness the massive expanse of the original foundations. The entrance to the underground interpretive center is located at bedrock. Here visitors could view many preserved artifacts from the twin towers: twisted steel beams, a crushed fire truck, and personal effects. The underground interpretive center would contain exhibition areas as well as lecture halls and a research library. •

In contrast with the public mandate of the underground interpretive center is the very private nature of the room for unidentified remains. It is situated at bedrock at the north tower footprint. Here a large stone vessel forms a centerpiece for the unidentified remains. A large opening in the ceiling connects this space to the sky above, and the sound of water shelters the space from the city. Family members can gather here for moments of private contemplation. It is a personal space for remembrance.

In this paragraph, Arad and Walker respond directly to the primary audience of judges and the memorial guidelines published by the Lower Manhattan Development Committee, an important element of the rhetorical situation for this proposal.

The authors anticipate and argue against possible objections to their plan of listing victims' names randomly. Their random arrangement is in keeping with the memorial guidelines, which caution against hierarchies.

These final paragraphs provide essential information addressing the challenges of memorializing the World Trade Center victims—and the feasibility of the design.

Proposals

The memorial plaza is designed to be a mediating space; it belongs both to the city and to the memorial. Located at street level to allow for its integration into the fabric of the city, the plaza encourages the use of this space by New Yorkers on a daily basis. The memorial grounds will not be isolated from the rest of the city; they will be a living part of it.

■ GUIDE TO RESPONDING TO THE RHETORICAL SITUATION

Understanding the Rhetorical Situation

When you want to argue for the best way to improve upon a situation, consider composing a proposal. Proposals commonly have the following features:

- There is a clear, identifiable problem that the proposal seeks to resolve.
- This problem is of concern to a significant number of people.
- The proposed solution will resolve the problem in a way these people will find acceptable.
- The proposal contains specific details about the costs and benefits of the solution.
- The proposal is directed to the appropriate audience and demonstrates a good understanding of that audience's needs and interests.
- The proposal clearly explains the steps or processes required to enact the solution.

The following sections will help you compose a proposal about a public space. To work with an online guide to the elements of the rhetorical situation, access your English CourseMate through CengageBrain.com.

Identifying an opportunity

Consider some public spaces you know: the mall, the campus, a local park, a town square, a suburban green belt, a public library, a parking lot, a train or bus station. What kinds of experiences have you had there? Are any of these spaces a focus of contention among different groups? Perhaps you have witnessed some group of people being asked to stop what they are doing or to leave—people selling items, teenagers skateboarding, individuals asking for spare change. Maybe you have felt unsafe in a particular space at particular times of the day or night. Or maybe you have had a wonderful experience, and you want others to be able to enjoy it, too. The following activities can help you identify an opportunity.

1. Make a list of public spaces with which you are familiar, including those you wrote about in response to the questions on page 226. For each space, list the experiences you have had there.

If the experiences were positive, explain why, providing as many details as possible. If anything could have made the experiences better, explain how. If the experiences were negative, describe the factors that made them difficult or unpleasant. Write down as many contributing factors as you can: the shape of the space, the number of people in the space, the posted rules for the space, and so forth.

2. Choosing one or two of the spaces you've listed, sketch pictures of the location(s), with labels that name and describe key features. Or take photos of the location(s) from various vantage points, paying particular attention to the features you find most intriguing.

3. Choose the public space you would like to write about and compose four or five descriptions of a problem you see in the space. Vary the ways you describe the problem. For example, one description might emphasize one group of people who are affected by the problem, and another might emphasize a different group. Another description might focus on the physical dimensions of the space, and yet another might identify uses the space seems to promote or prohibit.

Locating an audience

The following questions can help you locate your rhetorical audience as well as identify the relationship they have to the problem you've identified. Then, you'll be able to choose the best way to describe that problem.

1. List the names of the persons or groups who are in the best position to help with your problem. This step may require some research and some legwork.

2. Next to the name of each potential audience, write reasons that audience could have for acknowledging the existence of your problem. In other words, what would persuade these audiences that something needs to change?

3. What actions could these audiences reasonably be persuaded to perform? In other words, consider what each audience would be able to do to address the problem.

4. With your audience's interests and capabilities in mind, look again at the descriptions of the problem that you composed in the preceding section. Decide which description will best help your audience feel connected to the public space in question and invested in improving it. At this point, it may be necessary to revise your best description to tailor it to your audience. Remember

to consider whether the most fitting description will include images, video, or audio.

Identifying a fitting response

Identifying a problem and getting others to recognize it as a problem are only the first steps in responding to your rhetorical situation. You also need to identify and support a suitable solution to the problem. Your solution should consider the information you gathered about your audience, such as the limitations of their position. It should also be feasible in the sense that it provides an efficient and cost-effective way to go about making a positive change.

As you know, different purposes and different audiences require different kinds of texts—delivered through different media. For example, if a local shopping center doesn't provide enough accessible parking spaces for patrons with disabilities, you might write a letter of complaint to the owner. The threatened closing of a favorite coffee shop to make way for a chain restaurant might prompt a narrative essay or Facebook fan page that describes your experiences at the old hangout and evokes feelings of nostalgia in readers. Neither of these situations calls for the kind of extended, formal proposal that Michael Arad and Peter Walker submitted for the World Trade Center memorial. The point is that once you have identified your problem, audience, and purpose, you need to determine what kind of text will best respond to your rhetorical situation.

Use the following questions to help you narrow your purpose and shape your response:

1. How would you efficiently and effectively solve the problem you've identified?
2. What would this solution require of your audience?
3. Are you asking your audience simply to support your solution or to perform a particular action?
4. What is the best way to reach this audience? That is, what kind of presentation is this audience most likely to respond to? (Chapter 10 can help you explore options for media and design.)

Considering your proposal's acceptability and feasibility

The next step has to do with two concepts that are particularly important to proposals: acceptability and feasibility. Audiences are more likely to be persuaded by solutions that make responsible use of resources and that benefit some group rather than just a few individuals. Once you have identified and defined the problem for a particular audience, one that can affect the resolution of the problem by showing support or giving permission or by working on the solution, you can begin to consider the acceptability and feasibility of your proposal.

1. What resources—time, money, and human effort—are needed to accomplish the solution you're proposing? Write about each of these needs separately.
2. What positive consequences will follow from your proposed solution? List them.
3. What examples can you provide of other instances in which your proposed solution (or a similar one) has had positive results?
4. What logistical challenges does your solution face? List them.
5. What can be done to address each of these challenges?

Writing a Proposal: Working with Your Available Means

Shaping your proposal

As you have probably figured out, a proposal is arranged much like an argument. The introduction provides enough background information to describe and define the problem (perhaps in terms of its causes or consequences) and states your reasonable thesis, which conveys the essence of your proposed sensible solution, all of which helps establish your ethos.

page 310
pages 306–308

The body of a proposal provides supporting evidence for your proposed solution, particularly in terms of its consequences or results. The shape and content of your overall argument help establish your logos. In addition, the body accounts for the feasibility of the proposed solution in terms of time, money, and human effort. In other words, what resources are necessary for implementing your solution? What needs to be done first, second, and next? How much time will it take? How much will it cost? Who needs to do what? And when?

pages 318–320

Introduction
► Defines and describes the problem by offering necessary background
► Establishes common ground (ethos)
► States thesis (the writer's sensible solution)

Body
► Supports the proposed solution with evidence (logos)
► Discusses feasibility of the solution: the time, money, and effort required
► Addresses possible objections

Conclusion
► Predicts positive outcomes of the solution
► Makes an emotional connection with the audience, linking the solution to their interests (pathos)

Proposals

The body of a proposal also acknowledges possible objections and criticisms (whether they have to do with the disadvantages of your solution, the superiority of another alternative, or the costs) by including a point-by-point defense of the solution. Successful proposals often discuss trade-offs in this section.

Finally, the conclusion of a proposal predicts the positive consequences or improvements that will result from the proposed solution. Also, it's in the conclusion that you'll want to make an emotional connection with your audience, using the rhetorical appeal of pathos. Your goal is to identify your solution with the interests of your audience.

Revision and peer review

After you've drafted your proposal, ask one of your classmates to read it. You'll want your classmate to respond to your work in a way that helps you revise it into the strongest proposal it can be, one that addresses your intended audience, helps you fulfill your purpose, and is delivered in the most appropriate means available to you.

Questions for a peer reviewer
1. To what opportunity for change is the writer responding? How does the writer define the problem to which he or she is responding?
2. Who might be the writer's intended audience?
3. Where does the writer indicate how the problem will affect the audience?
4. Note the writer's thesis statement, in which the writer clearly states the solution he or she proposes. If you cannot locate a thesis statement, what thesis statement might work for this document?
5. Note the evidence the writer provides in support of the proposed solution. Where does the writer address potential objections to the solution?
6. Note the supporting ideas (presented through narration, cause-and-effect analysis, description, exemplification, process analysis, or definition) that the writer uses to support his or her assertions.
7. How feasible does the solution seem? What additional evidence could the writer provide to better support the solution's feasibility?
8. What does the solution ask of the audience? Is the requested action explicit or merely implied?
9. How does the writer make use of images? Are there places in which a graph or chart could be included, to lay out expenses or otherwise provide readers with a sense of what will be expected of them or the community?

10. How does the writer establish pathos?
11. What did you learn from the conclusion that you didn't already know after reading the introduction and the body? What information does the writer want you to take away from the proposal? Does the writer attempt to change your attitude, action, or opinion?
12. What section of the proposal did you most enjoy? Why?

PROPOSALS IN THREE MEDIA

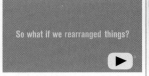

Online proposal with images	Spoken proposal or short film	Print proposal
This proposal by Fred Kent urges architects and designers to make public uses of space primary to their designs. Photographs illustrate both problems and solutions. Additionally, the Making Places Project for Public Spaces blog provides numerous examples of online proposals. To see both sites, find *Proposals in Three Media* in your English CourseMate, accessed through CengageBrain.com.	The short video "Built to Last" proposes a radical change in the ways we imagine public spaces. To view the video, find *Proposals in Three Media* in your English Course-Mate, accessed through CengageBrain.com.	In the following proposal, student Rupali Kumar explains her idea for creating an outdoor play area at her temple.
Image: Courtesy of Fred Kent and PPS.	*Image: Courtesy 1 standmain*	*Image: Courtesy of Rupali Kumar.*

Proposals

Instead of writing a proposal, Rupali Kumar might have decided to write a letter to an appropriate person or committee in response to the child's accident that was her rhetorical problem. Given her rhetorical context, she also could have composed a prayer for the child's speedy recovery. But, as she notes, the accident pointed to a larger problem—one that affects all members of the temple community. After thinking about possible solutions and their feasibility, she decided to write a proposal that presents a specific plan in words and images and describes its advantages.

Rupali Kumar

Professor Enoch

English 215

29 February 2010

Baal Leela[1]

It is quite common to see Srinivas Charyulu, the very lively and animated son of our priest, running around in the Sri Venkateswara Temple (SVT) parking lot. Surely he has to expend his abundance of energy somehow! However, things took an unfortunate turn last year, when the five-year-old collided with a parked car at his top speed. The sight of tiny Srinivas in a full-leg cast is one that the temple community will not soon forget.

Srinivas's case is not an isolated one. Our temple is regularly filled with dozens of equally active children. When they are not busy in music lessons or Sunday school, they are naturally inclined to play. Inside of the SVT, I often see kids tossing footballs in the small auditorium, chasing each other through the halls, and congregating in the coat closet. When it suits them, they venture outside to engage in parking lot Frisbee games and snowball fights on unfenced hills overlooking the road.

And naturally, the children's behavior is a source of constant tension for the parents and other adults. Some adults complain that the kids are treating the temple as their playground: they are being too noisy, congesting the halls, breaking ceiling tiles, denting cars with their Frisbees, and disrupting prayer services and important meetings. Most of all, many adults fear that children will suffer injuries like Srinivas's, or worse. Therefore, many of the temple's adults are of the opinion that the

Proposals

Rupali identifies a problem, a rhetorical opportunity that she can address, maybe even resolve, with words.

The problem she's identified is one that affects a good number of children and their parents.

children must be controlled. To prevent ruckus and injury in the temple, they believe that children's wild behavior must be stopped. They argue that parents ought to be more responsible and force their children to sit quietly, because after all, the temple is a place to pray, not a place to play.

I respectfully disagree with this opinion. Anyone well-acquainted with Sri Venkateswara Temple knows that it is more than merely a place to pray. It is a center for social interaction and therefore should allow for interaction among children as well as adults. Furthermore, it is as difficult as it is inappropriate to prohibit children from playing. In my experience with the SVT children, most of them equate being at the temple with having fun with their friends. Attempts to force children to behave contrary to their playful nature are usually unsuccessful. Thus, such an approach is ineffective in stopping the incidence of disruption and injury.

In its place, I propose an alternative solution: the creation of designated recreational areas for children in and outside of the temple. First, a portion of the temple's outdoor property must be designated for children to play on. Ideally, this area should be distant enough from the temple building to prevent children from breaking windows, yet close enough to be conveniently accessible from the building. It should be distant enough from the parking lot to prevent children from interfering with traffic flow, damaging cars, or having accidents like Srinivas's. Furthermore, this area should be fenced in or otherwise contained to avoid accidents such as those that might occur on the unfenced hills that the children currently play on.

Taking into account these factors, I find that the best place for this outdoor play area would be the region currently known as the Lower

Rupali mentions the one solution that has already been put forward, but it's a solution she thinks she can improve.

In this paragraph, Rupali provides sensible reasons for not accepting the original solution.

Proposals

Rupali proposes her own solution, one that will resolve the problem in a way that her temple family will find acceptable.

Parking Lot. The loss of those few parking spaces is sufficiently counterbalanced by the ample space in the newly constructed Upper Parking Lot. Because it is at a lower elevation, the Lower Parking Lot is set apart from the main parking lot and traffic artery while being sufficiently close to the building. The region can easily be fenced in for added security. Part of this outdoor play area could be a spacious field designated for the popular pastimes of Frisbee and football. Another part could contain safe playground equipment selected to appeal to the children's preferences.

For those times of year when Pittsburgh weather makes it unfavorable to be outdoors, an indoor children's recreational space must be designated. Such a room should be reasonably spacious to allow children to run around freely. Furthermore, the room's sole purpose should be for children to play in it. This will prevent children from playing in other places and disrupting temple happenings.

In light of recent construction developments, the creation of a children's recreational room in the body of the temple is highly feasible. New space is being added onto the building with the recently initiated

She works, paragraph by paragraph, to offer specific details about where and how her solution can be implemented— and by whom.

Courtesy of Rupali Kumar.

Fig. 1. Proposed space for outdoor play area (photograph by the author).

Proposals

Kitchen Annex Project. This project, as advertised in the temple calendar, aims to create a "modern kitchen and dining facility," a "community hall" for devotee use, and "classrooms for youth education" (*Sri Venkateswara Temple Calendar*). While all of these grand improvements to the temple are being made, the problem of inadequate safe play space can finally be solved by including a carefully designed recreational area in the final blueprint.●┈┈┈┈┈┈┈┈┈┈┈┈┈┈┈┈┈

Once the necessity and clear benefits of creating indoor and outdoor play areas are recognized by the members of the SVT, we will need to undergo a meticulous planning process to ensure the best results. Volunteers dedicated to this project must form a special committee. This committee will obtain input from the temple's administrative chairs, especially the Construction Committee members, as well as parents and children. Suggestions for the play areas, regarding such details as layout, types of play equipment present, safety precautions, and supervision, must be gathered, along with donations. The committee's main task will be to integrate the collected input into a detailed blueprint of both recreational areas. The next step, for which community participation will also be necessary, will be to construct the recreational areas. Volunteers could do some of the work, while construction firms, perhaps including the one currently working on the Kitchen Annex Project, can be employed for more difficult tasks.

Creating areas solely for children to play in, both indoors and outdoors, will prove exceedingly beneficial to the temple community.●┈┈┈┈┈┈┈┈┈┈┈┈┈ It will give respect and approval to children interacting in their natural, playful manner. It will reduce playing children's disturbance of other temple activities. Finally, it will save children from Srinivas's fate of

Rupali directs her proposal to the parents who belong to her temple and demonstrates a clear understanding of their needs, interests, and abilities.

Finally, Rupali offers the positive consequences of implementing her carefully thought-out proposal.

Proposals

getting hurt playing in areas not designed for playing. With the collaborated enthusiasm and efforts of all of the temple's devotees, the most fitting play areas for our purposes can be designed and built.

It has been over a year since Srinivas's accident, and it is still common to stumble across the priest's lively little son, along with dozens of kids like him, as they dart through the halls and driveways of Sri Venkateswara Temple. Nothing has changed. Nothing is being accomplished by those who point fingers at parents for failing to suppress children's natural playful tendencies, or those who stubbornly declare playing inappropriate at the social interaction center that is our temple. Instead, disentangling ourselves from the unproductive web of petty arguments, we must collectively redirect our focus onto creating play areas for the welfare of the temple community and its children.

Note

[1]Baal Leela refers to the delightful childhood nature of Lord Krishna, one of the human incarnations of the Hindu deity Vishnu (also known as Sri Venkateswara, the presiding deity of this temple). Accounts of Krishna's childhood always mention his endearing mischief and playful nature as a child. Thus, in our faith, God has shown by example that it is children's nature and duty to be playful.

Work Cited

Sri Venkateswara Temple Calendar. Etna, PA: Schiff Printing, 2006. Print.

Proposals

Alternatives to the Proposal

Fitting responses come in many forms, not just proposals. Your instructor might call upon you to consider one of the following opportunities for writing.

1. In a public space that is familiar to you, what uses emerged from the bottom up? Which uses were planned from the top down? In an essay of three to four pages, describe a familiar public space in terms of its use. Various rhetorical methods of development—process analysis, comparison and contrast, cause-and-consequence analysis, exemplification, classification and division—may help you conceptualize and then arrange your essay.

2. Pioneer Courthouse Square in Portland, Oregon, is considered a successful example of a planned public space, with its recurring activities (flower and fashion shows, musical events), inviting amenities (public art, flowers, trees), easy access (by foot, light rail, city bus, or automobile), and comfort (comfortable seating was incorporated in the architecture itself). Identify a public space—on campus or in your community—and in an essay of three to four pages evaluate it in comparison to Pioneer Courthouse Square or according to criteria of your own (function, identity or character, arrangement, access and circulation, seating, environment, food and drink, and so on). Be sure to specify the criteria on which you're basing your evaluation. As you write, consider your audience (who may or may not share your ideas about criteria), your purpose (which should align with your audience), and the constraints and resources of your rhetorical situation.

3. Consider a public space that you know well. Analyze how the space brings people together, keeps them apart, or otherwise controls how they interact. Along with this process analysis, determine whether some groups of people are encouraged to or discouraged from interacting in this space. Draft an essay of three to four pages, making certain to consider rhetorical opportunity, audience, purpose, constraints and resources, and available means.

8 Reviewing Visual Culture: Responding with Evaluations

It's more than likely that your first introduction to the college or university where you're now studying came through a brochure, a booklet, or a Web site describing the school's programs, its student body, and campus life. At the University of Kansas, prospective students can download the official KU app to their iPhones. Like the school's Web site, the iPhone app offers news, sports scores, campus photographs and maps, and a schedule of events, all awash in Jayhawk red and blue.

Students considering Lewis & Clark College in Portland, Oregon, can scroll through a host of photos and student blogs that depict "Real Life at Lewis & Clark College." Seeing images of real students and reading their

The Latest Posts

Maisha Foster-O'Neal: test run cooking

Springtime in Portland is always such a messy affair. In the past two weeks I've experienced shorts and mild sunburns, a series of deluges, cold winds, and a hail storm. Spring break itself tripped all over itself in the weather department. My brother came home from San Luis Obispo for spring break, and we spent our week just chilling out. We hiked to the top of **Multnomah Falls**, hill-walked Portland, threw sticks for our fetch-obsessed cocker spaniel Moki on **Sauvie Island** beach, and drank a lot of tea. I finally got around to seeing Avatar, but the 3-D glasses gave me a killer headache, because they didn't fit over my regular glasses very well. I also spent a good portion of break reading and researching for class.

A lot of the research I did over break was for my Gender in Relational Communication final project. I read academic articles

What is Real Life?

Real life is an online journal where students tell you their everyday — what it's like to live, breathe and study in Portland Oregon at Lewis & Clark. The Admissions Office has sponsored this journal since 2003. If you'd like, you can read some of the past five years of posts.

Topics

THE TOP THIRTY

dscn0151.JPG

See More

2009-10

April 2010

March 2010

February 2010

Courtesy of Lewis & Clark College

accounts of college life may persuade viewers that Lewis & Clark College is the place for them to pursue their undergraduate careers.

Web pages and phone apps—in addition to the countless brochures and pamphlets published in order to stimulate recruitment—are two means by which colleges and universities craft a recruitment message to send to prospective students and their parents. Each school wants potential students to appreciate all the available opportunities of that particular school and to imagine themselves as successful there. When you were a prospective student, it was up to you to decide how you were going to evaluate these highly visual messages.

Evaluations—spoken or written texts that argue whether something meets a particular set of criteria—are particularly useful for understanding how well individuals and groups portray themselves visually and what kinds of decisions readers or viewers make in response to those portrayals. Evaluations consider such questions as the following: What is the immediate overall effect of the visual? What are the specific parts of the visual? How are these parts pieced together? What is the overall effectiveness of the visual? These are the types of questions you will be asking and responding to in this chapter, questions that lead not only to detailed evaluations of images but also to thoughtful analyses of how the visual culture in which we are increasingly immersed is shaping our society.

Throughout this chapter, you will work to identify an opportunity to evaluate a visual element of our culture. As you determine the specific interest or appeal of this element (whether it's your school's or company's Web site, a product logo, an advertisement, the architecture of a familiar building, or a movie or video game), consider also the most fitting means of delivery for your evaluation:

▶ Print review, to be published in a community or campus newspaper or local 'zine

▶ Online review, to be published on a blog, a film review site (such as Rotten Tomatoes), a video game review site (such as Boomtown), or other Web site

▶ Evaluation using video, a slide show, or other presentation software

To begin, freewrite for five minutes in response to each of the following questions (or use any of the invention techniques presented on pages 306–320):

1. Look at the photographs on the next few pages of this chapter. Which of them represent a designed space or object that is familiar to you? Which ones represent something unfamiliar? How do you ordinarily interact with the familiar scenes or objects? How might you interact with the unfamiliar ones?

2. What kinds of images or designed spaces do you encounter in your everyday life? What details constitute these images or designs? How do you interact with or respond to these images or designs?

3. Which of the images in this section do you find especially interesting? Which ones would stimulate you to look twice or think more deeply were you to pass them on your way across campus?

4. What kinds of words would you use to describe the especially stimulating images? What specific details prompt you to think about these images in this particular way?

Real Situations

Once on campus, you are immersed in a sea of images, some that are portrayed in the official brochures and some that are not. On your walk to class, you may step over chalk drawings urging you to attend an upcoming lecture or pass by flyers urging you to participate in an upcoming Critical Mass bike ride. While visiting your friend's dorm room, you may spend a few moments looking at the posters of abstract art or the hundreds of photos of her family and friends that she has scattered over every available inch of wall space. And, when eating lunch at the student union, you may glance at posters encouraging you to sell your chemistry textbook back to the bookstore during finals week. You may read advertisements in the student newspaper persuading you to spend your hard-earned money on dinner-and-drink specials at restaurants in town. All of these kinds of visual texts use images as a means of capturing a particular mood, delivering a specific message, or provoking a specific action.

As you know well, personal computers, smart phones, and tablet computers are playing an increasingly central role in our leisure time, and as a result we are becoming ever more enmeshed in a world of images and multimedia, from the personal to the academic. Many students (maybe including you) present themselves through a careful construction of photos, videos, and text on a personal blog or on sites such as Facebook and Twitter. More students than ever before read about and watch the news on visually rich online magazines and newspapers, such as Salon.com, msnbc.com, FoxNews.com, and Yahoo! News. All of these sites offer visually intense environments, with photos and text situated alongside colorful banner ads, animated graphics, and links to sponsors' Web sites. And, in addition to tapping the resources of social and political sites, students are also taking advantage of the possibilities of academic-related multimedia sites by participating in online courses, viewing online slide shows for Art Appreciation 101, or creating, contributing to, and editing a course wiki.

The ways in which you and your fellow students experience visual culture do not end with the more obvious forms of photographs, posters, advertisements, Web pages, and movies. The visual design of the buildings, green spaces, and monuments on

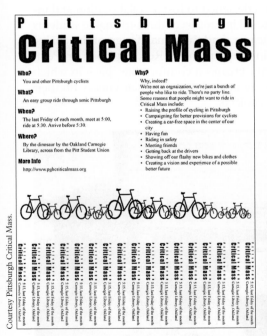

Courtesy Pittsburgh Critical Mass.

Flyers like this one are among the many visuals competing for attention on college campuses.

James Woodson/Digital Vision/Jupiter Images

Many dorm rooms are visual presentations of students' interests and self-image.

AP Photo/David J. Phillip

The Bonfire Memorial at Texas A&M University.

your college or university campus creates a particular atmosphere. For example, the prominent Bonfire Memorial at Texas A&M University seeks to reinforce a deep respect for that school's unique traditions. The visual design of the classrooms and labs on your campus creates particular types of learning environments. The digital writing classrooms at Stanford University have been redesigned to foster collaboration and innovation, with computers clustered in groups of three to enable students to work on writing projects in teams. And the visual design of the chairs, tables, lights, and bookshelves in the Humanities Reading Room in Penn State University's Pattee Library creates a comfortable space in which students and faculty members are invited to focus their energy on their individual reading and writing projects.

© Cheryl Glenn, 2007.

A redesigned digital writing classroom at Stanford University allows for effective collaboration.

The Humanities Reading Room in Penn State University's Pattee Library.

If you look around your own campus, you'll see an environment rich in visuals. Whether or not you have thought much about it, living within this visual culture shapes the ways you seek and communicate information every day. Charles A. Hill, a professor of rhetoric and writing at the University of Wisconsin, Oshkosh, describes the effects in this way:

> [T]he students now entering our classrooms have grown up with one hundred channels of television, and the World Wide Web is no longer a novelty, but part of their social, academic, and working lives. If we include nonelectronic sources of visual communication such as billboards, print advertisements, and the ubiquitous packaging that has taken such an important place in our consumer culture, then we have to conclude that most of the information our students are exposed to is in a visual form.

For Hill, this high level of immersion in an increasingly visual culture calls for both teachers and students to know how to read what images communicate.

DESCRIBING IMAGES ON CAMPUS

1. Choose two of the photographs in this section of the chapter and list the specific details you notice about the images—for example, the way objects and people are arranged, the lighting, or a contrast in color or sizes. Be prepared to share your answers with the rest of the class.

2. Who do you imagine designed the spaces or arranged the objects? Who produced the actual images?

3. What might be the rhetorical audience for and purpose of each image?

4. What adjectives come to mind when you consider these images? Which of the details that you used to answer question 1 illustrate each of those adjectives?

5. Translate the purposes, adjectives, and details into a single statement about each of the images. Then compose a list of criteria by which you might best evaluate each image. Be prepared to share your statement and list with the rest of the class.

Real Responses to Real Situations

One good way to explore visual culture in this country is to consider one of its most common forms: movies. In 2004, the average American watched more than two thousand hours of filmed entertainment, and the evaluation of movies in the United States is a mini-industry itself. We rely on the professional assessments of Roger Ebert and Gene Shalit, on publications such as *Entertainment Weekly* and Web sites such as rottentomatoes.com, and on the regular columns in our local and school newspapers. Every day, we have easy access to evaluations of this part of our visual culture—even though we don't always think in these terms when we search online for movie reviews or read an opinion piece about the latest crop of action films.

A reasonable and insightful movie evaluation includes judgments about overall quality, strengths and weaknesses, cast, setting, and technical features. In addition, a good evaluation might include a consideration of the cultural referents of the film, such as costumes or historical references in the movie's plot line. Whatever the reviewer argues, it is paramount that he or she supply specific evidence to support that claim (for example, that a movie is ground-breaking or derivative, suspenseful or confusing).

Evaluating the visual spectacle of a Hollywood film: *The Matrix*

One film that has generated an enormous amount of critical evaluation from a variety of perspectives is *The Matrix*, written and directed by Andy and Larry Wachowski. *The Matrix* was released in 1999 and was an instant box-office hit, generating $27.8 million in its opening weekend—the biggest opening weekend of that year. Not only was *The Matrix* widely reviewed, but it soon became the subject of

The cast of *The Matrix*, a film that continues to inspire critical evaluation.

articles, classroom discussions, and books. *The Matrix* proved to be one of those unusual films enjoyed by both casual moviegoers of a wide variety of ages, ethnicities, and regions and devoted fans who gave it cult status.

When *The Matrix* was first released, most people had never seen anything like it. The film combined cinematic techniques from popular Hong Kong action movies, kung fu films, and Japanese anime with sophisticated digital technology. One visual, what the directors call "bullet-time photography," gives key action sequences in the film a slow-motion, 360-degree view in which the characters appear to be able to halt or slow down time. This technique was combined with digital special effects and "wire" fighting scenes adapted from Asian martial arts movies to create a movie that was new and

startling. As one reviewer for the *Village Voice* observed, "It's that rare sci-fi film that actually looked like it was from the future."

According to critic Joshua Clover, *The Matrix*'s story is based on two popular premises in many science fiction stories: "the war between man and machine, and the possibility that reality is a hoax." The movie is set in what may be the twenty-second century, when intelligent machines have taken over the world, conquered humanity, and turned people into living "battery packs" farmed by the machines for energy. The plot centers around a small band of free rebels (played by Keanu Reeves, Laurence Fishburne, Carrie-Anne Moss, and Joe Pantoliano) who are searching for "The One" to help them conquer the ruling machines and end the virtual reality called "The Matrix" that they have created to fool humanity.

The Matrix won four Academy awards: Best Visual Effects, Best Film Editing, Best Sound, and Best Sound Effects Editing. It inspired two sequel films, *The Matrix Reloaded* (2003) and *The Matrix Revolutions* (2003), which most viewers judged to be disappointing in comparison with the original. Nonetheless, more than a dozen popular books on the film's cinematography, philosophy, religion, and artwork (just to name a few of the most common themes)—as well as countless reviews, fan sites, a comic book series, animated movies, and an online computer game—have since been published about *The Matrix*. The evaluative conversation about the meaning and merits of this movie is an active one.

In an early review of the film, professional film critic Kenneth Turan gave *The Matrix* a positive evaluation. Like many of the first reviewers, Turan praises the film primarily for its visual look and feel, its energy, and its action sequences. He clearly lays out all the criteria he uses to evaluate a film, and he provides vivid descriptions of scenes and characters to explain how he sees the film stacking up on these criteria. He acknowledges where *The Matrix* falls short, but he leaves readers with a strong sense that, overall, the movie's combination of interesting story line and innovative visual techniques makes it worth seeing.

> An Apocalypse of Kinetic Joy

Kenneth Turan

"Imagine you're feeling a little like Alice, tumbling down the rabbit hole," someone says in the dazzling and disorienting "The Matrix," and who has the strength to argue?

A wildly cinematic futuristic thriller that is determined to overpower the imagination, "The Matrix" combines traditional science-fiction premises with spanking new visual technology in a way that almost defies description. Like it or not, this is one movie that words don't come close to approximating.

Written and directed by the Wachowski brothers, Larry and Andy, "The Matrix" is the unlikely spiritual love child of dark futurist Philip K. Dick and the snap and dazzle of Hong Kong filmmaking, with digital technology serving as the helpful midwife.

Yet because this tale has been on the Wachowskis' minds for so long—it was written before their 1996 debut film, "Bound"—"The Matrix" never feels patched together. And its story, constructed though it is from familiar elements and pseudo-mystical musings, is nevertheless strong enough to support the film's rip-roaring visuals.

Thomas Anderson (Keanu Reeves), a software programmer in a world very much like our own who goes by his nighttime hacker moniker of Neo, has heard the Matrix whispered about his whole life, but no one knows what it is. All the beautiful Trinity (Carrie-Anne Moss of TV's "Dark Justice") can tell him is that "it's looking for you," which is certainly scary but not a great deal of help.

For that Neo has to turn to Trinity's partner, the legendary Morpheus (Laurence Fishburne), considered the most dangerous man alive by the authorities. What he says is more than frightening: What Neo thinks is the real world is no more than a computer-generated dreamscape, a virtual reality created by the artificial intelligence that really controls things to distract our human minds while our bodies are systematically plundered as an energy source to keep those nefarious machines up and running.

Sometimes those machines take human form as agents, robotic parodies of FBI men, like the chilling Agent Smith (Hugo Weaving of "Proof" and "The Adventures of Priscilla, Queen of the Desert"), who wear security earpieces, sunglasses and white shirts with ties and are terrifyingly close to indestructible.

These Matrix men have a special interest in Neo. There's a feeling in the air, one that Morpheus and his ragtag colleagues (including "Bound" veteran Joe Pantoliano) are tempted to share, that Neo might be the One, the foretold liberator who has the power to destroy the Matrix and free the human race. But only the Oracle (a fine cameo by Gloria Foster) knows for sure, and everything she says is, well, oracular.

Obviously, there's a great deal that's familiar about "The Matrix," starting with its sturdy themes of alternate realities, the deadly rivalry between men and machines, the resilient power of the human mind and the creeping dangers of conformity. And the film's fake-Zen dialogue, lines like "Don't think you are; know you are" and "There's a difference between knowing the path and walking the path," isn't going to win any ovations for originality.

On the other hand, the somber quality of the dialogue suits the apocalyptic quality of "The Matrix" story, and the gravity of the actors, especially the always magisterial Fishburne and the magnetically phlegmatic Reeves, makes the words more bemusing than bothersome.

continued

Helping most of all are the riveting visuals shot by Bill Pope. The Wachowskis do have a taste for the bizarre (witness an electronic bug that turns into a body-piercing insect) but this tendency pays off in bravura moments like a mesmerizing vista of a body farm without end (inspired by the work of comic-book artist Geof Darrow) where humans are relentlessly harvested for energy like so many replaceable Eveready batteries.

Just as exciting are "The Matrix"'s two kinds of action sequences. One . . . involves John Woo–type expenditures of massive amounts of ammunition shot in super slow-motion and the other uses both Hong Kong–style stunt work and a technique the press notes refer to as "bullet-time photography" that involved shooting film at the computer-aided equivalent of 12,000 frames per second.

"The Matrix" cast members who were involved in the film's eye-catching kung fu fight sequences also apparently committed to four months of pre-production work with Hong Kong director and stunt coordinator Yuen Wo Ping, someone who specializes in the technique, known as wire fighting, that gives H.K. films like "Drunken Master," "Once Upon a Time in China" and "Fist of Legend" their distinctive high-flying look.

Not everything in "The Matrix" makes even minimal sense, but the Wachowski brothers, said to be major fans of comic books and graphic novels, are sure-handed enough to smoothly pull us over the rough spots. When a film is as successful as this one is at hooking into the kinetic joy of adrenalized movie making, quibbling with it feels beside the point.

Taking a different position from Kenneth Turan's largely positive review, Bob Graham, senior writer for the *San Francisco Chronicle*, argues that *The Matrix*'s technology is all the movie actually is, calling the movie a "pretentious sci-fi thriller" that is "also a special effects spectacle" that doesn't create a memorable film. For him, special effects alone do not a movie make. "Technical expertise and visual imagination" should always be put in the service of plot development and character growth.

> Lost in the Matrix

Bob Graham

The Keanu Reeves cyberspace opera, "The Matrix," is a wonderful movie to chew up and spit out.

Larry and Andy Wachowski, the hotshot-brothers writing and directing team, clearly set out to astonish with this one, and they certainly do.

It's astonishing that so much money, talent, technical expertise and visual imagination can be put in the service of something so stupid.

Folly on such a monumental scale is almost exhilarating.

So this is what more than 100 years of cinema history has come to: special effects with no movie.

"The Matrix" is about nothing less than the nature of reality, heaven help us. The Wachowskis have discovered that there is a real world behind the apparent one. This may be a tremendous subject in the hands of somebody like Plato, but when the Wachowskis get their mitts on it, watch out. Somebody ought to adjust their medication.

If anybody ever wanted to see Reeves shaved naked and covered with slime, now is the chance.

He plays a computer hacker who stumbles into a vague awareness— with him, everything is vague—that this world is but the dim reflection of a controlling cyberworld "out there."

"The Matrix" is the film that asks the question, "Ever had that feeling you're not sure if you're awake or still dreaming?"

Frequently.

Characters have names like Neo, Morpheus, Trinity and Cypher that take us into the quagmire of allegory, and the unfortunate actors attached to these names have to deliver speeches accordingly.

"It's like a splinter in your mind driving you mad," someone says. Splinters in your mind will do that.

This movie is so pretentious that it invites speculation in kind. The neo-Wagnerian soundtrack score falsely raises hopes that "The Matrix" has aspirations of becoming the all-encompassing multimedia philosophical artwork that the German genius might have created if only moving pictures hadn't waited so long to be invented. In fact, the Wachowskis seem to be masters of the Wagnerian art of transition. In one stunning shot, the camera closes in on a static TV monitor view of Reeves in an interrogation room. The camera seamlessly merges into the shot on the monitor and then independently moves about the interrogation room. It is breathtaking, and there are other displays of visual virtuosity that almost equal it, including a shot into a fiber-optics cable. To say nothing of the insect-like monsters, among them one that enters Reeves' belly button.

As he moves back and forth between this world and that, Reeves materializes at one point as a kung fu artist. After the audience gets though digesting that one, he flies through the air like a refugee from some Hong Kong fantasy, more empty technical razzmatazz.

Maybe the DVD version will have an option to eliminate the dialogue, but in the meantime we have to put up with oppressive acting here.

We know that Reeves is puzzled about which reality he currently occupies because he squinches up his eyebrows. Laurence Fishburne has the chore, as a mysterious cyberworld overlord, of making absolute

continued

nonsense sound like he believes it. He does this by e-nun-ci-a-ting every syllable.

In a throwback to the Wachowskis' "Bound," Carrie-Anne Moss in black leather plays the Gina Gershon ambiguous lesbian character.

Australian actor Hugo Weaving ("The Adventures of Priscilla, Queen of the Desert") is a "Men in Black"-style special agent. His mannered performance is briefly fun until it becomes apparent that's all there is and he intends to go on and on with it.

As one of the overlord's underlings, Joe Pantoliano ("The Fugitive") at first seems to be the actor who will rescue the honor of the profession. He is the only one who has a spark of wit, but even he is eventually swamped by the hopeless muddle that "The Matrix" becomes.

Like Turan, Graham weighs various criteria (plot, visual effects, character development, and acting) in order to evaluate *The Matrix,* and he presents in clear terms how he sees the film meeting or falling short of each one. For him, the plot is "about nothing less than the nature of reality," which merits his scoff, "heaven help us." And the visual look that Turan found so stunning and difficult to put into words seems to Graham to consist of "money, talent, technical expertise, and visual imagination. . . . put in the service of something . . . stupid." Graham calls out the allegorical names of the characters (Neo, Morpheus, Trinity, and Cypher), lamenting that the "unfortunate actors attached to these names have to deliver speeches accordingly." And he criticizes the acting itself, citing Keanu Reeves' movie-long puzzlement, enacted by "squinch[ing] up his eyebrows," and Laurence Fishburne's demonstration of his mysterious character by "e-nun-ci-a-ting every syllable" of his nonsensical dialogue. Thus, even though Graham presents a set of evaluation criteria similar to those of Turan, Graham arrives at a markedly different conclusion, a negative conclusion that he supports with specific evidence and compelling examples. Ultimately, both Turan and Graham are trying to persuade their readers that the criteria they use to evaluate the film (and the examples from the film to which they apply the criteria) are the most important ones to consider.

> ANALYZING THE RHETORICAL SITUATION

1. State Kenneth Turan's main evaluative claim about *The Matrix* in one sentence. What reason(s) does Turan use to support his claim? What specific evidence does he provide to support his reason(s)?

2. State Bob Graham's main evaluative claim in one sentence. What reason(s) does he use to support his claim? What specific evidence does he provide to support his reason(s)? How is some of the same evidence used by Turan used differently in this evaluation?

3. You have read both a positive review of *The Matrix* (Turan's) and a negative one (Graham's). Which one seems more persuasive to you? Why? Be prepared to share your answer with the class.

COMMUNITY CONNECTIONS

1. Write for ten minutes about your response to one of the evaluations of *The Matrix*. How do the various elements of the movie that this evaluation explores coincide with or diverge from the elements that you normally consider when evaluating a movie?

2. Now write for ten minutes about the other evaluation of *The Matrix*. What criteria does the writer use to evaluate the movie, and how are these criteria similar to or different from the criteria that you use to evaluate a film?

3. What visually compelling images on your campus or in your community have grabbed your attention over the past few weeks? Write for ten minutes about your initial impressions of one visually compelling image. Describe, with as much detail as you can, the image and the context in which you first saw it.

4. Now consider the rhetorical situation for the image you've just described: Who created this image? Who was intended to see and respond to the image? What rhetorical opportunity might have prompted this image?

5. What criteria would you use to evaluate the image you've described? On what basis would you evaluate it?

6. What do you understand to be the purpose of evaluating the visual elements in our everyday lives? What particular kinds of rhetorical situations call for evaluation, and what does evaluation allow us to do in response to those situations?

Evaluating visual culture in our everyday lives

We tend to think first of television, movies, and computers when we consider visual culture. In doing so, we overlook other visual elements we encounter every day: an attractive chair in the student lounge, a sign on a storefront, a new laptop computer, the look of a coffee mug, a canvas tote bag, or a backpack. The designers who created these objects considered not only the object's function and purpose but also how the object's aesthetic dimensions influence the user's experience with it. Just as we can analyze and evaluate movies, we can assess the ways in which the design of everyday objects speaks to our needs for function and aesthetic pleasure.

One of the most everyday of everyday objects is the reusable tote bag. In response to the proliferation of those lightweight plastic bags that have replaced brown paper bags— and begun to clog our waterways, waterworks, landfills, and roadsides—grocery stores, discount retailers, and high-end boutiques are all pushing their own brands of reusable bags. Often artfully designed with catchy sayings, these tote bags are one way to "go green," now that going green has become fashionable. In the following essay written for the Design Observer blog, Dmitri Siegel, Web art director for Urban Outfitters, evaluates the trend in reusable tote bags.

> Paper, Plastic, or Canvas?

Dmitri Siegel

Amidst all the despair in the last few years about the slow extinction of various design-friendly formats—the vinyl LP, the newspaper, the book, etc.—one vehicle for graphic design has vaulted to almost instant ubiquity: the canvas tote. The medium is not new, of course. Public television stations have been giving them away during fundraisers for decades and L. L. Bean's "Boat and Tote" has been a New England staple even longer. But the timely environmental appeal of these reusable bags and the easy application of graphics catapulted the canvas tote from the health food store to the runway in a few short years. Graphic designers have embraced the form as a venue for their imagery and messages on par with the tee shirt. The ensuing glut of these bags, however, raises questions about the sustainability of any product regardless of the intention behind it, and the role that design plays in consumption.

© John Derian Co., 2008

Whale tote bag, Hugo
Guiness, 2008.

Evaluations

It's difficult to pinpoint when the recent canvas tote craze really started, but there was a pivotal moment two years ago when Anya Hindmarch released the "I'm Not a Plastic Bag" tote in collaboration with the global social change movement We Are What We Do. The bag was originally sold in limited numbers at Hindmarch boutiques, Colette and Dover Street Market in London, but when it went into wide release at Sainsbury's 80,000 people lined up to get one. When the bag hit stores in Taiwan, there was so much demand that the riot police had to be called in to control a stampede, which sent 30 people to the hospital. Suddenly the formerly crunchy canvas tote had cachet.

Marc Jacobs skewered his own eponymous empire with his "marc by marc for marc" tote. This fascination with cheap bags seemed like part reaction to and part extension of the high-end handbag frenzy that gripped the fashion industry for much of the 00s. It had all the same qualities of exclusivity and brand envy, but also seemed at least in part to be an acknowledgment that things had gone too far. Was Mr. Jacobs' self-mocking tote a *mea culpa* for the astronomical handbag prices he had helped engineer at Louis Vuitton or was it a sly attempt to mainstream the phenomenon?

Simultaneous with the fashion world's affair with the tote, the graphic design community seemed to rediscover this humble sack. The canvas tote is a great medium for graphic design because it is flat and easy to print on. The canvas provides a beautiful off-white ground and the material is as wonderfully suited to silk-screen printing as primed canvas is to oil paint. The recent show at Open Space in Beacon, NY demonstrated the material appeal of the bags and the adaptability of their flat surface. Short-run printing and the quick transfer of graphic files make it remarkably easy to produce a relatively high quality bag. Design blogs have become enthralled by the never-ending stream of canvas totes—each one made unique by a clever and/ or beautiful graphic.

But the primary reason that designers in both fields have embraced canvas totes so quickly and nearly universally is their compelling social benefits. Not only is canvas a renewable resource, but the bags are biodegradable and sturdy enough to stand up to years of use. Reusing canvas bags could reduce the number of plastic bags that are used and discarded every year. According to Vincent Cobb, founder of reusablebags .com, somewhere between 500 billion and a trillion plastic bags are consumed worldwide each year. The impact of the super-thin plastic bags given away free with purchase at supermarkets and shops is so severe

Jacobs by Marc Jacobs... tote bag

Jacobs by Marc Jacobs . . .
tote bag, Marc Jacobs, 2008.

continued

Evaluations

"Paper, Plastic, or Canvas?" *(continued)*

that governments from Ireland to San Francisco to China have banned their distribution altogether. With the devastating effects of global warming and pollution becoming a feature of everyday life, designers and consumers alike latched onto [the] reusable canvas tote as a tangible step they could take to help the environment. Canvas totes are often cited as an example of how good design can help the environment because of the promise that they will replace plastic bags.

Alphabet tote bag, Daniel Eatock, 2008.

Daniel Eatock/Eatock Ltd.

Ironically, however, [the] plastic bag problem can in large part be traced back to the quality of its design as well. Before the introduction of the ultra thin plastic bags in the 1980s groceries were packed almost exclusively in paper bags. Plastic bags were touted as a way to save trees. Within a few years plastic was dominant and now commands 80% of grocery and supermarket traffic. Comparing a plastic bag to a paper bag, it is easy to see why: the ultra thin plastic bag is a vastly superior design. It consumes 40 percent less energy, generates 80 percent less solid waste, produces 70 percent fewer atmospheric emissions, and releases up to 94 percent fewer waterborne wastes. A plastic bag costs roughly a quarter as much to produce as a paper bag and is substantially lighter so it takes a great [deal] less [. . .] fossil fuel to transport. Plastic bags are among the most highly reused items in the home and are just as recyclable as paper.

The problem is that what is marvelous about an individual plastic bag becomes menacing when multiplied out to accommodate a rapidly growing global economy. The low cost of the bags allowed merchants to give them away, and despite the strength of an individual bag, they are routinely packed with a single item or double-bagged unnecessarily. The bag was so cleverly designed that there is simply no barrier to their indiscriminate distribution. Their incredible durability means it can take up to hundreds of years for them to decompose (a process that releases hazardous toxins). Although plastic bags are recyclable, the evidence suggests that even after ten years, in-store recycling programs have barely managed to achieve a one percent recycle rate. It is simply too easy and efficient to keep making and distributing more plastic bags. Meanwhile consumers mistakenly try to recycle the bags through their curbside recycling programs (perhaps because of the recycle symbols printed on the bags), creating a sorting nightmare at recycling facilities across the country.

Are we headed for the same kind of catch-22 with the adoption of the cleverly designed canvas tote with its renewable materials and infinite potential for customization? I am certainly an outlier in this case but I recently found twenty-three canvas totes in my house. Most of them were given to me as promotional materials for design studios, start-ups, boutique shops; more than one came from an environmental event or organization; one even commemorates a friend's wedding. A local community group recently delivered a reusable shopping bag to every house in my neighborhood to promote local holiday shopping. On the one hand all this interest in reusable bags is inspiring, but just like the story of Anya Hindmarch's "I'm Not a Plastic Bag" it also reveals the fundamental contradiction of the canvas tote phenomenon. Best intentions are almost immediately buried under an avalanche of conspicuous consumption and proliferation of choice. The environmental promise of reusable bags becomes pretty dubious when there are closets and drawers full of them in every home.

Design: Tracy Jenkins of Village / Photo: Rey Banogon

For Like Ever tote bag, Village.

This contradiction can largely be traced back to the influence of graphic design. Once this gorgeous flat surface presented itself, it quickly became simply a substrate for messaging, branding, promotion, etc. Judging by the cost, producing one tote is roughly equivalent to producing 400 plastic bags. That's fine if you actually use the tote 400 times, but what if you just end up with 40 totes in your closet? Once the emphasis shifts from reusing a bag to having a bag that reflects your status or personality, the environmental goal starts drifting out of sight.

I could not find any data on the subject of how much the use of canvas totes has decreased the number of plastic bags, but at best the totes can only be a catalyst for the act of reusing. Designers are correct in thinking that making a more appealing bag increases the likelihood that it will be reused, but the environmental benefit does not come from people acquiring bags. It comes from people reusing them. Successful attempts to reduce the number of plastic bags have all focused on (not surprisingly) depressing the consumption of plastic bags. For example, in 2001, Ireland consumed 1.2 billion plastic bags, or 316 per person. In 2002 they introduced what they called a PlasTax—15 cents for every plastic bag consumed. The program reduced consumption of plastic bags in that country by 90%! This seems to undercut the whole strategy of selling canvas totes as a way to help the environment. Based on the Irish example, even a 15 cent price-tag might actually inhibit the use of canvas totes by 90%. In terms of actually reducing the number of plastic bags, programs like the one at IKEA, which charges customers 5 cents per plastic bag and donates the proceeds to a conservation group, are probably more likely to have an impact than selling a canvas alternative. The best thing for the environment is reuse and that can be accomplished just as easily by reusing plastic bags.

The canvas tote is a great example of the power and the paradox of design in a consumer society. On the one hand design has allowed for

continued

personal expression, and fantastic variation in an otherwise mundane object. Every well-designed tote has the potential to replace some of the estimated 1000 plastic bags that each family brings home every year. The aesthetic power of a single design raised more awareness about the impact of plastic bags on our environment than any government or non-governmental organization. On the other hand, it is unclear that a consumable can counteract the effects of consumption. The designs that make each bag unique contribute to an overabundance of things that are essentially identical and the constant stream of newness discourages reuse. Just as the remarkable efficiency of the plastic bag ended up making it a menace to the environment, graphic design's ability to generate options and choices may turn a sustainable idea into an environmental calamity.

The following essay, which appeared on the Art & Design blog of the British newspaper the *Guardian*, is twelfth in Jonathan Glancey's series of evaluations of everyday objects. In his series, Glancey asks readers to reappreciate the form and design of the ordinary paper clip, to pause a moment to admire the "smartly uniformed, practical, and long-lived" UPS trucks passing them on the street, and, in this blog, to share his pleasure in the neon light.

> Classics of Everyday Design No 12
Jonathan Glancey

Stepping out of Copenhagen station a few weeks ago in the winter dark, I felt welcomed by the colourful glow of the rooftops of the otherwise straight-laced office blocks and hotels of the close-by neighbourhood. These are crowned with neon advertisements. Nothing fancy, and yet warm, alive and happily cheerful in the otherwise biting winter gloom.

Here is an example of subtle neon lighting used to make a winter night in a dark and cold winter city shine like some modern, and urban, equivalent of Jacob's coat of many colours. Not exactly Piccadilly Circus, not quite Times Square, but rainbow-like, heart-warming and fun.

The neon sign is indeed one of the great everyday classic designs. It can be subtle. It can be all singing, all dancing, yet never ever dull.

The mastermind, and master eye, behind the cheerful neon sign was Georges Claude (1870–1960), a French chemist, engineer and inventor. Claude discovered that an electric charge applied to a sealed tube of neon gas would produce a joyous coloured light. Red. And, that other of the family of gases to which neon belongs, treated in the same way, would bring alive other colours, too. Blue in the case of mercury. White with CO2. Helium turned gas and electricity to gold. Phosphor-coated glass tubes could spin any number of colours—some 150 to date.

Neon itself had been identified by the British scientists, William Ramsey and M. W. Travers, in 1898; yet, it was up to Claude to suggest its popular and commercial potential. The gas was certainly special—just one part in 65,000 of the Earth's atmosphere—but once distilled, could enliven shops, arcades, squares and city centres from Los Angeles via London to Rome and Shanghai.

© iStockphoto.com/Valerie Loiseleux

Evaluations

Claude demonstrated the first neon sign in Paris at the World Expo of 1910, although the first commercial application—above the door of a Parisian barber's shop—had to wait another two years. Claude first exported the invention, or concept, to the US in 1923 when ritzy neon lamps showcased a Packard car dealer's showroom in Los Angeles, and the rest was colourfully-lit history.

Neon lighting can, of course, be wholly over-the-top, and absurdly vulgar; yet, at its best, it warms the cockles, and cornices, of any number of otherwise dark buildings and glum streets in winter, and whenever, in fact, the blazing sun, all hydrogen and helium, and only a tiny bit of neon, disappears.

> ANALYZING THE RHETORICAL SITUATION

1. Look again at the photographs of the various canvas tote bags. What do these images convey to you about the bags' surge in popularity?
2. What specific features of a tote bag does Siegel evaluate?
3. What criteria does he use to evaluate the simple tote bag? How does he describe the various totes in terms of these criteria?
4. Who is the specific audience for each of the two evaluations in this section? What purpose does each writer hope to achieve? How does that purpose relate to the audience for each evaluation?

5. What kinds of specific details and evidence does each writer provide in order to evaluate the everyday object? What rhetorical method(s) of development does each author use? What kinds of questions do the writers ask about tote bags or neon lights in order to draw out these types of details and evidence?

6. What rhetorical opportunity prompted each of the visual evaluations in this section? How would you characterize each one's contribution to the ongoing professional and public conversation about everyday design?

COMMUNITY CONNECTIONS

1. Write for ten minutes about your response to the evaluation of the tote bag. How do the criteria used by the writer coincide with or diverge from the criteria that you would apply to evaluate a tote bag you use every day? How do those criteria relate to those you consider most important for evaluating some other common object?

2. Write for ten minutes about the evaluation of the neon light. What criteria does the writer use to evaluate neon lights? How do these criteria relate to those you consider most important for evaluating a light or another common object?

3. What object other than a tote bag or a neon light that you encounter every day has a design that affects how you work or play? Who made the design decisions that shaped this object? How and why do you come into contact with this object?

4. Write for ten minutes about the design of the object you chose in question 3. Provide as many specific visual and tactile details as you can in describing it. Then, write for five minutes about the ways in which you use this object. Be sure to specify where and when (places and time of day) you use it. Finally, write for five minutes about how the visual design of this object affects your attitude toward the work or play that you do. Be prepared to share your answers.

Evaluations: A Fitting Response

The readings in this chapter illustrate the use of evaluation to understand how visual elements shape our everyday experiences. Visual effects in movies such as *The Matrix* can lead us, in the words of Morpheus, to "free our minds" and consider the limits of human thought.

A nighttime walk down a neon-lit city street can lead us, like Jonathan Glancey, to take pleasure in the efficient functioning of everyday objects. Clearly, evaluating visuals in our culture helps us to better understand the logical and emotional responses they produce in us.

An evaluation of images in contemporary culture

As you have seen throughout this chapter, there are many visual elements in our culture that affect the ways in which we live and work, whether we realize it or not. Critics compose evaluative essays as a means for exploring the ways in which our lives are shaped by images and design. In the following essay, critic Mike D'Angelo evaluates two movies in terms of the technique used in their creation.

Unreally, Really Cool: Stop-Motion Movies May Be Old School, but They Still Eat Other Animation for Breakfast

Mike D'Angelo

As a filmgoer, I have virtually no allegiances. My goal is basically to avoid things that suck. However brilliant the actor, I have no interest in watching him sort his laundry or demonstrate that even the mentally retarded can be wonderful parents, thereby teaching Michelle Pfeiffer the true meaning of family. You say your movie is about lesbian vampire Catholic schoolgirls on a submarine? It may take zero stars from every critic on the face of the planet to keep me away . . . but if it does get the pan of a lifetime, I can resist. Or at least wait for the DVD.

That said, no amount of negative buzz could keep me away from two of this season's tastiest offerings: Tim Burton's *Corpse Bride* . . . and *Wallace & Gromit: The Curse of the Were-rabbit*. . . .

Image by © Louis Quail/Corbis

If there's one thing in the vast world of cinema that qualifies as inherently compelling, that thing is stop-motion animation. Almost as old as the medium itself—you can see stop motion at work in Georges Méliès's classic short *A Trip to the Moon* (1902)—the basic process has remained unchanged. The original King Kong, the dueling skeletons in Ray Harryhausen adventures, the barnyard animals in *Chicken Run*—all involve miniature puppets being painstakingly manipulated one frame at a time.

Pixar may have the most consistently impressive track record since the glory days of Walt Disney, but a Pixar CG [computer-generated] movie with a mediocre script and generic voice characterizations would be . . . well, it'd be *Madagascar*. Traditional cel animation, too, no matter how beautiful, can be deadly dull. Stop motion is different. There is no such thing as a stop-motion film that isn't fascinating to watch. Obviously, some are better than others—and there's reason to hope that *Corpse Bride*, a typically macabre Burton fable about a man who inadvertently marries a cadaver, and *Were-rabbit*, the long-awaited feature debut of Nick Park's beloved duo, will both be terrific. But all of them share the same singular, outré visual allure. They're uncanny.

Consider Gromit. (I've been waiting years to say that.) If you've seen any of Park's Oscar-winning shorts about the adventures of a cheerful English nincompoop and his faithful, tolerant canine companion, you're familiar with the character's look and temperament: big floppy ears, deep-set goggle eyes, silently unperturbable demeanor. You probably have a favorite Gromit moment, and it probably involves nothing more dynamic than a single styptic blink in response to escalating lunacy. But I submit that Gromit would not be half as funny or as endearing were he hand drawn or computer generated, no matter how expertly the animators replicated his appearance and mannerisms. Whether we're conscious of it or not, his oddball charisma is rooted in a combination of tactility and artificiality that's unique to stop motion. It's a very different kind of response from the one we have to Dumbo or Buzz Lightyear. We love Gromit because he's at once real and not real.

Human beings are drawn to borders, gray areas, the mystery of the in-between. The director's favorite time of day is dusk, also known as the "magic hour": no longer light, not yet dark. Many movie stars have vaguely androgynous features (Julia Roberts looks exactly like Eric Roberts to me), and movies themselves tend to appeal to us the more they resemble our dreams, that world weirdly suspended between waking and sleeping. What makes stop motion so arresting, regardless of whether we're involved in the story or the characters, is that it pushes this dichotomy one step further, straddling the line

The writer provides a succinct definition of the phenomenon he will evaluate.

D'Angelo mentions some characteristics that he does not apply to stop-motion films: "mediocre scripts" and "generic voice characterizations."

D'Angelo introduces one criterion he will use to evaluate animated films— "outré" suggests that an animated film ought to be evaluated according to whether it's unconventional, eccentric, or bizarre.

The word "Consider" signals that the writer is going to begin providing evidence and examples to support his claim.

D'Angelo introduces two more criteria: the objects on the screen should combine tactility and artificiality.

Evaluations

that separates reality from imagination.•Cel animation and computer animation, no matter how aesthetically pleasing, never offer anything more than a simulacrum of reality; they are clearly make-believe. But when we look at one of the grandiosely morbid sets in Burton's *The Nightmare Before Christmas*, we can plainly see that those ornate tombstones and grinning jack-o'-lanterns and curlicue hills are really there, physically present.•(The next time you watch *Nightmare*, notice how many objects have grooves cut into them, or have surfaces that are stippled. That sort of three-dimensional detail works only in stop motion.) And there's something oddly riveting about watching puppets navigate this tactile landscape 1/24 of a second at a time.

That's another thing about stop motion: There are no short-cuts. Cel animation is exacting work, but there are numerous ways to economize, as any *Speed Racer* fan knows all too well. Computer animation allows for endless revision. But stop motion is always and only moving everything a fraction of an inch, taking a picture, moving everything a fraction of an inch, taking a picture—day in, day out, for years and years. Screw something up and you have to do it all . . . over . . . again. It's like building a skyscraper using a pair of tweezers. Consequently, the folks who toil in this nearly moribund field tend to be perfectionists—not just when it comes to technical matters but in every aspect of filmmaking.•*Corpse Bride* and *Were-rabbit* don't have to be good. But I bet you they will be.

■ GUIDE TO RESPONDING TO THE RHETORICAL SITUATION

Understanding the Rhetorical Situation

When you want to present your thoughts on a facet of visual culture, you want to consider composing an evaluation. Evaluations commonly have the following features:

- Evaluations describe the particular object or phenomenon in a way that the rhetorical audience will understand.

- Evaluations make clear why a particular object or phenomenon should be evaluated.

- Evaluations identify the precise category into which the object or phenomenon fits.

- The criteria on which the object or phenomenon is to be evaluated are presented clearly.

- Concrete evidence and examples illustrate the ways in which the object or phenomenon does or does not meet each evaluative criterion.

- Evaluations articulate a clear argument about whether or not the object or phenomenon meets the criteria on which it is being evaluated.

 The following sections will help you evaluate an element of visual culture. To work with an online guide to the elements of the rhetorical situation, access your English CourseMate through CengageBrain.com.

Identifying an opportunity

Consider your campus. Are there any buildings with unarguably unique architecture? Are there any pages on the school's Web site that are either visually compelling or aesthetically uninspired? Are there any advertisements in the campus newspaper, in a building stairwell, or on a campus bus that you think have particularly innovative imagery or layout? Is there any public artwork that made you do a double-take when you first walked by it? Are there any computer labs that make you feel mentally and physically exhausted—or all revved up? Are there any couches or chairs in the common area of your dormitory that seem to be particularly inviting—or just the opposite? Are any of your friends' dorm rooms creatively decorated?

1. Make a list of five interesting images or designs that you have noticed over the past week, a list that might include some elements you wrote about in response to the questions on page 262. For each one, write a few sentences describing your initial impressions. Were your impressions positive or negative? Provide as many details as you can to explain why. Also identify the contextual factors that may have shaped your impression of each image or design: where and when (place and time of day) you saw it, what you were doing at that time, the emotion or response evoked.

2. Choose two of the images or designs you listed and take photos of them. Pay particular attention to documenting the physical context in which the image or design appears.

3. Choose the image or design you want to write about and compose four or five sentences that describe its visual features in concrete, specific detail. After composing these descriptions, spend several minutes free-writing about the context of the image or design. Respond to questions such as these: What do you think the purpose of this image or design might be? When and where do you tend to interact with it in your everyday life? If you are writing about the visual design of an everyday object, what are the purposes for which you use the object? If you are writing about an image, how do you view it and in what ways do you interpret it and make sense of it?

Locating an audience

The following questions can help you locate your rhetorical audience as well as identify the relationship they have to the visual element you're writing about. Answering them can help you determine the best way to present your evaluation of that image or design.

1. List the names of the persons or groups—students, faculty, administrators, community members, alumni, parents—most likely to see and be affected by the visual element you've chosen. These are potential audiences for your evaluation.

2. Next to the name of each audience, write reasons that audience might have for thinking in greater depth about this particular image or design. In other words, what would persuade these audiences that the visual element needs to be evaluated?

3. How could each of these audiences reasonably be influenced by an evaluation of this image or design? In other words, what emotional responses could they be expected to have or what logical conclusions could they be expected to arrive at after reading your evaluative essay? Consider what motivations each group might

have for analyzing the specific details that make up an object's design or an image's composition.

4. With your audience's interests and motivations in mind, look again at the descriptions of the image or design that you composed in the preceding section. Which description(s) will enable your readers to feel engaged in your evaluation and invested in exploring this image or design in greater depth? The better description not only allows readers to create a vivid mental picture of the visual element but also helps them understand why and how it affects them. At this point, it may be necessary to revise your best description to tailor it to your audience's needs and interests.

Identifying a fitting response

As you know, narrowing your purpose is important, because different purposes require different kinds of texts, delivered through different media. For example, if you are evaluating an image such as a photograph or a painting, you might want to compose an essay that would appear as part of a museum display or in an exhibition catalog. Your evaluation of a visually uninspiring Web page could be crafted as a letter to the staff in the admissions or alumni relations office. Your evaluation of the dysfunctional design of a computer lab could take the form of a pamphlet or flyer to be distributed to other students in order to gain their support for change. The point is that once you have identified your opportunity, audience, and purpose, you need to determine what kind of text will best respond to your rhetorical situation.

Use the following questions to help you narrow your purpose and shape your response:

1. What kinds of facts or details about the image or design do you need to provide in order to precisely define the contexts in which it influences or interacts with people's everyday lives on campus?
2. What kinds of facts or details about the visual image or visual design make it particularly compelling?
3. What cultural, social, economic, or political details do you need to know in order to better understand the purpose of this visual design and its significance for the people who created it as well as for the people who interact with it, whether regularly or only once?
4. Are you asking the audience to adopt a new perspective on this particular object or image, or do you want the audience to perform a particular action in response to your writing?
5. What is the best way to reach this audience? That is, what kind of text is this audience most likely to respond to? (Chapter 10 can help you explore options for media and design.)

Writing an Evaluation: Working with Your Available Means

Shaping your evaluation

You are no doubt familiar with evaluations because you have seen many examples of this genre in the form of movie reviews in newspapers and magazines and product reviews in print and online publications such as *Consumer Reports* and *PC Magazine*. What you may not have noticed, however, are the ways in which evaluations use the rhetorical methods of development. For instance, the introduction of an evaluation provides readers with a concise definition of what is to be evaluated, the reasons it merits evaluation, and the particular ways in which it is to be evaluated. By the end of the introduction, then, the writer has begun to establish his or her expertise and good sense, asserting a position as a qualified evaluator and thereby establishing his or her ethos. For example, by the end of his second paragraph, Mike D'Angelo has provided a brief definition of stop-motion animation ("miniature puppets being painstakingly manipulated one frame at a time") and explained how he thinks animated films should be evaluated (by whether or not they provide compelling movie-going experiences). Writers of evaluations also use the introduction to show readers why they need to consider the evaluation. D'Angelo is no exception: he tells readers that two stop-motion movies will be released soon. By providing an in-depth explanation, D'Angelo establishes his expertise and knowledge.

pages 306–308

The body of an evaluation generally provides the criteria according to which the particular object or phenomenon will be evaluated. These

Introduction	Body	Conclusion
► Establishes the author's ethos by ► Defining the subject to be evaluated ► Explaining why the subject should be evaluated ► Identifying the ways in which the subject is to be evaluated ► Explaining why readers should pay attention to the evaluation	► Provides criteria for evaluating the subject ► Describes the subject in detail ► Offers specific facts, examples, and direct quotations to show how the subject meets or does not meet those criteria ► Explains the political, economic, social, or cultural context that gives the subject particular significance ► Establishes logos	► Synthesizes criteria and collected evidence ► Makes one final appeal for readers to adopt a specific attitude or opinion ► Establishes pathos

pages 318–320 criteria help make—and shape—the argument at the same time that they establish the logos (the logical appeals) of the evaluation. To accompany each criterion (and further emphasize logos), the writer offers facts and direct quotations to show how the object or phenomenon does or does not meet it. The body of an evaluation also describes the object or phenomenon in as much specific detail as possible, again maintaining the appeal to logos. Photos and audio or video clips can help provide page 310 details, as can careful verbal description. Readers of D'Angelo's essay, for example, can imagine Gromit's "big floppy ears, deep-set goggle eyes, silently unperturbable demeanor" and see the grooves cut into the tombstones in *The Nightmare Before Christmas.* These details grab and maintain the readers' interest. Just as important, sensory details help the writer to persuade his or her readers that the evaluation is based on a careful, complete analysis of all the elements that make up the object or phenomenon, and they provide the evidence to support the writer's argument and make the readers believe that it is based on sound reasons. Indeed, the reader of D'Angelo's essay is no doubt convinced that stop-motion animators "tend to be perfectionists—not just when it comes to technical matters but in every aspect of filmmaking."

The body of an evaluation often attempts to explain the political, economic, social, or cultural context that gives this object or phenomenon particular significance. D'Angelo, for example, argues that "movies themselves tend to appeal to us the more they resemble our dreams." Thus, stop-motion animation is particularly compelling because this method of composing visual imagery in a film "pushes this dichotomy [between waking and sleeping] one step further, straddling the line that separates reality from imagination." This contextual evaluation helps deepen readers' understanding of how the animated films fit into contemporary visual culture and influence their daily lives.

Finally, the conclusion of an evaluation brings together the various criteria and the collected evidence in order to make one final appeal for readers to adopt a specific attitude or opinion. D'Angelo connects with his readers on an emotional level (establishing pathos), urging them to appreciate the technical artistry of stop-motion animated movies and the "folks who toil" to create these films.

Revision and peer review

After you've drafted your evaluation, ask one of your classmates to read it. You'll want your classmate to respond to your work in a way that helps you revise it into the strongest evaluation it can be, one that addresses your intended audience, helps you fulfill your purpose, and is delivered in the most appropriate means available to you.

Evaluations

Questions for a peer reviewer

1. To what opportunity for change is the writer responding?
2. Who might be the writer's intended audience?
3. What might be the writer's purpose? How do audience and purpose come together in this evaluation?
4. What information did you receive from the introduction? How does the writer introduce the particular object or phenomenon he or she is exploring? How does the writer suggest why it needs to be evaluated? What suggestions do you have for the writer regarding the introduction?
5. Note the writer's thesis statement. If you cannot locate a thesis statement, what thesis statement might work for this evaluation?
6. Note the assertions the writer makes to support the thesis. (These may be in the form of criteria the writer establishes.) Are they presented in chronological or emphatic order? Does the writer use the order that seems most effective? How could the writer improve the order of these assertions?
7. If you cannot locate a series of assertions, what assertions could be made to support the thesis statement?
8. Note the concrete evidence and examples that the writer uses to show how the subject meets or does not meet the criteria established.
9. How does the writer establish ethos? How could the writer strengthen this appeal?
10. What material does the writer use to establish logos? How might the writer strengthen this appeal (see questions 6–8).
11. How does the writer make use of pathos?
12. What did you learn from the conclusion that you didn't already know after reading the introduction and body? What information does the writer want you to take away from the evaluation? Does the writer attempt to change your attitude, action, or opinion?
13. What section of the evaluation did you most enjoy? Why?

EVALUATIONS IN THREE MEDIA

Online evaluation

Stephanie Zacharek posted her evaluation of *Clash of the Titans* (2010) on the site Salon.com. To read the review, find *Evaluations in Three Media* in your English Course-Mate, accessed through CengageBrain.com.

Image: © Frank Trapper/Corbis

Evaluation using video

"EDU Checkup" is a video blog (vlog) that reviews college and university Web sites. To view the evaluation of Southwest Minnesota State University's Web site, find *Evaluation in Three Media* in your English Course-Mate, accessed through CengageBrain.com

Image: © Nick Denardis

Print evaluation

In the following essay, student Alexis Walker locates a rhetorical opportunity in the changing landscape of her city's downtown.

Image: Courtesy of Jim Kirkhuff.

- If Alexis had wanted to argue against the sale of a downtown shop to Dunkin' Donuts, she could have organized her thoughts into talking points and spoken at a city council meeting. Or, if she had wanted to focus on architectural details that were obscured by the new sign, she might have written a letter to the local preservation association. As a long-time resident witnessing a shift in the aesthetics of the downtown area, Alexis wanted to evaluate the effects of this latest change in order to influence the perceptions of other residents—so that they might use the criteria she establishes in her critical review to evaluate future developments.

Alexis Walker

Prof. Davis

English 251

September 27, 2009

Alexis opens her evaluation by describing the scene she plans to analyze in a way that all her readers can easily understand.

Donuts at Easton's Center Circle: Slam Dunk or Cycle of Deterioration?

•The way a city looks—its skyline, the buildings, the streets, even the greenery—affects how we feel in that city and the perception of what it has to offer. From the hectic environment of New York to the calming quality of a rural farm, these feelings are informed by what surrounds us.•With that in mind, the center of a city should, ideally, portray the best the city has to offer. Visual clues, such as the type of businesses that thrive in the area, indicate something about the town.

In a two-sentence thesis statement, Alexis asserts why the scene she describes merits evaluation.

A quick scan around downtown Easton on a winter weekday afternoon, however, makes clear that there is much to be desired in this eastern Pennsylvania town. For instance, the prominence of the Peace Candle, standing proudly in the center of the traffic circle, assumes a grandiosity that fails to actualize itself. No matter which direction one enters the circle from, the peace candle sits straight ahead. The off-white concrete representing the wax looks grungy and neglected. Some melted wax drips down the sides in light blue cascades of color encrusting each corner. The stiff flame of orange and red metal sits atop the structure, too unassuming to project the proper vibrancy. It's all supported by a series of black visible cables emphasizing the candle's behemoth existence as almost menacing. The display of fire intends to signify energy and soul, an attempt to spark downtown into a bustling hub of city commerce full of life rather than old and dull as the mostly rundown space actually is. Instead, darkened windowpanes and boarded up entrances encircle the mammoth centerpiece.

Fig. 1. Historic downtown's Dunkin' Donuts
(photograph courtesy of Jim Kirkhuff).

Freshly painted buildings and the presence of patrons constitute the two criteria for an appealing city center or, in this case, center circle.

•The bright white, freshly painted outside of the new Dunkin' Donuts provides a clear contrast to the lifeless grey buildings that surround it. The signature orange and pink lettering adorns both sides of this corner edifice, and its large windows showcase the patrons the establishment actually is attracting. All of these attributes, dissimilar to the dreary display downtown Easton usually offers, might suggest that the area is on the rise. Indeed, the revamped Dunkin' Donuts building and the business it brings are nice.

This and following paragraphs contain details that illuminate how well Easton is meeting each of the two criteria that Alexis is using to evaluate the overall appeal of the center circle.

•There are a few more exceptions to the lifeless environment intermittently placed among the abandoned properties. Pearly Baker's restaurant sits inconspicuously in one corner despite its neon green sign. Easton is also home to Crayola crayons, and across the street, a building complex dominates the scene, advertising all things Crayola (and a McDonald's to boot!); a giant crayon box acts as a sign to identify—if gaudily—the gift shop entrance. It is also a relatively new building with plenty of windows and one of the taller buildings in the circle.

Considering the already successful Crayola complex and built-in McDonald's, it is clear that bigger corporations are not new to downtown. Now, though, with the addition of a Dunkin' Donuts, the precedent is set for what kind of companies can be successful within the circle: anything with a brand name. Crayola and Dunkin' Donuts both have name recognition, which is a primary reason they are the most prominent attractions to Easton's center. The chance the center circle once had to become a thriving, eclectic neighborhood now seems impossible. Even if small businesses remain for a while, it is the Dunkin' Donuts that will draw the most business from Crayola's downtown existence and vice versa. The patronage these two businesses will bring to downtown might create some spillover business for the other establishments, but these two primary attractions seem to complement each other the most. And so the problem remains: less patronage for small businesses begets fewer attractions to offer Eastonians. There won't be any compelling postcards of the hustle and bustle of the charming city to sell. An image of a humdrum town with an emerging strip mall for a downtown region, however, is easily imaginable, if less compelling.

There are bright spots within this dismal image, though. During the summertime, provided good weather, Easton's center circle plays host to a farmers' market every week. Consisting of stands selling products from produce to freshly milled soap, it is a time when there is an alternative offering—transient as it may be—to draw a crowd. And that crowd is outside and socializing, delivering a livelier image than the downtown area used to.

Should one take a picture of these two different downtown environments, position them next to each other and then draw conclusions about what type of place Easton is to live in, the results would obviously be quite different. Whether one picture is more accurate, or

In this passage, Alexis explains what kinds of business will succeed in Easton's center circle.

Then she quickly points out the concrete reasons that the circle won't succeed: most businesses don't meet the criteria for success.

Evaluations

In mentioning the farmers' market, Alexis offers one concrete example of how the center circle might meet the second criterion, that of having patrons visit the downtown.

Finally and overall, Alexis articulates a clear argument that Easton is not meeting the criteria required for a thriving center circle.

whether the real Easton experience is somewhere in between ultimately is irrelevant. The fact remains that a city projects a certain experience through its surroundings. Is it welcoming, impressive, expansive, busy, or a combination? Usually a trip to Easton's center circle would not yield a particularly promising impression of what Easton has to offer. Maybe the recent addition of a Dunkin' Donuts will improve downtown's condition. On the other hand, maybe it will cement its deterioration.

Alternatives to the Evaluation

Fitting responses come in many forms, not just evaluations. Your instructor might call upon you to consider one of the following opportunities for writing.

1. What happens when a familiar image gets printed in a different medium or a familiar design appears in a different context? How does this new medium or context affect a viewer's or a user's experience of that image or that object? For example, how does the visual effect of a painting by Vincent van Gogh differ when the painting is displayed in a gallery and when it's reprinted on mugs and t-shirts? Or, how does a response to a urinal differ when it appears in a bathroom and when it appears in a museum? Compose an analysis of how the medium or the context affects a response to an image or object.

2. As you learned throughout this chapter, descriptive details are at the heart of any evaluation of visual culture. In a descriptive essay, help readers visualize a particular image or object and try to draw out a particular emotional response to the image or object.

3. Designers such as Marc Jacobs and Anya Hindmarch took up tote bags not only as a way to express their creative vision but also to solve a problem of everyday life—too much plastic waste. Identify a design problem that affects the work or play of people on your campus or in the surrounding community. In an investigative report, describe the problem and help readers better understand how it shapes their lives in negative ways and how their lives might be different if the design were improved.

Strategies ³ for Composing

Responsible writers always consider the rhetorical situation as they write. They realize the value of responding to an opportunity for change with a purposeful message directed at a specific audience and delivered by the most appropriate means available to them. By paying attention to these features of the rhetorical situation, effective writers are able to adjust their message until it comes as close to fulfilling their rhetorical purpose as conditions allow. Often, writers consider the various rhetorical methods for developing their ideas, turning to the broad categories of definition, comparison, relationship, and circumstance as resources for finding what to say and ways to say it. At the same time, effective writers also carefully consider the steps in their composing process, whether they are working online, on paper, or with videos, images, or audio. They know that successful communication takes time and effort—and more than one draft. To develop your writing skills further, you'll want to pay special attention to your own writing process.

9 Writing Processes and Strategies: From Tentative Idea to Finished Product

In this chapter, you'll move through the three general steps of the writing process: planning, drafting, and revising. These steps are the same whether you're working online or off. As you read about each of these steps, you'll learn when to consider the components of the rhetorical situation (components that include problem or opportunity for change, writer, purpose, message, audience, and context) and when to set those components aside and just write. You'll also learn about the rhetorical methods that are used for developing writing: definition, classification and division, exemplification, description, comparison and contrast, cause-and-effect analysis, process analysis, narration, and argument.

© Cindy Charles / Photo Edit

> WRITE FOR FIVE

Write for five minutes in response to each of the following questions. Be prepared to share your answers with the rest of the class.

1. What is your first reaction to receiving a writing assignment? What kinds of information do you look for in that assignment? Why? When do you actually start the assignment (however you define "start")?

2. Make a list of the kinds of writing you do regularly. Categorize the list according to whether the writing is work-related, school-related, or personal. Which of the available means of delivery do you use most often to deliver that writing?

3. Compare your responses to questions 1 and 2 with those of two classmates. What surprised you about their responses? Pick two things a classmate wrote that made you rethink your answers; then rewrite those answers.

Finding Pleasure in Writing

You've been writing almost all your life. When you were a small child, you grabbed crayons, felt-tip markers, or chalk and wrote on whatever surfaces you could find: paper, coloring books, sidewalks, chalk boards, table tops, walls, lampshades. You might not yet have been talking fluently or reading well, but you were already "writing" as well as your fine-motor skills and linguistic expertise would allow. Like the human animal you are, you were marking your territory—leaving messages for the people who entered your world. When you learned to write cursive or to use a keyboard, you may have felt the same kind of satisfaction that you felt when you scribbled on the sidewalk. You were moving forward into the adult world of writing, a world that feeds our primitive human need to communicate with others.

As you think back on your earliest memories of writing, keep in mind the process of writing that you practiced then. You gathered up your materials and set to work. The entire process—from start to finish—was simple, often fun. Many of you have been writing—and enjoying it—for years. Award-winning author Joyce Carol Oates cannot recall a time when she wasn't writing:

Before I could write what might be called human words in the English language, I eagerly emulated grown-ups' handwriting in pencil scribbles. My first "novels" . . . were tablets of inspired scribbles illustrated by line drawings of chickens, horses and upright cats.

—**Joyce Carol Oates**,
"To Invigorate Literary
Mind, Start Moving
Literary Feet"

© Cheryl Glenn, 2007.

What do you remember about early writing experiences?

Strategies

Like the writing you did as a child, college writing can also be satisfying, but that is not to say that it will *always* be fun, let alone easy. The process might at times seem demanding, but the results are often exhilarating, something you're proud of. If that weren't the case, you wouldn't worry about writing well or care what your teacher thought of your writing.

Perhaps the best way to make writing a pleasurable activity is to build on what you already do well and enjoy as you write. If you're a person who likes to explore a topic, you may already have a collection of special notebooks in which you jot down notes and observations, write freely about interesting topics, copy delicious phrases or sentences you've heard or read, and make rough outlines.

You may be a writer who especially likes composing the first draft—by hand or keyboard. Maybe you enjoy the tactile sensation of writing with a gel pen on a yellow legal pad or the friction of moving a felt-tipped pen across pulpy paper. Maybe you draft at your computer, entertaining yourself by connecting particular fonts with particular ideas in your draft. Quickly moving between word processing and on-line audio and video applications, you might share and get feedback on bits of your freewriting or get inspired to use digital media in your composition. At your keyboard, you can rewrite phrase after phrase, sentence after sentence, tinkering that may be especially comforting and pleasurable for you.

Or maybe you're one of those writers who are relieved when they finish a draft so that they can use their energy to work with and against that draft. You may like to print out your piece, sit back in a comfortable chair, and read it line by line, penciling in new sentences, crossing out entire sections, fiddling with your word choice, and drawing arrows to reorganize your paragraphs. You might keep a thesaurus, dictionary, and handbook in a stack nearby, resources for checking your words and punctuation; you might also keep one of your special notebooks nearby so you can weave into your writing some of your favorite phrases or thoughts. Writers who enjoy this final part of the writing process feel that the hardest part is over. These writers especially enjoy polishing their writing until they're proud to submit it. As internationally known writer Susan Sontag put it:

> You write in order to read what you've written and see if it's OK and, since of course it never is, to rewrite it—once, twice, as many times as it takes to get it to be something you can bear to reread.
>
> —**Susan Sontag**, *Writers on Writing*

For writers like Sontag, the enjoyment they get from rereading their revised work is the best part, whether or not they send it on to someone else to read.

Regardless of which parts of the process they enjoy most, all good writers move through a general, three-step writing process: planning,

Strategies

drafting, and revising. Each of these general steps has smaller steps within it, which is probably why no two writers move through these three basic stages in exactly the same way. Still, most experienced writers use some variation of the general writing process that we'll review in the rest of this chapter. Before we begin, take a few minutes to jot down answers to the following questions, which will reveal what parts of the writing process you already do well and already enjoy.

> YOUR WRITING EXPERIENCES

1. Of the many kinds of writing you do, which one gives you the most pleasure? Is it instant messages; planned, drafted, and revised essays; or some other writing? Why do you do this kind of writing?

2. Which of the means available to you for writing gives you the most pleasure (for example, do you prefer pen and paper or a keyboard)? Which one makes you feel most confident?

3. How would you describe the process you go through to accomplish this pleasurable writing?

4. What part(s) of your writing process do you most enjoy? Find most difficult? Spend the most time on? Spend the least time on? Can you imagine any ways to make the difficult part(s) easier or more enjoyable?

Recognizing an Opportunity for Change

As you learned in chapter 1, composing most often begins with an opportunity for change or a problem: a specific reason to use words in order to address an issue. You may think of a due date for a written assignment as a problem that can be addressed only through words—and it is. But even in this case, any authentic essay will be a direct response to a broader problem (for instance, "What makes for an effective PowerPoint presentation?" or "How do credit card companies make money?"). Often, the opportunity for change is more subtle: a problem that tugs at you for attention. After attending a school board meeting and listening to a discussion of budget cuts, you may feel the need to write a letter to the editor of your local newspaper about the importance of music classes for schoolchildren. At the movie theater, you might find yourself wanting to speak to the manager when you see the sorry state of the restrooms. Or you may be bothered by a controversy—such as that surrounding South African runner Caster Semenya's gender classification—and feel the need to post your opinion online. The problem you've identified establishes your starting point; it is the opportunity for change that prompts you to enter the conversation.

Planning a Response

Planning to write usually involves three steps: exploration, organization, and consideration of development methods. Experienced writers employ a variety of methods for exploring a topic or inventing things to say about it.

Exploration

The most commonly used methods of exploration (also known as *invention strategies*) are listing, keeping a journal, freewriting, and questioning. But experienced writers also regularly use conversation, meditation, reading, and listening as ways to discover good ideas. They realize that good ideas come to them in all sorts of ways, so they keep a pen and a notebook with them all the time, even at night, because ideas often come just as they're falling asleep. They grab the notebook, scribble down their idea, and sleep soundly, no longer worried that they'll forget the idea.

As you plan your college writing assignments, you'll probably continue to rely on the methods that have worked for you in the past. When you're stuck, however, you may want to try out a new method, if only as a way to jump-start your writing.

Listing As soon as you have some idea of what you're expected to write about, start a list of possibilities—and keep adding to it. Look over some of the lists you made in response to the questions on pages 296 and 297. These are the kinds of lists that can spark your thinking and writing.

On the first day of the semester, when her professor reviewed the syllabus for the "Writing and Technology" course, Stacy Simkanin learned about the requirements for her first essay. So during the first week of classes, she jotted down some tentative ideas, knowing that, as time went by, she'd keep adding possibilities for her formal essay. You can follow Stacy's example and keep your list going over the course of a few days. Or you can jot down all your ideas at one sitting, a kind of listing often referred to as **brainstorming**. What follows is the list Stacy made and kept adding to:

computers	Web searches	social networking
chat rooms	Statistical Universe	downloadable essays
visual culture class	plagiarism	forum discussions
photo essays	convenience	electronic requests
quality	online databases	Internet
constantly developing	online course notes	time saver
full-length journal articles	classroom computers	Google

Keeping a journal Some writing instructors expect you to keep a weekly journal, either in print or online. When you're writing in your journal, you don't need to be concerned with punctuation, grammar, spelling, and other mechanical features. If you write three pages a week for a journal or as part of your online class discussion, you may not be able to lift a ready-to-submit essay directly from your work, but you will have accumulated a pool of ideas from which to draw. Even more important, you will have been practicing getting thoughts into words.

In addition to using journal entries as a way to explore your topic, you might also use your journal to write out your understandings of and reactions to your reading and writing assignments and class discussions and lectures. As Stacy considered her own upcoming assignment, she wrote in her ongoing electronic journal:

> I think I tend to take modern advances for granted, but when I look at how much more I use technology as a college student than I did, say, eight years ago as a junior high student, it's amazing to think of how much my studies have become dependent on it. I need computer access for almost everything anymore, from writing papers to updating my Facebook status, to doing research on the Web. Not only that, but some of my favorite classes have been those that incorporated some form of technology into the course format. I think this is one of technology's major advantages—turning learning into something new and interactive, which gets students involved. I've had courses that used technology in basic ways, like my Biological Science class, in which the class lectures were recorded and saved online for students to listen to later. Some of my other courses, though, have used it in lots of interesting ways. In one of my English classes, for instance, we took a day to hold class in a chat room, and we all signed into the room from our computers at home. It was great as part of our discussions about literacy, because experimenting with computer literacy allowed us all to see how people communicate differently when they're not face to face. Of course, some people would argue that kids my age spend way too much time "chatting" and texting, and that Instant Messenger is one of a student's biggest distracters. I guess, like any good thing, technology also carries with it some disadvantages.

Freewriting Freewriting means just what it says: it's the writing you do that costs you nothing. You don't have to worry about spelling or grammar; you don't even have to worry about writing complete sentences, because no one is going to grade it. In fact, no one (except

Strategies

you) may ever even read it. It's the kind of writing you do to loosen up your thinking and your fingers; it's the kind of no-pressure writing that can yield an explosion of ideas.

When Stacy's teacher asked everyone in class to write for five minutes about the connection between technology and their college success, Stacy wrote the following:

Spanish 3: used chat room discussion.

English 202: used chat room discussion to analyze Internet communication as it relates to literacy.

English 202 and Phil 197: used ANGEL's online forums.

Being an English major, I tend to see the biggest advantages of modern technology as those that have most helped my writing. My courses require hours of writing from me each week, and I know that, without access to all the Web resources that have been available to me, the amount of time I have to spend working on a paper would probably double. For instance, technology helps me write a research paper before I've even typed the first word, because I can research my topic so much faster by first consulting the online catalogues, instead of going to the library and getting lost in the stacks. If there is material I need that this library doesn't have, I simply have it sent to me through interlibrary loan. Then, when I actually start writing, the process is made easier through referencing certain Web sites that I can't live without. And once I'm finished writing my paper, I can choose from plenty of Web pages designed to show the proper way to cite any resources I've used. Of course, there are also some things that students get from the Web that they'd be better to stay away from, such as downloadable essays and book notes that help you skip out of actually reading a text. With technology being so accessible, so fast, so convenient, so easy to use, so full of information, etc., it can be hard to make sure you don't rely on it *too much*. For instance, I don't think it's a good idea to always use information from the Internet as a replacement for going to the library, because sometimes I've found that the perfect resource for a paper I'm writing is sitting on a shelf in the University Library. I think the best way for students to make use of modern advances is to draw on them to help build their own ideas and abilities, and not use them as a means of avoiding any real work.

Notice how Stacy starts with a list of some courses that used technology. She doesn't seem to be heading in any one direction. Then suddenly she's off and running about how the use of technology affects her life as an English major.

After trying several methods of exploration (listing, keeping a journal, and freewriting) and tapping several rhetorical methods of development (process analysis, cause-and-effect analysis, narration, and exemplification), Stacy found that she was starting to repeat herself. She didn't yet have a point she wanted to make, let alone a **thesis**, a controlling idea for her essay. She needed to try a new tack.

Questioning Sometimes when you're in a conversation, someone will ask you a question that takes you by surprise—and forces you to rethink your position or think about the topic in a new way. By using structured questioning, you can push yourself to explore your topic more deeply.

You're probably already familiar with the **journalists' questions**, which can readily serve your purpose: *Who? What? Where? When? Why? How?* As Stacy answered these questions, she began to form an opinion about her topic.

Who is using technology? Teachers, students, librarians–everyone on campus, it seems. But I'm going to talk about how it affects me.

What technology is being used, and what is it being used for? All kinds of technology, from email and Web searches to PowerPoint presentations and voice mail, is being used, for instruction, homework, student-to-student communication, student-and-teacher communication, and research. I'm going to concentrate on my use of computer technology, mostly access to the Web.

Where is technology being used? At the library, in the classroom, but most often in my bedroom, where my computer is.

When is technology being used? Usually at night, after I come home from classes and am doing my homework.

Why do students use or not use technology? I use it because it's more convenient than walking over to the library and searching. Not all students have Internet access in their apartments; others may not know all the online research techniques that I know.

How are students using it? Some students are using it to advance their education; others are using it to subvert it (like downloading essays and cheating schemes).

Considering genre

Stacy didn't need to think much about the genre in which she would write: her instructor had already determined that fitting responses would take the form of an academic essay, rather than another genre, such as memoir, profile, report, argument, or proposal. But situations will arise when you need to determine which genre is most appropriate. The genre you choose should fulfill your purpose and be deliverable through a medium that will reach your intended audience. In other words, picking the most effective genre is key to making the best use of your available means.

Here are some tips for determining which genre is appropriate to your rhetorical situation:

► Consider who else has been faced with a similar rhetorical situation and what genre(s) they used in response.

► Locate one or more examples to identify common characteristics of a genre, such as the kind of language used (formal or informal, for example), where and how the rhetorical appeals of ethos, logos, and pathos appear, and what kind of evidence (facts, statistics, personal experience, scientific research) is employed.

► Ask yourself whether it is most appropriate to use a genre that has been used in similar situations or whether a variation on the expected characteristics of that genre might have a stronger effect.

► Finally, consider your available means. To what physical means of delivery do you have access—word processing, PowerPoint, podcast, printed document? What rhetorical methods would make good strategies—definition, classification and division, exemplification, description, comparison, cause-and-effect analysis, process analysis, narration, argument? And what physical and rhetorical means is your audience expecting from you? How do these factors influence your choice of genre and means of delivery?

Organization

Once you've explored your topic as thoroughly as you can, it's time to begin organizing your essay. Two simple methods can help you get started: clustering and outlining.

Clustering Clustering is a visual method for connecting ideas that go together. You might start with words and phrases from a list you compiled or brainstormed and link them with arrows, circles, or lines, the way Stacy did. Notice how Stacy used different sizes of type to accentuate the connections she wanted to make between technology and learning. (You might want to use color as well to help you make connections.) Interestingly, Stacy hasn't yet put herself into her essay's plan.

Outlining An outline establishes the limits of your topic at the same time as it lists the main parts. Outlining is a good way to plan, but only if you think of the result as a rough—not formal or final—outline. You'll want to allow yourself to add and delete points and move things around

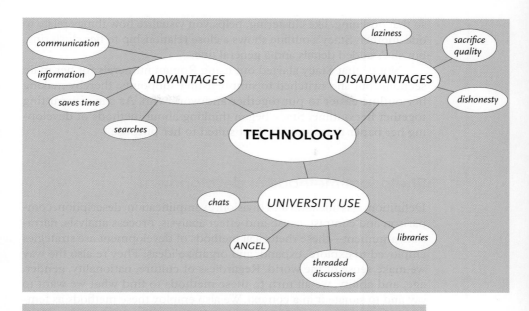

Technology and Learning

I. Advantages
    Information
        fast and convenient
        online catalogues
        eBay's First Edition or Rare Books page
        online concordances
        databases
    Communication
        ANGEL
        online forums
        new forms of interaction
        chat rooms
II. Disadvantages
    Academic laziness
        ignore traditional forms of research
        quality vs. convenience
        lose the value of a trip to the library
    Dishonesty
        free online book notes
        downloadable essays
        plagiarism

so that outlining, like clustering, helps you visualize how things relate to one another. Stacy's outline shows a close relationship to her clustering, but she's added details and a general title:

Notice that Stacy started out using Roman numerals for her main sections, but she switched to simply listing subpoints, thereby making her outline easier to put together and work with. As she was putting together her outline, Stacy began thinking about methods of developing her paper that would be best suited to her purpose.

Rhetorical methods of development

Definition, classification and division, exemplification, description, comparison and contrast, cause-and-effect analysis, process analysis, narration, argument—these rhetorical methods of development are strategies employed to explore, expand, and organize ideas. They're also the way we make sense of the world. Regardless of culture, nationality, gender, age, and ability, we all turn to these methods to find what we want to say and to situate it in a context. We also employ these methods as templates for interpreting what someone else is communicating to us. Each of these methods can stand alone, but more often they complement one another. When we use the method of *comparison*, for instance, we often need to *define* what exactly we are comparing.

Definition If you were to define the animal in the photograph, you might classify it as a "mammal" and then distinguish this mammal from others similar to it, describing its features and perhaps coming up with a definitive name for it. Thus, definition makes use of other strategies such as classification and division, exemplification, and description.

© Noel Rowe, 2007

Whenever we're introduced to something new—a new word, academic subject, sport, activity, or language—we need to develop a new vocabulary. Whether we're learning the vocabulary of cooking (*chop, slice, mince, stir, fold, whip, fry*), golf (*ace, birdie, bogey, chip, drive, duff*), or human evolution (*prosimians, hominoids, paleoanthropology, australopithecines, isotopes*), we're expanding our world with new concepts and ideas. Definition is essential to our learning and our understanding.

No matter what we're learning or learning about, we use definition.

And whether or not we're conscious of it, we always employ the three steps of definition:

1. We name the specific concept, action, person, or thing; in other words, we provide a term for it.
2. Then, we classify that term, or place it in a more general category. (See pages 308–309.)
3. Finally, we differentiate the specific term from all the other concepts, actions, persons, or things in that general category, often using examples. (See pages 309–310.)

For instance, if you're studying human evolution, you'll no doubt need to learn what distinguishes primates from other mammals.

Term	Class	Differentiation
Primates are	mammals	that have "a lack of strong specialization in structure; prehensile hands and feet, usually with opposable thumbs and great toes; flattened nails instead of claws on the digits; acute vision with some degree of binocular vision; relatively large brain exhibiting a degree of cortical folding; and prolonged postnatal dependency. No primate exhibits all these features, and indeed the diversity of primate forms has produced disagreement as to their proper classification" (*Encyclopedia Britannica*).

The preceding is a **formal** (or **sentence**) **definition**, the kind you'll find in a reference book. But it's not the only kind of definition. An **extended definition**, such as this one from primate.org, provides additional differentiating information:

> Primates are the mammals that are humankind's closest biological relatives. We share 98.4% of [our] DNA with chimpanzees. Apes, monkeys, and prosimians such as lorises, bush babies, and lemurs make up the 234 species of the family tree. About 90% of the primates live in tropical forests. They play an integral role in the ecology of their habitat. They help the forest by being pollinators, seed predators, and seed dispersers.

A **historical definition**, like this one from chimpanzoo.org/ history_of_primates, provides a longitudinal overview of what the term has described over time, offering additional concepts and terms:

65 mya [million years ago]: Paleocene epoch begins. . . . The earliest primates evolve. These primates were small insectivores who were most likely terrestrial. During this epoch, primates began to include food items such as seeds, fruits, nuts and leaves in their diet.

53.5 mya: Eocene epoch begins. Primates diversify and some become arboreal. Primates have developed prehensile hands and feet with opposable thumbs and toes and their claws have evolved into nails. Arboreal primates evolve relatively longer lower limbs for vertical clinging and leaping. Their eye sockets are oriented more frontally resulting in stereoscopic vision. Primates of this epoch belong to the prosimian family.

One of the best things about learning a new subject is that the initial vocabulary introduces more vocabulary, so the learning never ends.

Sometimes, you'll need to write a **negative definition** to clarify for your readers not only what a term means but also what it does not mean. In conversation, you might say, "When I talk about success, I'm not talking about making money." For you, success might instead involve having personal integrity, experiencing fulfillment in interpersonal relationships, and taking on exciting professional challenges. Even primates can be defined negatively, as W. E. Le Gros Clark wrote in *The Antecedents of Man*: "The Primates as a whole have preserved rather a generalized anatomy and . . . are to be mainly distinguished . . . by a negative feature—their lack of specialization."

Finally, you may come across or come up with a **stipulative definition**, which limits—or stipulates—the range of a term's meaning or application, thereby announcing to the reader exactly how the writer is using the term in the specific rhetorical situation. For instance, if you find yourself writing about success, you might define your meaning for your readers like this: "In this paper, *success* will be defined in terms of how quickly college graduates obtain employment in their chosen fields." Or if you're writing about primates, you might stipulate that you're concentrating on a twenty-first century conception of them. As you can see, definition provides the foundation for learning, understanding, and communicating. As you'll see in the following pages, classification and division, exemplification, and description all work in service of definition.

Classification and Division Like definition, **classification and division** first places something in a general category and then distinguishes it from other things within that category. Department stores, hospitals, telephone books, libraries, grocery stores, and book stores are all classified and divided in order to enhance accessibility to their information or contents. When you go into a hospital, for instance, you look at the directory by the entrance to find out how the areas in the building are classified (reception area, visitor information, emergency room, outpatient clinic, waiting room, obstetrics, patient rooms, gift shop, and cafeteria). Then, when you make your way to one of those areas (patient rooms, for instance), you look to see how that general area has been divided up (into floors and individual rooms on those floors). In important ways, the classification of hospital areas and the further division and distinction of those same areas define those locations. The hospital room you want to find is defined by belonging to the category of *patient rooms* and then differentiated from (or divided from) other patient rooms by being on the fifth floor, at the end of the hallway, to the left. Just as with definition, then, when you use classification and division, you provide a term and then place that term in its general category of origin.

Exemplification The rhetorical strategy of **exemplification** involves making a generalization and using an example or series of examples in support of that generalization. If you want to clarify why Veronica is the best sales clerk in your favorite sporting goods store, you can provide a series of examples that define *best sales clerk:* Veronica is herself a competitive athlete; she has positive energy and is knowledgeable about all the equipment, from running shoes and jackets to cycles and kayaks. She lets you know when items will be going on sale, and, best of all, she never pushes a sale. She realizes by now that if you really want it, you'll come back for it when you have the money. Or if you want to add interest to a generalization about your terrific Santa Fe vacation, you might talk about the clear blue skies, warm days, and cool nights; you could include anecdotes about the bargain rate you found online for your hotel room, running into Jessica Simpson at the Folk Art Museum, attending the Santa Domingo Pueblo feast day, and joining a Friday night art gallery walk and meeting artists; you could describe shopping on the plaza, where you found turquoise jewelry, Acoma Pueblo pottery, and Hopi-made Christmas presents. You could also include tantalizing, sensory descriptions of the delicious regional food—Frito pie, chocolate-covered chile creams, carne adovada, and natillas. All these examples not only add interest to the generalization that you had a "spectacular vacation" but also help define exactly what you mean by that phrase.

© Vulpix/Big Stock Photo

In the following passage, Pulitzer Prize–winner William Styron defines *suicidal* through his examples of suicidal thoughts.

> He asked me if I was suicidal, and I reluctantly told him yes. I did not particularize—since there seemed no need to—did not tell him that in truth many of the artifacts of my house had become potential devices for my own destruction: the attic rafters (and an outside maple or two) a means to hang myself, the garage a place to inhale carbon monoxide, the bathtub a vessel to receive the flow from my opened arteries. The kitchen knives in their drawers had but one purpose for me. Death by heart attack seemed particularly inviting, absolving me as it would of active responsibility, and I had toyed

with the idea of self-induced pneumonia—a long, frigid, shirt-sleeved hike through the rainy woods. Nor had I overlooked an ostensible accident . . . by walking in front of a truck on the highway nearby. These thoughts may seem outlandishly macabre—a strained joked—but they are genuine.

—**William Styron**, *Darkness Visible*

Styron admits to his physician that he is, indeed, depressed to the point of being suicidal, but he reserves the persuasive examples of his mental state for readers of his memoir.

Description Specific details converge in **description**, a verbal accounting of what we have experienced physically and mentally. Thus, our descriptions always carry with them **sensory details** having to do with our physical sensations (what we see, hear, smell, touch, or taste) or **sensibility details** having to with our intellectual, emotional, or physical states (alertness, gullibility, grief, fear, loathing, exuberance, clumsiness, relaxation, agitation, and so on).

José Antonio Burciaga's description (and extended definition) of *tortilla* relies heavily on sensory details:

> For Mexicans over the centuries, the *tortilla* has served as the spoon and fork, the plate and the napkin. . . . When I was growing up in El Paso, . . . I used to visit a *tortilla* factory in an ancient adobe building near the open *mercado* in Ciudad Juárez. As I approached, I could hear the rhythmic slapping of the *masa* as the skilled vendors outside the factory formed it into balls and patted them into perfectly round corn cakes between the palms of their hands. The wonderful aroma and the speed with which the women counted so many dozens of *tortillas* out of warm wicker baskets still linger in my mind. Watching them at work convinced me that the most handsome and *deliciosas tortillas* are handmade. Although machines are faster, they can never adequately replace generation-to-generation experience. There's no place in the factory assembly line for the tender slaps that give each *tortilla* character. The best thing that can be said about mass-producing *tortillas* is that it makes it possible for many people to enjoy them.
>
> —**José Antonio Burciaga**, "I Remember Masa"

The sensory details that infuse Burciaga's description of *tortilla* make it entertaining and memorable. Because description relies on details, it defines what is being described in specific ways.

Comparison and Contrast We use **comparison and contrast**, a two-part method of rhetorical development, from the moment we wake up (often comparing the advantages of getting up without enough rest with those of staying in bed) until we go to bed at night (comparing the option of getting rest with that of staying up and working). We use **comparison**

© Steven Lunetta Photography, 2007

to consider how two or more things are alike, and we use **contrast** to show how related things are different. This rhetorical strategy, which helps us clarify issues, can be used to explain, make a decision, shape an argument, open a discussion, or craft an entertaining narrative.

When you do decide to get up, you might want to choose a cereal to have for breakfast, knowing that you have Lucky Charms and Cheerios on your shelf. Because both of these share the characteristics of cold breakfast cereals, you have a **basis for comparison**. In order to decide which you want to eat, you'll intuitively set up **points of comparison** to clarify the ways in which the two are the same (both are cereals, served cold, eaten for breakfast) as well as the ways in which they are different (in terms of taste, nutrition, ingredients). You may already know the answers to the questions of which cereal tastes better, which one is better for you, and which one will sustain you until lunch. But you may not be familiar with the information that supports those answers, information that appears on the cereal boxes themselves.

The nutritional information panels on the boxes indicate that both cold cereals have been approved by the American Heart Association because both are low in saturated fats and cholesterol, with 0 grams of saturated fat and 0 milligrams of cholesterol. Both are also pretty low in sodium (200 milligrams and 210 milligrams), carbohydrates (25 grams and 22 grams), and protein (2 grams and 3 grams). But neither of the cereals comes close to fulfilling recommended daily allowances (RDAs) of carbohydrates and protein, as the charts on the boxes show. What about the recommended daily requirements (RDRs) for vitamins and minerals? The nutrition charts show that these cereals provide the same amounts of vitamins A, C, D, B_6, and B_{12}. In terms of other nutrients—calcium, thiamin, riboflavin, niacin, folic acid, and zinc—they are also the same. Cheerios, however, offers more iron (nearly half the RDR), phosphorus, magnesium, and copper. But will those differences affect your choice?

What distinctive contrast will be the deciding factor? The amount of sugar? Lucky Charms has 13 grams, whereas Cheerios has only 1 gram. The extra sugar might make Lucky Charms taste better, which may tip the scale. If you want enough energy to sustain you until lunch, however, you might choose Cheerios, so that you don't start your day with a sugar high and then crash midmorning.

The information you can glean from the side of a cereal box helps you understand the ingredients of the cereal and make an informed choice. If you wanted to discuss the choice of cereal with children and argue for the "right" choice, you could use much of that information. Whether you could ultimately persuade them to choose Cheerios over Lucky Charms is, of course, another story. You would, however, be informing them through the method of comparison and contrast.

Cause-and-Effect Analysis Whenever you find yourself concentrating on either causes or effects, explaining why certain events have occurred or predicting that particular events or situations will lead to specific effects, you're conducting a **cause-and-effect analysis**. The opportunity for change in these situations comes with your ability to use words to address your questions, to explore why some things happen, or to predict the effects of an event or situation. Cause-and-effect analysis can be used to explain (your opinion on why Ohio State is going to the Rose Bowl), to entertain (your description of what happens when the family gathers for Thanksgiving), to speculate (your thoughts on the causes of autism), or to argue a point (your stance on the effects of pollution).

We spend a good deal of time considering the causes of situations. For instance, when one of your bookshelves collapses, you check to see if the shelf braces are screwed into studs, if the books are too heavy, or if you need additional supporting braces. If you have a fender bender on the way to school, you think about what led to the accident. Some of the reasons may be outside your control: low visibility, an icy road, a poorly marked road, missing taillights on the car in front of you. Other causes may reside with you: your own tailgating, speeding, or inattention (eating, putting a CD in, talking or texting on your cell phone).

We spend just as much time—maybe even more—evaluating the effects of situations and events. You're enrolled in college and already considering the effects of having a college degree, most of them positive (you'll have to pay for your coursework and work hard, but you're likely to be well employed when you're finished). If you're considering marriage, you're analyzing the positive and not-so-positive effects of that decision (you'll live with the love of your life, but you'll have to relocate to Sacramento, where you may not be able to transfer all your credits). If you follow current events, you know that the effects of the controversial wars in Iraq and Afghanistan include the deaths of nearly 5,400 Americans, about 110,600 Iraqis, approximately 16,000 Afghanis (estimates vary), and a good deal of public discontent.

Image courtesy of NOAA.

Before-and-after photographs, such as the dramatic ones shown here, often lead us to wonder *what happened?* and *what was the cause?* The first of this pair of photographs shows a beautiful old church surrounded by big trees. It's Trinity Episcopal Church in Pass Christian, Mississippi, which was built in 1849. Set among live oaks and lush lawns, Trinity served as a landmark for over a century. In the second photo, some—but not all—of the big trees are still standing, but

Image courtesy of NOAA.

there's no church, just the stairs and pathway leading up to the church. This second photograph was taken on August 18, 1969, the day after Hurricane Camille smashed into the Mississippi Gulf Coast, with wind speeds in excess of two hundred miles per hour and water levels twenty-four feet above normal high tide, making it the strongest storm in U.S. history. The effects of Camille, by the time it had dissipated on August 22, included 256 deaths and $1.4 billion in damages, the equivalent of $8.4 billion in 2010. Even though chances are slim that anyone in your class will have heard of, let alone remember, Hurricane Camille, you understand its effects. Developing your ability to examine situations or events for their causes or effects, teasing out a relevant analysis, will help you better understand your world.

Process Analysis Whenever you develop your ideas in order to explain how something is done, you're engaging in **process analysis**. Process analysis involves dividing up an entire process into a series of ordered steps so that your audience can understand the relationship among those steps and maybe even replicate them. To that end, process analysis always includes a series of separate, chronological steps that provide details about a process and often reads like a narration. Many process analyses take the form of a list, with distinct and often numbered steps, as in recipes, instruction manuals (for tasks from using a small appliance to assembling a toy), and installation guides (for everything from shower heads and garbage disposals to computer software). Whether the purpose of the process analysis is to inform (how volcanoes erupt, how leukemia is treated), entertain (how to gain weight on vacation, how a ten-year-old boy makes hot chocolate), or argue a point (the best way to quit a job, learn to write, develop as a reader), the analysis itself responds to a problem: someone needs to know how to do something or wants to learn how something is done.

Television programs and DVDs present processes we can duplicate or appreciate: we can watch the Food Network to learn about Paula Deen's plan for an easy-to-prepare Thanksgiving dinner (one that includes deep-fried turkey and double-chocolate gooey cake) or be entertained by *Say Yes to the Dress*, a not-always-flattering analysis of the process brides-to-be move through in their search for the perfect wedding dress. We can view DVDs to learn how to compose an iron-clad will or *How to Draw Comics the Marvel Way*, although these analyses might not provide enough training for us to duplicate the processes they describe. Whether processes are conveyed orally, in writing, or visually, whether we're taking directions from our mom, reading a car-repair manual, or watching *The Ace of Cakes*, we're using process analysis.

Process analyses come in two basic forms. **Directive process analysis** is used to teach the audience how to do something, how to duplicate the process. **Informative process analysis**, on the other hand, is used to explain a process so that the audience can understand, enjoy, or be persuaded. Either kind of process analysis can constitute an entire message or be one part of a larger message (within a novel, proposal, report, or essay, for example).

If you've ever taken an airplane trip, you're familiar with directive process analyses. Both the passenger safety card found in the pocket of the seat in front of you and the oral instructions from the flight attendant serve as perfect examples. As you follow along with the card, the attendant recites and enacts the step-by-step directions for various safety procedures during takeoffs, landings, and emergencies: how to buckle and unbuckle your seat belt, how to put an oxygen mask on yourself and help a child do so, how to locate and inflate the life preserver, and so on. Many passengers can understand the language in which the flight attendant is giving the instructions, but, for those who cannot, the visuals on the card provide the details necessary for full understanding. Whether the passengers take in the information aurally, visually, or both aurally and visually, the directive process analysis allows them to duplicate the steps described.

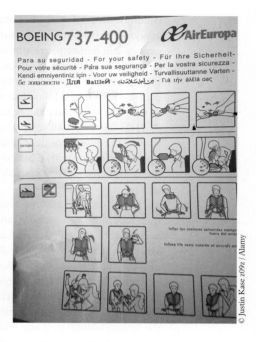

© Justin Kase z09z / Alamy

The following example of the second type of process analysis, informative process analysis, comes from a suspense novel. The author uses process analysis to address the problem emerging in the opening paragraph.

Detective Matt Chacon knew that unlike the TV cop shows—where actors sit in front of a computer monitor and instantaneously pull up a digital fingerprint record that matches a perp or a victim—trying to ID someone using prints in the real world can be mind-numbing work. There are thousands of prints that have never been entered into the computer data banks, and thousands more on file that, because of poor quality, are virtually unusable for comparison purposes. On top of that, figure in the small cop shops who haven't got the money, manpower, and equipment to transfer print records to computers, and the unknown number of print records that were left in closed felony cases and sit forgotten in basement archives at police departments all over the country, and you've got a data-bank system that is woefully inadequate and incomplete. Finally, while each fingerprint

Strategies

is unique, the difference between prints can be so slight that a very careful analysis must be made to confirm a perfect match. Even then, different experts can debate the results endlessly, since it isn't an exact science.

Chacon had started his career in law enforcement as a crime scene technician with a specialty in fingerprint and tool-mark identification, so of course Lieutenant Molina had sent him off to the state police headquarters to work the state and federal data banks to see if he could get a match.

He'd been at it all night long and his coffee was starting to taste like sludge, his eyes were itchy, and his butt was numb. Using an automated identification system, Chacon had digitally stored the victim's prints in the computer and then started scanning for a match against those already on file.

The computer system could identify possible matches quickly, but then it became a process of carefully analyzing each one and scoring them according to a detailed classification system. So far, Chacon had examined six dozen sets of prints that looked like possible equivalents and had struck out. But there was another baker's dozen to review.

He clicked on the next record, adjusted the monitor to enhance the resolution of the smudged prints, and began scoring them in sequence. Whoever had printed the subject had done a piss-poor job. He glanced at the agency identifier. It was a Department of Corrections submission.

Chacon finished the sequence and used a split screen to compare his scoring to the victim's print. It showed a match. He rechecked the scoring and verified his findings.

—**Michael McGarrity,** *Everyone Dies*

As it informs and entertains, this process analysis argues a point—that fingerprint matching is a complicated and often time-consuming procedure, not the quick fix depicted by popular media. Process analysis provides the overall structure of the passage—a thesis statement, chronological organization, and purposeful point of view. In addition, the passage uses several other rhetorical strategies for development: comparison and contrast, narration, description, exemplification, and cause-and-effect analysis.

In our culture, directions are no longer given and received only through print or face-to-face interaction. Instead of reading a cookbook, we might turn on the Food Channel; instead of hiring a plumber, we might visit homedepot.com. So whether you decide to convey a process analysis in English or another language, over the telephone or by email, in laborious detail or in shorthand, with or without an accompanying visual depends on your audience's native language, access to various means of communication, and understanding of the subject matter. With process analysis, as with other rhetorical methods, it's important to consider the physical means of delivering and receiving information.

Courtesy of the author.

Narration One of the rhetorical methods for development that you already know well is **narration**, which tells a story that has **characters** (people in the story), **dialogue** (direct speech by the characters), a **setting** (the time and place), **description** (selected sensory and sensibility details about the characters, dialogue, and setting), and **plot** (the sequence of events). Narrations help us make sense of the world for ourselves and for others—whether we're retelling a fairy tale or family legend or recounting the final minutes of the Super Bowl or our canyon-bottom tour of Canyon de Chelly (pictured above).

Narration can frame an entire story (*Robin Hood* or the first Thanksgiving), or it can provide an example (why you can depend on your brother) and support an argument (those final plays proved the Steelers to be the better team). Usually narrations are verbal—we want to tell "what happened." Verbal narration, which appears in newspapers, in movies, and in reports on television and radio, tells us, for example, about University of California students protesting tuition hikes, the latest child-abduction tragedy, the president's travels to the Middle East, a murder mystery or police procedural, a girl who's been sneezing for two weeks, obituaries, and the local school board meeting. Such verbal narrations might consist of one particular sequence of events or include a series of separate incidents that shape an overall narrative.

Were you to compose a narration about the photograph of the jeep and flood water at Canyon de Chelly, what might it be? Would your narration account for your entire vacation, beginning when you left home, or might you concentrate only on the canyon-bottom tour? In addition to tapping all the elements of a narration (characters, dialogue, setting, description, and plot), would you also use an **anecdote** (a brief, illustrative story that propels the narrative)? From what **point of view** would you tell the story? Your own, that of the Navajo guide, your parents', or your sibling's? And what might be the **climax** of your narration, the turning point toward a resolution? Would you recount your narration in chronological order, or might you use **flashback** to account for past events or **flashforward** to account for future events? Purposefully interruptive, these techniques add interest to a story, providing glimpses of other times, which illuminate the present as it is being recounted in an otherwise straightforward, chronological organization.

Whether used to supply information, explain, provide an example, set a mood, or argue a point, narration easily reaches most audiences and often serves as a fitting response to opportunities for change. Given its versatility, narration can serve as the basis for a good deal of your academic, personal, and work-related writing.

Argument The words *argument* and *persuasion* are often used interchangeably, despite the technical distinctions between the two terms. **Argument** refers to the verbal or visual delivery of a point of view and the use of logical reasoning to help an audience understand that point of view as true or valid. **Persuasion**, on the other hand, refers to the use of emotions as well as logical reasoning to move the audience a step or two beyond the understanding that accompanies successful argument. The goal of persuasion is to change the mind, point of view, or actions of the audience. Because any visual or verbal argument can easily include emotional appeals as well as logical reasoning and because any argument holds the potential for changing the collective mind or actions of an audience, the broader term *argument* will be used throughout this chapter and book.

We employ and respond to arguments all day long, as we work to understand and explain to others the world around or within us. Sometimes, our arguments focus on defending our opinions or questioning the opinions of others—opinions about whether Serena Williams should be punished for her foul-mouthed tirade at the U.S. Open, where to get the best pizza, which music venue offers the best nightlife, or whether a vegan diet is truly healthful. Sometimes, argument involves exploring and clarifying our own opinions, as we weigh all sides of an issue and various possible consequences of our final opinion. Often, we employ that kind of analytical argument when we're considering some of life's big issues: surgery, divorce, marriage, a new job, racism, sexism, and so on.

Other times, argument is invitational, in that it invites the audience to understand your position (even if they're not convinced to change their minds or action) and to explain their position to you (even if you're not convinced to change your mind or action). Invitational argument works especially well when the speaker and the audience need to work together to solve a problem (what to do about school violence, the spread of the AIDS virus, or unemployment), construct a position that represents diverse interests (for or against universal health

Strategies

coverage, the professionalization of college athletics, or affirmative action), or implement a policy that requires broad support (on establishing a draft system or allowing gay marriage).

When we analyze an argument—our own or one someone else is presenting to us—we can consider several elements: an identifiable issue, a claim, common ground, and rhetorical appeals.

An **identifiable issue** is the topic under discussion, one that we choose from a multitude of issues we confront daily, from limited service at the university health center to poverty, homelessness, poor-quality schooling, and so on. Often, we don't take the time to address any one of those problems in any productive way, perhaps because we cannot pinpoint the specific issue within that problem that we want to argue for or against. In other words, we cannot identify an opportunity for change that can be addressed with words.

But suppose you were experiencing both bad service and bad food at a restaurant. That experience might not be a very big deal unless you became violently ill and you thought it was from the salmon, which didn't taste quite right. Now you have identified a specific issue you can argue as you express your opinion that either the storage of the fresh seafood or the sanitary conditions of that restaurant are in need of improvement. Or suppose you've identified one specific issue that contributes to the poor test scores of your neighborhood school: most children don't eat breakfast before they come to school.

Once you've identified an issue (that schoolchildren test poorly), you can make a **claim** about it, an arguable position you take regarding that issue. Your claim could be that the school should launch a free breakfast program for students. The need for free school breakfasts would be the position you'd take in your argument to parents, teachers, administrators, and the school board. As you think through the various claims that could be made about the issue (parents should feed their children themselves; parents should provide better after-school support; children need to work harder; teachers need to concentrate on the basics, and so on), you'll want to make sure that your claim is one that can be argued and responded to. Citing research can be one of the most persuasive kinds of support, as the U.S. Department of Agriculture demonstrates in a flyer they produced:

There are many benefits of breakfast for children. Breakfast provides children with the energy and essential nutrients they need to concentrate on school work and learn. Studies show that breakfast provides as much as 25 percent of the recommended daily allowance for key nutrients, such as calcium, protein, vitamins A and B6, magnesium, iron and zinc.

Courtesy of the author

Research shows that children who eat breakfast have higher achievement scores, lower rates of absence and tardiness, and increased concentration in the classroom. . . .

Another important benefit of breakfast for children is that establishing the healthy habit of eating breakfast early in life could stave off many adulthood health problems associated with poor diet, such as diabetes and obesity.

Among all the possible views of school breakfast programs, yours—that school breakfast programs contribute to academic performance—will ground your thesis statement.

In addition to supplying support for your claim, you'll also need to establish **common ground:** the goal, belief, value, or assumption that you share with your audience. In this case, you might say that "academic performance needs to improve," and you could be reasonably certain that your audience would agree. Once you've established common ground, you've assured your audience that, despite any misunderstandings or disagreements, you both actually share a good deal, which provides a starting point for you to speak or write.

You'll also employ the rhetorical appeals of ethos, logos, and pathos to make connections with your audience (see pages 49–51). By establishing common ground and speaking to a nationwide problem involving children and their school performance, you've emphasized ethos. By citing research to support your assertion that eating breakfast improves students' health, behavior, and academic performance, you're employing logos. And by listing ten reasons children should eat breakfast, starting with the obvious one that no child should go hungry, you're employing pathos.

Argument is a common part of everyday life, whether we're negotiating to change an airline ticket, discussing why Notre Dame fired football coach Charlie Weis, or explaining why we don't want our roommate borrowing our clothes. In some ways, then, everything's an argument. Every time you transfer meaning or understanding from yourself to another person, you've made a successful argument. And every time you've understood what someone else is saying to you, you've responded to a successful argument. No matter what kind they are—visual or verbal, angry or informative, personal or bureaucratic—arguments work to fulfill one of three rhetorical purposes: to express or defend a position, to question or argue against an established belief or course of action, or to invite or persuade an audience to change an opinion or action.

You can find additional help with writing arguments in chapter 2, which discusses the rhetorical appeals of ethos, logos, and pathos; chapter 6, which discusses and gives examples of position arguments and rhetorical fallacies; and chapter 7, which discusses and gives examples of proposal arguments.

Strategies

Write for five minutes in response to each of the following questions. Be prepared to share your answers with the rest of the class.

1. What was the last opportunity for change you responded to in writing? Why did you choose to respond to it? What did you think your words could do?

2. How did you go about exploring possible responses? Which of the invention strategies did you employ?

3. How did you begin organizing your response? What organizational methods did you explore? How was your response organized in its final form?

4. What means did you use to deliver your response—words, visuals, paper, electronic files? Why did you choose that specific means of delivery?

5. Compare your answers with those of two classmates. What surprised you about their answers? List two things a classmate wrote that made you rethink your own answers. Then rewrite those answers.

Drafting a Response

Reconsidering audience, resources, and constraints

After you've explored your topic, loosely organized your paper, and considered which of the rhetorical methods of development are best suited to your purpose, you'll begin drafting. While some writers find the first draft the toughest part of the process, many others derive great pleasure from the two-step drafting process: drafting and evaluating. The joy of putting words together is exhilarating for many writers; they enjoy the freedom of combining an outline with a freewrite as they work to attend to all the elements of the rhetorical situation (see chapter 1). A first draft is just that—words you'll revisit again and again as you adjust your message to take into account all the elements in your rhetorical situation.

When you're drafting, you'll be considering your intended audience as well, particularly in terms of what you're hoping your audience can do to address (or help you address) the opportunity for change that sparked your writing in the first place. The following list may help you as you reconsider audience:

▶ Who can resolve the opportunity for change (or the problem) that you've identified?

▶ What exactly might that audience do to address, resolve, or help resolve it?

▶ What opportunities (if any) are there for you to receive feedback from that audience?

Answers to these questions will help you tie your purpose to your particular audience.

By thinking of her assignment as a rhetorical situation, Stacy developed a better idea of how to approach her draft. When an instructor doesn't write out an assignment, you should feel free to ask him or her to explain it in terms of the rhetorical situation—that is, ask your instructor specific questions about purpose, audience (or receiver), context, and constraints.

Here is Stacy's first draft.

Technology for teaching and learning is especially strong here at State. It provides many advantages for students and teachers alike, but it also brings with it some disadvantages. In this essay, I'm going to talk about my experiences with technology, the advantages I've experienced and the disadvantages I feel. I'll draw upon my experiences in Spanish 3, English 202, Philosophy 197, Biological Sciences, Art History, and my internship.

Technology is rapidly becoming increasingly advanced, and much of it is used to enhance learning and writing. Not only does it increase the amount of information available, but it allows for stronger writing. I can search libraries around the world, use eBay to find rare manuscripts, use interlibrary loan, and file electronic requests for needed items.

Technology also makes the writing process faster, more convenient. I often access online concordances, view library books on my PC, email librarians, and read full-text journal articles online. This technology is also allowing for more ways to develop ideas and new forms of written communication. For instance, I'm now experienced with chat room communication, forum discussions, and photo essays.

But at the same time that technology brings these advantages, it also inhibits learning and writing. I know that when I'm conducting online research I may be missing out on information or lowering the quality of information because I'm limiting my searching to electronic sources. Nowadays, students don't really have to learn to use the library, where often more information can be found than what appears on an online search. I fear that students are placing convenience over quality. I know I do sometimes. The information online isn't always reliable, either. Students don't often take the time to investigate sources.

For these reasons, campus technology may be promoting academic laziness in some students, and dishonesty as well. So much information is available that you can practically write a book report without ever reading the book. And online papers make plagiarism easy. In conclusion . . .

Stacy's first draft has begun to address the components of the rhetorical situation: she understands that she needs to talk about her own experiences with technology and describe the technology that she uses. In getting her thoughts down, she's beginning to sketch out an organizational structure that starts with the advantages of this technology and ends with the disadvantages. She has made certain to add that some students take advantage of technology only in a way that cheapens their learning experience. Notice that she hasn't begun to shape a strong thesis yet, let alone a conclusion. Still, she's ready to begin revising.

> WRITE FOR FIVE

1. What methods do you use to launch your first draft?
2. What's the easiest part of drafting for you? The most difficult? Why?
3. How does having a specific sense of audience help or hinder you?
4. Many writers concentrate on the big picture when drafting; others find themselves slowing down and filling in some details as well. How would you describe your process of producing a first draft? Be prepared to share your answers with the rest of the class.
5. How does your means of delivery (print, electronic file, visual, oral presentation) affect your process? In other words, which means of delivery help or hinder you?

Revising a Response

Revision means evaluating and rethinking your writing in terms of the rhetorical situation. Writers use several techniques during revision. Some put the draft aside for 24 hours or more in order to return to it with fresh ideas and a more objective viewpoint. Others like to print out the draft and actually cut it into different sections so that they can experiment with organization. One of the most popular—and most effective—revision techniques is peer evaluation.

Peer evaluation is a form of collaboration that provides productive advice and response from a fellow student writer. If the thought of letting a peer (a classmate or friend) read your first draft makes you uncomfortable, if you've tried peer evaluation before and it didn't work, or if you're worried that you won't receive good advice, please reconsider. All effective writing is the result of some measure of collaboration, whether between colleagues, editors and writers, publishers and writers, actors and writers, students and teachers, or friends. Just consider for a moment all the writing you read, hear, and see every day—newspapers, magazines, online chat, billboards, commercials, sitcoms, newscasts. A great majority of the words that you experience daily come to you as a result of collaboration and peer evaluation. Every day, experienced writers are showing their first drafts to someone else in order to get another point of view, advice, and evaluation.

Peer evaluation is a valuable step in the writing process that you, too, will want to experience. No matter how good a writer you are, you'll benefit from hearing what one or more real receivers have to say about your message. They may ask you questions that prompt you to clarify points you want to make, nudge you to provide more examples so that your prose comes alive, or point out attention-getting passages. When you respond to a peer's first draft, you are not only helping that writer but also strengthening your own skills as a reader and writer. As you discover strengths and weaknesses in someone else's writing, you also improve your ability to find them in your own. Most important, the successful writing of a peer will energize your own writing in ways that the successful writing of a professional might not. A peer can show you how attainable good writing can be.

Although it is sometimes helpful to get pointers on things like grammar and word choice, you'll usually want a peer reviewer to focus first on how well your draft responds to your rhetorical situation. The following set of ten questions can help guide a peer reviewer:

PEER EVALUATION QUESTIONS

1. What opportunity for change (or problem) sparked this essay?
2. What is the topic of this essay? What is the main idea the writer wants to convey about this topic?
3. What can you tell about the writer of this essay? What is his or her relationship to this topic?
4. Who is the audience? What information in the essay reveals the audience to you? What do you imagine are the needs and concerns of this audience? What might this audience do to address, resolve, or help resolve this problem?
5. What seems to be the relationship between the writer and the audience? How is the writer meeting the needs and concerns of this audience? What specific passages demonstrate the writer's use of the rhetorical appeals (ethos, pathos, and logos)?
6. What is the purpose of the writer's message? What is the relationship among the writer, the audience, and the writer's purpose? Do you have any other comments about the purpose?
7. What means is the writer using to deliver this message? How is this means appropriate to the situation?
8. What constraints are on the writer and this message?

9. What idea or passage in the essay is handled most successfully? Least successfully?

10. What are two questions you have for this writer?

These questions can be answered fairly quickly. Although you might be tempted to have your peer reviewer go through them quickly and orally, you'll be better served if you ask the peer reviewer to write his or her answers either on a separate piece of paper or directly on your draft. When it's your turn to evaluate a peer's draft, you may well come away from the experience surprised at how much you learned about your own writing. There's no better way to improve your own understanding than to explain something to someone else.

The peer reviewer of Stacy's paper offered her a good deal of advice, most of which had to do with large-scale revising, as you can see from his responses to questions 6 and 9:

6. I cannot tell for sure what your purpose is in writing this essay. You describe technology, but I'm not sure why. Do you want to explain the opportunities, or do you want to show how bad it can be for students? And I cannot tell who you're writing to—maybe just any reader? Still, I think you have a good start on a strong essay because you know so much neat stuff about all the technology here at school. I didn't know half this stuff.

9. The beginning of your essay is the least successful part; I can't tell by reading it where you're headed with your topic, so I think you're going to want to revise with a stronger purpose in mind. But as I said earlier, the strongest part of your essay is all the specific information you already know about using technology. No wonder you get such good grades. You don't have any conclusion yet. I think if you get a better start on your introduction that you can pull together your overall argument in your conclusion. Maybe talk about how technology is always thought of as being better, an improvement, but that it's not always, not really.

The peer reviewer confirmed what Stacy already thought: the introduction of the essay, especially the thesis statement, merited more of her attention. Earlier in this chapter, a **thesis** was defined as a controlling idea. More specifically, a **thesis statement** is a central idea stated in the form of an assertion, or claim, which indicates what you believe to be true, interesting, or valuable about your topic. A thesis statement also gives readers a clear idea of your purpose in writing, and it sometimes outlines the approach you'll take. Although it is often phrased as a single sentence, it doesn't need to be. Here is Stacy's first attempt at a thesis statement:

> Technology provides many advantages for students and teachers alike, but it also brings with it some disadvantages. In this essay, I'm going to talk about my experiences with technology, the advantages I've experienced and the disadvantages I feel.

Stacy identified her topic—use of technology by students and teachers—and forecast that she would be talking about both advantages and disadvantages. Her peer reviewer, though, was unclear about what Stacy's purpose was. So Stacy must concentrate on the connection between her purpose and audience as she creates a thesis statement that narrows her topic and makes a comment on that topic.

Editing and Proofreading a Response

Although the peer reviewer focused on Stacy's approach to the rhetorical situation, other evaluative responses had to do with smaller issues related to editing: improving word choice, adding specific details, and structuring sentences more effectively. Some writers revise, edit, and proofread simultaneously, while others focus their efforts on resolving the big issues (thesis statement, organization, supporting information) before tackling editing and proofreading.

After the peer reviewer finished responding to Stacy's essay (and she to his), Stacy took his advice, wrote two more drafts, and edited and proofread her way to her final draft. Like most writers, Stacy stopped revising because she'd run out of time—not because she thought her essay was perfect in every way. You can see Stacy's final draft, formatted according to MLA style, in your English CourseMate, accessed through CengageBrain.com.

> WRITE FOR FIVE

1. How do you define *revision?*
2. When do you revise? Can you name the last piece of writing that you revised? Why did you choose to revise that particular piece?
3. What are your strengths as a reviser? Your weaknesses?
4. What features of revision do you like to have help with?
5. What features of proofreading and editing are you good at? Which could you use help with? Be prepared to share your answers with the rest of the class.

Strategies

> YOUR WRITING EXPERIENCES

1. Where does your best writing appear? What qualities of this writing lead you to judge it to be your best?

2. What writing do you feel most proud of? Why does this writing make you feel proud?

3. What opportunities for change (or problems) spur your best writing? Who is your audience? What is your purpose? What is the context? What is your medium for writing?

4. After reading this chapter and studying Stacy's writing process, describe two specific ways in which you could improve your own writing process. Be prepared to share your answer with the rest of the class.

10 Responding with Multimedia

If you're thinking that multimedia responses include visually effective emails, Web sites, and text messages, you're right. As a college student, you're probably already composing multimedia—documents featuring some combination of words, visuals, and sound—using various composing technologies ranging from word processors and photo- and Web-page-editing software to video and audio recording equipment. You might even be one of those people who make impromptu compositions with cameraphones. If you're already fluent in multimedia composition, preparing your blog posts might include creating and uploading images or in-line video, making decisions about effective page layout, and even using Web code to produce exactly what you want. If your experience with technology is limited, you can still make effective multimedia compositions by adhering to the rhetorical principles covered in this book.

In this chapter, the general rhetorical approach to composing is applied more specifically to a digital environment. Because the principles of multimedia composing (planning and arrangement, for instance), are the same as those for composing with text, the guidelines in this chapter should be easy to implement. The goal is for you not only to understand *how* to create multimedia compositions, but also to appreciate *when* and *where* such multimedia compositions will be most effective.

The chapter is divided into two parts. The first introduces scenarios calling for multimedia responses, and the second addresses the composition process for Web sites, blogs, wikis, podcasts, Facebook posts, and even YouTube videos.

> WRITE FOR FIVE

Write for five minutes in response to each of the following questions. Be prepared to share your answers with the rest of the class.

1. Describe your reading and writing practices, listing the technologies you use with each of them. Keep in mind that pens and books are technologies in the sense that they are tools designed and created by humans with particular purposes in mind.

2. Which of your composing and reading experiences involve multimedia?

3. How is the writing you do on a Web site such as Facebook (or Twitter, a blog, or other online writing space) different from other kinds of writing you do? List as many differences as you can.

Multimedia and the Rhetorical Situation

The last few years have seen students use multimedia to address rhetorical opportunities in a number of inventive ways. "TXTmob," "coup de texte," "going mobile," "text brigades," "swarms"—these are some of the terms young people all over the world are using to describe the ways political mobilizations are conducted, allowing group leaders to control, minute by minute, the appearance and movements of demonstrators. You might be familiar with the 2006 swarm of Filipino university students, who organized and publicized a series of political rallies using text messages sent from cell phones. Similarly, after the 2009 Iranian presidential election, students in Tehran took to the streets in protest, relying on text

A young woman whistles as she films the scene around her at a 2009 election rally in Tehran, Iran.

One of Calpernia Addams's YouTube videos.

messaging and the online social networking service Twitter to synchronize their street-level swarm and to communicate with one another, the media, and the outside world. Twitter and texting were particularly important methods of communication during the Iran protests because they provided alternatives to the traditional news media, which were heavily censored by the Iranian government.

Not all of the situations that call for multimedia responses involve national-scale political movements, however. Some social situations invite multimedia responses as well. For instance, actress and activist Calpernia Addams uses YouTube videos to discuss transsexual issues that are often ignored by "mainstream" media outlets. She's posted a video entitled "Bad Questions to Ask a Transsexual" in order to achieve two goals: (1) to lampoon offensive questions people often ask her and (2) to promote transsexual resources and education programs. Addams's video also provides links to Web sites like Genderlife.com and to a response by one of her critics.

In addition to addressing political and sociocultural issues, multimedia composing can be used to address organizational issues, as many student groups have discovered. Student-run programs have come to rely on multimedia for organizing and advertising their events. As you read about the Texas A&M Visualization Science Program in the following pages, you'll see how the students chose among different media in order to organize and promote their art exhibition as well as to shape their ultimate message for their various audiences.

WAIT A MINUTE ...

What's so "multi" about "multimedia"? Whether you choose an audio recording, a video, still images, or written text, your medium affects your message. As more composing is done in digital environments (that is, on computers and online), the boundaries among the different media begin to blur. For example, a Web site usually consists at least of images and text working together to create meaning, and many now include audio and video as well. Considering all of your available means—and knowing how and when to mix and blur them—is an important rhetorical skill, just like arranging an essay.

Using multimedia to address a rhetorical opportunity

For over twenty years now, students in the Texas A&M Visualization Science Program have held Viza Go-Go, a visual art show that introduces multimedia student work to the student body and larger college-town community. Spreading the word about and attracting an audience

The Web site for Texas A&M's Viza Go-Go show reaches a large and diverse audience.

to the show are the task and rhetorical opportunity of Viza Go-Go's student organizers each year. And each year, the organizers brainstorm different options for their response to that opportunity. Consider two options, each requiring different media and having different advantages and disadvantages: the printed flyer and the Web page. Printed flyers could display event details in visible spots around campus, but they'd be competing for attention with any number of other flyers and visuals. A Web site, on the other hand, would allow organizers to take advantage of several types of media and reach a specific audience.

Using multimedia to address an audience

Once you decide to respond to a rhetorical opportunity or problem, you must consider your audience, a rhetorical audience who can resolve or help you resolve the problem that you've identified. The rhetorical opportunity for the Viza Go-Go organizers is figuring out how to attract an audience for their upcoming art show. They could use a blanket advertising campaign (such as the flyers) that might or might not attract interested audience members, or they could target an audience already inclined to respond. Although a printed flyer on a bulletin board in a café might reach hundreds of students, not all the students who pass by will be interested in coming to the art show (assuming they notice the flyer in the first place). At best, a few students might notice the quality

Multimedia

The Gallery lets visitors to the site preview the artists' work.

of the showcased artwork (if photos are included on the flyer), that one of the artists is someone they know (if artists are listed), or even that the art show provides a good date destination and then decide to attend (if the exhibition dates and times are prominently displayed). On the other hand, with a link to the Viza Go-Go Web site on the Visualization Science home page, organizers could reach other Visualization Science students and encourage them to circulate details about the event by pulling verbal, visual, or audio information from the site. The Web site could feature "teaser" video clips of animations, image galleries of sketches and video stills, and even a history page documenting the development of the show.

In giving individual artists and other interested students something to link to (via Twitter, Facebook, or an email message), the Web site could involve even more people in targeting a rhetorical audience (people who might attend the show). In fact, once the organizers decided on a Web site rather than a flyer, the site began to reach a wide audience, in part because program alumni who had moved on to careers shared the Web site with their coworkers at ILM, Dreamworks, Disney, and Microsoft. As the audience expanded, the rhetorical purpose of the Web site began to change as well.

Using multimedia with a rhetorical purpose

As you already know, purpose and audience cannot be separated. So when the designers of the Viza Go-Go Web site realized that their purpose had changed, from simply publicizing the art event to also promot-

Multimedia

ing themselves to potential employers, they decided that they needed to address their more complicated (dual) rhetorical purpose. Their new rhetorical situation opened a whole new range of rhetorical choices for the organizers. As they considered their options, they generated a list of possiblities: they could expand the gallery section of the Web site to showcase more talent online, include visual-audio bios of the artists themselves, feature online portfolios, describe the annual event as well as the current show, include a map and directions to the show, even add a travel page, with information on accommodations for out-of-town attendees. After they winnowed down their choices, they'd need to concentrate on how they would arrange the material on the Web site.

Using multimedia as a fitting response

If you were one of the early student organizers of Viza Go-Go, you and your fellow organizers might have weighed the ease of composing and circulating flyers against the time-consuming nature of composing with the more tantalizing multimedia. Or, together, you might have come to realize the advantage of adopting both approaches. After all, you can compose, print, and circulate flyers that include a link to your Web site, thereby enjoying the benefits of both media. You have the flyer's broad distribution combined with the Web site's detailed, engaging, and easily passed-on content. The overlapping of print and digital media has already become common: business cards often have Web and email addresses printed on them, while a company's Web site may make printable coupons available.

The combination of Web site and flyer has in fact proven successful for Viza Go-Go organizers, who plastered the Texas A&M campus with printed flyers weeks before the show and put "table tents" (small flyers that can be propped up on a table) in all of the student dining halls. They also ran television and radio ads, all of which directed potential audience members to their Web site for more information about the show. In recent years, as its target audience and available means have grown, Viza Go-Go has expanded its reach to social networking sites, with a Facebook profile that is now integrated into the show's main Web site (vizagogo.tamu.edu).

Using multimedia as an available means

Like all other kinds of composing, multimedia composing requires that you assess the resources and constraints of your available means of delivery. As you know well, multimedia compositions provide resources that traditional print documents do not. When the Viza Go-Go organizers incorporated video on their Web site, for example, they were able to display teaser videos of student work as well as clips of the television advertising about their event.

As a multimedia composer, you should be aware of the types of media you might encounter (text, images, audio, and video), as well as the variety of digital composing environments used to produce those media. A digital composing environment is any software or Web site that allows you to manipulate your composition. For example, Microsoft Word, Twitter, and Adobe Photoshop all offer different features for creating different types of compositions. Microsoft Word offers templates for managing long text-based documents, whereas Twitter won't let you type more than 140 characters. Meanwhile, Photoshop focuses on the visual features of composing multimedia documents, allowing you to edit still images but offering very limited text-editing capabilities. In practice, however, these composing environments often overlap: you might compose text in Word and edit photos in Photoshop before combining your work into a single blog post or Web page.

The following sections discuss different types of composing environments, focusing on how the rhetorical principles of invention and memory, arrangement, style, and delivery can inform your composing process in each environment.

A Rhetorical Approach to Web Sites

The best composers, whether working online or not, take their rhetorical situation into consideration as they shape their message. When breast cancer became a global issue—that is, when women and men all over the world realized that a greater awareness of symptoms and treatments could help prevent many deaths from breast cancer—activists generated ideas for how best to bring breast cancer to the public's awareness. As a result of their thinking, the Pink Ribbon movement was launched in 1991. Initially, the message of breast cancer awareness was delivered via the now-familiar small pink ribbon. The Komen Foundation (a charitable foundation that supports breast cancer research and awareness) distributed pink ribbons to all the participants in its "Race for the Cure"; celebrities wore the pink ribbon at gala events; and many people sported bumper stickers and car magnets shaped like pink ribbons. In a sense, those ribbons and the words that went with them were a form of multimedia, if a relatively low-tech form.

Given the opportunity to expand breast cancer awareness globally, organizers chose to build a Web site to address that opportunity in 1997. Pink Ribbon International organizers established a Web site (PinkRibbon.org) that was "available for all people in the world connected to breast cancer." Not only would a Web site allow for easy access to information about breast cancer, but it could do so using multimedia such as images and educational video. Of course, not all people have access to a computer, let alone to online Web sites like PinkRibbon.org. Many of the world's people have never used a computer, which is a constraint

Multimedia

in this rhetorical situation. A resource, however, might be that health care providers in relatively undeveloped areas of the world sometimes have online access (or did when they were being trained and thus may already have encountered the PinkRibbon.org site).

When organizations like Pink Ribbon International make use of online multimedia elements, their Web designers and content suppliers find themselves choosing from among a seemingly infinite assortment of images, texts, and layouts. Only by keeping their rhetorical situation—and the individual elements of that situation—in mind can they make the best decisions about their media options. The Web site PinkRibbon.org balances text and images, using a layout that helps readers immediately identify the most important information. As a fundraising organization, Pink Ribbon needs to solicit donations—a focus made prominent on its Web site. A visitor to the site is likely to be drawn first to the large top banner image urging readers to "donate now." Keeping additional text in small, contained blocks is a rhetorical decision that makes it easy for the audience to scan and absorb large amounts of information quickly—an important feature, considering the organization's educational goals.

To organize multimedia elements like images and menus, Web designers make use of the same fundamental principles of rhetoric

Pink Ribbon International's home page balances text and images to help its audience absorb information quickly.

that you use when writing an essay or drafting a speech—principles of invention and memory, arrangement, style, and delivery. As you compose, design, and format a Web site, you'll want to keep in mind these basic principles.

Invention and memory

Invention and memory are closely linked—they work together to provide you with the ideas and plans for any composition, including a Web site. Most broadly, "memory" refers to a storehouse of knowledge; the knowledge may be stored in a library, in an archive, on a bulletin board, or in your own memory. You draw from this storehouse when you work through invention (or exploration) strategies such as listing, freewriting, and clustering (see chapter 9). In digital environments, invention and memory can extend across space and time as you share ideas with coauthors around the world and examine historical documents in online archives.

Arrangement

You should arrange the elements of your document (including text and images) to create a "hierarchy of information"; that is, your arrangement should make obvious which information is most important and which is less so. For example, in this textbook, color-coded tabs, chapter titles, headings, and subheadings are used to visually organize the text. You've been taught to place your thesis in the introduction of your essays, and you'll follow that same procedure in your multimedia compositions—placing the most important piece of information wherever your readers will be drawn to first. Because we read from left to right and from top to bottom, the top left corner is often the first place we look. Thus, your decision about what to place there has especially important rhetorical effects. PinkRibbon.org uses that space for a logo; as a result, the organization's promotional materials are always prominent on the Web site.

Ultimately, arrangement is connected to logos. As you already know, logos is the logical appeal of your response to a rhetorical situation, and part of that appeal lies in the (literal) shape of the argument. A writer's attention to shape (or lack thereof) becomes especially evident on Web sites. Most Web sites use images to break up large blocks of text. The resulting shorter chunks of text, in conjunction with images, help your audience focus on the important elements of your composition. In addition, using headings to highlight major ideas can help your audience scan your composition more quickly as they scroll through your Web site. (Remember that most people don't linger over a Web page the way they might over a book page.)

Style

Style, the artful expression of ideas, is an important factor in any composition, especially a multimedia composition, where options for expression are verbal, visual, and aural. In terms of visual elements, font choice in particular makes an important (and immediate) rhetorical statement to your audience. Many advertisements use clean, professional-looking fonts like Helvetica, while informal and light-hearted documents might use **Comic Sans.** Whereas *serif* fonts like Times New Roman (with those little foot-like tips, called serifs, on the ends of some letter strokes) make reading printed documents easier, *sans serif* fonts like **Verdana** (with no serifs on the ends of the strokes) have become the standard for Web sites. When deciding between fonts, consider your purpose. A good place to start is with the questions "What do I want this composition to do?" and "What font best achieves that?"

The colors you choose also have rhetorical effects on your audience. Specifically, colors are closely connected to pathos appeals. You're probably already familiar with how colors in everyday life influence emotions (red, blue, and yellow might conjure up a mental image of an elementary school classroom; just red and yellow might make someone hungry for McDonald's). The same idea applies online: a color scheme featuring dark colors tends to be more professional looking, whereas a vibrant orange scheme might complement the mood of a humor blog. In the case of PinkRibbon.org, the Web site uses a subtle gray as a secondary color to balance the thematic pink menu and highlights. Ultimately, just as you wouldn't write a scholarship application in lime-green text, you should choose Web color schemes based on your purpose and audience.

Delivery

Like style, delivery is concerned with *how* something is said—in this case, how a composition is delivered. How you deliver a speech can be just as important as what you say. The same is true for a Web site. Not everyone will be able to stream videos or download podcasts. Some people might be browsing from a smartphone or a netbook; others might be using an older computer without the capacity to deal with large video or audio downloads. In other words, accessibility is rhetorical: the means of delivery influence what parts of your message an audience ultimately sees and hears. As a result, when you begin designing a multimedia composition such as a Web site, you should consider what information is accessible to which people in what ways. Just because some users can't access videos doesn't mean you should avoid them as a delivery method. After all, if your audience members are all digital movie aficionados, a video review would be completely appropriate.

WAIT A MINUTE . . .

You've probably heard about blogs and wikis, but how are they different from the Web sites we've discussed so far? For one thing, they offer different levels of interactivity for the audience. Web sites traditionally have offered few opportunities for the audience to contribute (though this is changing with the rise of social networking sites like Facebook and Web 2.0 sites like Amazon, which encourage reader reviews and contributions). Like Web sites, blogs are usually updated by one person (or a small group). However, most blogs also have a comment feature, allowing audience members to respond directly to blog posts, but not edit them. Wikis are the most interactive, as they are created *by* site visitors *for* other site visitors. Thus, anyone can contribute to a wiki—developing text, adding images, and rewriting awkward sentences.

Wikis and blogs often address different rhetorical opportunities than Web sites do. Because of their interactivity, wikis are excellent tools for collaboration. For example, if you are working on a group project, you might set up a wiki where all the group members can contribute ideas and revise each other's work. Likewise, blogs often have a different purpose than Web sites do. Most blogs act as public journals, and journal writing often differs in its conventions from the kind of concise, compressed writing you find on a Web site. You might use a blog to document your personal adventures in cooking, whereas a restaurant owner would probably choose a Web site to provide an appealing, unified image of his or her business. As you face the rhetorical decision of which genre to use (wiki, blog, or Web site), keep in mind that the distinctions discussed above often overlap—a Web site might have a blog component or a wiki might act like a collaborative journal.

You should simply realize that the delivery choices you make determine not only who constitutes your audience but also how your audience experiences your composition.

If all of this technical talk seems intimidating, don't worry—many Web sites today are built and updated using Content Management Systems (CMSs) and design templates, allowing you to focus more on the rhetorical principles behind composing and less on the technical execution. A CMS lets users create and maintain Web sites through an Internet browser, thus requiring little knowledge of HTML or the technical side of design. For example, Penn State University's Composition Web site (composition.la.psu.edu) is built and maintained using the open-source CMS *Plone*. In the screenshots in the Tricks of the Trade box, you can see that pages are edited using a WYSIWYG editor and

Multimedia

TRICKS OF THE TRADE

WYSIWYG Editors

WYSIWYG stands for "what you see is what you get," and WYSIWYG editors are a type of software that has become commonplace on Web sites, blogs, and wikis. The advantage of a WYSIWYG editor is its familiarity—most have a toolbar for formatting text similar to the toolbar in Microsoft Word. This means you don't need an understanding of a complicated mark-up language like HTML in order to create professional-looking content for a Web site. Because WYSIWYG interfaces make creating online documents so easy, hosts of blogs and wikis in particular have adopted them in order to increase their user base. The simple selling point of WYSIWYG is this: if you can send an email, you can build a Web site, start a blog, or update a wiki.

A page on the Penn State Composition Web site being updated with a WYSIWYG editor. Notice that aside from the editing icons and textboxes, this looks very much like the finished page shown below.

Courtesy of Pennsylvania State University

The finished page made public on the Composition Web site.

Courtesy of Pennsylvania State University

constructed by *Plone* to fit the design template of the Web site. This is not to say that all design elements are out of your control, however: you still need to be comfortable with the rhetorical dimensions of arranging images and formatting text, discussed earlier.

A Rhetorical Approach to Podcasting

In your first-year writing class, you might be asked to produce a basic recording, such as a podcast. Such assignments offer an alternative to printed essays and give you practice with oral presentations. For example, you might be assigned to compose a critical review of your favorite band, a review you'll deliver as a podcast. The podcast is a fitting medium for a music review, one that enhances the message itself. In addition, a podcast might better appeal to your audience than a print review would. If you have never done it, creating a podcast might seem technologically daunting—but it's not. In fact, composing a podcast is fairly easy, as you can use your personal computer and basic sound editing software like Apple's GarageBand or any of the audio editors available as free downloads, such as Audacity.

TRICKS OF THE TRADE

Recording Technologies

The technologies used to make audio recordings can be as simple as a computer with a built-in microphone or as complicated as a full studio setup. You probably already have experience with audio recording as a medium of delivery. Think of all the times that you've planned out an important voice message before recording it. You probably considered your audience and purpose before calling—you might have even practiced your delivery a few times. The point is that you're probably no stranger to audio recording as a rhetorical act.

Recording basic audio at home has become much easier in recent years, and recordings can even approach studio quality, as many personal computers come with pre-installed sound editing software such as Apple's GarageBand. This software provides a visual representation of multiple recorded tracks that you have created or drawn from other sources, which can then be manipulated by cutting, pasting, rearranging, and recording over the segments of audio. You can adjust volume and equalization (treble, bass, etc.) levels using the slider bars to the left of your tracks or add sound effects with a single click of the mouse. Because of its visual interface, software like GarageBand makes it easy for anyone to mix and layer multiple tracks into a professional audio composition.

Invention and memory

You learned in the previous section that invention and memory work together to provide knowledge and generate new ideas when you are composing a Web site. Techniques such as freewriting and clustering can help you prepare what you're going to say for podcasting too. Like many writers, you may find that the act of imagining and planning for a recording generates ideas that never would have occurred to you if you had been composing a traditional print essay.

At this stage, particularly if podcasting is new to you, it might be helpful to listen to one or several podcasts. As you do, try to think about what this medium makes possible and how you can best take advantage of this resource.

Arrangement

Compose and practice your script before you start. If you don't want to be tethered to a full script, write out a detailed outline of what you want to say (in order to avoid sounding panicky or rambling). Another good reason to practice is that written language often needs to be "translated" to spoken language. As you read aloud, you'll find that some passages go smoothly while other passages are too complicated to make for good speaking or listening and need to be rewritten. You might need to break up long sentences, enumerate your points, or repeat key phrases. It also helps to mark in your script occasional pauses, so that your audience has time to process what you've said. Finally, by preparing and arranging your talk ahead of time and considering your audience and purpose, you can ensure that your word choice is suitable for the spoken medium. For example, instead of using a word like *disparage*, you might simply say "make fun of" or "put down."

Style

One advantage of an audio recording is that you can make stylistic changes after you've recorded it—that is, you can use sound editing software to edit your composition later. At this stage you can also add effects. For example, if you are recording an album review, you might include background music from the album or small samples of songs to establish your ethos (that is, that you know a good deal about the music itself) or to illustrate a particular point in your review (which would also enhance your ethos). You can also make technical adjustments, such as lowering volume levels for individual tracks. Finally, with your editing software's visual interface, you can find and selectively edit out mistakes (much as you delete typos with a word processor). Just as you practice before live presentations and proofread your written essays before submitting them, you should always go back and make adjustments to recordings so that your finished composition sounds polished. After all, you already know the importance of a polished composition—whether it be written, spoken, or recorded—in building your ethos.

Delivery

Delivery has always been an important part of effective rhetoric. Once you've determined that your means of delivery will involve audio, you need to be sure your listening audience can understand you. But the decision to speak clearly is a rhetorical choice; a good many underground or indie bands (such as The White Stripes and T-Pain) purposefully distort their vocals. Their purposeful voice distortion challenges the mainstream convention of recording clarity exhibited by artists like Justin Timberlake or Taylor Swift. In most cases, however, your audience will appreciate it if you speak clearly and slowly into the microphone to ensure that it picks up the sound of your voice properly. In addition to considering your voice quality, you'll also want to consider how fast you read. If you keep in mind that good spoken delivery usually takes 2.5 minutes per double-spaced page, you'll know how to pace yourself. And if you've followed the advice on arrangement and style, you will already have revised your composition so that your language is simple and clear enough to be understood by your listening audience.

A Rhetorical Approach to Broadcasting on YouTube

Video provides yet another available means for composing and delivering multimedia documents. If you are going to review a movie, for example, you might decide to use the same medium as the piece you are reviewing: video. That's exactly what Grace Randolph did in a review of *Shutter Island* in her movie review program *Beyond the Trailer*; she then posted her review on YouTube.

Once you've mastered podcasting, you may want to try composing a video. Both of these media give you opportunities to apply the rhetorical principles you're learning to non-text-based compositions.

Invention and memory

Like a well-done audio recording, a well-composed video is based on the preparation that only invention and memory can supply. Thinking back to the videos you've enjoyed and replaying them online or on your television set may give you ideas about what you want to be sure to include visually and verbally in your own video composition. Plenty of good information is stored in your own memory, as well as in your

Multimedia

Grace Randolph hosts a review of Martin Scorsese's *Shutter Island* on YouTube.

video library. You can use these ideas as the seeds of fresh new visual, verbal, and musical concepts for your video composition. Invention and memory will work together to supply what you want to say.

Arrangement

The material resulting from invention and memory must be given purposeful arrangement. Regardless of who performs in the video (you, others, or some combination thereof), you'll want to prepare a script, cue cards, or a flowchart so that you can closely track the arrangement of the video. Some videos are animated, some are "mashups" (a splicing together or layering of several existing clips), and still others are montages set to music or a narration (or both). You'll need to consider the resources and constraints of your rhetorical situation as you choose among the variety of arrangement options. Multiple options, your own willingness to perform (or fear of performing), your access to video equipment—any of these might be your richest resource or your strongest constraint. All of them play a role in the arrangement of your composition, whether you add music, art, interviews, performers—whatever visual or audio elements you choose to employ.

The ability to compose with video is in and of itself a major resource, as video allows you to edit and polish your composition after the fact, just as you can with audio. With video editing software you can rearrange your video frame by frame, as well as cut scenes and control audio. So if you finish your composition and then decide a different arrangement might appeal to your audience more, you can cut and paste sections into a different order, just as you might do with a word-processed essay. You might also need to do "cleanup" work on scenes that run too long or select specific segments of film to compile into a final video while cutting others. After all, as the twentieth-century rhetorician Kenneth Burke put it, any composition is ultimately a selection, reflection, and deflection of reality.

Style

Once you have a draft of your video, you can enhance its style by adding soundtracks or special effects from your editing software's effects library. You'll want to keep in mind that every audio or visual enhancement has its own rhetorical as well as stylistic effect. Consider, for instance, James Cameron's *Titanic*, a pathos-drenched drama. Only a solemn, stately soundtrack could complement *Titanic*, whereas the lively musical score of *Mamma Mia!* brings the upbeat plot to life. As you consider and reconsider the various stylistic embellishments of your video, keep in mind that even feature-length movies go through an intense editing process designed to produce a polished, stylistically appealing product.

Delivery

Good delivery in a video depends on many of the principles of effective audio compositions—you should speak clearly into the microphone, pace yourself when delivering monologues, and practice your performance ahead of time. However, you must also consider the visual dimensions of video, including what you and the other performers wear and what material and visual elements you include. For instance, in the *Beyond the Trailer* example (which is shown on the Web site Indy Mogul), Grace Randolph wears a sci-fi chic *Battlestar Galactica* t-shirt and stands next to a giant digital movie poster while delivering her monologue. Even though Randolph is casually dressed, she has chosen her attire and props carefully: the combination of these visual elements immediately builds her ethos as a movie reviewer who focuses specifically on the sci-fi/indie genre. Her choices also display audience awareness, as the audience for the film she is reviewing—Martin Scorsese's paranormal thriller *Shutter Island*—would likely also be sci-fi fans.

Delivery doesn't just apply to your performance on film, however. You should also consider how you will distribute (or deliver) the video itself to your audience. YouTube and other sites that host streaming video have made distribution easier. However, because of the public nature of such sites, you may want to choose a different distribution method, such as email, in order to more carefully control who is in your audience. Even something as mundane sounding as file format can be a rhetorical issue: obscure video formats might limit who can view your composition, whereas more common file formats (with extensions like .avi and .mov) can be opened on most computers. These kinds of technical considerations can even affect your ethos. For example, the .wma file extension can be opened only on computers running Windows, so saving your video in this format aligns you with PC users. If you've seen the "Mac vs. PC" commercials, you know that this alignment might hurt your ethos among Mac users, who often view PCs as inferior computers. However, saving your composition as a .wma file might contribute to your ethos in an office environment, where PCs are often the professional standard. In any case, even something as "neutral" as choosing a file format is actually an important rhetorical decision.

TRICKS OF THE TRADE

Video Composing Technologies

Like those for audio recording, the technologies required to create video can range from the simple combination of a digital camera and basic editing software to a full-blown studio environment. Point-and-shoot digital video cameras make filming a surprisingly simple process and can often be borrowed from your university's media department or library. And programs like Apple's Final Cut Express offer affordable, easy-to-learn alternatives to expensive software packages. Final Cut Express relies on a visually intuitive interface, much like that of GarageBand. Video and audio tracks appear under your video as labeled rectangles that can be cut, copied, moved, synced, or edited in a visual interface. You can also control transitions, colors, and effects using the menus in the left-hand workspace, all while seeing the real-time effects in the video viewer.

© Patagonik Works/Jupiter Images

Multimedia

Facebook and Twitter as Multimedia

In the past decade, social networking sites like Facebook and Twitter have become hugely popular. These sites allow you to construct an online profile, stay in touch with friends, and let people know what is happening in your life. Whenever you update your Facebook profile or post a photograph to Twitter, you are engaging in multimedia composing. After all, a Facebook profile is usually some combination of text, links, images, and video that you construct with a specific rhetorical purpose in mind. For example, if you wanted to persuade viewers of your profile that you were well read, you might post a long "Favorite Books" list, perhaps accompanied by a picture of your overburdened book shelves.

Although you don't likely think of the rhetorical principles of invention and memory, arrangement, style, and delivery each time you tweet or update your Facebook status, these principles are always at work. As you examine the following examples, one of a group's Facebook page and one of a Twitter stream, consider the ways the writers combined various media to form fitting responses.

The Brazos Valley Poets Facebook page came about in response to a specific problem: the poetry community of East Texas was loosely organized, with poetry readings under-advertised by word of mouth and the poets themselves unaware of other poets in the area. Identifying this problem as a rhetorical opportunity, a group of student poets realized that on a Facebook page, local writers could discuss their work, organize readings, and share news that was important to the community. The group eventually grew to encompass local poets and writers from a variety of backgrounds and a range of ages.

Some rhetorical advantages of using Facebook for such a project were the wide potential distribution, familiar standardized interface, and interactivity of the platform. If you are familiar with Facebook, you will notice

The Brazos Valley Poets Facebook page provides an online space where local poets can discuss their work, plan upcoming events, and share photos of local poetry readings.

that the "Info" page for Brazos Valley Poets has the same familiar layout as other group pages and profiles—it provides a basic, easily accessible description and contact information for the group. This accessibility turned out to be very important early on for the group as it increased its visibility. However, another rhetorical purpose in forming the group was to build community among local poets. As a result, the group's formal discussion pages and informal wall began to develop as communication spaces.

For the Brazos Valley Poets, a high-traffic site like a Facebook page was ideal for building a network of local poets. But issues of audience can become complicated when you are working online with multimedia compositions, especially on sites like Facebook. The primary audience for your Facebook profile might be your friends, but unless you have adjusted your privacy settings, anyone with an account could be part of the audience. Having such a large potential audience isn't necessarily a bad thing—as long as you are aware of it. After all, social networking sites can be effective tools for distributing compositions you think are important. Consider the university students in Iran who used Twitter to distribute information about protests to other Iranians and the outside world, discussed earlier in this chapter. Or consider the Viza Go-Go art show organizers, who linked their Web site to a Facebook profile as a way to reach beyond their small local audience and display their work to family members and potential employers. In both of these examples, the writers took full advantage of social networking sites' interconnectedness and potential for rapid distribution of information.

The rhetorical constraints of social networking sites have also spawned some unique and creative composing practices. Consider @cookbook, a Twitter cookbook by Maureen Evans, where all the recipes are condensed into 140-character tweets. As you can see in the screenshot, Evans had to develop her own cooking shorthand in order to adapt to her space constraint: writing "Cvr30m" instead of "Cover for 30 minutes" saves 14 valuable characters. Because this shorthand can be confusing, however, Evans also developed a glossary, using a wiki

Courtesy of Maureen Evans, author of *Eat Tweet*, published by Artisan Books (2010).

@cookbook is a Twitter stream that provides condensed, 140-character recipes.

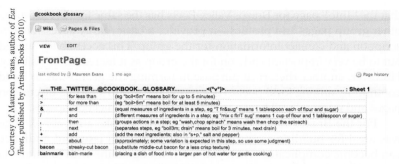

The companion wiki glossary to the @cookbook Twitter stream.

platform to define the shortened cooking terms she uses on Twitter. By connecting the two composing spaces (Evans created links to the wiki from @cookbook), Evans was able to work around one of the constraints of her rhetorical situation in a creative way.

One advantage of @cookbook's shortened recipes lies in the rhetorical principle of delivery: audience members can quickly and easily access these short recipes on small portable devices like smartphones. Such access may seem insignificant, but if you've ever been at the grocery store trying to remember the ingredients for your supper, you understand how important that access could be. That access is also handy in the kitchen: you can consult your phone rather than your laptop (which you want to protect from boiling liquids, thawing solids, and various other ingredients).

Challenges and Pleasures of Multimedia

Just as composing in traditional print media can be a challenge, so can composing with multimedia. In addition to requiring you to generate the most effective information and the most appropriate arrangement, multimedia composing asks you to consider new skills (using audio and visual technologies, for instance) as well as new audiences. You'll find yourself moving from writing for your instructor to writing for a much broader audience, many members of which you'll never meet. However, by paying attention to the rhetorical principles you've already learned—opportunity, audience, purpose, fitting response, available means—you can compose and deliver effective multimedia pieces. The multimedia examples referred to throughout this chapter were composed by students just like you, students who came to realize the power and potential of multimedia. They approached their compositions—a Facebook page for poets, a revolutionary text message, a multimedia art show Web site—with rhetorical savvy. As technology becomes an ever-present part of our lives, multimedia composing is becoming an important part of our rhetorical practices. Being familiar with multimedia is key to participating in the emerging conversations of the twenty-first century.

A Guide to Research

4

Throughout this part of the book, you'll use your knowledge of the rhetorical situation to understand the research process. Chapter 11 will help you use the elements of the rhetorical situation to get started on your research projects. Chapters 12 and 13 contain information on the many different types of sources available to you and where to find them. Chapter 14 provides strategies for managing the research process. Chapter 14 also explains how to evaluate and use sources. Chapter 15 provides detailed guidelines on acknowledging sources and formatting research papers, as well as a sample student paper.

Clues to Compulsive Collecting

SEPARATING USELESS JUNK FROM OBJECTS OF VALUE

AN INTRIGUING NEW STUDY MAY help researchers understand why some people are compelled to hoard useless objects. Steven W. Anderson, a neurologist, and his colleagues at the University of Iowa examined 63 people with brain damage from stroke, surgery or encephalitis. Before their brains were damaged, none had problems with hoarding, but afterward, nine began filling their houses with such things as old newspapers, broken appliances or boxes of junk mail, despite the intervention of family members.

WHY DO SOME PEOPLE COLLECT USELESS OBJECTS LIKE OLD NEWSPAPERS, BROKEN APPLIANCES AND JUNK MAIL?

Photo © WR Publishing/Alamy.

These compulsive collectors had all suffered damage to the prefrontal cortex, a brain region involved in decision making, information processing and behavioral organization. The people whose collecting behavior remained normal also had brain damage, but it was instead distributed throughout the right and left hemispheres of the brain.

Anderson posits that the urge to collect derives from the need to store supplies such as food—a drive so basic it originates in the subcortical and limbic portions of the brain. Humans need the prefrontal cortex, he says, to determine what "supplies" are worth hoarding. His study was presented at the annual conference of the Society for Neuroscience.

—Richard A. Lovett

1. In "Clues to Compulsive Collecting," Richard Lovett describes research first presented by Steven Anderson and his colleagues at a neuroscience conference. After reading this article, write a paragraph or two in which you discuss the article in terms of Lovett's and the original researchers' rhetorical situations. How are they similar? How are they different?

2. In answering question 1, you likely noted significant differences in the rhetorical situations of the article writer and the original researchers, even though their subject matter was the same. In order to prepare for the research you may have to do for college classes, describe a rhetorical situation you might encounter in one of your classes. Explain how research would help you prepare a fitting response.

An Overview of Research

When people hear the word *research,* they often think of laboratory experiments, archaeological digs, or hours spent in the library or on the library's Web site. They overlook the ordinary research they do every day as they decide what to buy, how to fix something, how to perform a function on their computer, what books to read, or where to spend their vacation. Research is common to everyone's experience.

When people move to a new place, they must find information about schools, clinics, stores, and other locations of importance or interest. They must also find out about dentists, doctors, veterinarians, and accountants. They obtain the information they need by doing research—that is, by talking with other people, visiting Web sites, and reading brochures and other materials.

Many people do research at work. Business owners must keep abreast of new technology, marketing trends, and changes in the tax code. Doctors must have current information on diagnostic procedures and effective treatments, therapies, and pharmaceuticals. Some types of research that professionals do may be surprising. Librarians, for example, have to know about the latest print materials and information technology, but in order to prepare their operating budgets, they also have to know the costs of items and numbers of library users. The types of research people do in the workplace depend on their jobs, but most professionals consult other people they consider knowledgeable, read materials on specific topics, and visit useful Web sites.

Students, of course, conduct many types of research, starting in elementary school and continuing through college. Their research enables them to prepare lab reports, posters, term papers, multimedia presentations, and other types of assignments. Some of their research entails laboratory experimentation. Other research takes place in the field, as students conduct surveys, make observations, and attend performances.

Much research focuses on written records such as articles and books, government documents, old letters, and personal journals.

Regardless of the form of the research or the context in which it takes place, all research is done in response to a *rhetorical opportunity:* a call or need for more information. Depending on the nature of the opportunity, you may or may not have to record the results of your research. Once you obtain the information on which store has the best prices for electronics, you simply go to that store. In contrast, research projects prepared in response to an assignment usually require writing— at all stages of the process. Researchers often freewrite to come up with ideas, create project designs and work plans, take notes, and eventually draft some kind of composition. It is hard to imagine a researcher in an academic setting without a pen, pencil, or keyboard.

For the results of research to be valuable, the process must be taken seriously. Researchers who chase down facts to attach to opinions they already have are doing only superficial research. These researchers are not interested in finding information that may cause them to question their beliefs or that may make their thinking more complicated. Genuine research, on the other hand, involves crafting a good research question and pursuing an answer to it, both of which require patience and care.

Rhetorical Opportunity and the Research Question

As you know from reading chapter 9, the starting point for any writing project is determining your rhetorical opportunity—what has prompted you to write. For research assignments, that opportunity (or problem) also includes what has prompted you to look for more information. Once you are sure of your opportunity, you can craft a question to guide your research.

To make the most of your time, choose a specific question early in your research process. Having such a question helps you avoid collecting more sources than you can possibly use or finding sources that are only tangentially related. A student who chooses a general topic— say, the separation of church and state—will waste time if he or she neglects to narrow the topic into a question, such as one of the following: What did the framers of the Constitution have in mind when they discussed the separation of church and state? How should the separation of church and state be interpreted in law? Should the Ten Commandments be posted in government buildings? Should the phrase *under God* be removed from the Pledge of Allegiance?

Good questions often arise when you try to relate what you are studying in a course to your own experience. For instance, you may start wondering about the separation of church and state when, after reading about this topic in a history class, you notice the number of times politicians refer to God in their speeches, you remember reciting the phrase *under God* in the Pledge of Allegiance, or you read in the newspaper that a plaque inscribed with the Ten Commandments has been removed from the State House in Alabama. These observations may prompt you to look for more information on the topic. Each observation, however, may give rise to a different question. You will choose the question that interests you the most and that will best help you fulfill the assignment.

To generate research questions, you may find it helpful to return to chapter 9, where you read about journalists' questions (Who? What? Where? When? Why? How?). Here are some more specific kinds of questions that commonly require research:

QUESTIONS ABOUT CAUSES

Why doesn't my college offer athletic scholarships?
What causes power outages in large areas of the country?

QUESTIONS ABOUT CONSEQUENCES

What are the consequences of taking antidepressants for a long period of time?
How would the atmosphere in a school change if a dress code were established?

QUESTIONS ABOUT PROCESSES

How can music lovers prevent corporations from controlling the development of music?
How does my hometown draw boundaries for school districts?

QUESTIONS ABOUT DEFINITIONS OR CATEGORIES

How do you know if you are addicted to something?
What kind of test is "the test of time"?

QUESTIONS ABOUT VALUES

Should the Makah tribe be allowed to hunt gray whales?
Would the construction of wind farms be detrimental to the environment?

Research

TRICKS OF THE TRADE

If the assignment doesn't specify a topic and you are not sure what you want to write about, you may need some prompting. Consider these questions:

▶ Can you remember an experience that you did not understand fully or that made you feel uncertain? What was it that you didn't understand? What were you unsure of?

▶ What have you observed lately (on television, in the newspaper, on your way to school, or in the student union) that piqued your curiosity? What were you curious about?

▶ What local or national problem that you have recently heard or read about would you like to help solve?

▶ Is there anything you find unusual that you would like to explore? Lifestyles? Political views? Religious views?

As you consider which question will most appropriately guide your research, you may find it helpful to discuss your ideas with other people. Research and writing both require a great deal of time and effort, and you will find the tasks more pleasant—and maybe even easier—if you are sincerely interested in your question. Moreover, enthusiasm about your work will motivate you to do the best you can; indifference breeds mediocrity. By talking with other people, you may find out that the question you have chosen is a good one. Or, you may discover that you need to narrow the question or change it in some other way. You may even realize that the question you initially chose really does not interest you very much. To get a conversation about your ideas started, have someone you are familiar with ask you some of the following questions. You may also use these questions for a focused freewriting exercise in your research log (see chapter 13 for more on research logs).

▶ Why is it important for you to answer the question? What is the answer's significance for you? How will answering the question help you? How is the question related to your rhetorical opportunity?

▶ Will the answer to your question require serious research? (A genuine research question does not have a simple or obvious answer.)

▶ What types of research might help you answer your question? (You may already have some ideas; see chapter 12 for ideas about library and online research and chapter 13 for suggestions on field research.) Will you be able to carry out these types of research in the amount of time you have been given?

Research and Audience

In part 1, you learned that a fitting response satisfies your audience. In order to meet the expectations of your readers, you must know something about them. First, you must find out who your audience is. If you are writing in response to a course assignment, your instructor may define your audience for you (usually, it is the instructor and your classmates). However, sometimes your instructor may ask you to imagine a different audience so that you have experience writing for a wider range of people. For example, your instructor might ask you to write a letter to the editor of your local paper. In this case, your audience is much broader. It still comprises your instructor and classmates, but it also includes the editor of the newspaper as well as all the newspaper's readers.

As your writing career progresses, the number of audiences you write for will increase. You may be able to easily name your audience—college students, science teachers, mechanical engineers, pediatricians, or the general public—but to make sure that you satisfy any audience you choose to address, you need to go beyond labels. When you do research, you must take into account what types of sources your audience will expect you to use and which sources they will find engaging, convincing, or entertaining.

Keep in mind that when you write for an audience, you are joining an ongoing conversation. To enter that conversation, you need to pay attention to what's being said and who the participants are. You can begin by reading the sources the participants in the conversation use. By reading what they read, you'll learn what information is familiar to them and what information may need to be explained in detail.

The brief article from *Bostonia,* Boston University's alumni magazine (on page 356), and the Web page for the Pucker Gallery (on page 357) contain information about the artist Joseph Ablow. The audience for each is different, however. In the *Bostonia* article, the abbreviation CFA is not explained, because the intended audience, alumni of Boston University, will know that it refers to the College of Fine Arts. If you were writing an article for an alumni magazine, you too would be able

Ablow's Objets d'Art

Large Still Life Frieze, oil on canvas, 32" x 66", 1986. Photograph by S. Petegorsky

IN A LECTURE this fall at Amherst College, Joseph Ablow described a major change in his artistic direction in the late 1950s. He had been working on large, classically inspired themes for a decade and "something did not feel right."

"My subjects no longer held much meaning for me," said Ablow, a CFA professor emeritus of art, "and I began to realize that painting and inventing from memory had left me visually parched. It was obvious to me that I had to start over."

The reevaluation pulled him back to the studio, where, he says, "simply as exercises, I returned to the subject of still life," something he had avoided since art school. "But it was not long before the motley collection of objects I had assembled began quietly to organize themselves into configurations that suggested unexpected pictorial possibilities to me.

"I soon discovered that these objects may be quiet, but that did not mean that they remained still. What was to have been a subject that suggested ways of studying the look of things within a manageable and concentrated situation became an increasingly involved world that could be surprisingly disquieting and provocative. I may have been the one responsible for arranging my cups and bowls on the tabletops, but that did not ensure that I was in control of them.

"The ginger jars and the compote dishes were real, particular, and palpable and yet had no inherent significance. Their interest or importance would be revealed only in the context of a painting."

Born in 1928, Ablow studied with Oskar Kokoschka, Ben Shahn, and Karl Zerbe. He earned degrees from Bennington and Harvard and taught at Boston University from 1963 until 1995. He is currently a visiting artist at Amherst College, which hosted the exhibition of his paintings that is coming to BU.

Still lifes painted over some thirty-five years highlight Joseph Ablow: A Retrospective, *from January 13 through March 5 at the Sherman Gallery, 775 Commonwealth Avenue.* ♦

to use abbreviations and acronyms familiar to those who attended that college or university. However, if your audience were broader, such abbreviations and acronyms would have to be explained the first time you used them. The same criterion can be used to make decisions about content. If you were researching one of Joseph Ablow's still life paintings, you would find that sources on Ablow's work do not define what a still life painting is; the authors of these sources assume that their readers are familiar with the term. However, if you were writing for readers who knew next to nothing about painting, you would provide a definition for the term.

Pucker Gallery

HOME

EXHIBITIONS

ARTISTS

DIRECTOR'S CHOICE

SHOP AT THE GALLERY

PUBLICATIONS

ABOUT US

JOSEPH ABLOW

Represented by Pucker Gallery since 1979

BORN: 1928 in Salem, Massachusetts
RESIDES: Brookline, Massachusetts

Most Recent Exhibition:
Together 10 February 2007 - 20 March 2007

Joe Ablow was born in Salem, Massachusetts and has lived, worked and taught in the Boston area his entire life. After studying painting at the School of the Museum of Fine Arts, Boston, receiving his Bachelors from Bennington College and his Masters from Harvard University, Ablow continued his instruction in painting with names such as Oskar Kokoschka and Ben Shahn. In addition to his own exhibitions, Ablow has been a professor at Boston University for thirty-five years and written countless academic articles on Art in the Twentieth Century.

Joseph Ablow
The Usual Suspects
Oil on Canvas
19 x 42"
JA210

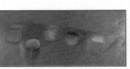

Joseph Ablow
A Gathering,
2006
Watercolor
w/gouache on
paper
7 x 11"
JA201

Joseph Ablow
Grey Forms,
2006
Watercolor w/
white over
Graphite
15 x 11 7/8"
JA213

Joseph Ablow
In the Balance, 2001
Oil on canvas
34 x 36"
JA194

Research

Readers of an academic research paper expect the author to be knowledgeable. You can demonstrate your knowledge through the types of sources you use and the ways you handle them. Because you aren't likely to have established credibility as an expert on the topic you are researching, you'll usually have to depend on the credibility of the sources you use. Once you have done enough research to understand your audience, you'll be better able to select sources that will give you credibility. For example, to persuade your readers of the value of a vegetarian diet, you could choose among sources written by nutritionists, ethicists, religious leaders, and animal rights proponents. Your decision would be based on which kinds of sources your audience would find most credible.

Readers of an academic research paper also expect the author to be critical. They want to be assured that an author can tell whether the source information is accurate or deceptive, whether its logic is strong or weak, and whether its conclusions are justifiable. Your readers may accept your use of a questionable source as long as you show why it is problematic. You will learn ways of establishing your credibility and demonstrating your critical abilities in chapter 14.

WAIT A MINUTE ...

When you read sources critically, you are considering the rhetorical situation from the perspective of a reader. Since you're also thinking about how the sources might be used in your own writing, you're involved in a second rhetorical situation as a writer. Rarely will the rhetorical situation that led to the creation of the source you are consulting be the same as the rhetorical situation you confront in writing for a class. Of course, there may be overlap, particularly in audience, but the rhetorical opportunity and purpose of the two pieces of writing are likely to be different.

Research and Purpose

In chapter 1, you saw how your rhetorical audience and your rhetorical purpose are interconnected. They cannot be separated. In general, your rhetorical purpose is to have an impact on your audience; more specifically, your aim may be to entertain them, to inform them, to explain something to them, or to influence them to do something. Research can help you achieve any of these purposes. For example, if you are writing a research paper on the roots of humor for a psychology class, your primary purpose is to inform. You may want to analyze a few jokes, in order to show how their construction can incite laughter, but you'll need research to support your claim. Your audience will be more inclined to believe you if you show them, say, experimental results indicating that people routinely find certain incidents funny.

Writers of research papers commonly define their rhetorical purposes in the following ways:

▶ *To inform an audience.* The researcher reports current thinking on a specific topic, including opposing views but not siding with any particular one.

Example: To inform the audience of current guidelines for developing a city park

▶ *To analyze and synthesize information and then offer tentative solutions to a problem.* The researcher analyzes and synthesizes information on a subject (for example, an argument, a text, an event, a technique, or a statistic), looking for points of agreement and disagreement and for gaps in coverage. Part of the research process consists of finding out what other researchers have already written about the subject. After presenting the analysis and synthesis, the researcher offers possible ways to address the problem.

Example: To analyze and synthesize various national health-care proposals

▶ *To persuade an audience or to issue an invitation to an audience.* The researcher states a position and backs it up with data, statistics, texts illustrating a point, or supporting arguments found through research. The researcher's purpose is to persuade or invite readers to take the same position.

Example: To persuade people to vote for a congressional candidate

Often, these purposes co-exist in the same piece of writing. A researcher presenting results from an original experiment or study, for instance, must often achieve all of these purposes. In the introduction to a lab report, the researcher might describe previous work done in the area and identify a research niche—an area needing research. The researcher then explains how his or her current study will help fill the gap in existing research. The body of the text is informative, describing the materials used, explaining the procedures followed, and presenting the results. In the conclusion, the researcher may choose, given the results of the experiment or study, to persuade the audience to take some action (for example, give up smoking, eat fewer carbohydrates, or fund future research).

The sources you find through research can help you achieve your purpose. If your purpose is to inform, you can use the work of established scholars to enhance your credibility. If your purpose is to analyze and synthesize information, sources you find can provide not only data for you to work on but also a backdrop against which to highlight your own originality or your special research niche. If your purpose is to persuade, you can use sources to support your assertions and to counter the assertions of others.

Research and a Fitting Response

Like any other kind of writing you do, your research report needs to address the rhetorical situation. There are many different kinds of research, just as there are many different ways to present research findings. Shaping a fitting response means considering the following kinds of questions:

▶ *Is your researched response appropriate to the problem?* The focus, and thus the kind of research called for (library, Internet, naturalistic, laboratory, or some combination of these), depends on the nature of the problem. Engineers studying the question of how to prevent future natural disasters from causing the kind of damage wrought in New Orleans by Hurricane Katrina in 2005 would need to be sure their research focused on environmental and geographical conditions specific to that area. Research on the success of levees built along the Danube in Europe might not be applicable. The researchers would also likely need to combine many different kinds of research in order to determine the best method of prevention.

▶ *Is your researched response delivered in a medium that will reach its intended audience?* Writers presenting research findings want to be sure their work finds its way into the right hands. Engineers researching the issue of how best to rebuild the levees in New Orleans could certainly summarize their findings in a letter to the editor of the New Orleans *Times Picayune*. However, if they wanted approval from a government agency for future work, they would likely need to present the research in a document addressed directly to that agency, such as a written application for funding or a proposal in the form of a multimedia presentation.

▶ *Will your researched response successfully satisfy the intended audience?* Research papers in different academic disciplines have different types of content and formats. To help make sure their audience will be satisfied, researchers take care to notice the research methods used in the discipline and deliver writing that is presented and

Research

documented according to the accepted style of the discipline. (For information on different kinds of documentation styles, see chapter 15.)

As always, a fitting response must also be considered in terms of the available means.

Research: Constraints and Resources

In chapter 1, you learned how the means available to you for responding are shaped by both the *constraints* (obstacles or limits) and the *resources* (positive influences) of the rhetorical situation. In reviewing the brief *Psychology Today* article that opened this chapter, you saw how one writer, Richard Lovett, worked with specific constraints and resources. You may have identified the primary elements of the rhetorical situation, noting constraints such as the need to deliver complex and specialized information from the field of neurology to readers of a popular magazine. To address this constraint, Lovett made allowances for his readers' perhaps limited knowledge of how the brain works by defining unfamiliar terms (*prefrontal cortex,* for example). You may also have noted some of the resources available to Lovett in writing for this kind of publication. The image that accompanies his text is a resource that allows readers to absorb the topic at a glance, while the pull-quote (the quotation in large type in the middle of the article) makes the scientists' research question explicit.

As a researcher in an academic setting, you are no doubt aware that many of your rhetorical situations share various constraints. For instance, an academic research assignment usually involves some kind of specifications from an instructor. Following are some common constraints for such writing assignments:

- ▶ *Expertise.* As a student, you rely to some degree on documenting what others have said in order to build credibility.

- ▶ *Geography.* Although the Internet gives researchers unprecedented access to materials not available locally, most students are still somewhat constrained by what's close at hand.

- ▶ *Time.* In most cases, your research will be subject to a time limit. Your readers—whether they are instructors, colleagues, or other decision makers—need to see your research before it goes out of date and before the deadline to make a decision (about what action to take or what grade to assign) has passed.

Constraints such as these can, however, suggest resources. What primary documents might you have access to in your geographical location? What unique opportunities do you have for reaching your audience that a recognized expert might not have? Can working within a particular time frame provide motivation?

Of course, each rhetorical situation is different. Every time you begin research, you'll face a new set of constraints and resources. To participate effectively in an ongoing conversation, you'll need to identify specific resources to help you manage your particular set of constraints.

Research

Pop Cultures

REFRESCOS IN SPANISH, MASHROOB GHAZI in Arabic, kele in Chinese: the world has many words, and an unslakable thirst, for carbonated soft drinks. Since 1997 per capita consumption has nearly doubled in eastern Europe. In 2008 Coca-Cola tallied soda sales in some 200 countries. Even the global recession, says industry monitor Zenith International, has merely caused manufacturers to lean on promotional offers and try cheap social-networking ads.

But some are sour on all this sweetness. U.S. obesity expert David Ludwig calls aggressive marketing in emerging nations—where people tend to eat more and move less as they prosper—"deeply irresponsible. That's the time of greatest risk for heart disease, diabetes, and obesity."

As that thinking catches on, places including New York and Romania are mulling levies on sugared drinks. Others argue that taxing a single product isn't the fix: promoting healthy lifestyles and zero-calorie drinks is. Fizz for thought?

—Jeremy Berlin

Consumption of carbonates*
12-ounce servings per person, 2008

U.S.	529
Mexico	501
Malta	425
Czech Republic	413
Chile	391
Norway	381
Australia	377
Iceland	333
Canada	311
Belgium	300

*INCLUDES REGULAR AND LOW-CALORIE SODAS

Rebecca Hale/National Geographic Stock

1. Why do you think Jeremy Berlin (and the editors at *National Geographic*) decided to use a photograph and a list of statistics with the article "Pop Cultures"? What kind of research do you think he and his editors did to prepare this article and the accompanying graphics? In other words, what might they have read or observed, whom might they have questioned, and so on? If you wanted to check their facts, what would you do?

2. Think back to a research paper you wrote. What kind of research did you conduct for that project? Where did you go to find your sources? Given more time and more resources, what additional kinds of research might you have done?

Research

Sources for Research

Although the library will probably play an important role in your research, it often will not be the only location in which you conduct research. During the research process, you might find yourself at home using the Internet, in your instructor's office getting suggestions for new sources, or even at the student union taking notes on what you observe about some aspect of student behavior. More than likely, the authors of the sources you gather did not confine themselves to one particular kind of research either—or do it all in one particular location. Responding to their own rhetorical situations, the authors of your sources specified a goal for their research, a group of readers who might be interested in their findings, and the type of document that would best express their thoughts. Based on their purpose, audience, and genre, the authors determined what kinds of research would be most suitable. Like the authors of your sources, you need to consider your rhetorical situation when determining which kinds of research to conduct. In order to make effective decisions, you need to know what kinds of research you will be able to do at the library and on the Internet. (Research in the field, another option, is covered in the next chapter.)

Library and Internet research continue to evolve, as librarians find new ways to make emerging research technologies more accessible and scholars and other authors find new ways to use the Internet to deliver information. In general, though, the types of sources available through the library and the Internet can be broken down into three main categories: books, periodicals, and online and audiovisual sources.

Books

Three types of books are often consulted in the research process. **Scholarly books** are written by scholars for other scholars in order to advance knowledge of a certain subject. Most include original research. Before being published, these books are reviewed by experts in the field (in a process referred to as a peer review). **Trade books** may also be written by scholars, though they may be authored by journalists or freelance writers as well. But the audience and purpose of trade books differ from those of scholarly books. Rather than addressing other scholars, authors of trade books write to inform a popular audience, often about research that has been done by others; thus, trade books are usually **secondary sources**—as opposed to **primary sources**, which contain original research. **Reference books** such as encyclopedias and dictionaries provide factual information. Reference books often contain short articles written and reviewed by experts in the field. The audience for these secondary sources includes both veteran scholars and those new to a field of study.

General encyclopedias and dictionaries such as the *Encyclopedia Britannica* and the *American Heritage Dictionary* provide basic information on many topics. Specialized encyclopedias and dictionaries cover topics in greater depth. In addition to overviews of topics, they also include definitions of technical terminology, discussions of major issues, and bibliographies of related works. Specialized encyclopedias and dictionaries exist for all major disciplines. Here is just a small sampling:

Art	*Grove Dictionary of Art, Encyclopedia of Visual Art*
Biology	*Concise Encyclopedia of Biology*
Chemistry	*Concise Macmillan Encyclopedia of Chemistry, Encyclopedia of Inorganic Chemistry*
Computers	*Encyclopedia of Computer Science and Technology*
Economics	*Fortune Encyclopedia of Economics*
Education	*Encyclopedia of Higher Education, Encyclopedia of Educational Research*
Environment	*Encyclopedia of the Environment*
History	*Dictionary of American History, New Cambridge Modern History*
Literature	*Encyclopedia of World Literature in the 20th Century*
Music	*New Grove Dictionary of Music and Musicians*
Philosophy	*Routledge Encyclopedia of Philosophy, Encyclopedia of Applied Ethics*
Psychology	*Encyclopedia of Psychology, Encyclopedia of Human Behavior*
Religion	*Encyclopedia of Religion*
Social sciences	*International Encyclopedia of the Social Sciences*
Women's studies	*Women's Studies Encyclopedia, Encyclopedia of Women and Gender*

You can find these kinds of sources by doing a title search of your library's online catalog. For other specialized encyclopedias, contact a reference librarian or consult *Kister's Best Encyclopedias*.

Periodicals

Periodicals include scholarly journals, magazines, and newspapers. Because these materials are published more frequently than books, the information they contain is more recent. Like scholarly books, **scholarly journals** contain original research (they are primary sources) and address a narrow, specialized audience. Many scholarly journals have the word *journal* in their names: examples are *Journal of Business Communication* and *Consulting Psychology Journal*. **Magazines** and **newspapers** are generally written by staff writers for the general public. These secondary sources carry a combination of news stories, which are intended to be objective, and essays, which reflect the opinions of editors or guest contributors. Both national newspapers (such as the *New York Times* and the *Washington Post*) and regional or local newspapers may have articles, letters, and editorials of interest to researchers.

TRICKS OF THE TRADE

by Alyse Murphy Leininger, English major

Once I've found an article or book that really works for my research, I always look at its bibliography to see what sources the author used for his or her research. Usually I'm able to use one or two of those sources as well and get different ideas or quotes that weren't in the original article.

Online and audiovisual sources

Books, journals, magazine articles, and newspaper articles can all be found online. But when you read documents on Web sites, created specifically for access by computer, you need to determine who is responsible for the site, why the site was established, and who the target audience is. To find answers to these questions, you can first check the domain name, which is at the end of the main part of the Internet address. This name will give you clues about the site. An Internet address with the domain name **.com** (for commerce) tells you that the Web site is associated with a profit-making business. The domain name **.edu** indicates that a site is connected to an educational institution. Web sites maintained by the branches or agencies of a government have the domain name **.gov**. Nonprofit organizations such as Habitat for Humanity and National Public Radio have **.org** as their domain name.

You can also find out about the nature of a Web site by clicking on navigational buttons such as "About Us" or "Vision." Here is an excerpt from a page entitled "About NPR" on the National Public Radio Web site:

> What is NPR?
> NPR is an internationally acclaimed producer and distributor of noncommercial news, talk, and entertainment programming. A privately supported, not-for-profit, membership organization, NPR serves more than 770 independently operated, noncommercial public radio stations. Each member station serves local listeners with a distinctive combination of national and local programming.

Research

The most common audiovisual sources are documentaries, lectures, and interviews. **Documentary films and television programs** are much like trade books and magazines. They are created for a popular audience, with the purpose of providing factual information, usually of a political, social, or historical nature. **Lectures** generally take place live at universities and in public auditoriums or are recorded as podcasts or for distribution through iTunes U or university Web sites. Lectures sponsored by a university are usually more technical or scholarly than those given in a public auditorium. Lecturers, who are usually experts in their field of study, deliver prepared speeches on a variety of topics. Sometimes lectures are like editorials in that the creator's perspective is presented in high profile. **Interviews** are a special type of conversation in which a reporter elicits responses from someone recognized for his or her status or accomplishments. Interviews, which are aired for a general audience, aim to provide information about the interviewee's achievements or about his or her views on a specific issue.

Research

Finding Sources in Print and Online

In the first part of this chapter, you learned about the different types of sources available to you. You'll find it easier to select your sources once you have a basic understanding of the genre, audience, and purpose of potential sources. For example, for an advanced course in your discipline, you'll want to consult primary sources, such as online or printed journal articles that present original research. However, if you have chosen a topic that is brand new to you, it may be more productive to consult secondary sources along with primary sources, as the primary sources may contain so much technical terminology that you might misunderstand the content. The rest of this chapter will help you find different types of sources in your library and online.

Finding books

The easiest way to find books on a particular topic is to consult your library's online catalog. Once you are logged on, navigate your way to the Web page with search boxes similar to those shown below. An author search or title search is useful when you already have a particular author or title in mind. When a research area is new to you, you can find many sources by doing either a keyword search or a subject search. For a keyword search, choose a word or phrase that you think is likely to be found in titles or notes in the catalog's records.

An advanced search page such as the one on page 370 allows the user to specify a language, a location in the library, a type of book (or a type of material other than a book), how the results should be organized, a publisher, and a date of publication. A keyword search page also provides some recommendations for entering words. By using a word or part of a word followed by asterisks, you can find all sources that have that word or word part, even when suffixes have been added. For example, if you entered *environment**, the search would return not only sources with *environment* in the title but also sources whose titles included *environments, environmental,* or *environmentalist*. This shortening technique is called **truncation**. You can enter multiple words by using operators such as *and* or *or*. You can exclude words by using

Search box from a library online catalog.

Research

and not. When you enter multiple words, you can require that they be close to each other by using *near;* if you want to specify their proximity, you can use *within,* followed by a number indicating the greatest number of words that may separate them.

Subject searches in most libraries are based on categories published by the Library of Congress. You may be able to find sources by entering words familiar to you. However, if your search does not yield any results, ask a reference librarian for a subject-heading guide or note the subject categories that accompany the search results for sources you have already found.

Once you locate a source, write down or print out its call number. The call number corresponds to a specific location in the library's shelving system, usually based on the classification system of the Library of Congress. Keys to the shelving system are usually posted on the walls of the library, but staff members will also be able to help you find sources.

In addition to using your library's online catalog, you can also access books online, downloading them as PDFs or in other formats for use on handheld devices such as a Kindle or an iPad. Over 35,000 free books are listed on the University of Pennsylvania's Online Books Page (onlinebooks.library.upenn.edu).

TRICKS OF THE TRADE

Searching Google Books (books.google.com) or using Amazon .com's Search Inside This Book feature can give you more information about books not available locally. Both sites allow you to search for keywords inside certain virtual texts. If the search locates the keywords, you can then preview the relevant pages of the text to determine if you want to purchase the book or order it from an interlibrary loan service. If the book is in the public domain, you may be able to access the entire text through Google Books.

Finding articles

Your library's online catalog lists the titles of periodicals (journals, magazines, and newspapers); however, it does not provide the titles of individual articles within these periodicals. Although many researchers head straight to an Internet search engine or Web browser (Google, Bing, Yahoo, Internet Explorer), type in the name of the desired article, and locate a copy, many others end up frustrated by such a broad search. You may find that the best strategy for finding reliable articles on your topic is to use an electronic database, available through your library portal. A database (such as ERIC, JSTOR, and PsycINFO) is similar to an

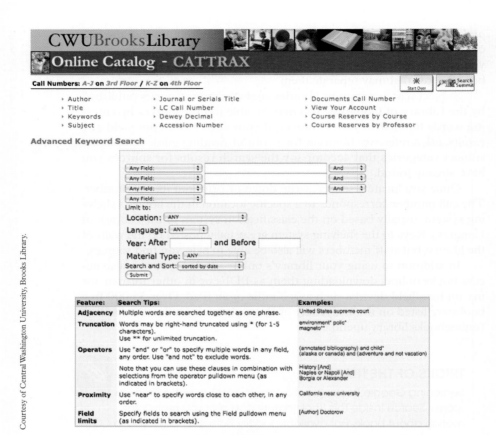

Advanced keyword search page from a library online catalog.

online catalog in that it allows you to search for sources by author, title, subject, keyword, and other features. Because so much information is available, databases focus on specific subject areas.

You can access your library's databases from a computer in the library or, if you have a password, via an Internet link from a computer located elsewhere. Libraries subscribe to various vendors for these services, but these are some of the most common database vendors:

OCLC FirstSearch or EBSCOhost: Contains articles and other types of records (for example, electronic books and DVDs) on a wide range of subjects.

ProQuest: Provides access to major newspapers such as the *New York Times* and the *Wall Street Journal* and to consumer and scholarly periodicals in areas including business, humanities, literature, and science.

LexisNexis: Includes articles on business, legal, and medical topics and on current events.

The EBSCOhost database allows you to search various smaller databases, such as ERIC.

To find sources through a database, you can use some of the same strategies you use for navigating an online catalog. However, search pages often differ, so there is no substitute for hands-on experimentation. Your library may use a general database, such as OCLC First-Search or EBSCOhost. The first box on the EBSCOhost search page asks you to specify a subject area. Just underneath that box is a drop-down menu that lets you choose among several databases, including ERIC (Educational Resources Information Center), MLA (Modern Language Association), and PsycINFO (Psychology Information). After you choose the particular database you would like to search, you can search by keyword, author, title, source, year, or a combination of these attributes. You click on the question-mark icon to the right of the search entry box to get directions for searching according to that attribute. In the Refine Search menu, you can click on a checkbox to limit a search to full texts only. In this case, your search will bring back only sources that include the complete text of an article, which can be downloaded and printed. Otherwise, the database search generally yields the source's bibliographic information and an **abstract**, which is a short summary of an article's content. To find the full text, you note the basic bibliographic information and then look up that book or periodical in the library's online catalog, as described earlier.

Finally, some periodicals are available online. Highwire is a service that lists many science journals that offer free issues; you can find this list by going to highwire.stanford.edu/lists/freeart.dtl. Global Development Network lists journals from a wide range of academic disciplines at www.gdnet.org. Online articles are not always free, however. Be sure to check for subscription services that are available through your library's Web site before paying for an archived article on a newspaper's home page. You might save yourself a good deal of money!

Finding images

Internet and database searches yield all kinds of images for writers. You can search for images on the Web by using a search engine such as http://images.google.com. Also consider visiting the Web sites of specific libraries, museums, and government agencies, such as the Library of Congress, the Smithsonian Institute, and the U.S. Census Bureau; they often have databases of special collections.

Once you find an image that suits your purpose, download it from the Web site onto your desktop by right-clicking on the image and selecting Save Image As (or Save This Image As). To insert the image from your desktop into your paper, use the Insert command from your word processor's pull-down menu. (Some programs may allow you to drag the image into your text.) If you need to resize the image you have chosen, click on its corners and drag your mouse to enlarge it or reduce it. Hold down the Shift key while you are resizing the image to retain its original proportions.

The last step in using an image is to give credit to its creator and, if necessary, acquire permission to use it. If you are not publishing your paper in print or online, fair-use laws governing reproduction for educational purposes might allow you to use the image without permission. If you are uploading your paper to a Web site or publishing it in

Research

any other way, determine whether the image is copyrighted; if so, you'll have to contact its creator for permission to use it and then include a credit line underneath the image, after the caption.

Keep in mind that before you decide to include an image in your paper, you should be sure to identify your purpose for doing so. Avoid using images as mere decoration.

Finding government documents

You can find government documents by using library databases such as Marcive and LexisNexis Academic. In addition, the following Web sites are helpful:

FedWorld Information Network	fedworld.gov
Government Printing Office	gpoaccess.gov
U.S. Courts	uscourts.gov

Finding resources in special collections

Most academic libraries have special collections that you might also find useful, such as art collections, including drawings and paintings; audio and video collections, including records, audiotapes, CDs, videotapes, and DVDs; and computer resources, usually consisting of programs that combine text, audio, and video. You can find these resources by navigating through your library's Web site or by asking a reference librarian for help.

Additional advice for finding sources online

To find text, image, video, and audio sources relevant to your project, your first instinct might be to look online. Although searching the Internet is a popular research technique, it is not always the most appropriate technique. Search engines cover only the portion of the Internet that allows free access. Many books available at your school's library or periodicals available through the library's database materials cannot be found using a search engine because library and database services are available only to paid subscribers (students fall into this category). If you do decide to use the Internet, remember that no one search engine covers all of it, and surprisingly little overlap occurs when different search engines are used to find information on the same topic. Thus, using more than one search engine is a good idea. The following are commonly used search engines:

Ask.com	ask.com
Google	google.com
WebCrawler	webcrawler.com
Yahoo!	yahoo.com

When using a search engine for research, you'll probably want to check the Help links to learn about advanced search options. Using these options will allow you to weed out results that are not of interest to you. Advanced searches are performed in much the same way with search engines as they are with online catalogs and databases. You can specify words or phrases, how close words should be to each other, which words should be excluded, and whether the search should return longer versions of truncated words.

TRICKS OF THE TRADE

by Cristian Nuñez, history and economics major

To stay abreast of new developments on a particular topic, I create a Google Alert for it. Google Alerts are email updates of the latest relevant Google results from news Web sites and blogs based on your choice of query or topic.

Metasearch engines are also available. *Meta* means "transcending" or "more comprehensive." Metasearch engines check numerous search engines, including those listed above. Try these for starters:

Dogpile	dogpile.com
Mamma metasearch	mamma.com
MetaCrawler	metacrawler.com

Finally, be aware that sometimes when you click on a link, you end up at a totally different Web site. You can keep track of your location by looking at the Internet address, or URL, at the top of your screen. URLs generally include the following information: server name, domain name, directory and perhaps subdirectory, file name, and file type.

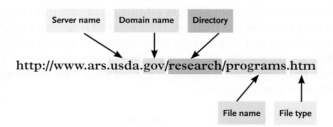

Be sure to check the server and domain names whenever you are unsure of your location. (See chapter 14 for help in evaluating Web sites.)

USING RESEARCH IN YOUR WRITING

Using the same keywords, perform a database search and then a Web search. For each type of search, print the first screen of results you get. Compare the two printouts, explaining how the results of the two searches differ.

13 Research in the Field

© AP Photo/David Kohl

1. You may have used a self-checkout machine at the supermarket. Even if your local store doesn't have a machine that allows customers to check out their groceries by themselves, you're no doubt familiar with various technologies designed to make our hectic lives a little easier by making routine tasks more efficient. Take a moment to list several such technologies that you've encountered recently.

Research

2. Choose one item on your list and consider its effect(s): What or whom does it replace? How is it changing human behavior? To take this activity further, go to a place where the technology is in use. Observe the scene for twenty minutes or so, noting effects of the technology on human behavior. Do your observations differ from your assumptions? If so, what is unexpected or surprising?

Basic Principles of Naturalistic Study

By now, you are familiar with the rhetorical situation and how it supports reading, writing, speaking—and research. In this chapter, you'll apply your knowledge of the rhetorical situation to develop an understanding of a local situation, an understanding that usually cannot be easily reached through traditional library, online, or laboratory research. Although these methods are effective, they cannot address all research questions.

Some research questions can be answered only by **fieldwork**, research carried out in the field, rather than in a library, laboratory, or some other controlled environment. Fieldwork usually takes place in a real-world or a naturalistic environment. Following are some research questions calling for the collection of data in a naturalistic environment:

What nights of the week are busiest at the student union?
How popular is the foreign film series shown on campus, in terms of both attendance and satisfaction? How do the responses of students, faculty, and staff differ?
What do hair stylists do at work?
What is the effect of self-checkout machines in local grocery stores?
How do mothers and adult daughters communicate?
How has the day-to-day nature of nurses' work changed during the last 40 years?
How useful is the library's help desk? Who uses it? How often? When? Why?

All of these questions call for careful observation in the field (even though the field is actually the library in the case of the final question) and some means of data collection.

Observation in a real-world environment

A **naturalistic study** is based on observation in a real-world environment. The researcher observes and records some human behavior or phenomenon in its natural setting. Whether the goal is to establish the learning patterns of museum visitors, the daily driving habits of commuters, or the benefits of home schooling, the researcher conducting a naturalistic study observes, employing any or all of the following research methods:

- ► Watching the behavior or phenomenon and recording what he or she sees
- ► Using audiovisual equipment, such as digital recorders or video cameras
- ► Listening in on conversations or comments and taking notes
- ► Distributing questionnaires or administering pretests and posttests about a situation, phenomenon, or behavior
- ► Conducting interviews with individuals or focus groups

Whichever of these methods is employed, the researcher himself or herself is the most significant instrument for the collection and analysis of data.

Testing assumptions

Researchers often undertake a naturalistic study because they want to investigate an **assumption**, an idea taken for granted or accepted as true without proof. Whether expressed as a problem ("English majors dominate class discussion"), a question ("How much do hair stylists think as they do their job?"), or a belief ("The student union is always busy"), the assumption may be the researcher's alone or be commonly held. By collecting and analyzing data, the researcher compares the assumption with possible conclusions. The researcher tests the assumption with two goals in mind: (1) to interfere as little as possible with the subject or phenomenon under observation and (2) to minimize systematically the ways in which mere participation in the study influences patterns and outcomes. In other words, the fact that the researcher is observing, listening, or conducting interviews should not affect the behavior or beliefs of the participants. The researcher's goals overlap with the researcher's ethics.

Triangulation

To minimize inaccuracies and distortions, a researcher usually sets up a three-way process for gathering information, referred to as **triangulation**. When the process depends on using different sets of information from a variety of sources, it is called **data triangulation**. For instance, to triangulate responses to the question of how useful the library's help desk is, you might gather opinions from several different groups of people, looking for commonalities in their responses. When two or more researchers work together in order to compare their observations and findings, the approach is known as **investigator triangulation**. And, finally, **methodological triangulation** involves using multiple methods (observation, questionnaires, and so on) to study a single problem, person, or phenomenon.

Basic principles at work:
Deborah Tannen's naturalistic study

After publishing a book about adult family relationships, *I Only Say This Because I Love You,* Deborah Tannen discovered that her readers were most interested in the chapter on communication between mothers and adult daughters. With that knowledge, she launched the naturalistic study that became the book *You're Wearing That?* Tannen's preresearch assumption was that mothers and their adult daughters have a uniquely intense relationship; she felt sure this was true, given her own relationship with her mother. Tannen observed, recorded, and then transcribed many conversations; she also conducted interviews (or what she refers to as "focused conversations"), asked people she knew for examples from their own lives, and drew on her own ongoing communication with her mother. This process of observing, talking, asking questions, recording, and listening to the opinions of others was an example of methodological triangulation.

Deborah Tannen, author of *You're Wearing That?*

Courtesy of Deborah Tannen.

As Tannen observed and recorded, she also began to analyze what she was witnessing, an analysis based on her expertise in sociolinguistics (and on her status as an adult daughter). Toward the end of her research process, she compared her preresearch assumption (that the mother–adult daughter relationship is uniquely intense) with the emerging conclusion that mother–adult daughter communication "continues to evoke powerful emotions long after it has ceased."

Like all experienced researchers, Tannen knows that naturalistic studies may be generalizable—but only to a point. Naturalistic studies are like the rhetorical situation itself: time-bound and context-bound, with all the entities of the study (observer or recorder, analysis, and subject or behavior under observation) shaping one another simultaneously.

Research

Methods for Fieldwork

Observing, taking notes, and asking questions are the three activities at the heart of a naturalistic study, as you have probably gathered from reading about Deborah Tannen's research and trying your hand at a brief study of your own. In his study of the intellectual processes necessary for conducting ordinary kinds of work, Mike Rose describes these three elements at work together:

> When at a job site or in a classroom, I observed people at work, writing notes on their activity and, when permissible, taking photographs of the task at hand. Once I got a sense of the rhythms of the work—its moments of less intense focus and its pauses—I would begin asking questions about what people were doing and why, trying to gain an understanding of their behavior and the thinking that directed it. As they got more familiar with me and I with them and their work, I was able to ask increasingly specific questions, probing the reasons for using one implement rather than another, for a particular positioning of the body, for the benefits of this procedure over that one. I wondered aloud how they knew what to do, given the materials and constraints of the present task, what they had in mind to do next, how they knew something was wrong. . . . Over time, the exchanges became more conversational, and frequently people on their own began explaining what they were doing and what their thinking was for doing it, a kind of modified think-aloud procedure, long used in studies of problem solving.
>
> —**Mike Rose**, *The Mind at Work*

Notice how Rose talks about the material conditions of his observation: he watches, takes notes, sometimes takes photographs, and asks ever-more-sophisticated questions as he begins to understand the procedures more and more. Each activity occurs in coordination with the others, but we'll look at them one at a time.

Using observation

Observation—watching closely what is happening and trying to figure out why—plays a central role in naturalistic studies of all kinds. After all, a naturalistic study depends most heavily on the researcher himself or herself, which is its advantage. The researcher is right there on the scene, conducting the research, with direct access to the person or phenomenon.

By the time Rose was ready to write up his observation, he was able to describe the results of his naturalistic study with style, grace, and a good deal of detail. In the following passage, he writes about the thinking that goes into the hair styling that Vanessa does.

Excerpt from

The Mind at Work

Mike Rose

Vanessa works in a trendy salon but also cuts hair in her apartment—
for a few friends and friends of friends. Her client Lynn sits in a small
barber's chair by the window, the place where you'd imagine a breakfast table, a mirror leaning against the wall in front of her. On the floor
by the mirror there is a small bowl for Vanessa's dog and a vase with
three yellow flowers. Vanessa stands behind Lynn, asking her questions
about her hair, chitchatting a little. She keeps her eyes on Lynn's hair
as she moves her fingers through it, lifting up, then pulling down one
section, then another, then gesturing with her hands around the hair,
indicating shape and movement. "How did you like the last haircut?"
she asks. How did it handle? Was it easy to manage? What's bugging
you now? Does it feel heavy up front? Lynn answers these questions,
describing what she wants, relying on adjectives that have more to
do with feeling than shape. She wants the cut "freshened," wants it
"sassy."

> Already readers can see how much information Rose has gleaned by talking with Vanessa as he observes her.

> Rose includes details that could be retained only with careful note taking or tape recording.

A pair of scissors, a comb, and a round hand mirror sit on the stove,
to Vanessa's side. She reaches for the scissors and begins. She starts
at the crown and moves around Lynn's head, picking a strand of hair,
pulling it down gently along Lynn's face, eyeballing it, then elevating it,
cutting into it, "point cutting," she calls it, not a "blunt" cut, her scissors angling into the hair, layering it, "giving it a softer look."

> Rose has taken the time to learn the vocabulary of the people he's observing.

Vanessa likes to cut dry hair—at least hair like Lynn's, baby fine,
short—because she "can see what it's doing immediately . . . where it's
heavy, where it needs to be cut into." ("You can comb hair and cut it,"
she explains, "only to have it move into a different shape than the one
you just cut.") When she does cut hair wet, because a particular style
demands it, she "can't wait to dry it and then go in and do *my* work. . . .
The initial shape might be there, but the whole interior can change.
Eighty percent of the haircut is after you dry it."

> This information could have been obtained only by asking interview questions, not by observation.

As Vanessa continues, cutting, comparing one length of hair to another, her gaze circling her client's head, she tells me more about her
work. Though she can do "technical, precise" cuts, like a graduated
bob (a bob tapered at the nape of the neck), she most likes to cut "free-
hand," as she is doing now, a more "flowing" cut, and flowing process.
"I don't like authority," she laughs, "so I love cutting this way." Even
with that graduated bob, she adds, after it's dry, she'll "go in and add
my own touch, a signature."

> You can almost hear Rose asking the questions that elicited these specific answers.

Rose invokes his library research, which underpins the assumption he is exploring with his study.

Notice how Rose is weaving in his results, conclusions, and inferences.

Readers do not know whether Vanessa actually told Rose these things; he seems to be making inferences based on his naturalistic study.

Vanessa certainly has an idea of how a haircut should look, an idea based on the characteristics of the hair she's cutting and the client's desires, discerned from those opening questions, and, if the client's a regular, from their history together. And she is methodical. But she does not plan her cut in advance to the degree that some stylists do; cognitive psychologists would characterize her planning style as incremental or opportunistic. As the cut progresses, she observes what the hair is doing, how it's falling and moving, and reacts to that. "I do a lot of visual when I cut." And, in fact, about two-thirds of the way through Lynn's haircut, Vanessa exclaims, "Oh, this is starting to look really cute!" Moments like this are pivotal to Vanessa, aesthetically and motivationally. It excites her, is the art of it all, to use her skill in a way that is responsive to, interactive with, the medium of hair, watching the cut emerge, shaping it incrementally, guided by her aesthetic sense and enabled by her repertoire of techniques. Lynn is pleased with the outcome. It *is* a "sassy" cut. "Vanessa understands hair like mine."

> ANALYZING THE RHETORICAL SITUATION

With a classmate or two, reread Rose's description of Vanessa's work and then answer the following questions:

1. What assumption, problem, or question is Rose exploring?
2. Why is observation a necessary component of his research?
3. Whom is Rose observing? Why?
4. What behaviors or actions is Rose observing? Why?
5. Where is he conducting his observations? Why?
6. How does he use observation to advance his exploration of the assumption?
7. Why does Rose need to use more than observation to conduct his study?

Be prepared to share your answers with the rest of the class.

USING OBSERVATION IN YOUR WRITING

Now apply the questions in the preceding Analyzing the Rhetorical Situation to a naturalistic study that you would like to conduct. Provide written answers and be prepared to share them with the class.

Taking notes

Lisa F. Young

The second part of the naturalistic research process is **note taking**, writing down what you observe or hear. You can tell by reading Rose's account of his observations that he took copious notes as he watched Vanessa work. Otherwise, he would not have been able to compose such a realistic and compelling narrative about his observations. An important feature of note taking, however, is what Krista Ratcliffe refers to in her book *Rhetorical Listening: Identification, Gender, Whiteness* as "rhetorical listening": "a stance of openness that a person may choose to assume in relation to any person, text, or culture." We all have a tendency to allow our expectations and experiences to influence how we process what we encounter. The openness that we adopt when listening rhetorically keeps us aware of difference and newness. Rhetorical listening also helps researchers translate what they observe and hear into spoken and written language (questions and research drafts). If we listen with the intent to understand (rather than waiting for a spot to insert our own voice), we'll have an easier time writing and speaking about unfamiliar topics from a standpoint of authentic knowledge and goodwill. Thus, careful observing, listening, and note taking all support the researcher's perceptions—and improve the results.

Researchers like Rose take notes during observations for two reasons: to record very specific detail and to record their own reactions to what they observe. Without notes, few people can remember all the details of what they have observed. While observing, researchers can experience a range of reactions: they might find what they've observed to be in line with what they expected, or they might find it comforting, puzzling, or even infuriating or distressing. By jotting down their reactions as they occur, researchers can minimize the degree to which their preconceptions influence those reactions. Some naturalistic researchers simply (or not so simply) take notes about what they observe, trying to jot down snatches of conversation and specialized terms or insider phrases that they will need to ask about later. They might also record specific actions or sequences of movements.

Whether you keep your notes in a notebook, on separate note cards or pieces of paper, or on your laptop, you can choose among various ways of recording what you observe and your responses. You might write notes that combine narration, description, and evaluation. In the following passage, student Bethanie Orban uses a

Research

combination of narration, description, and evaluation to focus on the question "Who talks the most, and what are the different ways of communicating?"

> Cody, Andrea, and Tom are friends who eat lunch together. Andrea comes to the table first, followed by Tom. Both wait for Cody to join them before they start to eat. Cody comes to the table humming. As soon as he sits down, he immediately begins talking about his history exam. "I don't know where the professor got the questions!" Cody says. Andrea assures Cody he did fine, trying to comfort him. Tom makes a joke that Cody probably didn't study. Cody begins gesturing with his hands that he did study a lot. Tom laughs and holds up his hand. He tells Cody it was a joke. Cody begins to eat his soup and Tom takes a drink of his milk. Andrea begins telling them about her weekend in New York with her friend. She describes the Broadway show she saw. Andrea keeps describing how great it was. Cody begins a story about going to a movie over the weekend. Tom says he saw the movie a while back. Cody thinks it was the best movie he ever saw. "It was awesome." Cody looks around at the other tables to see if anyone is listening to what he's saying, which makes him look like he likes to be the center of attention. Andrea excuses herself to go get a cookie. She asks if anyone else wants anything, but both Tom and Cody say they are full.

You might begin by describing what you observe and then go back later to add your evaluation of what you saw, as Bethanie Orban did in the following passage from her double-entry notebook. A **double-entry notebook** is a journal that has two distinct parts: observational details and personal response to those details. The double-entry notebook thus allows researchers to keep their observations separate from their responses (including biases and preferences) toward what they observe. In addition, it encourages researchers to push their observations further, with responses to and questions about what they see or think they see. Some researchers draw a heavy line down the middle of each page of the notebook, putting "Observations" at the top of the left-hand side of the page and "Response" at the top of the right-hand side. Others lay the notebook flat and use the right-hand page for recording their observations and the left-hand page for responding to those observations. If you're using a computer, you can format your entries the way Bethanie did:

OBSERVATIONS

Andrea, Cody, and Tom meet up for lunch. Andrea thinks they need to find a table first before they get food. Cody thinks it would be nice to sit by the window, so they put their stuff down. Andrea is the first back to the table and waits for everyone else before eating. Cody tells the other two about his exam. He doesn't think he did well. Andrea thinks he probably did fine, but Tom makes a joke about it. Eventually Andrea begins talking about her weekend in New York. Cody tells about the movie he saw. When he's done, Andrea goes to get a cookie. Tom and Cody continue to talk about their weekends. The dining commons smells like fried food and cookies. Everyone thinks the food tastes good. The tables feel a little sticky. There is the constant noise of students talking. Andrea returns with her cookie while Tom and Cody continue their conversation about the weekend.

RESPONSE

I felt that Cody seems to talk the most. However, my response could be based on my own opinions about Cody. Cody is shorter and has glasses—and he really likes to be the center of attention, possibly because he wants to make up for something (his height, maybe?). He tends to be loud and look around at other tables to see if anyone else heard. Andrea waits her turn to speak, but gets really passionate when she talks about Broadway. I feel like maybe she feels out of place with two guys, but wants to engage others in conversation. Tom seems the most laid back and likes to joke around. He has really curly hair so he doesn't mind teasing, perhaps to take it off himself. I believe many of my observations were colored by my own take on each student: Cody wanting attention, Andrea feeling uncomfortable, and Tom's use of humor.

Like all human beings, Bethanie brings her personal experience and disposition to every research situation. Bethanie labels one student's excitement about Broadway "passionate" while she characterizes another's loud speaking as evidence that he "likes to be the center of attention." She suspects that a third student uses jokes to relieve social pressure. Chances are many observers would agree with Bethanie, but few would come to the same conclusion that she does about the very same scene. The double-entry notebook Bethanie chose to use helped her separate her observations from her responses and judgments.

Our biases and preferences sometimes prevent us from seeing what is going on right in front of our eyes. Besides bringing our personal preferences to what we observe, we also bring our personal understanding—or lack thereof. Our level of expertise with procedures, history, and terminology can enhance our understanding or prevent us from understanding what we are seeing. For these reasons, most of us need to train ourselves to become better observers of our surroundings, better at seeing and hearing, more attuned to all of our senses. As award-winning writer Diane Ackerman reminds us in *A Natural History of the Senses,* "There is no way in which to understand the world without first detecting it through the radar-net of our senses."

Researchers conducting naturalistic studies have to push themselves to see more clearly, and questioning often helps. The best researchers ask many questions before, during, and after their observations. Successful researchers also rely on other means to triangulate what they think they are seeing and hearing: interviews, questionnaires, tape recordings, or the work of another researcher.

Asking questions

The third part of the naturalistic research process consists of asking questions. Researchers may ask their questions all at once or over an extended period of time during their observations and afterward. They may ask questions face to face, over the phone, online, or in a distributed questionnaire. We'll first consider face-to-face interviews and then explore methods for preparing and distributing questionnaires. Understanding how to prepare for and conduct interviews will advance your ability to carry on conversations all through your research study and beyond. This understanding will also help you think through the design of a questionnaire, if you decide to compose one.

Interviews An interview conducted as part of a naturalistic study can be formal, based on a set of predetermined questions, or more casual, almost like a conversation. But the friendly nature of good conversational interviews belies the serious planning that goes into them. After all, asking questions (interviewing) is an important component of data collection, often just as valuable as observing and taking notes.

Whatever method you decide to use for your interview, you must obtain permission to conduct the interview, schedule the interview, and obtain permission to tape record or take notes during the interview. After the interview (or series of conversations) is complete, you'll want to send a thank-you note to the person and include a complimentary copy of your study.

Perhaps the most important element of interviewing is choosing **interview subjects,** the specific people who can provide useful information for your naturalistic study. In other words, whom do you want to interview and why? Your interview subjects might be **key participants** in the phenomenon you are studying, or they might be experts on the subject you are studying. Whatever rationale you use for choosing interview subjects, the most important criterion should be that each person can provide you with information you need to proceed with your research.

All successful questioning involves **background research**—in other words, doing your homework before you begin asking questions. Many television programs, from shows on MTV and BET to *The Today Show* and *Oprah*, feature interviews. When you watch an interview (especially one in the guise of a casual conversation), you can see how well or badly the interviewer prepared. The burden is on the researcher or interviewer to know enough about the person or phenomenon to ask intelligent questions, just as Rose did when studying the hairstylist. Good interview questions will help guide your research.

Your **interview questions** should serve your research in two ways. First, they should put your subjects at ease so that they willingly talk, amplify their answers, and provide rich examples. Second, your interview questions should pro-gress purposefully from one subject to another. Successful researchers write out a series of questions to which they want answers, arranging them so that one question leads logically to the next. In addition, your interview questions should indicate that you have done your homework about the interviewee and the process or phenomenon you are studying—and that you have been paying close attention during your observations. They should also demonstrate that you appreciate the time and information the interviewee is giving you.

Interview questions that can be answered with yes or no will not yield much information unless they are followed with a related question. For example, if you follow a question like "Do you like your job?" with a journalist's question ("Why?" "When?" or "How?"), you give your interviewee a chance to elaborate. Effective interviews usually contain a blend of open, or broad, questions and focused, or narrow, questions. Here are a few examples:

OPEN QUESTIONS

What do you think about _____?
What are your views on _____?
Why do you believe _____?

FOCUSED QUESTIONS

How long have you worked as a _____?
When did you start _____?
What does _____ mean?
Why did you _____?

Whatever kind of interview you conduct—face to face, telephone, email, or online—you should not rely on your memory alone, no matter how good it is. You need to take notes or record the conversation in order to keep track of the questions you pose and the responses you receive. Many researchers use a tape recorder during face-to-face interviews so that they can focus their attention on the interviewee, establishing the personal rapport that invigorates any interview. During telephone interviews, you may want to use the speakerphone function so that you can tape the interview or take notes. Because taking notes and transcribing recordings are both time-consuming (and sometimes tedious) tasks, some researchers conduct email or online interviews. These electronic techniques have the advantage of providing a written record of your questions and the answers. They also allow you a convenient way to "meet" the person. Perhaps the biggest disadvantage of electronic interviews is the burden they place on the interviewee, who has to take the time and energy to think through and then compose cogent answers. Talking is often much easier for the interviewee.

After the interview, you need to read through your notes and listen to any recordings. Many researchers find this to be the best point in the process for transcribing recordings. As you read your materials, consider a number of questions:

▶ What information surprised you? Why?

▶ How does that reaction affect your study?

▶ What do you now understand better than you did? What was said that illuminated your understanding?

▶ What specific passages best forward the purpose of your research? How does that information help answer or address your research assumption?

▶ What exactly would you like to know more about?

When you have answered these questions, you'll know what else needs to be done. You may find that you need to make further observations, go to the library, or conduct more interviews.

After you have read through your notes and listened to any recordings, you can begin writing up results, based on what you have observed, listened to, asked about, and perhaps researched in other ways. Writing up results launches the analysis that will shape your final report.

Gillian Petrie, interview of Jan Frese

The following selections are written transcripts of an interview conducted by Gillian Petrie, a student who decided to interview a long-time nurse, Jan Frese, about the changes she had seen in the profession during the course of her thirty-eight years on the job. Gillian's first question is open-ended and aimed at making her interviewee comfortable.

> GILLIAN: Would you like to tell me, How did you get into nursing in the first place, Jan?
>
> JAN: I was a little late getting into nursing, because I was married and I had four children and . . . things were not going well at home and I was going to get a divorce. Well now, how am I going to take care of my children? Sooo, a friend of mine told me about this LPN [Licensed Practical Nurse] school and, um, it was only a year, it only took a year to be a licensed practical nurse, and I thought that—that sounds like a good idea. So, I went to the school and, um, graduated from there, and was an LPN for, er, 10 years, and most of that time I worked in a nursing home.
>
> But at the nursing home, um, there wasn't a—there was like one RN [Registered Nurse], and I worked night shift and there were no RNs and I ended up doing pretty much everything the RNs did but still getting the LPN pay. And I thought, This isn't a good idea! I'm going to do RN work, even though it was a nursing home, which isn't as complicated as a hospital, of course. I, er, thought I'll go back to school and be an RN; and I had every intention of going back to work at the nursing home. Go to school, be an RN, go back to the nursing home [laughs], do pretty much what I was doing before, but at least I'll get paid for it!

As the interview progresses, Gillian steers her subject to the topic of changes that she has seen over the years in patients' perception of nurses. Gillian now mixes prepared questions with follow-up prompts that encourage her subject to expand on her responses.

JAN: When I worked, um, as an LPN, in fact, we had to wear white dresses, white socks, white shoes, *and* a *cap*. You *absolutely had* to wear a cap. And, er, people respected you. They—they knew you were a nurse. They knew you were a nurse and they res—respected what you did. They could tell the difference between, er, um, a nurse's aide [laughs], because you dressed differently and you looked quite respectable. Neat. Uh huh, very neat, hair up [laughs] 'cos I learnt that when I went to school: you keep your hair up, you keep your fingernails short [laughs]. And we didn't wear much makeup either. And, er, people just seemed to respect you then. They'd say, Well, this is a nurse, she *knows* what she's doing.

GILLIAN: As opposed to . . . ?

JAN: As opposed to now. Well, working in Intensive Care I wear scrubs, which looks like pajamas. You can wear, well—I hate to tell you what I wear on my feet! I've gotten lax in my old age [laughs]. Sloppy old shoes . . . .

GILLIAN: So you think the change in dress has, er—we've sacrificed a little . . .

JAN: I think it has *something* to do with it.

GILLIAN: . . . professional authority?

JAN: When I go into a patient's room, *they* don't know *who* I am. I could be the housekeeper, 'cos they have to wear scrubs too. I could be the housekeeper; I could be dietary, bringing them their tray. They don't know *what* I am and I just, erm, . . . I *long* for the old days when I really *looked* like a nurse [laughs]! Because now I—I—I look like somebody who just got out of bed [laughs]!

Toward the end of the interview, Gillian asks if Jan sees any differences in how well people take care of themselves. This question leads into a discussion of nurses' roles as educators. Notice that in the following passage and elsewhere, Gillian summarizes or rephrases what her subject has said to demonstrate that she is listening rhetorically ("So you feel that *now* it is a continuous process . . .").

GILLIAN: An important part of the RN, erm, *job* is supposed to be *educating* people. . . .

JAN: Well, I did that, when I was first graduated from RN and went to telemetry. Darn, I was pretty good at it too, I'm tellin' you! I never—I saw a lot of open heart surgeries and that helped, because when I was a—a student that's what I loved to do. So I had a flip chart that had all the information on it, and I really liked doing that. I really liked, erm, . . . and the *people*—they—they *looked* at me with *respect*. Like, *Wow!* *She* knows what she's *talking* about. Although I'd never taken care of a open heart patient *after* surgery, until I went to these, um, ICU classes. But I could *tell* them about what to *expect,* and it was—I—I thought I was pretty good at it. I *liked* it. Was a good job.

GILLIAN: Do you find it more difficult to educate people now?

JAN: Errrm, well, I don't do *that* anymore because I don't work on te-lemetry. But you just *automatically educate* people as you go. You don't sit down with the *flip* chart like I used to, and educate the whole *family* sittin' there in *front* of yer. You just, erm, . . . *talk* to 'em when they come out of—of surgery, you just *tell* 'em what's gonna happen. You know, "You've got this breathing tube and when you're a little more awake and your blood gases are good and the tube will come out and then you'll be able to talk. You can't talk now because of the tube." And you just *talk* to 'em. You know, but it isn't like sittin' down, givin' a lesson. But you *teach* all the *time.*

GILLIAN: Mm huh. So you feel that *now* it is a continuous process . . .

JAN: It *is!*

GILLIAN: . . . rather than a sit down, formalized . . .

JAN: Well, that's, you know—it *was* kinda fun [laughs], sitting down and—and being "the teacher." But now it's just like a continuous pro-cess; you're right.

You can listen to the full interview, which Gillian recorded, at your English CourseMate, accessed through CengageBrain.com.

Questionnaires Whereas an interview elicits information from one person whose name you know, questionnaires provide information from a number of anonymous people. To be effective, questionnaires need to be short and focused. If they are too long, people may not be willing to take the time to fill them out. If they are not focused on your research, you'll find it difficult to integrate the results into your paper.

The questions on questionnaires take a variety of forms:

▶ Questions that require a simple yes-or-no answer

Do you commute to work in a car? (Circle one.)
   Yes No

▶ Multiple-choice questions

How many people do you commute with? (Circle one.)
   0 1 2 3 4

▶ Questions with answers on a checklist

How long does it take you to commute to work? (Check one.)
   ___ 0–30 minutes   ___ 30–60 minutes
   ___ 60–90 minutes   ___ 90–120 minutes

▶ Questions with a ranking scale

If the car you drive or ride in is not working, which of the following types of transportation do you rely on? (Rank the choices from 1 for most frequently used to 4 for least frequently used.)

___ bus ___ shuttle van ___ subway ___ taxi

▶ Open questions

What feature of commuting do you find most irritating?

The types of questions you decide to use will depend on the purpose of your project. The first four types of questions are the easiest for respondents to answer and the least complicated for you to process. Open questions should be asked only when other types of questions cannot elicit the information you want.

Be sure to begin your questionnaire with an introduction stating what the purpose of the questionnaire is, how the results will be used, and how long it will take to complete the questionnaire. In the introduction, you should also assure participants that their answers will be kept confidential. To protect participants' privacy, colleges and universities have committees set up to review questionnaires. These committees are often referred to as **institutional review boards**. Before you distribute your questionnaire, check with the institutional review board (IRB) on your campus to make certain you are following its guidelines.

Administering a questionnaire can sometimes be problematic. Many questionnaires sent through the mail are never returned. If you do decide to mail out your questionnaire, provide a self-addressed envelope and directions for returning the questionnaire. It is always a good idea to send out twice as many questionnaires as you think you need, because the response rate for such mailings is generally low. If you are on campus, questionnaires can sometimes be distributed in dormitories or in classes, but such a procedure must be approved by campus officials.

Once your questionnaires have been completed and returned, tally the results for all but the open questions on a single unused questionnaire. To assess responses to the open questions, first read through them all. You might find that you can create categories for the responses. Answers to the open question "What feature of commuting do you find most irritating?" might fall into such categories as "length of time," "amount of traffic," or "bad weather conditions." By first creating categories, you'll be able to tally the answers to the open questions.

To put the results of a questionnaire to work in your research, ask yourself questions similar to the ones you reflect on after an interview:

▶ What information surprised you? Why?

▶ How does that reaction affect your study?

▶ What do you now understand better than you did? Which particular results illuminated your understanding?

▶ What exactly would you like to know more about?

These reflective questions will guide you in determining what else needs to be done, such as to make further observations, go to the library, or conduct interviews. The questions will also help with your analysis. Analysis is part of a naturalistic study from the beginning, when you conceive an assumption you want to explore. But analysis becomes particularly important as you bring together all three parts of your methodology (observing, note taking, and asking questions) and begin the final step of writing up your research.

Organizing a Field Research Study

Like other kinds of research papers, a report on a naturalistic study is arranged into distinct sections. Many effective writers use headings to differentiate among the sections of a long piece of writing. Besides making reading easier, headings make writing easier. You can end one section and start another one, rather than spending time on building transitions between sections.

- The **introduction** conveys the assumption under investigation, expressed as a problem, a question, or a belief. You might also use the introduction to explain the significance of your assumption.

- A **literature review** can be part of the introduction or can form a separate section. In the literature review, you demonstrate that you have conducted some library or online research about the assumption under examination. In fact, your assumption might even have grown out of that prior work.

- A **methodology** section explains the process you used to study the assumption you set out in your introduction. In the case of a naturalistic study, you explain how you gathered information. Whatever method of triangulation you used is also explained in this section.

- In the **results** section, you report your findings. Your findings might be a solution to a problem, an explanation or answer to a question, or an evaluation of an assumption. In this section, you might include graphs, photographs, or other kinds of visuals that help support your verbal explanation of your results.

- A **discussion** section provides a place to interpret your findings, compare them with what others have discovered or believe, and relate them to the assumption with which you started.

- Finally, a **conclusion** closes a research report. One way to shape a conclusion is to break it into three subsections: (1) the clear-cut, obvious conclusions you can draw from your study; (2) the inferences you can draw, given your current knowledge of the subject under study; and (3) the implications of your research in terms of further research or practical application.

Many research studies also merit a references or a works-cited list (see chapter 15).

14 Reading, Evaluating, and Responding to Sources

The following is an excerpt from an interview conducted by Sharifa Rhodes-Pitts with Debra Dickerson, author of *The End of Blackness: Returning the Souls of Black Folks to Their Rightful Owners (New York: Pantheon, 2004).*

RHODES-PITTS: You've spoken about how *The End of Blackness* grew out of your frustration with the way racial politics get played out in what you call "black liberal" sectors. Can you elaborate a bit on what you mean?

DICKERSON: Part of what brought about the book in the first place was a lifetime spent having to bite my tongue because of the way black liberals wage the battle on race. It doesn't need to be a battle. It ought to be a dialogue—it ought to be a family discussion. Instead you're either with them or you're against them. If you don't think exactly like them you're the enemy or you're insane.

   I think that comes from a couple of things. The moral urgency that there once was—when people were being lynched or were sitting in the back of the bus or being defrauded of their citizenship—is no more. But even though it's 2004 and we don't confront the same problems, people go at it as if it's still 1950 and nothing has changed. A lot of people read about what Fannie Lou Hamer and Martin Luther King went through and slip into an us-against-the-world kind of mode and pretend that things are more dire than they are. There's a temptation to want to feel like you're waging a crusade and the forces of evil are arrayed against you. But I think there's a real sloppiness of thought there.

1. In one paragraph, summarize the interview excerpt as objectively as you can.
2. Look over your paragraph and reflect in writing on the following questions: (a) What strategies did you use to put the source's ideas into your own words? (b) How did you indicate the source of any direct quotes you included? (c) How did you respond to the ideas expressed in the interview? (d) How did you credit and cite the source? If you were expanding your written response, which parts of your summary paragraph would you include? How would you alter those parts, if at all?

Reading with Your Audience and Purpose in Mind

Now that you've considered what kinds of sources might be useful to you and where to find them, you need a plan for proceeding with the research process. Keeping purposeful notes as you read sources can save you from having to scramble the night before your paper is due. Not even experienced researchers attempt to remember which sources they've consulted, how those sources fit into their research, and what their next steps will be. In the first part of this chapter, you'll learn how to keep a research log and how to summarize, paraphrase, and quote from your sources. Each of these techniques for recording information can help you achieve your purpose and satisfy your audience. In the second part of this chapter, you'll learn strategies for evaluating and responding to your sources.

Keeping a Research Log

Research logs come in different forms, but whatever their form—electronic or printed, detailed or brief—they help researchers stay focused. The items included on a log depend on the particular kind of research. For instance, a sociologist's log of field observations might include spaces for recording descriptions of the location, the time, and even the weather conditions—in addition to comments about what he observed and notes about what steps should be taken next. (See chapter 13 for more on conducting observations.) An architect working on a proposal for renovating an old courthouse might use a log to document her findings on the history of the building, noting locations and details of the photographs, sketches, and correspondence she comes across. A psychology student beginning his research with the library's PsycINFO database may save himself time in the long run by recording keyword combinations he uses in his searches, circling the keywords he wants to plug into similar databases. (See pages 368–369 for help in choosing keywords.)

Researchers make decisions about what to include in their logs by anticipating what kind of information will be most important in helping them answer their research question and document their results. Generally, entries in a research log relate to one of the following activities:

▶ Establishing the rhetorical opportunity, purpose, and research question
▶ Identifying the sources
▶ Taking notes
▶ Responding to notes
▶ Establishing the audience

Your research log may also be where you keep track of progress on the following activities, which are important to the writing process:

- ▶ Preparing a working bibliography
- ▶ Annotating a bibliography
- ▶ Crafting a working thesis
- ▶ Dealing with areas of tension in the research

Depending on your assignment, you may want to include entries related to all of these types of activities or just a few of them. We'll discuss several kinds of entries in this chapter.

Before you start to take notes from any source, jot down important identifying features of the source, in case you need to return to it or cite it. If you expect to have only a few sources, you may want to include complete bibliographic information with your notes. If you will be consulting a number of sources, create an entry in your working bibliography (see pages 412–413) and then include with your content notes only basic information, such as the author's name and the page number.

TRICKS OF THE TRADE

by Keith Evans, history major

Color-coding by source is a great means of keeping different sources and information (and your research log) organized as you go. As I move information from my notes to a word processor, I first type the source's page number that this note came from, and then highlight each source in a different color. This way, as I create a bibliography or footnotes, I can immediately recognize what information is coming from what source, as well as the page number of the source itself.

Most of your entries, whether in a research log or on note cards, will consist of detailed notes about the research you have done. Often these notes will be based on your reading, but they may also cover observations, interviews, and other types of research. As you take notes, you may choose to quote, paraphrase, or summarize your sources.

Summarizing

Summarizing an entire source in your research log can help you understand the source and present it to your audience. Researchers regularly use summaries in their writing to indicate that they have done their homework—that is, that they are familiar with other work done on a topic. In summarizing sources, researchers restate the information they have read as concisely and objectively as they can, thereby demonstrating their understanding of it and conveying their own credibility. Researchers may have additional reasons for using summaries. For instance, they may use the information to support their own view, to deepen an explanation, or to contest other information they have found. In academic research papers, summaries appear most frequently as introductory material.

Using function statements

Depending on your purpose, you may decide to summarize an entire source or just part of it. Summarizing an entire source can help you understand it. To compose such a summary, you may find it useful to first write a **function statement** for each paragraph. A function statement goes beyond restating the content of the paragraph; it captures the intention of the author. For example, an author may introduce a topic, provide background information, present alternative views, refute other writers' positions, or draw conclusions based on evidence provided.

The words you use to indicate who the author is and what he or she is doing are called **attributive tags** because they attribute information to a source. Attributive tags help you assign credit where credit is due. Most tags consist of the author's name and a verb. These verbs are often used in attributive tags:

acknowledge	criticize	insist
advise	declare	list
agree	deny	maintain
analyze	describe	note
argue	disagree	object
assert	discuss	offer
believe	emphasize	oppose
claim	endorse	reject
compare	explain	report
concede	find	state
conclude	illustrate	suggest
consider	imply	think

Other attributive tags are phrases, such as *according to the researcher, from the author's perspective,* and *in the author's mind.*

Jacob Thomas used function statements to develop a summary of the following article. Jacob chose the article as a possible source for a

Research

research project addressing the question "How do the media use language to deceive the public?" His function statements follow the essay.

> Doubts about Doublespeak
William Lutz

During the past year, we learned that we can shop at a "unique retail biosphere" instead of a farmers' market, where we can buy items made of "synthetic glass" instead of plastic, or purchase a "high-velocity, multipurpose air circulator," or electric fan. A "wastewater conveyance facility" may "exceed the odor threshold" from time to time due to the presence of "regulated human nutrients," but that is not to be confused with a sewage plant that stinks up the neighborhood with sewage sludge. Nor should we confuse a "resource development park" with a dump. Thus does doublespeak continue to spread.

Doublespeak is language which pretends to communicate but doesn't. It is language which makes the bad seem good, the negative seem positive, the unpleasant seem attractive, or at least tolerable. It is language which avoids, shifts or denies responsibility; language which is at variance with its real or purported meaning. It is language which conceals or prevents thought.

Doublespeak is all around us. We are asked to check our packages at the desk "for our convenience" when it's not for our convenience at all but for someone else's convenience. We see advertisements for "pre-owned," "experienced" or "previously distinguished" cars, not used cars, and for "genuine imitation leather," "virgin vinyl" or "real counterfeit diamonds." Television offers not reruns but "encore telecasts." There are no slums or ghettos, just the "inner city" or "substandard housing" where the "disadvantaged" or "economically nonaffluent" live and where there might be a problem with "substance abuse." Nonprofit organizations don't make a profit, they have "negative deficits" or experience "revenue excesses." With doublespeak it's not dying but "terminal living" or "negative patient care outcome."

There are four kinds of doublespeak. The first kind is the euphemism, a word or phrase designed to avoid a harsh or distasteful reality. Used to mislead or deceive, the euphemism becomes doublespeak. In 1984 the U.S. State Department's annual reports on the status of human rights around the world ceased using the word "killing." Instead the State Department used the phrase "unlawful or arbitrary deprivation of life," thus avoiding the embarrassing situation of government-sanctioned killing in countries supported by the United States.

A second kind of doublespeak is jargon, the specialized language of a trade, profession or similar group, such as doctors, lawyers, plumbers or car mechanics. Legitimately used, jargon allows members of a group to communicate with each other clearly, efficiently and quickly. Lawyers and tax accountants speak to each other of an "involuntary conversion" of property, a legal term that means the loss or destruction of property through theft, accident or condemnation. But when lawyers or tax accountants use unfamiliar terms to speak to others, then the jargon becomes doublespeak.

In 1978 a commercial 727 crashed on takeoff, killing three passengers, injuring 21 others and destroying the airplane. The insured value of the airplane was greater than its book value, so the airline made a profit of $1.7 million, creating two problems: the airline didn't want to talk about one of its airplanes crashing, yet it had to account for that $1.7 million profit in its annual report to its stockholders. The airline solved both problems by inserting a footnote in its annual report which explained that the $1.7 million was due to "the involuntary conversion of a 727."

A third kind of doublespeak is gobbledygook or bureaucratese. Such doublespeak is simply a matter of overwhelming the audience with words—the more the better. Alan Greenspan, a polished practitioner of bureaucratese, once testified before a Senate committee that "it is a tricky problem to find the particular calibration in timing that would be appropriate to stem the acceleration in risk premiums created by falling incomes without prematurely aborting the decline in the inflation-generated risk premiums."

The fourth kind of doublespeak is inflated language, which is designed to make the ordinary seem extraordinary, to make everyday things seem impressive, to give an air of importance to people or situations, to make the simple seem complex. Thus do car mechanics become "automotive internists," elevator operators become "members of the vertical transportation corps," grocery store checkout clerks become "career associate scanning professionals," and smelling something becomes "organoleptic analysis."

Doublespeak is not the product of careless language or sloppy thinking. Quite the opposite. Doublespeak is language carefully designed and constructed to appear to communicate when in fact it doesn't. It is language designed not to lead but mislead. Thus, it's not a tax increase but "revenue enhancement" or "tax-base broadening." So how can you complain about higher taxes? Those aren't useless, billion dollar pork barrel projects; they're really "congressional projects of national significance," so don't complain about wasteful government spending. That isn't the Mafia in Atlantic City; those are just "members of a career-offender cartel," so don't worry about the influence of organized crime in the city.

New doublespeak is created every day. The Environmental Protection Agency once called acid rain "poorly buffered precipitation," then

continued

dropped that term in favor of "atmospheric deposition of anthropo-
genically-derived acidic substances," but recently decided that acid rain
should be called "wet deposition." The Pentagon, which has in the past
given us such classic doublespeak as "hexiform rotatable surface com-
pression unit" for steel nut, just published a pamphlet warning soldiers
that exposure to nerve gas will lead to "immediate permanent incapaci-
tation." That's almost as good as the Pentagon's official term "servicing
the target," meaning to kill the enemy. Meanwhile, the Department of
Energy wants to establish a "monitored retrievable storage site," a place
once known as a dump for spent nuclear fuel.

Bad economic times give rise to lots of new doublespeak designed to
avoid some very unpleasant economic realities. As the "contained depres-
sion" continues, so does the corporate policy of making up even more new
terms to avoid the simple, and easily understandable, term "layoff." So it
is that corporations "reposition," "restructure," "reshape" or "realign" the
company and "reduce duplication" through "release of resources" that
involves a "permanent downsizing" or a "payroll adjustment" that results
in a number of employees being "involuntarily terminated."

Other countries regularly contribute to doublespeak. In Japan, where
baldness is called "hair disadvantaged," the economy is undergoing a
"severe adjustment process," while in Canada there is an "involuntary
downward development" of the work force. For some government
agencies in Canada, wastepaper baskets have become "user friendly,
space effective, flexible, deskside sortation units." Politicians in Canada
may engage in "reality augmentation," but they never lie. As part of
their new freedom, the people of Moscow can visit "intimacy salons,"
or sex shops as they're known in other countries. When dealing with
the bureaucracy in Russia, people know that they should show officials
"normal gratitude," or give them a bribe.

The worst doublespeak is the doublespeak of death. It is the language, wrote George Orwell in 1945, that is "largely the defense of the
indefensible designed to make lies sound truthful and murder respectable, and to give an appearance of solidity to pure wind." In the doublespeak of death, Orwell continued, "defenseless villages are bombarded
from the air, the inhabitants driven out into the countryside, the cattle
machine-gunned, the huts set on fire with incendiary bullets. This is
called pacification. Millions of peasants are robbed of their farms and
sent trudging along the roads with no more than they can carry. This
is called transfer of population or rectification of frontiers." Today, in a
country once called Yugoslavia, this is called "ethnic cleansing."

It's easy to laugh off doublespeak. After all, we all know what's going on, so what's the harm? But we don't always know what's going on,
and when that happens, doublespeak accomplishes its ends. It alters
our perception of reality. It deprives us of the tools we need to develop, advance and preserve our society, our culture, our civilization. It

Research

breeds suspicion, cynicism, distrust and, ultimately, hostility. It delivers us into the hands of those who do not have our interests at heart. As Samuel Johnson noted in 18th century England, even the devils in hell do not lie to one another, since the society of hell could not subsist without the truth, any more than any other society.

SAMPLE FUNCTION STATEMENTS

Paragraph 1: Lutz begins his article on doublespeak by providing some examples: a "unique retail biosphere" is really a farmers' market; "synthetic glass" is really plastic.

Paragraph 2: Lutz defines *doublespeak* as devious language–"language which pretends to communicate but doesn't" (22).

Paragraph 3: Lutz describes the wide use of doublespeak. It is used in all media.

Paragraph 4: Lutz defines the first of four types of doublespeak—euphemism, which is a word or phrase that sugarcoats a harsher meaning. He provides an example from the U.S. State Department.

Paragraph 5: Lutz identifies jargon as the second type of doublespeak. It is the specialized language used by trades or professions such as car mechanics or doctors. But Lutz believes the use of jargon is legitimate when it enables efficient communication among group members. Jargon is considered doublespeak when in-group members use it to communicate with nonmembers who cannot understand it.

Paragraph 6: Lutz shows how an airline's annual report includes devious use of jargon to camouflage a disaster.

Paragraph 7: According to Lutz, the third type of doublespeak has two alternative labels: *gobbledygook* or *bureaucratese*. The distinguishing feature of this type of doublespeak is the large number of words used.

Paragraph 8: Lutz states that the final type of doublespeak is inflated language.

Paragraph 9: Lutz is careful to note that doublespeak is not the product of carelessness or "sloppy thinking" (23) but rather an attempt to deceive.

Paragraph 10: Lutz emphasizes that instances of doublespeak are created on a daily basis and provides examples.

Paragraph 11: Lutz attributes increases in the use of doublespeak to a bad economy. Doublespeak serves to gloss over the hardships people experience.

Paragraph 12: Lutz notes that doublespeak is also used in other countries.

Paragraph 13: Lutz singles out the doublespeak surrounding the topic of death as the worst type of doublespeak.

Paragraph 14: Lutz concludes his article by establishing the harmfulness of doublespeak, which can leave us without "the tools we need to develop, advance and preserve our society, our culture, our civilization" (24).

Clustering and ordering

After you have written a function statement for each paragraph of an essay, you may find that statements cluster together. For example, the statements Jacob Thomas wrote for paragraphs 4 through 8 of William Lutz's article all deal with the different categories of doublespeak. If an essay includes subheadings, you can use them to understand how the original author grouped ideas. By finding clusters of ideas, you take a major step toward condensing information. Instead of using a sentence or two to summarize each paragraph, you can use a sentence or two to summarize three paragraphs.

Summaries often present the main points in the same order as in the original source, usually with the thesis statement of the original source first, followed by supporting information. Even if the thesis statement appears at the end of the original source, you should still state it at the beginning of your summary. If there is no explicit thesis statement in the original source, you should state at the beginning of your summary the thesis (or main idea) that you have inferred from reading that source. Including a thesis statement, which captures the essence of the original source, in the first or second sentence of a summary provides a reference point for other information reported in the summary. The introductory sentences of a summary should also include the source author's name and the title of the source.

After you finish your summary, ask yourself the following questions to ensure that it is effective:

Have I included the author's name and the title of the source?

Have I mentioned the thesis (or main idea) of the original source?

Have I used attributive tags to show that I am referring to someone else's ideas?

Have I remained objective, not evaluating or judging the material I am summarizing?

Have I remained faithful to the source by accurately representing the material?

Direct quotations can be used in summaries, but they should be used sparingly. Guidelines for quotations are discussed in more detail on pages 405–407. All quotations and references to source material require accurate citation and documentation. In-text citation and documentation formats are presented in chapter 15.

Partial summaries

Using his function statements for the paragraphs, Jacob Thomas could have summarized the entire article. Depending on his purpose and the expectations of his audience, he might instead have chosen to write a partial summary. Partial summaries of varying size are frequently found in research papers. A one-sentence summary may be appropriate when the researcher wants to focus on a specific piece of information. If

Jacob had been interested in noting what various writers have said about doublespeak, he could have represented William Lutz's ideas as follows:

> In "Doubts about Doublespeak," William Lutz describes abuses of language and explains why they are harmful.

Partial summaries of the same source may vary depending on the researcher's purpose. The following partial summary focuses on William Lutz's reference to George Orwell's work, rather than on the uses of doublespeak.

SAMPLE PARTIAL SUMMARY

Authors frequently cite the work of George Orwell when discussing the abuses of language. In "Doubts about Doublespeak," William Lutz describes different types of doublespeak—language used to deceive—and explains why they are harmful. He quotes a passage from Orwell's "Politics and the English Language" in order to emphasize his own belief that the doublespeak surrounding the topic of death is the worst form of language abuse: "defenseless villages are bombarded from the air, the inhabitants driven out into the countryside, the cattle machine-gunned, the huts set on fire with incendiary bullets. This is called pacification. Millions of peasants are robbed of their farms and sent trudging along the roads with no more than they can carry. This is called transfer of population or rectification of frontiers" (qtd. in Lutz 24).

Paraphrasing

A **paraphrase** is like a summary in that it is a restatement of someone else's ideas, but a paraphrase differs from a summary in coverage. A summary condenses information to a greater extent than a paraphrase does. When you paraphrase, you translate the original source into your own words; thus, your paraphrase will be approximately the same length as the original. Researchers usually paraphrase material when they want to clarify it or integrate its content smoothly into their own work.

A paraphrase, then, should be written in your own words and should cite the original author. A restatement of an author's ideas that maintains the original sentence structure but substitutes a few synonyms is not an adequate paraphrase. In fact, such a restatement is plagiarism—even when the author's name is cited. Your paraphrase should contain different words and a new word order; however, the content of the original source should not be altered. In short, a paraphrase must be accurate. Any intentional misrepresentation of another person's work is unethical.

Research

Below are some examples of problematic and successful paraphrases. The source citations in the examples are formatted according to MLA guidelines.

SOURCE

Wardhaugh, Ronald. *How Conversation Works*. Oxford: Basil Blackwell, 1985. Print.

ORIGINAL

Conversation, like daily living, requires you to exhibit a considerable trust in others.

PROBLEMATIC PARAPHRASE

Conversation, like everyday life, requires you to show your trust in others (Wardhaugh 5).

SUCCESSFUL PARAPHRASE

Ronald Wardhaugh compares conversation to everyday life because it requires people to trust one another (5).

ORIGINAL

Without routine ways of doing things and in the absence of norms of behaviour, life would be too difficult, too uncertain for most of us. The routines, patterns, rituals, stereotypes even of everyday existence provide us with many of the means for coping with that existence, for reducing uncertainty and anxiety, and for providing us with the appearance of stability and continuity in the outside world. They let us get on with the actual business of living. However, many are beneath our conscious awareness; what, therefore, is of particular interest is bringing to awareness just those aspects of our lives that make living endurable (and even enjoyable) just because they are so commonly taken for granted.

PROBLEMATIC PARAPHRASE

Without habitual ways of acting and without behavioral norms, life would be too uncertain for us and thus too difficult. Our routines and rituals of everyday life provide us with many of the ways for coping with our lives, for decreasing the amount of uncertainty and anxiety we feel, and for giving us a sense of stability and continuity. They let us live our lives. But many are beneath our awareness, so what is of interest is bringing to consciousness just those parts of our lives that make life livable (and even fun) just because we generally take them for granted (Wardhaugh 21–22).

Research

Notice how the attributive tags in the successful paraphrases help the writer vary sentence structure.

Quoting Sources in Your Paper

Whenever you find a quotation that you would like to use in your paper, you should think about your reasons for including it. Quotations should be used only sparingly; therefore, make sure that when you quote a source, you do so because the language in the quotation is striking and not easily paraphrased. A pithy quotation in just the right place can help you emphasize a point you have mentioned or, alternatively, set up a point of view you wish to refute. If you overuse quotations, though, readers may decide that laziness prevented you from making sufficient effort to express your own thoughts.

TRICKS OF THE TRADE

by Keith Evans, history major

After completing a developed draft of my paper, I identify all the direct quotes I have used and critically analyze their effectiveness. I try to remember that a paraphrase will work *better* than a quote if all the quote's information is useful but couched in difficult or inexpressive language, and a summary will be preferable if the quote is taking too long to arrive at its crucial point. Only if the exact wording of the quote is what makes it so valuable should it be kept.

Using attributive tags

The direct quotations in your paper should be exact replicas of the originals. This means replicating not only the words but also punctuation and capitalization. Full sentences require quotation marks and usually commas to set them off from attributive tags. Such a tag can be placed at the beginning, middle, or end of your own sentence.

Research

Including question marks or exclamation points

If you choose to quote a sentence that ends with a question mark or an exclamation point, the punctuation should be maintained; no comma is necessary.

"Why are New Yorkers always bumping into Charlie Ravioli and grabbing lunch, instead of sitting down with him and exchanging intimacies, as friends should, as people do in Paris and Rome?" asks Adam Gopnik (106).

"Incompatibility is unacceptable in mathematics! It must be resolved!" claims William Byers (29).

Quoting memorable words or phrases

You may want to quote just a memorable word or phrase. Only the part of the sentence you are quoting appears within quotation marks, and generally no comma is necessary.

Part of what Ken Wilber calls "boomeritis" is attributable to excessive emotional preoccupation with the self (27).

Modifying quotations with square brackets or ellipsis points

In order to make a quotation fit your sentence, you may need to modify the capitalization of a word. To indicate such a modification, use square brackets:

Pollan believes that "[t]hough animals are still very much 'things' in the eyes of American law, change is in the air" (191).

Research

You can also use square brackets to insert words needed for clarification:

> Ben Metcalf reports, "She [Sacajawea] seems to have dug up a good deal of the topsoil along the route in an effort to find edible roots with which to impress Lewis and Clark . . ." (164).

For partial quotations, as in the example above, use three ellipsis points to indicate that some of the original sentence was omitted.

Using block quotations

If you want to quote an extremely long sentence or more than one sentence, you may need to use a block quotation. MLA guidelines call for a block quotation to be set off by being indented one inch from the left margin. You should use a block quotation only if the quoted material takes up more than four lines on your paper's page. No quotation marks are used around a block quotation.

> Francis Spufford describes her experience reading *The Hobbit* as a young child:
>
>> By the time I reached *The Hobbit*'s last page, though, writing had softened, and lost the outlines of the printed alphabet, and become a transparent liquid, first viscous and sluggish, like a jelly of meaning, then ever thinner and more mobile, flowing faster and faster, until it reached me at the speed of thinking and I could not entirely distinguish the suggestions it was making from my own thoughts. (279)

APA guidelines call for using a block format when quoting forty or more words. The page number for the in-text citation follows *p.* for "page." More information about in-text citations can be found in chapter 15.

Evaluating and Responding to Your Sources

To incorporate sources effectively, you should not only summarize, paraphrase, quote, and document them but also respond to them. Your research log is a good place to record your initial responses. You can then craft more complete responses to your sources during the process of writing your paper.

In your research log, you may wish to comment on what you agree or disagree with, what you question, why you find some item of information particularly interesting, and what connections you draw between one source and another. Like your notes, your responses should be purposeful. When you find a source with which you agree or disagree, you'll probably copy down or paraphrase excerpts you wish to emphasize or dispute; if you do not also note *why* you agree or disagree, however, you may not be able to reconstruct your initial response later when you are composing your essay. If you take the time to carefully record your responses to sources, you will be able to make a smooth transition from taking notes to composing your essay.

Especially when you are recording source notes and your responses to those notes in the same place, it's crucial to have a system for making clear which ideas come from the source and which are your own. Even professional authors have damaged their research—and their credibility—by assuming they would remember which ideas came from their sources and which were their responses to those sources. Guard against this danger by writing your responses in a different color ink or in a different font, enclosing your responses in brackets, or using some other technique to make the distinction. You might want to use a double-entry notebook, as described in chapter 13.

TRICKS OF THE TRADE

by Alyse Murphy-Leininger, English major

After reading eight or nine articles, I tend to forget where I read each quote or idea, so I always use several methods to annotate my sources as I'm researching. I like using different colored Post-it notes, highlighting, underlining, and taking notes in the margins. I also put the especially important quotes that I know I want to use on a separate document on the computer so I can just search through the document instead of having to read all the articles again to find what I'm looking for.

Your response to a source will be based on your evaluation of it. Readers of academic research papers expect the authors to be critical. They want to know whether facts are accurate or erroneous, whether logic is apt or weak, whether plans are comprehensive or ill-conceived, and whether conclusions are valid or invalid. Thus, researchers evaluate their sources to ensure that their readers' concerns are being addressed.

Research

However, they also critique sources to set up their own research niche. They try to show that previous research is lacking in some way in order to establish a rhetorical opportunity for their study.

Questions that can help you evaluate your sources fall into five categories: currency, coverage, reliability, reasoning, and author stance. In the following sections, you'll learn more about these categories and read brief sample responses to research.

Currency

Depending on the nature of your research, the currency of sources or of the data they present may be important to consider. Using up-to-date sources is crucial when you are writing about events that have taken place recently or issues that have arisen recently. However, if you are doing historical research, you may want to use primary sources from the period you are focusing on.

QUESTIONS ABOUT CURRENCY

Do your sources and the data presented in them need to be up to date? If so, are they?

If you are doing historical research, are your sources from the relevant period?

Since you began your project, have events occurred that you should take into account?

Do you need to find new sources?

> **SAMPLE RESPONSE TO A SOURCE'S CURRENCY**
>
> According to the author, only 50 percent of all public schools have Web pages (23); however, this statistic is taken from a report published in 1997. A more recent count would likely yield a much higher percentage.

Coverage

Coverage refers to the comprehensiveness of research. The more comprehensive a study is, the more convincing are its findings. Similarly, the more examples a writer provides, the more compelling are the writer's conclusions. Claims that are based on only one instance are likely to be criticized for being merely anecdotal.

QUESTIONS ABOUT COVERAGE

How many examples is the claim based on?

Is this number of examples convincing or are more examples needed?

Are the conclusions based on a sufficient amount of data?

Reliability

Research, especially research based on experiments or surveys, must be reliable. Experimental results are reliable if they can be replicated in other studies—that is, if other researchers who perform the same experiment or survey get the same results. Any claims based on results supported by only one experiment are extremely tentative.

Reliability also refers to the accuracy of data reported as factual. Researchers are expected to report their findings honestly, not distorting them to support their own beliefs and not claiming others' ideas as their own. Researchers must resist the temptation to exclude information that might weaken their conclusions.

Sometimes, evaluating the publisher can provide a gauge of the reliability of the material. As a rule, reliable source material is published by reputable companies, institutions, and organizations. If you are using a book, check to see whether it was published by a university press or a commercial press. Books published by university presses are normally reviewed by experts before publication to ensure the accuracy of facts. Books published by commercial presses may or may not have received the same scrutiny, so you will have to depend on the reputation of the author and/or postpublication reviews to determine reliability. If you are using an article, remember that articles published in journals, like books published by academic presses, have been reviewed in draft form by two or three experts. Journal articles also include extensive bibliographies so that readers can examine the sources used in the research. Magazine articles, in contrast, seldom undergo expert review and rarely include documentation of sources. If you decide to use an online source, be sure to consider the nature of its sponsor. Is it a college or university (identified by the suffix *.edu*), a government agency (*.gov*), a nonprofit organization (*.org*), a network site (*.net*), or a commercial business (*.com*)? There is no easy way to ascertain the reliability of online sources. If you are unsure about an online source, try to find out as much as you can about it. First click on links that tell you about the mission of the site sponsor and then perform an online search of the sponsor's name to see what other researchers have written about the company, institution, or organization.

Research

QUESTIONS ABOUT RELIABILITY

Could the experiment or survey that yielded these data be replicated?

Are the facts reported indeed facts?

Is the coverage balanced and the information relevant?

Are the sources used acknowledged properly?

Are there any disputes regarding the data? If so, are these disputes discussed sufficiently?

Was the material published by a reputable company, institution, or organization?

> **SAMPLE RESPONSE TO A SOURCE'S RELIABILITY**
>
> The author blames business for practically all of our nation's woes without providing details to bolster her argument. It is not clear how business has the impact on health care and education that she says it does.

Soundness of reasoning

When writing is logical, the reasoning is sound. Lapses in logic may be the result of using evidence that does not directly support a claim, appealing primarily (or exclusively) to the reader's emotions, or encouraging belief in false authority. Faulty logic is often due to the presence of rhetorical fallacies. These fallacies occur often enough that each one has its own name. Some of the most common rhetorical fallacies are listed below; after each is a question for you to ask yourself as you consider an author's reasoning. (See chapter 6 for a more detailed discussion of rhetorical fallacies, with examples of each of the following.)

Ad hominem (Latin for "toward the man himself"). Has the author criticized or attacked the author of another source based solely on his or her character, not taking into account the reasoning or evidence provided in the source?

Appeal to tradition. Does the author support or encourage some action merely by referring to what has traditionally been done?

Bandwagon. Does the author claim that an action is appropriate because many other people do it?

False authority. When reporting the opinions of experts in one field, does the author incorrectly assume that they have expertise in other fields?

False cause (sometimes referred to as the Latin *post hoc, ergo propter hoc,* which translates as "after this, so because of this"). When reporting two events, does the author incorrectly believe (or suggest) that the first event caused the second event?

False dilemma (also called the *either/or fallacy*). Does the author provide only two options when more than two exist?

Hasty generalization. Are the author's conclusions based on too little evidence?

Oversimplification. Does the author provide unreasonably simple solutions?

Slippery slope. Does the author predict an unreasonable sequence of events?

Research

Stance of the author

All authors have beliefs and values that influence their work. As you read a work as part of your research, it is your job to decide whether the author is expressing strong views because of deep commitment or because of a desire to deceive. As long as authors represent information truthfully and respectfully, they are acting ethically. If they twist facts or otherwise intentionally misrepresent ideas, they are being dishonest.

QUESTIONS ABOUT THE STANCE OF THE AUTHOR

Has the author adequately conveyed information, or has the author oversimplified information or ignored relevant information?

Has the author been faithful to source material, or has the author distorted information and quoted out of context?

Has the author adequately supported claims, or has the author used unsupported generalizations?

SAMPLE RESPONSE TO AN AUTHOR'S STANCE

The author believes that artificial environments are detrimental to the natural environment because they draw people away from the outdoors. In his mind, one must spend time outside in order to be an environmentalist (78). The author, though, owns a rafting service and thus is promoting his own business, which occurs in a natural environment. He fails to account for the many benefits of artificial environments, such as providing exercise opportunities to people who do not live near natural areas.

Preparing a Working Bibliography

Whenever you plan to consult a number of sources in a research project, dedicate a section of your research log to your working bibliography. A **working bibliography** is a preliminary record of the sources you find as you conduct your research. The working bibliography will serve as a draft for your final list of references or works cited.

The following sample templates indicate what bibliographic information you should record for books, articles, and Web sites. You may not use all of the information in a source citation, but it will come in handy if you need to return to the source for any reason. To save yourself work later as you prepare the bibliography for your paper, you may find it useful to take a few moments to look at how bibliographic information is conventionally recorded in your field. If you have been asked to follow the conventions of the Modern Language Association (MLA) or the American Psychological Association (APA), see chapter 15.

BOOKS

Author(s) and/or Editor(s): _____

Title: _____

Publisher: _____

Place of Publication: _____

Date of Publication: _____

Page Numbers of Particular Interest: _____

For online books, also provide as much of the following information as possible:

Title of the Internet Site: _____

Editor of the Site: _____

Version Number: _____

Date of Electronic Publication: _____

Name of Sponsoring Institution or Organization: _____

Date of Access: _____

URL for Book: _____

ARTICLES

Author(s): _____

Title of Article: _____

Title of Journal or Magazine: _____

Volume and Issue Numbers: _____

Date of Publication: _____

Page Numbers of Entire Article: _____

Page Numbers of Particular Interest: _____

For articles from a database, also provide as much of the following information as possible:

Name of Database: _____

Name of Service: _____

Date of Access: _____

URL for the Service's Home Page: _____

Digital Object Identifier (DOI), if any: _____

WEB SITES

Name of Site: _____

Name of Sponsoring Entity: _____

Author(s) or Editor(s) (if any): _____

URL: _____

Date of Publication: _____

Date of Last Update: _____

Date of Access: _____

Research

Annotating a Bibliography

An **annotated bibliography** is a list of works cited, or sometimes works consulted, that includes descriptive or critical commentary with each entry. By preparing an annotated bibliography, you show that you have understood your sources and have thought about how to incorporate them into your paper. Some instructors require students to include annotated bibliographies with their papers. However, even if an annotated bibliography is not required, you might want to create one if you are working on a research project that will take several weeks to complete, as it can help you keep track of sources. To prepare entries that will help you solidify your knowledge of sources and your plans for using them, follow these guidelines:

► Begin each entry with bibliographic information. Follow the guidelines on pages 421–440 for MLA documentation style or those on pages 444–457 for APA documentation style if your instructor requires you to use one of these styles.

► Below the bibliographic information, write two or three sentences that summarize the source.

► After summarizing the source, write two or three sentences explaining the usefulness of the source for your specific research project.

Planning a Research Paper

Strategies for planning a research paper are not that different from the general strategies you learned in chapter 9: listing, keeping a journal, freewriting, questioning, clustering, and outlining. If you have been keeping a research log, you have already used many of these methods. When writing the first draft of your paper, you may want to use some of these methods to generate or organize ideas.

Crafting a working thesis

The most important step to take as you begin to prepare your first draft is to write your thesis. If you started the research process with a question, now is the time to answer that question. A **working thesis** is a tentative answer to a research question. By forming such a thesis, you can test a possible framework for your fitting response.

Keep in mind that once you have written a working thesis, you may find that you need to adjust it. You can test your thesis as you try to support it in the body of your paper. Do not be concerned if you change your mind; writers often do. Writing a thesis is just a starting point in the drafting process.

Dealing with areas of tension in the research findings

As you sifted through all your information in an attempt to find an answer to your research question, you probably encountered information that was at odds with other information. Perhaps two authors disagreed, perhaps one study contradicted another, or perhaps your own experience provided evidence counter to another author's thesis. You may also have found flaws in the reasoning or gaps in the evidence. Look closely at these areas of tension, because they can provide an opportunity and a purpose for your writing. You may even find ways to introduce them into your thesis. Kendra Fry's experience provides an illustration.

Kendra had been studying how mathematics is taught in elementary schools and observing students in a fifth-grade classroom. Her research question was "What are the most effective methods for teaching mathematics to students in elementary school?" Both in the articles Kendra read and in the classes she observed, she found a great deal of emphasis placed on writing. Students were often asked to write down explanations for their answers to math problems. The initial working thesis she drafted was "Although language arts and mathematics are often kept separate in coursework, writing may be key to teaching mathematics in elementary school." When observing students, though, Kendra found that some students who were able to solve math equations easily still had difficulty explaining the process. She thought this difficulty made a few of them dislike their math lessons. As Kendra started to draft her paper, she changed her thesis to take into account the tension between the type of mathematics teaching that was prescribed and the effect on learning that she was witnessing: "Although students in elementary schools are encouraged to explain their mathematical reasoning, this practice may have an adverse effect on some students' motivation to study math." In the process of trying to answer a broader question, Kendra found a rhetorical opportunity and a purpose for a research paper she was really interested in writing.

Like Kendra, you can find a genuine research agenda when you pay attention to what doesn't fit neatly into an early outline you have or into your initial plans for what you will say.

15 Acknowledging Sources

The Way I See It #248

Imagine a world in which every single person on the planet is given free access to the sum of all human knowledge. Wikis give us a place where anyone who is kind, thoughtful and intelligent can come and join us in building a better and more rational world.

-- Jimmy Wales
Founder of Wikipedia and Wikia.com.

This is the author's opinion, not necessarily that of Starbucks. To read more or respond, go to www.starbucks.com/wayiseeit

The Way I See It #261

All the darkness of the world cannot extinguish the light of a small candle.

-- Reza Deghati
Photographer, humanitarian and National Geographic Fellow.

This is the author's opinion, not necessarily that of Starbucks. To read more or respond, go to www.starbucks.com/wayiseeit

The Way I See It #220

Evolution as described by Charles Darwin is a scientific theory, abundantly reconfirmed, explaining physical phenomena by physical causes. Intelligent Design is a faith-based initiative in rhetorical argument. Should we teach I.D. in America's public schools? Yes, let's do – not as science, but alongside other spiritual beliefs, such as Islam, Zoroastrianism and the Hindu idea that Earth rests on Chukwa, the giant turtle.

-- David Quammen
Author. His books include The Song of the Dodo *and* The Reluctant Mr. Darwin.

This is the author's opinion, not necessarily that of Starbucks. To read more or respond, go to www.starbucks.com/wayiseeit

1. The coffee cups pictured here may be a familiar sight, but you may not have thought of them as demonstrating the use of sources. How does Starbucks credit the sources of the quotations? What information is given? What does that information tell you? What information about the sources is left out?

2. Even if you're not used to seeing quotations on coffee cups, you've likely seen them elsewhere; they appear on everything from teabags to t-shirts, bumper stickers to baseball caps. If you wanted to place a quotation on something you own, what item and what quotation would you choose? What source information, if any, would you provide to accompany it?

Why Acknowledge Sources?

Just as you decide whether authors of sources are credible, your readers will decide whether your work is trustworthy. One of the most important ways to demonstrate credibility as an author is to acknowledge the sources from which you have drawn. Writers who do not provide adequate acknowledgment are accused of **plagiarism**, the unethical and illegal use of others' words and ideas. By acknowledging your sources, you also give your readers the information they need to find those sources in case they would like to consult them on their own. Such acknowledgment should occur in the body of your paper (in-text citations) and in the bibliography at the end of your paper (documentation). The Modern Language Association (MLA) and the American Psychological Association (APA) provide guidelines for both formatting papers and acknowledging sources. These guidelines are summarized in the following sections.

Which Sources to Cite

If the information you use is considered common knowledge, you do not have to include an in-text citation. Common knowledge is information that most educated people know and many reference books report. For example, you would not have to include an in-text citation if you mentioned that New Orleans was devastated by Hurricane Katrina. However, if you quoted or paraphrased what various politicians said about relief efforts following Katrina, you would need to include such citations.

You should include citations for all facts that are not common knowledge, statistics (whether from a text, table, graph, or chart), visuals, research findings, and quotations and paraphrases of statements made by other people. Be sure that when you acknowledge sources you include the following:

▶ The name(s) of the author(s); if unknown, include the title of the text

▶ Page number(s)

▶ A bibliographic entry that corresponds to the in-text citation

▶ Quotation marks around material quoted exactly

Common Citation Errors

To avoid being accused of plagiarism, be on the lookout for the following errors:

▶ No author (or title) mentioned

▶ No page numbers listed

- No quotation marks used
- Paraphrase worded too similarly to the source
- Inaccurate paraphrase
- Images used with no indication of the source
- No bibliographic entry corresponding to the in-text citation

MLA Guidelines for In-Text Citations

If you are following the style recommended by the Modern Language Association, you will acknowledge your sources within the text of your paper by referring just to authors and page numbers. If the author's name is unknown, you use the title of the source in the in-text citation. By providing in-text citations and a works-cited list at the end of your paper, you offer your readers the opportunity to consult the sources you used.

You will likely consult a variety of sources for any research paper. The following examples are representative of the types of in-text citations you might use.

1.   Work by one to three authors

Although New York State publishes a booklet of driving rules, **Katha Pollit** has found no books on "the art of driving" (**217**).

No books exist on "the art of driving" (**Pollit 217**).

Other researchers, such as **Steven Reiss and James Wiltz,** rely on tools like surveys to explain why we watch reality television (**734–36**).

Survey results can help us understand why we watch reality television (**Reiss and Wiltz 734–36**).

Citizens passed the bond issue in 2004, even though they originally voted it down in 2001 (**Jacobs, Manzow, and Holst 120**).

The authors' last names can be placed in the text or within parentheses with the page number. The parenthetical citation should appear as close as possible to the information documented—usually at the end of the sentence or after any quotation marks. When citing a range of page numbers of three digits, do not repeat the hundreds' digit for the higher number: 201–97.

2. Work by four or more authors

When citing parenthetically a source by more than three authors, you can either include all the authors' last names or provide just the first author's last name followed by the abbreviation *et al.* (Latin for "and others"): (Stafford, Suzuki, Li, and Brown 67) or (Stafford et al. 67). The abbreviation *et al.* should not be underlined or italicized in citations.

3. Work by an unknown author

The Tehuelche people left their handprints on the walls of a cave, now called Cave of the Hands (**"Hands of Time" 124**).

If the author is unknown, use the title of the work in place of the author's name. If the title is long, shorten it, beginning with the first word used in the corresponding works-cited entry ("Wandering" for "Wandering with Cameras in the Himalaya"). If you use the title in the text, however, you do not have to place it in the parenthetical reference.

4. An entire work

Using literary examples, **Alain de Botton** explores the reasons people decide to travel.

Notice that no page numbers are necessary when an entire work is cited.

5. A multivolume work

President Truman asked that all soldiers be treated equally (**Merrill 11: 741**).

The volume number and page number(s) are separated by a colon.

6. Two or more works by the same author(s)

Kress refers to the kinds of interpretive skills required of children who play video games to argue that we should recognize multiple forms of reading, not just those already encouraged in our school systems (*Literacy* 174).

Marianne Celce-Murcia and Diane Larsen-Freeman claim that grammar involves three dimensions (*Grammar Book* 4).

To distinguish one work from another, include a title. If the title is long (such as *Literacy in the New Media Age*), shorten it, beginning with the first word used in the corresponding works-cited entry.

7. Two or more works by different authors with the same last name

If the military were to use solely conventional weapons, the draft would likely be reinstated (**E. Scarry** 241).

To distinguish one author from another, use their initials. If the initials are the same, spell out their first names.

8. Work by a corporate or government author

Strawbale constructions are now popular across the nation (**Natl. Ecobuilders Group** 2).

Provide the name of the corporate or government author and a page reference. If the author's name is extremely long, you may use common abbreviations—for example, *assn.* for "association" and *natl.* for "national."

9. Indirect source

According to **Sir George Dasent**, a reader "must be satisfied with the soup that is set before him, and not desire to see the bones of the ox out of which it has been boiled" (**qtd. in Shippey** 289).

Use the abbreviation *qtd.* to indicate that you found the quotation in another source.

10. Work in an anthology

"Good cooking," claims **Jane Kramer**, "is much easier to master than good writing" (153).

Either in the text or within parentheses with the page number, use the name of the author of the particular section (chapter, essay, or article) you are citing, not the editor of the entire book, unless they are the same.

11. Poem

The final sentence in **Philip Levine's** "Homecoming" is framed by conditional clauses: "If we're quiet / if the place had a spirit" (**38–43**).

Instead of page numbers, provide line numbers, preceded by *line(s)* for the first citation; use numbers only for subsequent citations.

12. Drama

After some hesitation, the messenger tells Macbeth what he saw: "As I did stand my watch upon the hill / I looked toward Birnam and anon methought / The wood began to move" (**5.5.35–37**).

Instead of page numbers, indicate act, scene, and line numbers.

13. Bible

The image of seeds covering the sidewalk reminded her of the parable in which a seed falls on stony ground (**Matt. 13.18–23**).

Instead of page numbers, mention the book of the Bible (using the conventional abbreviation), chapter, and verse.

14. Two or more works in one parenthetical citation

Usage issues are discussed in both academic and popular periodicals (**Bex and Watts 5; Lippi-Green 53**).

Use a semicolon to separate citations.

15. Material from the Internet

Alston describes three types of rubrics that teachers can use to evaluate student writing (**pars. 2–15**).

McGowan finds one possible cause of tensions between science and religion in "our cultural terror of curiosity."

If an online publication numbers pages, paragraphs, or screens, provide those numbers in the citation. Precede paragraph numbers with *par.* or *pars* and screen numbers with *screen* or *screens.* If the source does not number pages, paragraphs, or screens, refer to the entire work in your text by citing the author.

MLA Guidelines for Documenting Works Cited

To provide readers with the information they need to find all the sources you have used in your paper, you must prepare a bibliography. According to MLA guidelines, your bibliography should be entitled *Works Cited* (not in italics). It should contain an entry for every source you cite in your text, and, conversely, every bibliographic entry you list should have a corresponding in-text citation. (If you want to include entries for works that you consulted but did not cite in your paper, the bibliography should be entitled *Works Consulted.*)

The 2009 guidelines in the *MLA Handbook for Writers of Research Papers,* 7th edition, require that titles of books, magazines, Web sites, and other sources be italicized. MLA format also requires that the medium of publication you consulted be given at the end of each entry, including *Print, Web, CD-ROM, LP, Television,* or *Radio,* none of which are italicized. Alphabetize the entries in your works-cited list according to the author's (or the first author's) last name. When the author is unknown, alphabetize according to title. Use the first major word of the title; in other words, ignore any initial article (*a, an,* or *the*). If a source was written by four or more authors, you have two options: either list all the authors' names or provide just the first author's name followed by the abbreviation *et al.* (not italicized). Many people prefer to list all the authors so that their contributions are recognized equally.

Double-space the entire works-cited list. The first line of each entry begins flush with the left margin, and subsequent lines are indented one-half inch. If you have used more than one work by the same author (or team of authors), alphabetize the entries according to title. For the first entry, provide the author's name; for any subsequent entries, substitute three hyphens (---).

Rodriguez, Richard. *Brown: The Last Discovery of America.* New York: Viking, 2002. Print.

---. *Hunger of Memory: The Education of Richard Rodriguez.* New York: Bantam, 1982.
    Print.

If two or more entries have the same first author, alphabetize the entries according to the second author's last name.

Bailey, Guy, and Natalie Maynor. "The Divergence Controversy." *American Speech* 64.1
    (1989): 12-39. Print.

Bailey, Guy, and Jan Tillery. "Southern American English." *American Language Review*
    4.4 (2000): 27-29. Print.

For more details on various types of sources, use the following directory to find relevant sections. For an example of a works-cited list, see page 177. If you would like to use a checklist to help ensure that you have followed MLA guidelines, see page 440.

DIRECTORY OF WORKS-CITED ENTRIES ACCORDING TO MLA GUIDELINES

Books

1. Book by one author 426
2. Book by two or three authors 426

(Continued)

Books

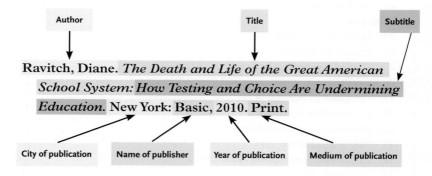

Author — Title — Subtitle

Ravitch, Diane. *The Death and Life of the Great American School System: How Testing and Choice Are Undermining Education.* New York: Basic, 2010. Print.

City of publication — Name of publisher — Year of publication — Medium of publication

Most of the information you need for a works-cited entry (see above) can be found on a book's title page. If you cannot find the date of publication on the title page, turn to the copyright page. Works-cited entries for books generally include three units of information: author, title, and publication data.

Author The author's last name is given first. Use a comma to separate the last name from the first, and place a period at the end of this unit of information. When two or more authors are listed, only the first author's name is inverted. For a source by more than three authors,

Research

either list all the authors' names or provide just the first author's name followed by the abbreviation *et al.* (not italicized).

Atherton, Lewis.

Blyth, Carl, Sigrid Becktenwald, and Jenny Wang.

Rand, George, Peter Mathis, Sali Hudson, and Victor Singler.

OR

Rand, George, et al.

Title Include the title and, if there is one, the subtitle of the book. Use a colon to separate the subtitle from the title. *Italicize* every part of the title and subtitle, including any colon.

Visual Explanations: Images and Quantities, Evidence and Narrative.

Publication data For the third unit of information, list the city of publication, the publisher's name, the copyright date, and the medium of publication you consulted (in this case, *Print*). Place a colon between the city of publication and the publisher's name, a comma between the publisher's name and the copyright date, a period between the date and the medium of publication, and a period at the end of this unit of information. When more than one city appears on the title page, use only the first one listed. You can usually shorten a publisher's name by using the principal name (*Random* for Random House or *Knopf* for Alfred A. Knopf) or by using the abbreviation *UP* for University Press (*Yale UP* for Yale University Press).

Medium of Publication (Print)

THE DEATH AND LIFE OF THE GREAT

AMERICAN SCHOOL SYSTEM

Title

How Testing and Choice Are Undermining Education

Subtitle

DIANE RAVITCH

Author

Name of publisher

A Member of the Perseus Books Group
New York

City of publication

Title page of *The Death and Life of the Great American School System.*

Copyright © 2010 by Diane Ravitch
Published by Basic Books,
A Member of the Perseus Books Group

year of publication

All rights reserved. Printed in the United States of America. No part of this book may be reproduced in any manner whatsoever without written permission except in the case of brief quotations embodied in critical articles and reviews. For information, address Basic Books, 387 Park Avenue South, New York, NY 10016-8810.

Books published by Basic Books are available at special discounts for bulk purchases in the United States by corporations, institutions, and other organizations. For more information, please contact the Special Markets Department at the Perseus Books Group, 2300 Chestnut Street, Suite 200, Philadelphia, PA 19103, or call (800) 810-4145, ext. 5000, or e-mail special.markets@perseusbooks.com.

Designed by Pauline Brown

Library of Congress Cataloging-in-Publication Data

Ravitch, Diane.
The death and life of the great American school system : how testing and choice are undermining education / Diane Ravitch.
    p. cm.
Includes bibliographical references and index.
ISBN 978-0-465-01491-0 (alk. paper)
1. Public schools—United States. 2. Educational accountability—United States.
3. Educational tests and measurements—United States. 4. School choice—United States. I. Title.
LA217.2.R38 2009
379.1—dc22
                        2009050406

10 9 8

Copyright page of *The Death and Life of the Great American School System.*

Research

1. Book by one author

You, Xiaoye. *Writing in the Devil's Tongue: A History of English Composition in China.* Carbondale: Southern Illinois UP, 2009. Print.

2. Book by two or three authors

Gies, Joseph, and Frances Gies. *Life in a Medieval City.* New York: Harper, 1981. Print.

List the authors' names in the order in which they appear on the title page, not in alphabetical order. Include full names for all of the authors, even if they have the same last name. Invert the name of only the first author.

3. Book by four or more authors

Belenky, Mary, Blythe Clincy, Nancy Goldberger, and Jill Tarule. *Women's Ways of Knowing: The Development of Self, Voice, and Mind.* New York: Basic, 1986. Print.

Belenky, Mary, et al. *Women's Ways of Knowing: The Development of Self, Voice, and Mind.* New York: Basic, 1986. Print.

Provide the names of all the authors in the order in which they appear on the title page, with the first author's name inverted, or list only the first author's name, followed by a comma and *et al.*

4. Book by a corporate author

American Heart Association. *The New American Heart Association Cookbook.* 6th ed. New York: Clarkson Potter, 2001. Print.

Omit any article (*a, an,* or *the*) that begins the name of a corporate author, and alphabetize the entry in the works-cited list according to the first major word of the corporate author's name.

5. Book by an anonymous author

Primary Colors: A Novel of Politics. New York: Warner, 1996. Print.

Alphabetize the entry according to the first major word in the title of the work.

6. Book with an author and an editor

Dickens, Charles. *Pickwick Papers.* Ed. Malcolm Andrews. Boston: Tuttle, 1997. Print.

Begin the entry with the author's name. Place the editor's name after the title of the book, preceded by *Ed.* for "edited by."

7. Book with an editor instead of an author

Baxter, Leslie A., and Dawn O. Braithwaite, eds. *Engaging Theories in Interpersonal Communication: Multiple Perspectives.* Los Angeles: SAGE, 2008. Print.

Begin the entry with the name(s) of the editor(s), using the abbreviation *ed.* for "editor" or *eds.* for "editors."

8. Second or subsequent edition

Cameron, Rondo, and Larry Neal. *A Concise Economic History of the World: From Paleolithic Times to the Present.* 4th ed. New York: Oxford UP, 2003. Print.

After the title, place the number of the edition in its ordinal form, followed by *ed.* for "edition." Note that the letters *th* following the number appear in regular type, not as a superscript.

9. Introduction, preface, foreword, or afterword to a book

Peri, Yoram. Afterword. *The Rabin Memoirs.* By Yitzhak Rabin. Berkeley: U of California P, 1996. 422–32. Print.

Begin the entry with the name of the author of the introduction, preface, foreword, or afterword, followed by the name of the part being cited (e.g., *Afterword*). If the part being cited has a title, include the title in quotation marks between the author's name and the name of the part being cited. Provide the name of the author of the book, preceded by *By,* after the title of the book. Provide the page number(s) of the part being cited after the publication information and complete the entry with the medium of publication.

10. Anthology

Ramazani, Jahan, Robert O'Clair, and Richard Ellman, eds. *The Norton Anthology of Modern and Contemporary Poetry.* 3rd ed. New York: Norton, 2003. Print.

The entry begins with the anthology's editor(s), with the first (or only) editor's name inverted. Use the abbreviation *ed.* for "editor" or *eds.* for "editors."

11. Single work from an anthology

Muños, Gabriel Trujillo. "Once Upon a Time on the Border." *How I Learned English.* Ed. Tom Miller. Washington, DC: National Geographic, 2007. 141–48. Print.

Begin the entry with the name of the author of the work you are citing, not the name of the anthology's editor. The title of the work appears in quotation marks between the author's name and the title of the anthology. The editor's name is preceded by *Ed.* for "edited by." (Note that because *Ed.* stands for "edited by," not "editor," there is no need to make the abbreviation plural for multiple editors, as you do when listing editors before the title.) After the publication information, include the numbers of the pages on which the work appears and conclude with the medium of publication.

12. Two or more works from the same anthology

Miller, Tom, ed. *How I Learned English*. Washington, DC: National Geographic, 2007.
> Print.

Montero, Mayra. "How I Learned English . . . or Did I?" Miller 221–25.

Padilla, Ignacio. "El Dobbing and My English." Miller 237–41.

When citing more than one work from the same anthology, include an entry for the entire anthology as well as entries for the individual works. In entries for individual works, list the names of the author(s) and the editor(s) and the title of the work, but not the title of the anthology. Then specify the page or range of pages on which the work appears. Note that only the first, complete entry ends with the medium of publication.

13. Book with a title within the title

Koon, Helene Wickham. *Twentieth Century Interpretations of* Death of a Salesman:
> *A Collection of Critical Essays*. Englewood Cliffs: Prentice Hall, 1983. Print.

When an italicized title includes the title of another work that would normally be italicized, do not italicize the embedded title. If the embedded title normally requires quotation marks, it should be italicized as well as enclosed in quotation marks.

14. Translated book

Rilke, Rainer Maria. *Duino Elegies*. Trans. David Young. New York: Norton, 1978. Print.

The translator's name appears after the book title, preceded by *Trans.* However, if the material cited in your paper refers primarily to the translator's comments rather than to the translated text, the entry should appear as follows:

Young, David, trans. *Duino Elegies*. By Rainer Maria Rilke. New York: Norton, 1978. Print.

15. Republished book

Alcott, Louisa May. *Work: A Story of Experience*. 1873. Harmondsworth, Eng.: Penguin,
> 1995. Print.

Provide the publication date of the original work after the title.

16. Multivolume work

Banks, Lynne Reid. *The Indian in the Cupboard*. Vol. 3. New York: Morrow, 1994. Print.

Feynman, Richard Phillips, Robert B. Leighton, and Matthew L. Sands. *The Feynman Lectures on Physics*. 3 vols. Boston: Addison, 1989. Print.

Provide only the specific volume number (e.g., *Vol. 3*) after the title if you cite material from one volume. Provide the total number of volumes if you cite material from more than one volume.

17. Book in a series

Restle, David, and Dietmar Zaefferer, eds. *Sounds and Systems.* Berlin: Walter de
    Gruyter, 2002. Print. Trends in Linguistics. 141.

After the medium of publication at the end of the entry, provide the name of the series and the series number, separated by a period.

Articles

ARTICLE IN A JOURNAL

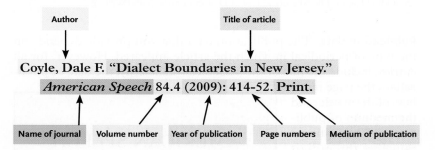

You can generally find the name of the journal, the volume number, and the year of publication on the cover of the journal. Sometimes this information is also included in the journal's page headers or footers. To find the title of the article, the author's name, and the page numbers, you'll need to locate the article within the journal.

ARTICLE IN A MAGAZINE

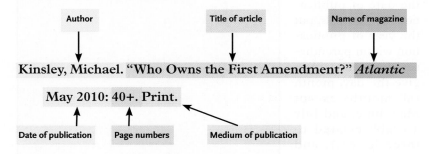

To find the name of the magazine and the date of publication (ignore volume and issue numbers), look on the cover of the magazine. Sometimes this information is also included in the magazine's page headers or footers. To find the title of the article, the author's name, and the page numbers, you'll have to look at the article itself.

Works-cited entries for articles generally include three units of information: author, title of article, and publication data.

Author List the author, last name first. Use a comma to separate the last name from the first, and place a period at the end of this unit of information. If there is more than one author, see the information given for book entries on pages 424–425.

Title of article Include the title and, if there is one, the subtitle of the article. Use a colon to separate the subtitle from the title. Place the entire title within quotation marks, including the period that marks the end of the unit of information.

"Sounding Cajun: The Rhetorical Use of Dialect in Speech and Writing."

Publication data The publication data that you provide depends on the type of periodical in which the article appeared. However, for all entries, include the title of the periodical (italicized), the date of publication, the page numbers of the article, and the medium of publication. When citing a range of three-digit page numbers, do not repeat the hundreds' digit (154-59). If you are using a journal, include the volume and issue numbers as well. Next, provide the date of publication. For journals, put the year of publication within parentheses. For magazines, give the day, month (all months except May, June, and July are abbreviated to three letters), and year. No punctuation separates the title and the date of publication. After the date of

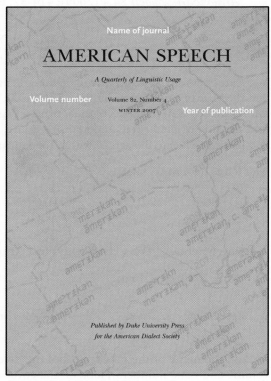

Cover of an academic journal

publication, place a colon and then the page numbers for the article. Conclude with the medium of publication. Note that current MLA guidelines no longer make a distinction between journals that are numbered continuously (e.g., Vol. 1 ends on page 208, Vol. 2 starts on page 209) and those numbered separately (that is, each volume starts on page 1). No matter how the journal is paginated, all entries must contain volume and issue numbers. One exception is journals with issue numbers only; simply cite the issue number alone as though it were a volume number.

18. Article in a journal

Burt, Susan Meredith. "Solicitudes in American English." *International Journal of Applied Linguistics* 13.1 (2003): 78–95. Print.

Place the title of the article in quotation marks between the author's name and the name of the journal. Provide the volume and issue numbers separated by a period (xx.x), the year of publication (in parentheses and followed by a colon), the range of pages on which the article appears, and the medium of publication.

19. Article in a monthly magazine

Moran, Thomas E. "Just for Kicks Soccer Program." *Exceptional Parent* Feb. 2004: 36–37. Print.

Provide the publication month and year after the title of the magazine. Abbreviate the names of all months except May, June, and July.

20. Article in a weekly magazine or newspaper

Gonzalez, Jennifer. "Community-College Professor, Visiting Yale, Explores the Ethics of Treating Animals." *Chronicle of Higher Education* 23 Apr. 2010: A4. Print.

Provide the day, month, and year of publication after the title of the publication.

21. Article in a daily newspaper

Lewin, Tamara. "Teenage Insults, Scrawled on Web, Not on Walls." *New York Times* 6 May 2010: A1+. Print.

Provide the day, month, and year of publication. If the article does not appear on consecutive pages, add a plus sign after the first page number.

22. Unsigned article

"Beware the Herd." *Newsweek* 8 Mar. 2004: 61. Print.

Alphabetize the entry according to the first major word in the title, ignoring any article (*a, an,* or *the*).

Research

23. Editorial in a newspaper or magazine

Marcus, Ruth. "In Arizona, Election Reform's Surprising Consequences." Editorial.
    Washington Post 5 May 2010: A21. Print.

Place the word *Editorial,* followed by a period, between the title of the editorial and the name of the newspaper or magazine.

24. Book or film review

Morgenstern, Joe. "See Spot Sing and Dance: Dog Cartoon 'Teacher's Pet' Has Enough
    Bite for Adults." Rev. of *Teacher's Pet*, dir. Timothy Björklund. *Wall Street Journal* 16
    Jan. 2004: W1+. Print.

Place the reviewer's name first, followed by the title of the review (if any) in quotation marks. Next, provide the title of the work reviewed, preceded by *Rev. of* for "review of," and then mention the name of the author, translator, editor, or director of the original work. The word *by* precedes an author's name, *trans.* precedes a translator's name, *ed.* precedes an editor's name, and *dir.* precedes a director's name.

Other print sources

25. Letter to the editor

Willens, Peggy A. Letter. *New York Times* 5 May 2010: A30. Print.

Following the author's name, use *Letter.* Then provide the name of the periodical, the date of publication, the page number, and the medium of publication.

26. Encyclopedia entry

"Heckelphone." *The Encyclopedia Americana.* 2001. Print.

Begin with the title of the entry, unless an author's name is provided. Provide the edition number (if any) and the year of publication after the title of the encyclopedia. Conclude with the medium of publication. Other publication information is unnecessary for familiar reference books.

27. Dictionary entry

"Foolscap." Def. 3. *Merriam-Webster's Collegiate Dictionary.* 11th ed. 2003. Print.

A dictionary entry is documented similarly to an encyclopedia entry. If the definition is one of several listed for the word, provide the definition number or letter, preceded by *Def.* for "definition."

28. Government publication

United States. Executive Office of the President and Council of Economic Advisors.
    Economic Report of the President. Washington: GPO, 2010. Print.

If no author is provided, list the name of the government (e.g., *United States, Montana,* or *New York City*), followed by the name of the agency issuing the publication, in this case, the Government Printing Office.

29. Pamphlet or bulletin

Ten Ways to Be a Better Dad. Gaithersburg: National Fatherhood Institute, 2000. Print.

An entry for a pamphlet is similar to one for a book. List the author's name first, if an author is identified.

30. Dissertation

Eves, Rosalyn Collings. "Mapping Rhetorical Frontiers: Women's Spatial Rhetorics in
    the Nineteenth-Century American West." Diss. Penn State U, 2008. Print.

If the dissertation has been published, proceed as for a book, but add *Diss.* for "dissertation" after the title, followed by the name of the institution that issued the degree and the year the degree was granted. If the dissertation has not been published, enclose the title of the dissertation in quotation marks rather than italicizing it.

Live performances and recordings

31. Play performance

Roulette. By Paul Weitz. Dir. Tripp Cullmann. John Houseman Theater, New York. 9 Feb.
    2004. Performance.

Begin with the title of the play (italicized), followed by the names of key contributors such as author, director, performers, and/or translator. The location of the performance (the theater and the city), the date of the performance, and the word *Performance* complete the entry.

32. Lecture or presentation

Joseph, Peniel. "The 1960's, Black History, and the Role of the NC A&T Four." Gibbs
    Lecture. General Classroom Building, North Carolina A&T State University,
    Greensboro. 5 Apr. 2010. Lecture.

Ryken, Leland. Class lecture. English 216. Breyer 103, Wheaton College, Wheaton. 4
    Feb. 2010. Lecture.

Provide the name of the speaker, the title of the lecture (if any) in quotation marks, the sponsoring organization (if applicable), the location and date of the lecture or presentation, and the form of delivery. If the lecture or presentation is untitled, provide a description after the name of the speaker.

33. Interview

Blauwkamp, Joan. Telephone interview. 14 Mar. 2010.

Kotapish, Dawn. Personal interview. 3 Jan. 2009.

Provide the name of the interviewee, a description of the type of interview conducted (e.g., *Telephone interview* or *Personal interview*), and the date on which the interview occurred.

34. Film

Bus Stop. Dir. Joshua Logan. Twentieth Century Fox, 1956. Film.

Monroe, Marilyn, perf. *Bus Stop.* Screenplay by George Axelrod. Dir. Joshua Logan.
    Twentieth Century Fox, 1956. Film.

Give the title of the film, the name of the director (preceded by *Dir.* for "directed by"), the distributor, the year of release, and the medium consulted. To highlight the contribution of a particular individual, start with the individual's name, followed by an indication of the nature of the contribution, abbreviated if possible. For example, *perf.* means "performer."

35. Radio or television program

"Blue Blood and Beans." Narr. Garrison Keillor. *A Prairie Home Companion.* Natl.
    Public Radio. KJZZ, Phoenix. 21 Feb. 2004. Radio.

Simon, Scott, narr. *Affluenza.* Prod. John de Graaf and Vivia Boe. PBS. KCTS, Seattle.
    2 July 1998. Television.

Provide the title of the segment (in quotation marks), the title of the program (italicized), the name of the network, the call letters and city of the broadcasting station, the date of the broadcast, and the medium of reception. Information such as the name of an author, performer, director, or narrator may appear after the title of the segment. When referring especially to the contribution of a specific individual, however, place the individual's name and an abbreviated identification of the contribution before the title.

36. Sound recording or compact disc

The White Stripes. *Under Great White Northern Lights.* Warner Bros., 2010. CD.

Begin with the name of the performer, composer, or conductor, depending on which you prefer to emphasize. Then provide the title of the recording, the manufacturer's name, the date of the recording, and the medium (in this case, *CD*). Other types of media include *LP, Audiocassette,* and *DVD.* When referring to an individual song, provide its name in quotation marks after the name of the performer, composer, or conductor. Note that the above entry would be alphabetized under *w*, not *t*.

Images

37. Work of art

Vermeer, Johannes. *Woman Holding a Balance*. 1664. Oil on canvas. Natl. Gallery of Art,
Washington.

Begin with the artist's name and the title of the work (italicized). Then provide the date the work was created (if not available, use the abbreviation
n.d. for *no date*) and the medium of composition. End your citation with
the location where the artwork is housed (that is, the name of the museum
or institution that owns the piece) and the city in which it is located.

38. Photograph

Lange, Dorothea. *Migrant Mother*. 1936. Photograph. Prints and Photographs Division,
Lib. of Congress, Washington.

Provide the photographer's name, the title of the work (italicized), the medium of composition, and the name and location of the institution that
houses the work. If the photograph has no title, briefly describe its subject.

39. Cartoon or comic strip

Cheney, Tom. "Back Page by Tom Cheney." Cartoon. *New Yorker* 12 Jan. 2004: 88. Print.

The description *Cartoon* appears before the title of the publication.

40. Advertisement

McCormick Pure Vanilla Extract. Advertisement. *Cooking Light* Mar. 2004: 177. Print.

Identify the item being advertised, and then include the description *Advertisement* before the usual publication information.

41. Map or chart

Scottsdale and Vicinity. Map. Chicago: Rand, 2000. Print.

Treat the map or chart as you would an anonymous book, including the
description *Map* or *Chart* before the usual publication information.

Online sources and databases

Current MLA guidelines do not require you to include a Web address
(URL) if your readers can easily locate the online source by searching for the author's name and the title of the work. For cases in which
your readers cannot easily locate a source, provide the complete URL
(between angle brackets) following the date of access and a period. The
closing angle bracket should also be followed by a period.

JOURNAL ARTICLE FROM A LIBRARY SUBSCRIPTION SERVICE

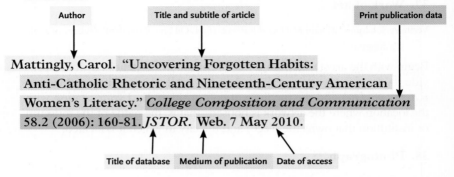

Author | Title and subtitle of article | Print publication data

Mattingly, Carol. "Uncovering Forgotten Habits: Anti-Catholic Rhetoric and Nineteenth-Century American Women's Literacy." *College Composition and Communication* 58.2 (2006): 160-81. *JSTOR*. Web. 7 May 2010.

Title of database | Medium of publication | Date of access

You can usually find much of the information you will need for your works-cited entry at the beginning of the article. Works-cited entries for online periodicals generally include six units of information: author, title (and subtitle, if any) of the article, print publication data, electronic publication data, medium of publication, and date of access (URL if needed).

Author The author's name is given, last name first. Use a comma to separate the last name from the first, and place a period at the end of this unit of information. If there is more than one author, see the information given for book entries on pages 424–425.

Title of article Include the title and, if there is one, the subtitle of the article. Use a colon to separate the subtitle from the title. Place the entire title within quotation marks, including the period that marks the end of the unit of information.

Print publication data The publication data that you provide depends on the type of periodical in which the article appeared. For detailed information, see the discussion of publication data for periodicals on pages 430–431.

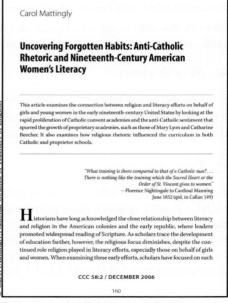

Carol Mattingly

Uncovering Forgotten Habits: Anti-Catholic Rhetoric and Nineteenth-Century American Women's Literacy

This article examines the connection between religion and literacy efforts on behalf of girls and young women in the early nineteenth-century United States by looking at the rapid proliferation of Catholic convent academies and the anti-Catholic sentiment that spurred the growth of proprietary academies, such as those of Mary Lyon and Catharine Beecher. It also examines how religious rhetoric influenced the curriculum in both Catholic and proprietor schools.

> *"What training is there compared to that of a Catholic nun?... There is nothing like the training which the Sacred Heart or the Order of St. Vincent gives to women."*
> —Florence Nightingale to Cardinal Manning June 1852 (qtd. in Callan 149)

H istorians have long acknowledged the close relationship between literacy and religion in the American colonies and the early republic, where leaders promoted widespread reading of Scripture. As scholars trace the development of education farther, however, the religious focus diminishes, despite the continued role religion played in literacy efforts, especially those on behalf of girls and women. When examining these early efforts, scholars have focused on such

CCC 58:2 / DECEMBER 2006

160

First page of article in an online journal

Electronic publication data If possible, include the name of the database in which the periodical can be found.

Medium of publication The medium of publication identifies the medium consulted, in this case, Web.

Date of access (with URL if needed) The date of access is the date on which you consulted a source. It can be found on any printout of the material you used. For cases in which your readers cannot easily locate a source, place the URL—the Internet address at which the source is located—between angle brackets (< >). Be sure to include its access-mode identifier (*http*, *ftp*, or *telnet*) and all punctuation. If the address must continue onto a second line, break it after a slash. If the URL is excessively long or complicated (more than one full line), provide just the search page you used to find the article. If there is no search page, use the site's home page.

Electronic sources vary significantly; thus, as you prepare your works-cited list, you'll need to follow the models shown here closely. On occasion, you may not be able to find all the information mentioned. In such cases, provide as much of the information as you can. When no publication date is available, use the abbreviation *n.d.* for *no date*. When no publisher or sponsor is available, use *N.p.* for *No publisher*.

42. Online book

Austen, Jane. *Emma*. London: Murray, 1815. *Gutenburg.net*. 1994. Web. 20 Nov. 2009.

Begin with the information you always provide for an entry for a book (author, title, and publication information, if available). Then provide as much of the following electronic publication information as possible: title of the Internet site (italicized), version number (if provided), date of electronic publication, and name of any sponsoring organization. Conclude with the medium of publication and the date of access.

43. Article in an online journal

Ballard, Karen. "Patient Safety: A Shared Responsibility." *NursingWorld* 8.3 (2003). Web.
    15 Jan. 2010.

Begin with the information you provide for an entry for an article in a print journal, and conclude with the medium of publication and the date of access.

44. Article in an online magazine

Cloud, John. "The Gurus of YouTube." *Time*. Time, 16 Dec. 2006. Web. 18 Dec. 2009.

Begin with the information you provide for an entry for an article in a print magazine, adding the name of any sponsor. Conclude with the medium of publication and the date of access.

45. Article in an online newspaper

Connelly, Joel. "Lessons from the Gulf Oil Spill." *Seattle Post-Intelligencer.* Hearst Seattle
    Media, 3 May 2010. Web. 7 May 2010.

Begin with the information you provide for an entry for an article in a print newspaper, adding the name of any sponsor before the date. Conclude with the medium of publication and the date of access.

46. Review in an online newspaper

Safire, William. "Not Peace, but a Sword." Rev. of *The Passion of the Christ*, dir. Mel
    Gibson. *New York Times.* New York Times, 1 Mar. 2004. Web. 6 Sept. 2009.

Begin with the information you provide for an entry for a review in a print newspaper, adding the name of any sponsor before the date. Conclude with the medium of publication and the date of access.

47. Article from a library subscription service

Fenn, Donna. "Can the Boss Make the Grade?" *Inc.* May 1996: n. pag. *ABI/INFORM.*
    Web. 11 Mar. 2010.

After providing the usual information for the article, include the italicized name of the database, the medium consulted, and the date of access. If a complete range of pages is not known for the original publication, indicate "n. pag."

48. Online work of art

Picasso, Pablo. *Guitar.* 1912. Museum of Modern Art, New York. Web. 17 Feb. 2010.

Begin with the information you always provide in an entry for a work of art and conclude with the medium of publication and the date of access. Note that the medium of composition is omitted.

49. Online government publication

United States. Dept. of Health and Human Services. *2008 Physical Activity Guidelines for
    Americans.* 22 Sept. 2008. Web. 13 Apr. 2010.

Begin with the information you provide for an entry for a print government publication and conclude with the publication medium and the date of access.

50. Web site

OMBWatch. OMB Watch, 2010. Web. 19 Apr. 2010.

Provide the title of the site (italicized), the version number (if provided), the name of any sponsoring organization, and the date of publication or latest update. Conclude with the medium of publication and the date of access.

51. Section of a Web site

"Creating a 21st Century Environmental Right-to-Know Agenda." *OMB Watch*. OMB
Watch, 2010. Web. 20 Apr. 2010.

Provide the information you include in an entry for an entire Web site, but place the title of the section you are citing in quotation marks before the title of the Web site. If the section has an author, list his or her name (inverted) first.

52. Course home page

Owens, Kalyn. General Chemistry. Course home page. Jan. 2010-Mar. 2010. Chemistry
Dept., Central Washington U. Web. 18 Feb. 2010.

List the instructor's name (inverted), the course title, the description *Course home page,* the course dates, the name of the department offering the course, and the name of the institution. Conclude with the medium consulted and the date of access.

53. Podcast

DiMeo, Nate. "The Sisters Fox." *The Memory Palace*. 12 Mar. 2010. Web. 14 Apr. 2010.

Provide the information you include in an entry for a section of a Web site. List the producer's name first, if available.

54. Online video clip

First+Main Media. *Built to Last*. 7 May 2009. *YouTube*. Web. 8 May 2010.

55. E-mail message

Kivett, George. "Hydrogen Fuel Cell Technology." Message to Theodore Ellis. 28 Jan.
2010. E-mail.

Give the name of the author of the message, the title (taken from the subject line of the message and enclosed in quotation marks), a description of the communication (including the recipient's name), the date the message was sent, and the medium of transmission.

56. Posting to discussion group or forum

Everett, Rebecca. "Searching for a Perfect Life 'In That House'." Online posting. 5 May
2010. Talk of the Nation. Web. 8 May 2010.

Provide the name of the author (inverted) and the title of the posting (in quotation marks), followed by the description *Online posting*.

Include the date the material was posted, the name of the forum, the medium consulted, and the date of your access.

57. Synchronous communication

Bruckman, Amy. 8th Birthday Symposium. "Educational MOOs: State of the Art." 17

    Jan. 2001. MediaMOO. Web. 10 Mar. 2005.

Provide the name of the writer (inverted) and a description of the discussion. Indicate any discussion title in quotation marks. The name of the forum appears between the date of the communication and the medium. The entry concludes with your date of access.

58. CD-ROM

Ultimate Human Body. Camberwell, Austral.: DK, 2002. CD-ROM.

Provide all the information you include for a print book. Add a description of the medium (e.g., *CD-ROM, Diskette, Magnetic tape*), followed by a period, after the publication information.

CHECKING OVER A WORKS-CITED LIST

✓ Is the title, *Works Cited* (not italicized), centered one inch from the top of the page? Is the first letter of each word capitalized?

✓ Is the entire list double-spaced?

✓ Are initial lines of entries flush with the left margin and subsequent lines indented one-half inch?

✓ Is there a works-cited entry for each in-text citation? Is there an in-text citation for each works-cited entry?

✓ Are the entries alphabetized according to the first author's last name? If the author of an entry is unknown, is the entry alphabetized according to title (ignoring any initial *a, an,* or *the*)?

✓ If the list contains two or more entries by the same author, are the entries alphabetized according to title? After the author's full name is used for the first entry, are three hyphens substituted for the name in subsequent entries?

✓ Are book and periodical titles italicized? Are names of databases italicized?

✓ Are quotation marks used to indicate article titles?

✓ Are URLs (when needed) enclosed in angle brackets?

Formatting an MLA Research Paper

The MLA recommends omitting a title page (unless your instructor requires one) and instead providing the identification on the first page of the paper. One inch from the top, on the left-hand side of the page, list your name, the name of the instructor, the name of the course, and the date—all double-spaced. Below these lines, center the title of the paper, which is in plain type (no italics, underlining, or boldface). On the right-hand side of each page, one-half inch from the top, use your last name and the page number as a header. Double-space the text throughout the paper, and use one-inch margins on the sides and bottom. Indent every paragraph (including the first one) one-half inch.

For an example of a research paper written in MLA style, see the investigative report by Kelly McNeil on pages 172–177, the position argument by Alicia Williams on pages 215–222, or the proposal by Rupali Kumar on pages 253–258.

APA Guidelines for In-Text Citations

If you are following the style recommended by the American Psychological Association, your in-text citations will refer to the author(s) of the text you consulted and the year of its publication. In addition, you must specify the page number(s) for any quotations you include; the abbreviation *p.* (for "page") or *pp.* (for "pages") should precede the number. For electronic sources that do not include page numbers, specify the paragraph number and precede it with the abbreviation *para.* or the symbol ¶. When no author's name is listed, you provide a shortened version of the title of the source. If your readers want to find more information about your source, they will look for the author's name or the title of the material in the bibliography at the end of your paper.

You will likely consult a variety of sources for your research paper. The following examples are representative of the types of in-text citations you might use.

DIRECTORY OF IN-TEXT CITATIONS ACCORDING TO APA GUIDELINES

1. Work by one or two authors 442
2. Work by three, four, or five authors 442
3. Work by six or more authors 442
4. Work by an unknown author 443
5. Two or more works by the same author 443
6. Two or more works by different authors with the same last name 443
7. Work by a group 443
8. Work by a government author 443
9. Indirect source 444
10. Two or more works in one parenthetical citation 444
11. Personal communication 444

Research

1. Work by one or two authors

Wachal (**2002**) discusses dictionary labels for words considered taboo.

Dictionary labels for taboo words include *offensive* and *derogatory* (**Wachal, 2002**).

Lance and Pulliam (**2002**) believe that an introductory linguistics text should have "persuasive power" (**p. 223**).

On learning of dialect bias, some students expressed outrage, often making "a 180-degree turn-around" from their original attitudes toward a standard language (**Lance & Pulliam, 2002, p. 223**).

Authors' names may be placed either in the text, followed by the date of publication in parentheses, or in parentheses along with the date. When you mention an author in the text, place the date of publication directly after the author's name. If you include a quotation, provide the page number(s) at the end of the quotation, after the quotation marks but before the period. When citing a work by two authors, use the word *and* between their names; when citing two authors in parentheses, use an ampersand (&) between their names. Always use a comma to separate the last author's name from the date.

2. Work by three, four, or five authors

First Mention

Johnstone, Bhasin, and Wittkofski (**2002**) describe the speech of Pittsburgh, Pennsylvania, as *Pittsburghese*.

The speech of Pittsburgh, Pennsylvania, is called *Pittsburghese* (**Johnstone, Bhasin, & Wittkofski, 2002**).

Subsequent Mention

Johnstone et al. (**2002**) cite *gumband* and *nebby* as words used in *Pittsburghese*.

The words *gumband* and *nebby* are used by speakers of *Pittsburghese* (**Johnstone et al., 2002**).

When first citing a source by three, four, or five authors, list all the authors' last names. In subsequent parenthetical citations, use just the first author's last name along with the abbreviation *et al.* (Latin for "and others"). The abbreviation *et al.* should not be italicized in citations.

3. Work by six or more authors

Taylor et al. (**2001**) have stressed the importance of prohibiting the dumping of plastic garbage into the oceans.

In both the first and subsequent mentions of the source, use only the first author's last name and the abbreviation *et al.*

4. Work by an unknown author

A recent survey indicated increased willingness of college students to vote in national elections (**"Ending Apathy," 2004**).

The documents leaked to the press could damage the governor's reputation (**Anonymous, 2010**).

When no author is mentioned, use a shortened version of the title instead. If the word *Anonymous* is used in the source to designate the author, use that word in place of the author's name.

5. Two or more works by the same author

Smith (**2001, 2003, 2005**) has consistently argued in support of language immersion.

Bayard (**1995a, 1995b**) discusses the acquisition of English in New Zealand.

In most cases, the year of publication will distinguish the works. However, if the works were published in the same year, distinguish them with lowercase letters, assigned based on the order of the titles in the bibliography.

6. Two or more works by different authors with the same last name

J. P. Hill and Giles (**2001**) and **G. S. Hill and Kellner** (**2002**) confirmed these findings.

When two or more authors have the same last name, always include first initials with that last name.

7. Work by a group

Style refers to publishing guidelines that encourage the clear and coherent presentation of written text (**American Psychological Association [APA], 2009**).

Spell out the name of the group when you first mention it. If the group has a widely recognizable abbreviation, place that abbreviation in square brackets after the first mention. You can then use the abbreviation in subsequent citations: (APA, 2009).

8. Work by a government author

Taxpayers encounter significant problems with two different taxes: the sole proprietor tax and the alternative minimum tax (**Internal Revenue Service [IRS], 2010**).

Spell out the name of the government entity when you first mention it. If the entity has a widely recognizable abbreviation, place that abbreviation in square brackets after the first mention. You can then use the abbreviation in subsequent citations: (IRS, 2010).

9. Indirect source

According to Ronald Butters, the word *go* is frequently used by speakers born after 1955 to introduce a quotation (**as cited in Cukor-Avila, 2002**).

Use *as cited in* to indicate that you found the information in another source.

10. Two or more works in one parenthetical citation

A speaker may use the word *like* to focus the listener's attention (**Eriksson, 1995; Ferrar & Bell 1995**).

When you include two or more works within the same parentheses, order them alphabetically. Arrange two or more works by the same author by year of publication, mentioning the author's name only once: (Kamil, 2002, 2004).

11. Personal communication

Revisions will be made to the agreement this month (**K. M. Liebenow, personal communication, February 11, 2010**).

Letters, email messages, and interviews are all considered personal communications, which you should cite in the text of a paper. Because personal communications do not represent recoverable data, you should not include entries for them in the references list.

APA Guidelines for Documenting References

To provide readers with the information they need to find all the sources you have used in your paper, you must prepare a bibliography. According to APA guidelines, your bibliography should be titled *References* (not italicized). It should contain all the information your readers would need to retrieve the sources if they wished to consult them on their own. Except for personal communications, each source you cite in your text should appear in the references list.

Alphabetize your references according to the author's (or the first author's) last name. If the author is unknown, alphabetize according to title (ignoring any initial article—*a, an,* or *the*). When you have more than one source by the same author(s), order them according to the year of publication, with the earliest first.

Frazer, B. (2000).

Frazer, B. (2004).

If two or more works by the same author(s) have the same year of publication, the entries are ordered alphabetically according to the works' titles, and lowercase letters are added to the date to distinguish the entries.

Fairclough, N. (1992a). The appropriacy of "appropriateness."

Fairclough, N. (1992b). *Critical language awareness.*

Fairclough, N. (1992c). *Discourse and social change.*

When an author you have cited is also the first of two or more authors of another entry, list the source with a single author first.

Allen, J. P. (1982).

Allen, J. P., & Turner, E. J. (1988).

When two or more entries have the same first author, alphabetize the list according to the names of subsequent authors.

Fallows, M. R., & Andrews, R. J. (1999).

Fallows, M. R., & Laver, J. T. (2002).

Double-space all of your entries, leaving the first line flush with the left margin and indenting subsequent lines one-half inch. (Your word processor may refer to the indented line as a *hanging indent*.)

For more details on various types of sources, use the following directory to find relevant sections. For an example of a references list, see pages 463–464. If you would like to use a checklist to help ensure that you have followed APA guidelines, see pages 456–457.

DIRECTORY OF REFERENCES ENTRIES ACCORDING TO APA GUIDELINES

Books

1. Book by one author 448
2. Book by two or more authors 448
3. Book with editor(s) 448
4. Book with an author and an editor 448
5. Book by a corporate author 448
6. Book by an anonymous author 448
7. Second or subsequent edition 448
8. Translated book 449
9. Republished book 449
10. Multivolume work 449
11. Government report 449
12. Selection from an edited book 449
13. Selection from a reference book 450

Research

Books

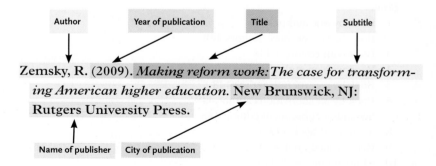

Author	Year of publication	Title	Subtitle

Zemsky, R. (2009). *Making reform work: The case for transforming American higher education.* New Brunswick, NJ: Rutgers University Press.

Name of publisher   City of publication

You can find most of the information you need to write a reference entry on a book's title page. If you cannot find the date of publication on the title page, turn to the copyright page. Reference entries for books generally

Research

include four units of information: author, year of publication, title, and publication data.

Author The author's last name appears first, followed by the first and (if given) the second initial. Use a comma to separate the last name from the initials, and place a period at the end of this unit of information. If there is more than one author, invert all the authors' names, following the pattern described for a single author. Separate the names with commas, adding an ampersand (&) before the name of the last author.

Hooker, R.

Montgomery, M., & Morgan, E.

McCrum, D., Kurath, H., & Middleton, S.

Year of publication Place the year of publication in parentheses after the author's name. Mark the end of this unit of information with a period.

Title Include the title and, if there is one, the subtitle of the book. Capitalize *only* the first word of the title and the subtitle, plus any proper nouns. Use a colon to separate the subtitle from the title. Italicize the title and subtitle.

Social cognition: Key readings.

Publication data For the fourth unit of information, start with the city of publication, followed by the common two-letter state abbreviation. Place a colon between the state abbreviation and the publisher's name. Use a shortened version

Making Reform Work
Title

The Case for Transforming American Higher Education
Subtitle

ROBERT ZEMSKY
Author

Name of Publisher

RUTGERS UNIVERSITY PRESS
New Brunswick, New Jersey, and London
City of Publication

Title page of Zemsky book

Library of Congress Cataloging-in-Publication Data

Zemsky, Robert, 1940–
Making reform work: the case for transforming American higher education / Robert Zemsky.
    p. cm.
    Includes bibliographical references and index.
    ISBN 978-0-8135-4591-2 (hardcover : alk. paper)
    1. Education, Higher—United States. 2. Educational change—United States. I. Title. II. Title: Case for transforming American higher education.
LA227.4.Z45 2009
378.73—dc22
                                                    2008048062

A British Cataloging-in-Publication record for this book is available from the British Library.

Copyright © 2009 by Robert Zemsky   Year of Publication

All rights reserved

No part of this book may be reproduced or utilized in any form or by any means, electronic or mechanical, or by any information storage and retrieval system, without written permission from the publisher. Please contact Rutgers University Press, 100 Joyce Kilmer Avenue, Piscataway, NJ 08854–8099. The only exception to this prohibition is "fair use" as defined by U.S. copyright law.

Visit our Web site: http://rutgerspress.rutgers.edu

Manufactured in the United States of America

Copyright page of Zemsky book

Research

of the publisher's name if possible. Although the word *Press or Books* should be retained, *Publishers, Company* (or Co.), and *Incorporated* (or *Inc.*) can be omitted.

1. Book by one author

Gladwell, M. (2008). *Outliers: The story of success.* New York, NY: Little, Brown.

2. Book by two or more authors

Alberts, B., Lewis, J., & Johnson, A. (2002). *Molecular biology of the cell.* Philadelphia, PA: Taylor & Francis.

If there are more than seven authors, provide the names of the first six authors, inverted, followed by an ellipsis and the name of the final author.

3. Book with editor(s)

Good, T. L., & Warshauer, L. B. (Eds.). (2002). *In our own voice: Graduate students teach writing.* Needham Heights, MA: Allyn & Bacon.

Provide the abbreviation *Ed.* or *Eds.* in parentheses after the name(s) of the editor(s).

4. Book with an author and an editor

Lewis, C. S. (2003). *A year with C. S. Lewis: Daily readings from his classic works* (P. S. Klein, Ed.). Grand Rapids, MI: Zondervan.

Provide the editor's name and the abbreviation *Ed.* in parentheses after the title of the book.

5. Book by a corporate author

Modern Language Association of America. (1978). *International bibliography of books and articles on the modern languages and literatures, 1976.* New York, NY: Author.

Alphabetize by the first major word in the corporate author's name. List the publisher as *Author* when the author and the publisher are the same.

6. Book by an anonymous author

Primary colors: A novel of politics. (1996). New York, NY: Warner.

List the title of the book in place of an author. Alphabetize the entry by the first major word of the title.

7. Second or subsequent edition

Cember, H. (1996). *Introduction to health physics* (3rd ed.). New York, NY: McGraw-Hill.

Maples, W. (2002). *Opportunities in aerospace careers* (Rev. ed.). New York, NY: McGraw-Hill.

Provide the edition number in parentheses after the title of the book. If the revision is not numbered, place *Rev. ed.* for "revised edition" in parentheses after the title.

8. Translated book

De Beauvoir, S. (1987). *The woman destroyed* (P. O'Brien, Trans.). New York, NY: Pantheon. (Original work published 1969)

Insert the name(s) of the translator(s) in parentheses after the title, and conclude with the original publication date. Note the absence of a period at the end of the entry. In the text, provide both publication dates as follows: (De Beauvoir, 1969/1987).

9. Republished book

Freire, P. (1982). *Pedagogy of the oppressed* (2nd ed.). London, England: Penguin. (Original work published 1972)

Conclude the entry with the original publication date. Note the absence of a period at the end of the entry. In the text provide both dates: (Freire, 1972/1982).

10. Multivolume work

Doyle, A. C. (2003). *The complete Sherlock Holmes* (Vols. 1–2). New York, NY: Barnes & Noble.

Maugham, S. W. (1977–1978). *Collected short stories* (Vols. 1–4). New York, NY: Penguin.

Include the number of volumes after the title of the work. If the volumes were published over a period of time, provide the date range after the author's name.

11. Government report

Executive Office of the President. (2003). *Economic report of the President, 2003* (GPO Publication No. 040-000-0760-1). Washington, DC: U.S. Government Printing Office.

Provide the publication number in parentheses after the name of the report. If the report is available from the Government Printing Office (GPO), that entity is the publisher. If the report is not available from the GPO, use *Author* as the publisher.

12. Selection from an edited book

Muños, G. T. (2007). Once upon a time on the border. In T. Miller (Ed.), *How I learned English* (pp. 141–148). Washington, DC: National Geographic.

The title of the selection is not italicized. The editor's name appears before the title of the book. Provide the page or range of pages on which the selection appears.

13. Selection from a reference book

Layering. (2003). In W. Lidwell, K. Holden, & J. Butler (Eds.), *Universal principles of
design* (pp. 122–123). Gloucester, MA: Rockport.

Provide the page number or range of pages after the title of the book. If
the selection has an author, give that author's name first.

Bruce, F. F. (1991). Hermeneutics. In *New Bible dictionary* (p. 476). Wheaton, IL:
Tyndale.

Articles in print

ARTICLE IN A JOURNAL

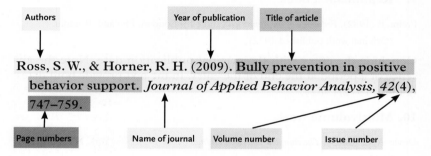

You can generally find the journal title, the volume and issue numbers,
and the year of publication on the cover of the journal. Sometimes this
information is also included in the journal's page headers or footers. To
find the title of the article, the author's name, and the page numbers,
you'll have to locate the article within the journal.

ARTICLE IN A MAGAZINE

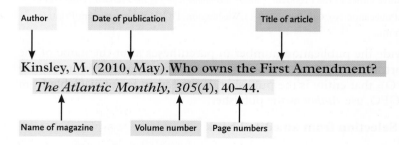

To find the name of the magazine, the volume and issue numbers,
and the date of publication, look on the cover of the magazine. Sometimes this information is also included in the magazine's page headers

Cover of an academic journal showing year of publication, volume and issue numbers (vertically, on left-hand side), and title of journal.

The Journal of
Applied Behavioral Science

Volume 46 Number 1 March 2010

Courtesy of The Journal of Applied Behavioral Science

Special Issue: *Organizational Discourse and Change*
Guest Editors: *Cliff Oswick*
David Grant
Bob Marshak
Julie Wolfram-Cox

NTL INSTITUTE

Published for NTL Institute by $SAGE

or footers. For the title of the article, the author's name, and the page numbers, look at the article itself. Reference entries for articles generally include four units of information: author, date of publication, title of article, and publication data.

Author The author's last name appears first, followed by the first and (if given) the second initial. Use a comma to separate the last name from the initial(s), and place a period at the end of this unit of information. For articles with more than one author, see the information given for book entries on pages 447–448.

Date of publication For journals, place just the year of publication in parentheses after the author's name. For magazines, also specify the month and the day (if given). Mark the end of this unit of information with a period.

Title of article Include the title and, if there is one, the subtitle of the article. Capitalize *only* the first word of the title and the subtitle, plus any proper nouns. Use a colon to separate the subtitle from the title. Place a period at the end of this unit of information.

Publication data The publication data that you provide depends on the type of periodical in which the article appeared. However, for all entries, include the title of the periodical (italicized), the volume number (also italicized), and the page numbers of the article. If you are using a magazine or a journal that paginates each issue separately, include the issue number as well. Place the issue number (not italicized) in parentheses following the volume number. After the issue number, place a comma and then the article's page numbers.

Research

14. Article in a journal with continuous pagination

McCarthy, M., & Carter, R. (2001). Size isn't everything: Spoken English, corpus, and
     the classroom. *TESOL Quarterly, 35,* 337–340.

Provide the volume number in italics after the title of the journal.
Conclude with the page number or page range.

15. Article in a journal with each issue paginated separately

Smiles, T. (2008). Connecting literacy and learning through collaborative action
     research. *Voices from the Middle, 15*(4), 32–39.

16. Article with three to seven authors

Biber, D., Conrad, S., & Reppen, R. (1996). Corpus-based investigations of language
     use. *Annual Review of Applied Linguistics, 16,* 115–136.

If there are seven or fewer authors, list all of the authors' names.

17. Article with more than seven authors

Stone, G. W., Ellis, S. G., Cox, D. A., Hermiller, J., O'Shaughnessy, C., Mann, J. T., . . .
     Russell, M. E. (2004). A polymer-based, paclitaxel-eluting stent in patients with
     coronary artery disease. *The New England Journal of Medicine, 350,* 221–231.

Provide the names of the first six authors, inverted, followed by an
ellipsis and the name of the final author.

18. Article in a monthly or weekly magazine

Gross, D. (2010, May 3). The days the Earth stood still. *Newsweek,* 46–48.

Warne, K. (2004, March). Harp seals. *National Geographic, 205,* 50–67.

Provide the month and year of publication for monthly magazines or
the day, month, and year for weekly magazines. Names of months are
not abbreviated. Include the volume number (italicized), if any, issue
number (not italicized), and the page number or page range (not italicized) after the name of the magazine.

19. Anonymous article

Ohio police hunt for highway sniper suspect. (2004, March 16). *The New York Times,* p. A4.

Begin the entry with the title of the article, followed by the date of
publication.

20. Article in a newspaper

Lewin, T. (2010, May 6). Teenage insults, scrawled on Web, not on walls. *The New York
     Times,* pp. A1, A18.

Use *p.* or *pp.* before the page number(s) of newspaper articles. If the article appears on discontinuous pages, provide all of the page numbers, separated by commas: pp. A8, A10–11, A13.

21. Letter to the editor

Richard, J. (2004, March 8). Diabetic children: Every day a challenge [Letter to the
    editor]. *The Wall Street Journal,* p. A17.

Include the description *Letter to the editor* in square brackets after the title of the letter.

22. Editorial in a newspaper

Marcus, R. (2010, May 5). In Arizona, election reform's surprising consequences.
    [Editorial]. *The Washington Post,* p. A21.

Include the description *Editorial* in square brackets after the title.

23. Book review

Kakutani, M. (2004, February 13). All aflutter, existentially [Review of the book *Dot in*
    the universe]. *The New York Times,* p. E31.

In square brackets after the title of the review, indicate that the work cited is a review, provide a description of the medium of the work (e.g., book, film, or play), and include the title of the work.

Sources produced for access by computer

JOURNAL ARTICLE FROM A DATABASE

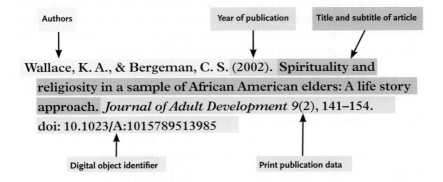

You can usually find much of the information you will need for your reference entry on the first page of the article. Each entry generally includes five units of information: author, year of publication, title and subtitle of the article, print publication data, and digital object identifier (DOI).

Author The author's last name appears first, followed by the first and (if given) the second initial. Use a comma to separate the last name from the initials, and place a period at the end of this unit of information. For articles with more than one author, see the information given for book entries on pages 447–448.

Date of publication For journals, place just the year of publication in parentheses after the author's name. Mark the end of this unit of information with a period.

Title of article Include the title and, if there is one, the subtitle of the article. Capitalize only the first word of the title and subtitle, plus any proper nouns. Use a colon to separate the subtitle from the main title. Place a period at the end of this unit of information.

Print publication data The publication data that you provide depends on the type of periodical in which the article appeared. See the information on publication data for periodicals on page 451.

Digital object identifier Rather than provide a URL for the database or article, include the digital object identifier (DOI), if available. A DOI is assigned to many scholarly articles found online and has the great advantage of being stable. You will usually find the DOI on the first page of the article, near the copyright notice. In cases in which a DOI is unavailable, provide the URL for the source's home page after the words *Retrieved from* (not italicized).

Electronic sources vary significantly; therefore, as you prepare your list of references, follow the models below closely. On occasion, you may not be able to find all the information presented in a particular model. In such cases, just provide as much of the information as you can.

24. Article from a database or from a journal published only online

Moore, A. C., Akhter, S., & Aboud, F. E. (2008). Evaluating an improved quality preschool program in rural Bangladesh. *International Journal of Educational Development, 28*(2), 118–131. doi:10.1016/j.ijedudev.2007.05.003

After the print publication data, include the DOI, if available.

Andersson, G., Carlbring, P., & Cuijpers, P. (2009). Internet interventions: Moving from efficacy to effectiveness. *E-Journal of Applied Psychology, 5*(2), 18–24. Retrieved from http://ojs.lib.swin.edu.au/index.php/ejap/index

If no DOI is assigned, end the citation with the URL of the journal's home page.

25. Article in an online newspaper

Connelly, J. (2010, May 3). Lessons from the Gulf oil spill. *Seattle Post-Intelligencer*. Retrieved from http://www.seattlepi.com

Provide the full date of the article after the author's name. Conclude with the URL of the newspaper's home page.

26. Message posted to a newsgroup, forum, or discussion group

Skrecky, D. (2004, February 27). Free radical theory of aging falsified [Newsgroup message]. Retrieved from news://ageing/bionet.molbio.ageing

Bradstreet, J. (2010, May 6). The over diagnosis of ADHD and why. [Electronic mailing list message]. Retrieved from http://groups.google.com/group/natural-health/browse_thread/thread/690cbd531a1ea39e

If the author's name is unavailable, the author's screen name may be used. A brief description of the source (such as *online forum comment*) should be provided in square brackets after the subject line of the message.

27. Document from a Web site

Robinson, J. (2010). *Grass-fed basics*. Retrieved from http://www.eatwild.com/basics.html

Slow Food USA. (2010). *Slow food on campus*. Retrieved from http://www.slowfoodusa.org/index.php/programs/details/slow_food_on_campus/

If no author is given, use the name of the organization hosting the Web site as the author of the document. Provide the date, the name of the document, and the URL for the specific page where the document can be found.

28. Email message

Personal communications such as email messages, letters, telephone conversations, and personal interviews do not appear in the references list, but should be cited in the text as follows: (S. L. Johnson, personal communication, September 3, 2009).

29. Podcast

DiMeo, N. (Producer). (2010, March 12). The sisters Fox. *The memory palace*. [Audio podcast]. Retrieved from http://thememorypalace.us

Other sources

30. Motion picture

Jurow, M. (Producer), & Edwards, B. (Writer/Director). (1963). *The pink panther*
    [Motion picture]. United States: United Artists.

Begin with the name of the producer or the director, or both. Include the description *Motion picture* in square brackets after the title of the film. Conclude with the country of origin and the name of the movie studio.

31. Television program

Godeanu, R. (Producer). (2004, March 17). *In search of ancient Ireland* [Television
    broadcast]. Alexandria, VA: Public Broadcasting Service.

Begin with the name of the producer. Italicize the title of the program, and follow the title with the description *Television broadcast* in square brackets.

32. Music recording

Porter, C. (1936). Easy to love [Recorded by H. Connick, Jr.]. On *Come by me* [CD].
    New York, NY: Columbia. (1999)

White, J. (2003). Seven nation army [Recorded by The White Stripes]. On *Under great
    white northern lights* [CD]. Burbank, CA: Warner Bros. Records. (2010)

Start with the name of the songwriter and the date the song was written. If someone other than the songwriter recorded the song, add *Recorded by* and the singer's name in square brackets after the song title. Indicate the medium of the recording in square brackets after the album title. Conclude the entry with the year the song was recorded, in parentheses, if that date is not the same as the date the song was written.

33. Interview

Brock, A. C. (2006). Rediscovering the history of psychology: Interview with Kurt
    Danziger. *History of Psychology, 9*(1), 1–16.

For a published interview, follow the format for an entry for an article. If you conducted the interview yourself, cite the name of the person you interviewed in the body of your paper and include in parentheses the words *personal communication,* followed by a comma and the interview date. Do not include an entry for a personal interview in the list of references.

CHECKING OVER A REFERENCES LIST

✓ Is the title, *References* (not italicized), centered one inch from the top of the page? Is the first letter capitalized?

✓ Is the entire list double-spaced?

- ✓ Are initial lines flush with the left margin and subsequent lines indented one-half inch?
- ✓ Is there an entry in the references list for each in-text citation (except for personal communications)? Is there an in-text citation for each entry in the references list?
- ✓ Are the entries alphabetized according to the first author's last name? If the author of an entry is unknown, is the entry alphabetized according to title (ignoring any initial *a, an,* or *the*)?
- ✓ If the list contains two or more entries by the same author, are the entries arranged according to year of publication (earliest one first)?
- ✓ Are book and periodical titles italicized?
- ✓ Is capitalization used for only the first words of book and article titles and subtitles and any proper nouns they contain?

Sample APA Research Paper

The APA provides the following general guidelines for formatting a research paper. The title page is page 1 of your paper. In the upper left-hand corner, place a shortened version of your title (no more than fifty characters), all in capital letters; on page 1 only, precede the header with the words *Running head:*. In the upper right-hand corner, put the page number. This manuscript page header should appear on every page, one-half inch from the top of the page and one inch from the left and right edges. Place the full title in the center of the page, using both uppercase and lowercase letters. Below it, put your name and affiliation (double-spaced)—unless your instructor asks you to include such information as the date and the course name and number instead of your affiliation.

If your instructor requires one, include an abstract—a short summary of your research—as the second page of your paper. The abstract should be no longer than 250 words. The word *Abstract* (not italicized) should be centered at the top of the page.

The first page of text is usually page 3 of the paper (following the title page and the abstract). The full title of the paper should be centered one inch from the top of the page. Double-space between the title and the first line of text. Use a one-inch margin on all sides of your paper (left, right, top, and bottom). Do not justify the text; that is, leave the right margin uneven. Indent paragraphs and block quotations one-half inch. Double-space your entire paper, including block quotations.

The page header
has a running head
(no more than
50 characters) on
the left and page
number on the
right. The words
Running head:
appear only on
page 1.

Perceptions of Peers' Drinking Behavior⦁

Catherine L. Davis

Central Washington University ⦁

The title is typed
in uppercase and
lowercase letters
and is centered.

An instructor
may require such
information as the
date and the course
name and number
instead of an
affiliation.

PERCEPTIONS OF PEERS' DRINKING BEHAVIOR   2

Abstract⦁

This study is an examination of how students' perceptions of their peers' drinking behavior are related to alcohol consumption and alcohol-related problems on campus. Four hundred nine randomly selected college students were interviewed using a modified version of the Core Survey (Presley, Meilman, & Lyeria, 1995) to assess alcohol consumption and its related problems.

The abstract
appears on a
separate page,
with the heading
centered on the
page width. The
abstract should not
exceed 250 words.

Research

Perceptions of Peers' Drinking Behavior •·································

The full title of the paper is centered on the page width.

Studies typically report the dangers associated with college students' use of alcohol (Beck et al., 2008). Nonetheless, drinking is still highly prevalent on American campuses. Johnston, O'Malley, and Bachman (1998) found that 87% of the college students surveyed reported drinking during their lifetime. Most of the students are 21 or 22 years old and report frequent episodes of heavy drinking (i.e., binge drinking).

When six or more authors are cited, *et al.* is used in the citation.

Heavy episodic drinking is particularly problematic. Johnston et al. (1998) found that 41% of college students engage in heavy episodic drinking, which they defined as having at least five or more drinks in a row at least once in the 2 weeks prior to being surveyed. Heavy episodic drinking is related to impaired academic performance, interpersonal problems, unsafe sexual activity, and sexual assault and other criminal violations (Moore, Smith, & Catford, 1994). The magnitude of such problems has led Neighbors, Lee, Lewis, Fossos, and Larimer (2007) to conclude that binge drinking is a widespread problem among college students.

This is a subsequent mention of a work by three authors.

When authors are named in the text, the year of publication is placed in parentheses after the names.

Massad and Rauhe (1997) report that college students engage in heavy episodic drinking in response to social pressure or physical discomfort. Almost half of college students in a survey stated their reason for drinking was to get drunk (Jessor, Costa, Krueger, & Turbin, 2006). Recent research suggests that students' misperceptions of their peers' drinking behavior contribute to increased alcohol consumption (Perkins, 2002).

College students commonly perceive their social peers as drinking more often and in greater quantities than they actually do (Neighbors et

Research

al., 2007). When these students see their peers as heavy drinkers, they are

more likely to engage in heavy drinking (Neighbors et al., 2007; Perkins

& Wechsler, 1996). The goal of this study was to determine whether

students' perceptions of their peers' use of alcohol are related to alcohol

consumption and alcohol-related problems on campus.

Method

Participants

For the purposes of this study, a randomly selected sample ($N =$ 409) of undergraduate students from a university in the Pacific Northwest was drawn. The mean age of participants, 55.8% of whom were female, was 24 years; 54.5% of participants were White, 19% were Hispanic, 14.8% were Asian/Pacific Islander, 5% were African American, 0.5% were American Indian, and 6.3% indicated "Other" as their ethnicity.

Instrument

The study used a modified version of the short form of the Core Survey (Presley, Meilman, & Lyeria, 1995). The Core Survey measures alcohol and other drug (AOD) use as well as related problems experienced by college students. For the purposes of this study, the Core was modified from a self-administered format to an interview format.

Procedure

Interviews were conducted by telephone. Each interview took an average of 16 minutes to complete. The refusal rate for this survey was 12%, and those refusing to participate were replaced randomly.

Alcohol use was defined as the number of days (during the past 30 days) that respondents drank alcohol. *Heavy episodic drinking* was defined as five or more drinks in a single setting, with a drink consisting of one beer, one glass of wine, one shot of hard liquor, or one mixed drink (Presley et al., 1995). Respondents indicated the number of occasions in the past 2 weeks that they engaged in heavy episodic drinking. *Alcohol-related problems* were defined as the number of times in the past 30 days respondents experienced any of 20 specific incidents.

To determine alcohol-related problems, the interviewer asked students how many times they (a) had a hangover, (b) damaged property, (c) got into a physical fight, (d) got into a verbal fight, (e) got nauseous or vomited, (f) drove a vehicle while under the influence, (g) were criticized by someone they knew, (h) had memory loss, or (i) did something they later regretted. To determine their perceptions of their peers' drinking, students were asked to respond on a 7-point ordinal scale that ranged from 0 = never to 6 = almost daily.

[The data analysis and statistical report of results have been omitted.]

Discussion

The relationship found here concerning the normative perception of alcohol use is somewhat consistent with past research (Baer & Carney, 1993; Perkins, 2002) that suggested drinking norms are related to alcohol use. Readers should note, however, that respondents' perceptions of the drinking norm were consistent with the actual norm for 30-day use. This indicates that students are fairly accurate in assessing their peers' drinking frequencies. Unfortunately, the current study did not include a perception question for heavy episodic drinking, making it unclear whether respondents accurately perceive their peers' drinking quantity. Conceptually, misperceptions of drinking quantity might be better

Research

predictors of heavy episodic drinking. That is, students might falsely believe that their peers drink heavily when they drink. Such a misperception would be compounded by the fact that most students accurately estimate frequency of their peers' drinking. The combination of an accurate perception of frequency coupled with an inaccurate perception of quantity might result in an overall perception of most students being heavy, frequent drinkers. As expected, this study also revealed a positive and moderately strong pathway from alcohol use, both heavy episodic drinking and 30-day drinking, to alcohol-related problems.

This study represents an effort to add to the literature concerning college students' alcohol consumption and its related problems. The results of the study suggest that students' perceptions of their peers' drinking habits are important predictors of drinking or drinking-related problems. Future studies along similar lines might help prevention specialists better design media campaigns related to drinking norms and high-risk behaviors.

References

Baer, J. S., & Carney, M. M. (1993). Biases in the perceptions of the consequences of alcohol use among college students. *Journal of Studies on Alcohol, 54,* 54–60.

Beck, K. H., Arria, A. M., Caldeira, K. M., Vincent, K. B., O'Grady, K. E., & Wish, E. D. (2008). Social context of drinking and alcohol problems among college students. *American Journal of Health Behavior, 32*(4), 420–430.

Jessor, R., Costa, F. M., Krueger, P. M., & Turbin, M. S. (2006). A developmental study of heavy episodic drinking among college students: The role of psychosocial and behavioral protective and risk factors. *Journal of Studies on Alcohol, 67,* 86–94.

Johnston, L. D., O'Malley, P. M., & Bachman, J. G. (1998). *National survey results on drug use from the Monitoring the Future Study. 1975-1997: Vol. 11* (NIH Publication No. 98-4346). Washington, DC: U.S. Government Printing Office.

Massad, S. J., & Rauhe, B. J. (1997). Alcohol consumption patterns in college students: A comparison by various socioeconomic indicators. *Journal for the International Council of Health, Physical Education, Recreation, Sport, and Dance, 23*(4), 60–64.

Moore, L., Smith, C., & Catford, J. (1994). Binge drinking: Prevalence, patterns and policy. *Health Education Research, 9,* 497–505. doi:10.1093/her/9.4.497

Neighbors, C., Lee, C. M., Lewis, M. A., Fossos, N., & Larimer, M. E. (2007). Are social norms the best predictor of outcomes among

References begin on a new page. The heading is centered on the page width.

The entries are alphabetized according to the first author's last name. If two or more entries have the same first author, the second author's last name determines the order of the entries.

All entries have a hanging indent of one-half inch and are double-spaced.

When available for an article accessed through a database, a DOI is included in the entry.

Research

heavy-drinking college students? *Journal of Studies on Alcohol and Drugs, 68,* 556–565.

Perkins, H. W. (2002). Social norms and the prevention of alcohol misuse in collegiate contexts. *Journal of American Studies on Alcohol, 14,* 164–172.

Perkins, H. W., & Wechsler, H. (1996). Variation in perceived college drinking norms and its impact on alcohol abuse: A nationwide study. *Journal of Drug Issues, 26,* 961–974.

Presley, C. A., Meilman, P. W., & Lyeria, R. (1995). Development of the Core Alcohol and Drug Survey: Initial findings and future directions. *Journal of American College Health, 42,* 248–255.

Entries with a single author come before entries with that author and one or more co-authors.

Research

Credits

p. 11: Email courtesy of Collin Allan.

pp. 12–14: Judy Brady, "Why I Want a Wife," *Ms.* magazine, inaugural issue, 1971. Used by permission of the author.

pp. 25–27: From *Life As We Know It* by Michael Bérubé, copyright © 1996 by Michael Bérubé. Used by permission of Pantheon Books, a division of Random House, Inc. and by The Doe Covver Literary Agency.

p. 29: Christopher Cokinos, from *Hope Is the Thing with Feathers: A Personal Chronicle of Vanished Birds* (New York: Grand Central Publishing, 2001).

pp. 32–33: www.Chooseresponsibility.org. Used by permission.

pp. 36–37: Statement of George A. Hacker, "Support 21" Coalition Press Conference on Minimum Drinking Age Law. Used by permission of Center for Science in the Public Interest.

pp. 39–40: Academic Senate of San Francisco State University, "Resolution Regarding the Rodney King Verdict," http://sfsu.edu/~senate/documents/resolutions/RS92-107.pdf

pp. 42–43: Barbara Smith, from *The Truth That Never Hurts*, pp. 102–105 (New Brunswick, NJ: Rutgers University Press, 1998).

pp. 50, 51: Sojourner Truth, from speech given at 1851 Women's Rights Convention in Akron, Ohio.

p. 55: "Susan Orlean Delivers 2001 Johnston Lecture," *Flash: Newsletter of the School of Journalism and Communication*, vol. 16, no. 3 (2001), http://flash.uoregon.edu/S01/orlean.html

pp. 56–58: From "The American Man, Age Ten," in *The Bullfighter Checks Her Makeup* by Susan Orlean, copyright © 2001 by Susan Orlean. Used by permission of Random House, Inc.

p. 64: Taryn Plumb, *Boston Globe*, May 4, 2006.

p. 64: Jonathan Kibera, from "Fond Memories of a Congenital Glutton," http://www.epinions.com/educ-review-229A-80FFD6-388E720C-bd3, January 5, 2000.

p. 67: Clotilde Dusoulier, "Happiness (A Recipe)," http://chocolateandzucchini.com/archives.2003/10/happinessarecipe

pp. 67–68: Ruth Reichl, "The Queen of Mold," from *Tender at the Bone*, copyright © 1998 by Ruth Reichl. Used by permission of Random House, Inc. and Random House, UK.

p. 68: Eric Schlosser, *Fast Food Nation* (Boston: Houghton Mifflin, 2001).

pp. 70–72: Transcript of Ruth Reichl: Favorite Food Memoirs. Steve Inskeep/Morning Edition Copyright © 2009 National Public Radio®

p. 72: Quote within interview from *The Kitchen Diaries: A Year in the Kitchen with Nigel Slater*, Gotham; First Printing edition (October 19, 2006).

p. 74: Julie Powell, from "The Julie/Julia Project," July 8, 2003, http://blogs.salon.com/0001399/2003/07/08.html

pp. 77–78: Margaret Mead, from "The Wider Food Situation," *Food Habits Research: Problems of the 1960s*, National Research Council's Committee for the Study of Food Habits Update.

pp. 78–79: Margaret Mead, from "The Changing Significance of Food," *American Scientist* 58 (March/April 1970): 176–81.

pp. 81–82: Corby Kummer, from "Good-bye Cryovac," *The Atlantic Monthly*, vol. 294, no. 3 (October 2004): p. 197+. Copyright 2004 The Atlantic Monthly Group, as first published in *The Atlantic Monthly*. Distributed by Tribune Media Services.

pp. 84–90, 95: Pooja Makhijani, "School Lunch," from *Women Who Eat*, edited by Leslie Miller, pp. 41–49 (New York: Seal Press, 2003). Reprinted by permission of Seal Press, a member of Perseus Books Group.

pp. 99–103: Courtesy of Anna Seitz Hickey.

p. 104: Reprinted by arrangement with The Heirs to the Estate of Martin Luther King Jr., c/o Writers House as agent for the proprietor New York, NY. Copyright 1963 Dr. Martin Luther King Jr; copyright renewed 1991 Coretta Scott King.

pp. 109–112: "What Would Obama Say?" by Ashley Parker, from the *New York Times*, Style Section, 1/20/2008, Section ST, Page 1. New York Times/PARS International. Used by permission and protected by the Copyright Laws of the United States. The printing, copying, redistribution, or retransmission of the Material without express written permission is prohibited.

pp. 112–114: Transcript of Senator Barack Obama's address to supporters after the Iowa caucuses, as provided by *Congressional Quarterly* via The Associated Press.

pp. 115–117: From *What I Saw at the Revolution*, by Peggy Noonan, copyright © 1989 by Peggy Noonan. Used by permission of Random House, Inc. and the William Morris Agency.

pp. 118–120: "Confessions of a TED Addict" by Virginia Heffernan, from the *New York Times*, Magazine Section, 1/25/2009 page 13. New York Times/PARS International. Used by permission and protected by the Copyright Laws of the United States. The printing, copying, redistribution, or retransmission of the Material without express written permission is prohibited.

pp. 121–123: "Uncovering Steve Jobs Presentation Secrets," by Carmine Gallo. *Business Week*, October 6, 2009. Used by permisison.

pp. 125–127, 132: Marisa Lagos, "Successes Speak Well for Debate Coach" (*Los Angeles Times*, October 6, 2004, Home edition, p. B2).

pp. 135–140: Courtesy of Matthew Glasgow.

pp. 150–152: Don Hammonds, "Honda Challenges Students to Market Its Latest Car to Younger Buyers." From the *Pittsburgh Post-Gazette*, March 31, 2006.

pp. 153–155: Eyal Press and Jennifer Washburn, from "The Kept University," *The Atlantic Monthly*, vol. 285 (March 1, 2000), p. 39. Copyright 2000 The Atlantic Monthly Group, as first published in *The Atlantic Monthly*. Distributed by Tribune Media Service.

pp. 155–158: "Building a Buzz on Campus" by Sarah Schweitzer from *The Boston Globe* (October 24, 2005). Used by permission of author.

pp. 159–162: "Riding the Trojan Horse" by Mike Fish, ESPN, Inc. (1/11/06).

pp. 164–165: "Big Oil Buys Berkeley" by Jennifer Washburn. *LA Times*, March 24, 2007. Used by permission.

pp. 173–177: Courtesy of Kelly E. McNeil.

pp. 178, 179: Barbara Wallraff, "Word Court," *The Atlantic Monthly*, vol. 295, no. 3 (2005), p. 136. Copyright 2007 The Atlantic Monthly Group, as first published in *The Atlantic Monthly*. Distributed by Tribune Media Services.

p. 181: Zitkala-Sa, "Impressions of an Indian Childhood," *The Atlantic Monthly*, vol. 85, no. 507 (January 1900), pp. 37–47.

pp. 181–182: From "Not Neither" by Sandra Mariá Esteves, quoted in Juan Flores, *From Bamboo to Hip-Hop: Puerto Rican Culture and Latino Identity* (New York: Columbia University Press, 2000), p. 56.

p. 184: Lines from "Nuestro Himno" by Adam Kidron, Urban Box Office/Beyond Oblivion. Used by permission.

p. 185: "Sen. Alexander to Introduce Senate Resolution on Singing National Anthem in English." Press release of U.S. Senator Lamar Alexander. 28 Apr. 2006. 19 May 2006.

pp. 188–190: Cited in *Language Loyalties: A Source Book on the Official English Controversy*, edited by James Crawford (Chicago: University of Chicago Press), pp. 94–100. Used by permission of The Regional Oral History Office, Berkeley, CA.

p. 190: U.S. Senate, Bill 992, http://www.govtrack.us/congress/billtext.xpd?bill=s111-992

p. 191: Quote from EPIC on English Plus from "The English Plus Alternative," in James Crawford (ed.), *Language Loyalties: A Source Book on the Official English Controversy* (Chicago: University of Chicago Press, 1992), pp. 151–53.

pp. 191–192: Geoffrey Nunberg, "The Official English Movement: Reimagining America." From *Language Loyalties: A Source Book on the Official English Controversy*, edited by James Crawford (Chicago: University of Chicago Press, 1992), pp. 479–494.

pp. 193–194: Hyon B. Shin, with Rosalind Bruno, from *Language Use and English-Speaking Ability: Census 2000 Brief*. Washington, DC: U.S. Dept. of Commerce, 2003.

pp. 196–198: "Los Olvidados: On the Making of Invisible People" by Juan F. Perea, 70 *N.Y.U. Law Review*, 965 (1995).

pp. 199–200: "Hunger of Memory" by Richard Rodriguez, from *Hunger of Memory: The Education of Richard Rodriguez* (New York: Bantam Books, 1982) pp. 19–20.

pp. 202–204, 208, 209: Gabriela Kuntz, "My Spanish Standoff," *Newsweek*, May 4, 1998, p. 22. © Newsweek, Inc. All rights reserved. Used by permission and protected by the Copyright Laws of the United States. The printing, copying, redistribution, or retransmission of the Material without express written permission is prohibited.

p. 211: Generation Rescue / 13636 Ventura Blvd. #259 / Sherman Oaks, CA 91423.

pp. 216–222: Courtesy of the author.

pp. 231–232, 237: "We Are Rebuilding New York" from *Working for the People* by Robert Moses (New York: Harper, 1956), pp. 557–560.

pp. 234–236: From *The Power Broker: Robert Moses and the Fall of New York* by Robert A. Caro. © 1974 by Robert A. Caro. Used by permission of Alfred A. Knopf, a division of Random House, Inc.

pp. 238–239: From *The Death and Life of Great American Cities* by Jane Jacobs, published by Jonathan Cape. Copyright © 1961, 1989 by Jane Jacobs.

Reprinted by permission of Random House, Inc. and The Random House Group Ltd.

pp. 240–241: Adina Levin, "Ants and Jane Jacobs," February 18, 2003, http://alevin.com/weblog/archives/000966.html

p. 243: Quote from guidelines for World Trade Center site memorial competition, http://www.wtcsitememorial.org/p1

pp. 244–246: Michael Arad and Peter Walker, "Reflecting Absence," World Trade Center Site Memorial Competition, http://www.wtcsitememorial.org/fin7.html. Used by permission of the National September 11 Memorial & Museum at the World Trade Center.

pp. 254–258: Courtesy of Rupali Kumar.

p. 265: Charles A. Hill, *Intertexts: Reading Pedagogy in College Writing Classrooms* (Mahwah, NJ: Lawrence Erlbaum, 2003), p. 123.

pp. 268–270: "An Apocalypse of Kinetic Joy" by Kenneth Turan from the *Los Angeles Times* (March 31, 1999): 1.

pp. 270–272: "Lost in the Matrix" by Bob Graham. *San Francisco Chronicle* March 31, 1999.

pp. 274–278: Paper, Plastic, or Canvas? by Dmitri Siegel. Originally published on Design Observer. Used by permission, Winterhouse, Falls Village, CT.

pp. 278–279: "Classics of Everday Design No 12" by Jonathan Glancey. Art & Design Blog of *The Guardian*, 13 March 2007. Used by permission.

pp. 281–283, 287, 288: Mike D'Angelo, "Unreally, Really Cool: Stop-Motion Movies May Be Old School, but They Still Eat Other Animation for Breakfast," *Esquire*, October 2005, pp. 72–73. Used by permission of the author.

pp. 291–294: Courtesy of Alexis Walker.

p. 297: Joyce Carol Oates, "To Invigorate Literary Mind, Start Moving Literary Feet," in *Writers on Writing: Collected Essays from The New York Times* (New York: Times Books/Holt, 2001), 165–71.

p. 298: Susan Sontag, in *Writers on Writing: Collected Essays from The New York Times* (New York: Times Books/Holt, 2001), 223–9.

pp. 300, 301, 302, 303, 305, 322, 326: Courtesy of Anastasia Simkanin.

p. 307 (top): Britannica definition of "primates," http://www.britannica.com/eb/article-9105977/primate

p. 307 (bottom): Primate Conservation, Inc., http://www.primate.org/about.htm

p. 308: ChimpanZoo: Research, Education and Enrichment 2003, www.chimpanzoo.org/history%20of%20primates.html

p. 308: W. E. Le Gros Clark, *The Antecedents of Man*, 3rd ed. (Chicago: Quadrangle Books, 1971).

pp. 309–310: William Styron, *Darkness Visible* (New York: Random House, 1990), p. 52.

p. 310: Burciaga, José Antonio, "I Remember Masa" from *Weedee Peepo*. Published by Pan American University Press, Edinburgh, TX (1988).

pp. 315–316: From Michael McGarrity, *Everyone Dies* (New York: Dutton-Penguin, 2003), pp. 169–71.

pp. 319–320: http://www.fns.usda.gov/cnd/Breakfast/expansion/10reasons-breakfast_flyer.pdf

p. 350: REPRINTED WITH PERMISSION FROM PSYCHOLOGY TODAY MAGAZINE, (Mar/Apr 2004) p. 29. Copyright © 2004 Sussex Publishers, LLC.

p. 356: *Bostonia* magazine, Winter 2003–2004, page 16.

p. 363: Jeremy Berlin/*National Geographic* Magazine.

p. 366: Tricks of the Trade courtesy of Alyse Murphy Leininger.

p. 366: "What is NPR?" from www.npr.org/about/

p. 374: Tricks of the Trade courtesy of Christian Nuñez.

pp. 380, 381–382: Mike Rose, from *The Mind at Work* (New York: Viking, 2004), pp. 31–32, 85–86, 219–20.

pp. 384, 385: Courtesy of Bethanie Orban.

pp. 389–391: Courtesy of Gillian Petrie.

p. 394: From interview with Debra Dickerson, author of *The End of Blackness: Returning the Souls of Black Folks to Their Rightful Owners*, in Sharifa Rhodes-Pitts, "Getting Over Race," *The Atlantic*, vol. 293, no. 1 (February 27, 2004).

p. 396: Tricks of the Trade courtesy of Keith Evans.

pp. 398–401: William Lutz, "Doubts about Doublespeak." From *State Government News* (July 1993), pp. 22–24. Used by permission of the author.

pp. 401, 403: Courtesy of Jacob Thomas.

p. 405: Tricks of the Trade courtesy of Keith Evans.

p. 408: Tricks of the Trade courtesy of Alyse Murphy Leininger.

pp. 458–464: Courtesy of Catherine L. Davis.

Index